MUSIC IN MEDIEVAL BRITAIN

STUDIES IN THE HISTORY OF MUSIC

EDITED BY EGON WELLESZ
C.B.E., F.B.A., Hon. D. Mus. Oxon.
Fellow of Lincoln College

MUSIC
IN MEDIEVAL
BRITAIN

by
FRANK Ll. HARRISON
Senior Lecturer in Music in the University of Oxford

Published in the U.S.A.
by
DOVER PUBLICATIONS, INC.
180 Varick Street
New York 14, New York

Routledge and Kegan Paul
LONDON

First published 1958
by Routledge & Kegan Paul Limited
Broadway House, Carter Lane, E.C.4.
Printed in Great Britain
by Butler & Tanner Limited
Frome and London
© *Frank Ll. Harrison 1958*

TO NORA

CONTENTS

CONTENTS

LIST OF ILLUSTRATIONS

ILLUSTRATIONS

LIST OF LINE DRAWINGS IN THE TEXT

PREFACE

THE period covered by this book begins with the establishment of Norman constitutions and liturgies following the Conquest and ends with the liturgical and institutional changes brought about at the Reformation. The last two decades of this period saw the end of the monastic orders in Britain, the destruction of many of their houses and the secularization of the rest. The Latin liturgy of the secular churches survived until the Edwardian Prayer Book of 1549, and had a brief revival during the reign of Queen Mary. Both in liturgy and music the end of the Latin rite marks the close of the medieval period, for English music was intimately bound up with the ritual tradition and held to its established styles and functions as long as the medieval liturgy remained. Though Renaissance features began to appear in English music, particularly in its secular forms, in the early sixteenth century, the transition from medieval to Renaissance concepts of structure and style, which took place on the continent in the fifteenth and early sixteenth centuries, was not fully accomplished in England until after the mid-sixteenth century. This is not the division between the Middle Ages and Renaissance usually adopted by musical historians, but I believe it to be justified in the case of the English ecclesiastical arts, both visual and musical, in which medieval styles showed no fundamental change until the new religious ideas became established.

In style and function the secular music of the early Tudor courts was the vanguard of the spirit of the Renaissance in England, and so does not come within the scope of this book. Its early history was cut short by Henry VIII's preoccupation with weightier matters of state after *c.* 1530, and its place in English music is that of a harbinger of developments to come. Earlier examples of secular music are few and of minor importance, and I have not dealt with them here. Nothing identifiable as minstrel music has survived, and the history of minstrelsy belongs to the study of social life and customs rather than of actual music. The history of musical instruments other than the organ is in much the same case, for there is no evidence that any instruments but the organ were normally played in church, and the musical remains are restricted to a small group of instrumental dances. I have touched only briefly on the subject of musical theory in connection with the education of singers in descant, and the history of notation needs more detailed and specialized study than could be given it in a survey of this kind.

On the other hand, I have gone more fully into the history of choirs and their liturgical customs than is usual in writing on medieval music. Although records of local institutions have in recent years become an important part of the study of social history and of the history of the visual arts, little use has yet been made of the records of the musical side of medieval institutions. Besides being the chief sources of biographical information, these records throw light on the place of musicians in the varied communities which made up the medieval church, and on the opportunities which life in these communities gave to composers and singers. The demands of institutional life have in their turn a direct bearing on changes and developments in musical style and practice. The history of choral foundations also serves to show how much the musical life of Britain owes to such great patrons of the ecclesiastical arts as Grandisson, Wykeham, Wayneflete and the Lancastrian kings, whose names, apart from the royal composer who goes under the name Roy Henry, do not normally figure in histories of music.

Because the polyphonic music of the Middle Ages was the ancestor of all the techniques of composition which have been developed since the sixteenth century, there is a tendency to overestimate its place in the liturgy and in the musical life of the time, as distinct from its historical importance from our point of view. It is not always realized that ritual plainsong was the staple fare of the medieval musician, the material of his musical education and the basis of his professional qualifications. The place of polyphony among the liturgical arts of poetry, music, ceremonial, vestment and ornament cannot be seen in its true proportion apart from the order and forms of the liturgy, nor can the special characteristics of its style and design be understood apart from the ritual which was its fount and origin. Viewed as a whole, the liturgy had a devotional function and a didactic purpose which resembled and complemented those of the buildings in which it had its place. As the Gothic cathedral was both 'a strictly architectural monument of the spirit of its age' and a '*Summa*, another *Speculum*, an encyclopedia carved in stone',[1] so the yearly cycle of the liturgy was both a *Gesamt-kunstwerk* of the liturgical arts and an aural and visual representation of Christian doctrine and history. The place of polyphony in this union of the liturgical arts and crafts is analogous to that of the finer carving of an image, a chantry chapel, a choir-stall or a fan-vault in the *Speculum* which was the medieval cathedral.

Since the greater part of the English polyphony of the medieval period is still unpublished, most of my musical examples have been transcribed from the manuscripts. At the same time the debt of such a survey as this to previous musical scholarship is bound to be a large one. More than fifty years ago W. Barclay Squire did pioneer service in giving detailed accounts of the contents of the Old Hall and Eton manuscripts. Among writing on medieval music in general, H. W. Wooldridge's volumes in the original *Oxford History of Music* were a remarkable achievement for their time, and still have value. The researches of Friedrich Ludwig and Heinrich Besseler on the manuscript sources of medieval music, and those of Jacques Handschin on many details of medieval style and practice remain indispensable, while Gustave Reese's *Music in the Middle Ages* and *Music in the Renaissance* are mines of information and marvels of thoroughness. In the publication of English medieval music little was done until the Plainsong and Mediaeval Music Society brought out editions of the Mass *O Quam Suavis* by H. B. Collins, of a selection of the Worcester remains by Dom Anselm Hughes, and of the Old Hall manuscript by A. Ramsbotham (completed by Collins and Hughes). The support of the Carnegie United Kingdom Trust made possible the issuing of ten volumes of *Tudor Church Music* under a group of editors, making available from among pre-Reformation composers

[1] N. Pevsner, *An Outline of European Architecture* 1953, p. 79.

the complete works of Taverner, Aston and Merbeck and the Latin music of Tallis, but leaving a great quantity of early Tudor music still in manuscript.

With the launching of the series *Musica Britannica* publication of some of the hitherto unrevealed monuments of English music has been undertaken in a systematic way. In medieval music there have appeared editions of the *Mulliner Book* by D. Stevens, of the complete corpus of fifteenth-century carols by J. Stevens, and of the complete works of Dunstable by M. F. Bukofzer, whose lamentable death in mid-career has taken away one whose exact and wide-ranging scholarship had illuminated some of the obscure phases of English medieval music. With the study and publication, now in progress, of the Eton Choirbook it has become abundantly clear that a new assessment of the work of English composers in the later Middle Ages is necessary and overdue. It has been part of my purpose to attempt this reassessment and to place it in the larger context of the history of medieval music in Britain.

For the history of musical foundations I have drawn on a variety of printed sources, most of which are in the publications of societies concerned with local and county history, as well as on the manuscript archives of institutions. For permission to study and transcribe from their archives I have to thank the institutions concerned and their curators. I am grateful to Mr. L. S. Colchester, Mrs. Audrey Erskine, Mr. John Harvey and Dr. Albert Hollaender for bringing useful documentary sources to my notice, and to Dr. Jocelyn G. Dickinson, Mme. Solange Doumic, Mr. A. B. Emden, Dr. J. R. L. Highfield, Dr. R. W. Hunt, Mr. Neil Ker, Dr. A. R. Myers, Mr. R. L. Rickard, Mr. John Saltmarsh, Dr. B. Schofield, Sir Wasey Sterry, Dr. Frank Taylor, Canon J. E. W. Wallis and Mr. W. L. Webb for information or help on special points.

My chief sources for liturgical history have of course been the publications of the Henry Bradshaw Society and the editions of and articles on the English uses by Christopher Wordsworth, W. H. Frere and others. On the musical side the published material has been supplemented by manuscripts and early prints of service-books, for some important sources of the music of the English liturgies are still unpublished. It is to be hoped that the splendid lead given by Frere in his facsimiles of the Sarum Gradual and Antiphonal will be followed up, and that we may soon have similar publications of the Hymnal, Sequentiary and Processional.

I am indebted to Professor J. A. Westrup for kindly reading through my typescript and making suggestions, to Miss Margaret Nielsen for invaluable help with proof-reading and indexes, to Dr. Egon Wellesz, to whose initiative is due the launching of the series of which this is the first volume, and to Mr. Colin Franklin, whose interest and encouragement have attended it at every stage.

F. Ll. H.

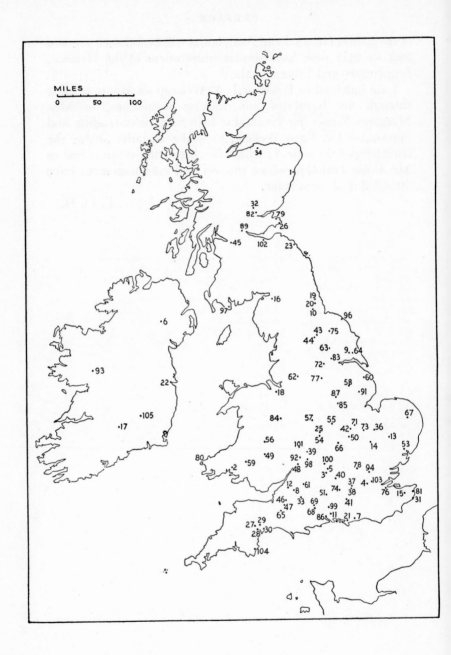

MILES

0   50   100

KEY TO MAP OF THE BRITISH ISLES

1. Aberdeen
2. Abergwili
3. Abingdon
4. London (and West-minster)
5. Oxford (and Oseney)
6. Armagh
7. Arundel
8. Bath
9. Beverley
10. Bishop Auckland
11. Bishop's Waltham
12. Bristol
13. Bury St. Edmund's
14. Cambridge
15. Canterbury
16. Carlisle
17. Cashel
18. Chester
19. Chester-le-Street
20. Durham
21. Chichester
22. Dublin
23. Coldingham
25. Coventry
26. Crail
27. Crediton
28. Exeter
29. Plymtree
30. Ottery St. Mary
31. Dover
32. Dunkeld
33. Edington

34. Elgin (and Spyny)
36. Ely
37. Eton
38. Windsor
39. Evesham
40. Ewelme
41. Farnham (and Waverley Abbey)
42. Fotheringhay
43. Ripon
44. Fountains Abbey
45. Glasgow
46. Wells
47. Glastonbury
48. Gloucester
49. Hereford
50. Higham Ferrers
51. Highclere
53. Ipswich
54. Kenilworth
55. Leicester
56. Leominster
57. Lichfield
58. Lincoln
59. Llangadoc
60. Louth
61. Malmesbury
62. Manchester
63. York
64. Meaux Abbey
65. Muchelney
66. Northampton
67. Norwich
68. Salisbury

69. Old Sarum
71. Peterborough
72. Pontefract
73. Ramsey
74. Reading
75. Rievaulx Abbey
76. Rochester
77. Rotherham
78. St. Alban's
79. St. Andrew's
80. St. David's
81. Sandwich
82. Scone
83. Selby
84. Shrewsbury
85. Sibthorpe
86. Southampton
87. Southwell
89. Stirling
91. Tattershall
92. Tewkesbury
93. Tuam
94. Waltham Holy Cross
96. Whitby
97. Whithorn
98. Winchcombe
99. Winchester (and Hyde Abbey)
100. Woodstock
101. Worcester
102. Edinburgh
103. Barking
104. Dartmouth
105. Kilkenny

I

THE INSTITUTIONS AND
THEIR CHOIRS

Unlike their modern counterparts, the medieval composer
and performer did not purvey their talents to an anonymous
public as private individuals. The life of a medieval musician
was always that of a member of a community which existed
for a wider purpose than a purely musical one, and which imposed definite rules and requirements not only on his musical
activities but also on the form and manner of his daily life. If
he were a member of a monastic community, the rule and duties
of the order applied to him no less than to its other members,
and the musical traditions and customs of his community determined the scope of his creative work. Membership in a secular
community brought demands and opportunities of a different
kind. The singers in a secular cathedral or minster, though
not living a cloistered life under strict vows, were the *ministri
inferiores* of their institution, bound by its statutes to be in holy
orders and to live as members both of the community as a
whole and of their particular corporation or *collegium* within
that community. Since, however, their duties were concerned
only with the observance of the ritual and its plainsong, they
had greater opportunities than members of a monastic community to develop their musical talents and to contribute to
the elaboration of the liturgical music. The enlightened patron-
age and support of some of the Bishops and higher clergy

I

brought about a gradual improvement in the organization and musical standards of the secular cathedral choirs, and enabled them to play a large part in the growth in the practice of polyphony which took place in the later Middle Ages.

The leadership in this development, however, lay neither with the monasteries nor the secular cathedrals, but with the more recent foundations of collegiate churches, colleges and private household chapels. In many of these newer institutions the singing of polyphonic music was a daily observance rather than, as hitherto, the special mark of great festivals. Consequently the composition and balance of their choirs took on a different aspect, the qualifications of their singers were more exacting, provision was made for training their boy choristers in polyphony, and the demands on their composers increased significantly. With these new foundations came changes in the social position of musicians. This is especially true of household chapels, where the singers ranked in the household organization as 'gentlemen' (*generosi*) and were no longer required to be in lower orders, as were singers in most of the collegiate churches and colleges. Curiously enough, the monasteries, too, were responsible for the increase in the number of lay singers in the later Middle Ages, for many of the larger abbeys supported choirs of laymen and boys who were put under the charge of a lay cantor. This multiplicity and variety in the character of the choral foundations—secular and monastic, cathedral and collegiate, royal and aristocratic, educational and charitable—which participated in the cultivation of polyphonic music is the most striking feature of the rich pattern of English musical life in the centuries before the Reformation.

Secular Cathedrals

When the Normans came to England they found little uniformity in the constitutions and organization of the cathedrals and larger churches. Some cathedrals were served by Benedictine monks, under an abbot who was also the bishop of the diocese. This was the case at Winchester, where the Benedictine rule was adopted by St. Ethelwold in 964, and at Worcester, where it had been established by St. Oswald (d. 992). The clergy of some other cathedrals lived under the rule of St.

Chrodegang, Bishop of Metz from 742 to 760 and the founder of its famous school of plainsong, which bound them to live in common without the right to own personal property, though not by a strict monastic rule. Bishop Leofric (d. 1072), who moved his see from Crediton to Exeter c. 1050, required his canons, a term which originally meant clergy who lived under some rule or 'canon', to follow the rule of Chrodegang, as did Bishop Giso of Wells (d. 1088) about the same time. The canons of the northern minsters of York, Southwell, Beverley and Ripon also lived in common, while those of St. Paul's, London, observed their own *Regula Sancti Pauli*, which was similar to the rule of Chrodegang.[1]

The Normans were accustomed to a cathedral chapter (so called from the *capitulum* or head of the eastern end of the church where originally the bishop sat surrounded by his clergy) in which the canons were secular, not monastic, priests who lived in separate houses and had individual incomes from the endowments of the church. As a result of reorganization by Norman bishops this type of cathedral government was adopted at Salisbury, York, Wells, St. Paul's, Lincoln, Exeter, Hereford, Lichfield and Chichester, which became the nine secular cathedrals of medieval England. During the same period nine cathedrals, some of which were new foundations, came under Benedictine rule, chiefly through the influence of Lanfranc, the first Archbishop of Canterbury under the Normans, and his successor Anselm (1093–1114). These nine, Canterbury, Bath (under the Bishop of Wells), Coventry (with Lichfield), Durham (founded 1083), Ely (separated from Lincoln c. 1109), Norwich (1096), Rochester (1077), Winchester and Worcester remained monastic cathedrals until they were refounded with secular chapters by Henry VIII in 1540–1. The house of Augustinian canons at Carlisle, which observed the rule of St. Augustine of Hippo in a form approved by the Pope in 1118, became a cathedral when the diocese was formed in 1133, and was the only English cathedral run by the order known as Austin or Black Canons.

The new constitution of the chapters of York and Lincoln was completed in 1090, and in the following year St. Osmund (Bishop of Salisbury, 1078–99) laid down for his cathedral the pattern of organization which York and Lincoln had adopted

[1] Edwards, *English Secular Cathedrals*, pp. 9–10.

3

and which was followed in due course by the other secular cathedrals. At the head of the chapter were the four 'principal persons' or 'dignities' of Dean, Precentor, Chancellor and Treasurer. As defined in St. Osmund's Institutes,[1] the functions of the dean were to govern the canons and vicars in all that concerned their spiritual and moral welfare and conduct, of the precentor to supervise the choir and direct their singing of the liturgical music (*potest cantus elevare et deponere*), of the treasurer to keep the plate, ornaments and other contents of the treasury and provide candles for the services, and of the chancellor to be responsible for teaching, apart from music, and for the care of non-musical books. In later and more detailed constitutions the precentor was given the duties of regulating the admission and instruction of the boy choristers, of providing and caring for the books of chant, and of entering the singers on the *tabula* or board on which the names and duties of singers and readers were posted, while the chancellor was made responsible for entering on the *tabula* the names of readers of lessons and assistants at the altar.[2] It became customary to appoint one of the canons sub-dean to act as the dean's deputy, another as succentor to carry out the routine duties of the precentor, and others to be sub-treasurer and vice-chancellor.

St. Osmund's *Institutio* required the four dignities to be in continuous residence, and allowed other canons to be absent only to study at the schools, to serve the king or bishop or to attend to the affairs of the cathedral or of his prebend. Non-residence, however, became the rule rather than the exception, and only the comparatively small number of canons necessary to maintain the services and carry on the business of the chapter resided in the cathedral close. The system of absenteeism, which led to pluralism, the holding of a number of canonries simultaneously, was made possible by dividing the church's income and endowments into a part reserved for the common fund and an amount assigned to each of the canons as a prebend (*praebere*, to supply), while the maintenance of the services was ensured by the provision of canons' vicars, or deputies. Vicars are mentioned in the *Institutio Osmundi* and were a part of the Norman constitutions from the beginning. With the recognition

[1] *Use of Sarum*, i, pp. 259–61; *Lincoln Statutes*, ii, pp. 7–10.
[2] Ibid., i, pp. 283–5.

4

of non-residence it became the general practice to require every canon, whether resident or not, to provide the stipend for a substitute (*vicarius*), nominally to carry out his duties in choir. In the course of time the vicars-choral developed their own independent organization within the framework of the cathedral constitutions, and eventually formed themselves into self-governing colleges.

The admission, duties and conduct of the vicars-choral were regulated by statutes drawn up from time to time by the cathedral chapters. At Salisbury Richard Poore (Dean, 1197–1215; Bishop, 1217–28) ordered that vicars should serve for a year on probation and learn the Psalter and Antiphonal by heart. Richard de Kareville (Treasurer of Salisbury, 1246–67) gave money to increase the stipends of the vicars and to ensure that there would always be at least thirteen vicars on each side of the choir.[1] Salisbury had already won special renown for its music, for Bishop Giles de Bridport began his statute of *c*. 1256 on the admission of vicars with a tribute to its pre-eminence.

'The church of Salisbury', he wrote, 'shines as the sun in its orb among the churches of the whole world in its divine service and those who minister in it, and by spreading its rays everywhere makes up for the defects of others. Therefore, lest through our neglect its splendour should be diminished by the unworthiness of its ministers, we ordain that hereafter none shall be presented to the office of vicar in this church unless he has a good and musical voice and skill in plainsong, besides the merits of character required in such ministers.'[2]

In 1472 Bishop Richard Beauchamp laid down new rules for the examination of Salisbury vicars, which required them to know by heart before their admission the first and last 'nocturns', or groups of psalms, in the Psalter, the *Commune Sanctorum*, the antiphons of the *Temporale* and the *Sanctorale* and the Commemorations of the Virgin and of St. Osmund, and to learn the remaining nocturns of the Psalter during their year of probation.[3] By the Lincoln statutes of 1236 every vicar was to be examined in reading and chanting before being admitted

---

[1] *Statutes of Sarum*, pp. 54, 56.
[2] *Statutes and Customs of Salisbury*, p. 88.
[3] Ibid., pp. 212–14; also in *Ceremonies of Salisbury*, pp. 274–5.

5

on probation for a year, during which he was to learn by heart the Antiphonal and the Hymnal. This achieved, he was to serve a second year of probation and memorize the Psalter.[1]

Vicars were expected to be in deacon's or sub-deacon's orders at least, and most of the older vicars were priests. In addition to the vicars and below them in rank there were singers known as clerks of the choir (*clerici chori*), who could not be priests, but must be in lower orders. Besides singing in choir they helped the chantry priests, some of whom were vicars, in serving Mass and took care of the altars at which chantry masses were celebrated. At Salisbury they were called 'altarists', at Exeter 'secondaries' and at Lincoln 'poor clerks', but the usual name for them was 'clerks of the second form', in reference to their place in choir. They were expected to be competent in reading and plainsong.

All the colleges of vicars-choral and the college of minor canons at St. Paul's were incorporated by royal charter during the fourteenth and fifteenth centuries.[2] The charters confirmed the rights of inheriting and administering property, electing their own officers and making their own 'domestic' rules which most of them had already exercised. In 1252 the vicars of York were given the right to administer property by the Archbishop and the Dean and Chapter, and this was confirmed by a charter of Henry III in 1268, though their college was not formally incorporated until 1421.[3] In the meantime they had acquired their own buildings, having been given land for their house in 1268, built their hall by 1328-9 and dedicated their chapel in 1349.[4] Similar developments took place elsewhere. At Lincoln the 'poor clerks' were given a house towards the end of the thirteenth century and Bishop Oliver Sutton (1280-1300) made provision for the building of the Vicars' Court, which was begun after his death and finished in 1328.[5] Bishop Walter Langton gave a house to the vicars of Lichfield in 1315,[6] and Ralph of Shrewsbury, Bishop of Wells, built and

---

[1] *Lincoln Statutes*, ii, p. 145.
[2] For dates of incorporation, see Edwards, *English Secular Cathedrals*, pp. 290-1.
[3] Ibid., p. 281.   [4] Harrison, *Life in a Medieval College*, pp. 29-38.
[5] *Lincoln Statutes*, i, p. 349; ii, p. l.
[6] Edwards, *English Secular Cathedrals*, p. 283.

endowed the vicars' close and hall at Wells *c.* 1350.[1] John Wylliot (d. 1369), Chancellor of Exeter, left money to provide a house for the vicars of Exeter, and Thomas de Brantyngham (Bishop, 1369-94) gave them a hall.[2] The vicars of Hereford had a common hall by 1375, while the college of vicars at Chichester was built between 1394 and 1403. Some of the vicars of Salisbury lived in separate houses in the close, and there is evidence that they had a common hall in 1409.[3]

In some cases the colleges came to assume responsibility for the standard of admission of their members. At York the elected head of the college, who was called the *succentor vicariorum* as distinct from the *succentor canonicorum* or *succentor major*, and five of his colleagues formed a committee which conducted the examination of new vicars.[4] Probationary vicars of Wells were presented to the chapter on the recommendation of the permanent vicars, one of whom was appointed supervisor (*ascultor*) of the new vicar during his trial year.[5] Under an order made *c.* 1343 by the Bishop of Lincoln three 'knowledgeable and skilled' vicars were deputed to test candidates and were required to swear to the faithfulness of their examination when they presented a new vicar to the chapter.[6]

Most of the colleges had a code of domestic statutes which governed their organization and discipline. The vicars of York imposed fines on their own members for absence from service as well as for such offences as brawling in hall, chattering in church, stealing from the college buttery, absence from college meetings and failure to read at dinner. The court of the Dean and Chapter dealt with neglect of chantry duties by vicars who were also chantry priests, with immorality and habitual drunkenness and, in general, with offences against Canon Law.[7] Irregularities of various kinds were also brought before the bishop at his visitation. It was reported to Bishop Chandler at his visitation of Salisbury in 1418 that the vicars sang

[1] Reynolds, *Wells Cathedral*, p. xxix; Palmer, *Collectanea I*, p. 55.
[2] Oliver, *Lives of the Bishops of Exeter*, pp. 450, 91.
[3] Edwards, *English Secular Cathedrals*, pp. 283-4.
[4] Harrison, *Life in a Medieval College*, pp. 53, 63.
[5] *Dean Cosyn and Wells Cathedral Miscellanea*, p. 5.
[6] *Lincoln Statutes*, i, p. 396.
[7] Harrison, *Life in a Medieval College*, pp. 60-2, 67-72.

'balades and cantalenes in their divine services',[1] and to Bishop Beauchamp in 1454 that three vicars were in the habit of 'running off into the town to play tennis and go to taverns, where they sat drinking and singing'.[2]

Disputes between the vicars and the residentiary canons, some of whom disliked the increasing independence of the singers, were fairly frequent during the thirteenth and four-teenth centuries. The vicars defended their privileges with some success, so that such principles as permanency of appointment and the right to nominate vicars as chantry priests, who had additional payments, when it was so provided by the founder of the chantry, became generally recognized. Cases of dis-missal were quite uncommon, and occurred only after a period of suspension and refusal to submit to public penance. In 1504 John Braddon, a vicar of Wells, who had been suspended for six weeks two years before, was accused of neglecting to cele-brate the morning Mass, keeping company with Johanna Mill-ward, speaking disrespectfully to the Sub-dean and Chapter and entering the choir without his habit and there insulting the Sub-dean. He pleaded guilty and submitted to correction. His punishment was that

'with bare feet and head and only a surplice over his gown, and with a candle of one pound weight in his hand *more poenitentis*, he should go before the procession of the church on two days, the sixth and thirteenth of October, and when the procession entered the choir he should stand in the choir and say the psalter of the Blessed Virgin Mary, or the seven peni-tential psalms, which devoutly said he should offer his candle to the image of St. Andrew'.

This penance could be remitted if he found an acceptable surety for his future conduct. Braddon did not appear to do his penance, pleading in a letter 'it is soo I have a litill besinesse to do', and after further charges and further postponements was formally dismissed by the Dean and Chapter with the signed consent of five of his colleagues.[3]

As a general rule the statutory number of vicars was the

[1] Robertson, *Sarum Close*, p. 97.
[2] *Statutes and Customs of Salisbury*, p. 332.
[3] Reynolds, *Wells Cathedral*, pp. 213–15.

same as the number of canons in the chapter. Lincoln, where only non-residentiary canons were bound to provide vicars, and St. Paul's, where the constitution differed from that of the other cathedrals, were exceptions. In the thirteenth century the numbers of canonries established were fifty-four at Wells and Lincoln (where there were thirty-four vicars in 1437),[1] fifty-two at Salisbury, thirty-six at York, twenty-eight at Hereford and Chichester, twenty-four at Exeter and twenty-one at Lichfield.[2] In the fifteenth century some cathedrals were having difficulty in keeping the number of vicars at the statutory figure. The value of endowments was falling, and in some cases the vicars themselves took steps to keep their numbers down.[3] There were only thirty-one vicars at Salisbury in 1468,[4] and at Bishop Beauchamp's visitation in 1475 it was observed that enough skilled and worthy men could not be found to maintain the statutory number, and that the Bishop's recent statute on the requirements for admission was not being observed.[5] The ever-increasing demand for competent singers for the new university colleges, collegiate churches and household chapels may have been one of the reasons why the cathedrals were unable to attract enough good men to their choirs.

Boys are mentioned in the *Institutio Osmundi*, and had important functions in the liturgical customs of the secular cathedrals. The precentor was responsible for their musical education, although the direct control of the *schola cantus* was in the hands of the succentor or his official, who taught the boys to memorize their parts in the services. The succentor also supervised the boys who carried candles, a cross or a censer when they conducted the reader of the Gospel to the lectern, while the chancellor or his deputy rehearsed them in the reading of lessons. The writer of the York statutes observed that a boy who was musical and had a good voice could in the course of time become a censer-bearer (*thurifer*), a sub-deacon, a deacon and, if he were worthy, a vicar.[6]

Until the fourteenth century the choristers lived in the houses

---

[1] At the examination by the Bishop's Commissary. *Lincoln Statutes*, iii, pp. 392-414.

[2] Edwards, *English Secular Cathedrals*, p. 33.   [3] Ibid., p. 288.

[4] Ibid., p. 274.   [5] *Ceremonies of Salisbury*, pp. 157, 154.

[6] *Lincoln Statutes*, ii, p. 103.

of the canons and acted as their personal and domestic servants. The change to a new arrangement was made, perhaps for the first time, at Lincoln in 1264 when Bishop Richard de Gravesend ordered that the choristers, who had hitherto existed on the charity of the canons, should in future live in one house under the supervision of a master, who would administer the income the Bishop had assigned to them and render an annual account to the Dean and Chapter, and that their number should be twelve, including two thurifers.[1] In 1322 Bishop Roger de Mortival of Salisbury, who had been Dean of Lincoln from 1310 to 1315, observed that the boys of Salisbury were 'compelled of necessity to go round flocking to crave a beggar's dole each day in the dwellings of resident canons', and ordered that they should no longer be used as servants but should 'give themselves to the ministries of the church and to liberal studies only'. They were put under the charge of a residentiary canon, who should act as their warden (*custos*) and control the use of their income, including the rentals which Bishop Simon of Ghent had given in 1314 'for the sustenance of fourteen chorister boys of the church and of a master to instruct them in grammar'.[2] Bishop Ralph of Shrewsbury found a similar situation at Wells in 1349, where there were 'boys called choristers serving in divine offices . . . at the day and night hours, for whose meat and raiment no rents have been assigned, so that by reason of indigence they must absent themselves to seek a living elsewhere'. He gave the choristers a yearly income and built a house for them and their master.[3]

In some cases the housing of the choristers was looked after by a canon-master and their musical training by the succentor or a vicar, while in others the posts of master and *informator* were combined. After 1400 the formal appointment of one of the vicars as instructor of the choristers became more common, and usually included the duty of teaching polyphonic music. At Lincoln, where the posts remained separate, John of Thetford was *magister choristarum in cantu et musica* in 1395.[4] J. Retford is referred to as *magister sive informator vicariorum et choristarum in cantu* in 1429, and W. Foukys, a vicar, was put in charge of

[1] *Lincoln Statutes*, iii, p. 162.   [2] Robertson, *Sarum Close*, pp. 39–40.
[3] Palmer, *Collectanea I*, pp. 55–6.
[4] Maddison, *Vicars-choral of Lincoln*, p. 29.

the *scholae cantus et grammatices* in 1431.[1] The composer William Horwood was appointed instructor in 1477, with the specific duty of teaching the choristers polyphonic music.[2] Horwood's successors in this office before the Reformation included the composers Thomas Ashewell and Thomas Appleby. At Wells the duties of master and instructor were combined, and were set out in full and interesting detail in Bishop Bekynton's *Regulae et ordinationes pro virtuose regendis et dirigendis pueris Ecclesiae nostrae Choristis* of 1460.[3] The Master of the Choristers was to be a priest, knowledgeable in grammar, and skilled in plainsong and polyphonic music (*in cantu tam plano quam organico*). In the preamble to his formulation of the rules Bekynton observed that they had been instituted by Robert Catour (Catur), whom he refers to as *choristarum praeceptor ac magister*, and who appears in the cathedral records as vicar-choral and organist between 1445 and 1462. When the composer Richard Hygons was appointed Master in 1479 the duties of his position were put down in even more detail in a lengthy indenture,[4] which granted him, in addition to his stipend, a quarterly sum for the support of the choristers and the occupation of one of the houses Bekynton had built on the south side of the cathedral close. In a Salisbury Chapter Act of 1462 John Thatcher or Catherow is referred to as *instructor choristarum in cantu*, and John Kegewyn was appointed to the position in the following year.[5] The composer Thomas Knyght was one of Thatcher's successors in the sixteenth century, and the teaching of polyphony was prescribed among his duties.[6] Provision for an *informator* at Chichester was made in Bishop Sherborne's 'Donations' of 1531–4,[7] and a surviving account of 1544 records a payment to William Samford *pro informatione choristarum*.[8]

At some cathedrals the number of choristers was increased in the later Middle Ages. Wells had six choristers and three

---

[1] *Lincoln Statutes*, iii, p. 470.   [2] *Lincoln Chapter Acts 1536–47*, p. 31, n.

[3] English translation in *Dean Cosyn and Wells Cathedral Miscellanea*.

[4] Printed as Appendix I below, p. 425.

[5] Salisbury Muniments, Newton Register, pp. 39, 57 (January 9, 1462; May 7, 1463).

[6] See below, p. 179.

[7] Copies in the County Hall, Chichester, in Winchester College, and in New College, Oxford.

[8] County Hall, Chichester, Chapter Act Book C.L.12, fo. 57.

'tabulars', a term used there for older boys who recorded attendance, in 1430–1, and twelve choristers in 1534–5.[1] The Chichester constitutions of 1232 provided for ten *pueri in tertia forma*;[2] in 1481 Bishop Storey increased the number to twelve, eight of whom were singers and the four oldest thurifers.[3] York had seven choristers according to statute, twelve by 1472.[4] Under Bishop Grandisson's statutes of 1337 there were to be twelve choristers at Exeter from that time on;[5] Lichfield also had twelve, while five was the number laid down by the Hereford statutes of 1280.[6] Comparison of these figures with the numbers of vicars given above makes it clear that the singers in a medieval cathedral were not thought of as a balanced choir in the modern sense. Their numbers were determined by the size and history of the particular institution, and their primary function was the rendering of the plainsong chants and lessons of the ritual. Polyphony was used to add distinction to the ritual of festivals and was sung by a small group of expert singers, while the regular teaching of polyphonic music to a larger group of vicars and choristers was a development of the later Middle Ages. The discussion of these points and their relation to the form and history of the liturgy will be taken up in subsequent chapters.

The constitution of St. Paul's differed from that of the other secular cathedrals in several ways, and seems to have retained some pre-Norman features. The 'great chapter' consisted of the bishop, dean and thirty canons, and there was also a college of twelve minor or 'petty' canons, all priests, which was presided over by a *custos* and was endowed and incorporated in 1394. The most skilled musician among the minor canons was chosen as sub-dean, and was in charge of the choir, while the second and third minor canons, who were called 'cardinals', a name which existed at St. Paul's before the conquest and is not found elsewhere, were responsible for the discipline and order of the singers.[7] Richard Cotell, who is known as the

---

[1] Reynolds, *Wells Cathedral*, p. lxxxv.
[2] *Statutes and Constitutions of Chichester*, pp. 3 sqq.
[3] *Early Statutes of Chichester*, p. 41.
[4] Harrison, *Life in a Medieval College*, p. 102.
[5] *Ordinale Exon*, i, p. 7.   [6] *Lincoln Statutes*, ii, p. 83.
[7] Statutes of 1386 in *Charter and Statutes of the Minor Canons of St. Paul's*, p. 23; also in *Registrum Statutorum Ecclesiae S. Pauli*, pp. 329 sqq.

PLATE I

2. Wells Cathedral: stairway from the Cathedral to the Chapter-house and Vicars' Hall

1. Salisbury Cathedral in 1754. The choir-screen was removed by James Wyatt c. 1790

PLATE II

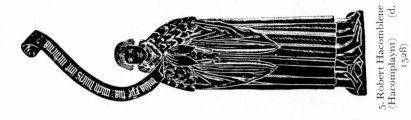

5. Robert Hacomblene (Hacomplaynt) (d. 1528)

4. John Grandisson, Bishop of Exeter, 1327-1369

3. Archbishop Talbot with his minor canons and choristers

writer of a short treatise on descant,[1] appears as a member of the college in the charter of 1394, and as cardinal in a document of the following year which signified the acceptance by the minor canons of their obligations under the charter.[2] In addition to the minor canons there was a body of thirty vicars-choral, inferior to them in rank, who took part in the work of the choir and, as elsewhere, served for their first year on probation. The statutes and customs drawn up by Ralph de Baldock (Dean, 1294–1305) and carried down to his own time by Thomas Lisieux (Dean, 1441–56) mention boys both as *pueri elemosinarii* and as *garciones*, the latter being helpers about the church under the direction of the sacrist.[3] The proposed statutes of John Colet (Dean, 1505–19), though never adopted, probably represent arrangements for the choristers which had been in force for some time. He provided for eight boys to be under the supervision of an almoner (*elemosinarius*), who was to see that they were taught singing and reading 'so that they can be in every way fit for the service of God in the choir'.[4] The most famous holder of this post was the composer John Redford (d. 1547). Philip Ap Rhys, a composer of organ music of the same period as Redford, is described in a musical manuscript as 'off saynt poulls in london'.

A grammar school attached to the cathedral was founded by Richard de Belmeis, who became Bishop of London in 1108. The statutes refer to a *magister de artibus scholis grammaticis* who acted under the chancellor, and also to a *magister scholae cantus in ecclesia Sancti Gregorii*, which was at the south-west side of the cathedral. In Colet's statutes the duties of the master of the song school were 'to instruct those who cannot sing and diligently to teach the boys'.[5] Colet's foundation of St. Paul's School was a new and separate institution, which he put under the control of a lay body, the Mercers' Company, while the almonry and choristers' school of the cathedral continued to exist through and after the Reformation. By the early sixteenth century the number of boys had been increased to ten, though there were now only six vicars-choral, for the grant approved

---

[1] In Oxford, Bodleian Library, MS. Bodl. 842, under the heading 'Opinio Ricardi Cutell de London'.

[2] *Registrum Statutorum Ecclesiae S. Pauli*, p. 362.

[3] Ibid., p. 109.   [4] Ibid., p. 228.   [5] Ibid., pp. 22, 226.

by Henry VII in 1507 for the foundation of the Guild of Jesus provided that 'twelf Petichanons if there be so many, viii Chauntry Preestis, six Vicars and tenne Queresters' should attend the services on the feast of the Name of Jesus.[1] However, the choir was supplemented by sixteen chantry priests, according to the numbers given in the statutes drawn up by Wolsey after he became Cardinal in 1515, which are twelve minor canons, sixteen chantry priests who also served in choir (*ad officium et sectam chori adstrictus*), six vicars and ten choristers.[2]

All but two of the Scottish cathedrals adopted constitutions similar to those of the English secular cathedrals before the end of the thirteenth century. The exceptions were St. Andrew's, which was a community of Augustinian Canons, and Whithorn, the cathedral of Galloway, which was run by canons of the order of St. Norbert of Prémontré, called Premonstratensians or White Canons.[3] The diocese of Moray formed its chapter on the model of Lincoln in 1212 when its cathedral was at Spyny, some twelve years before the new cathedral of Elgin was begun. Elgin had seventeen vicars-choral in 1489.[4] The chapter of Glasgow cathedral, which was dedicated in 1136, adopted the 'liberties of the cathedral church of Salisbury' in 1258,[5] and St. Machar's cathedral, Aberdeen, adopted the English form of constitution in 1256. At Aberdeen there were four boys to assist in the services of Matins and High Mass, two as taperers (*ceroferarii*) and two as thurifers.[6] In 1506 Robert Blacader, Archbishop of Glasgow, assigned a vicarage to maintain six boys whose voices had broken (*puerile sua voce jam destitutos*) so that they could continue to serve in the choir of his cathedral.[7]

Contemporary with his founding of Aberdeen University in 1495 Bishop William Elphinstone drew up some new statutes for Aberdeen cathedral. He ordered that there should be

[1] *Registrum Statutorum Ecclesiae S. Pauli*, p. 435.

[2] Ibid., p. 253. There were fifty-four chantry priests in St. Paul's when chantries were suppressed in 1547. Cook, *Mediaeval Chantries*, p. 114.

[3] Dowden, *The Medieval Church in Scotland*, pp. 58–9.

[4] *Use of Sarum*, i, pp. xxiii–xxiv; Dowden, *The Medieval Church in Scotland*, pp. 56, 59.

[5] *Registrum Episcopatus Glasguensis*, i, p. 166.

[6] *Registrum Episcopatus Aberdonensis*, ii, p. 49.

[7] *Liber Protocollorum*, ii, pp. 133–4.

twenty priest-vicars 'skilled and learned in Gregorian chant at least', two deacons and two sub-deacons, eleven boys who were to be maintained only as long as their voices were unbroken, and a sacristan.[1] A song school for the choristers was probably founded about the same time, for in the title of an agreement of 1537 William Myrtone is referred to as *praeceptor scholae cantationis Aberdonensis*, and in the body of the agreement he is called 'maister of the sang schuyll of the cathedrall kyrk of Aberdene'.[2] At Dunkeld cathedral Bishop George Brown endowed *c*. 1500 an altar of the Blessed Virgin, and chose seven vicars-choral to serve seven altars which were to be founded later. Alexander Myln (*c*. 1474–*c*. 1549), who wrote the lives of the fifteenth-century bishops of Dunkeld, records that in his day several of the canons were skilled in music, particularly John Stevenson, who excelled 'in music and in the playing of the organs', and Thomas Bettoun, who was 'highly trained in the theory of music as well as in the art of singing'.[3]

The Bishop of St. David's, the foremost cathedral of Wales, was the actual president of the chapter, there being no dean, and he was also the head of the collegiate churches which were founded by Thomas Beck (Bishop, 1280–93) at Llangadoc, which had twenty-one canons and twenty-one vicars, and Abergwili, where there were twelve canons and twelve vicars.[4] Beck built a house for the cathedral vicars, who numbered thirteen in the fourteenth century, and Adam Houghton (Bishop, 1362–89, and previously Precentor) founded *c*. 1382, with the help of John of Gaunt, the College of St. Mary, which formed a part of the cathedral buildings and establishment. He ordered that the Master and seven priests 'should live together in a collegiate manner and perform the Divine Offices in their Choir according to the Salisbury Missal', and that they 'should assist on Sundays and double festivals at High Mass and Vespers in the Cathedral among the Vicars there'. Houghton also made provision for 'two choristers under the Precentor's

[1] *Registrum Episcopatus Aberdonensis*, ii, pp. 92–101 (May 7, 1506). The term *cantus Gregorianus* seems not to have been used in England.
[2] Ibid., ii, p. 412.
[3] *Rentale Dunkeldense*, pp. xxxix, 302 sqq. Other musicians mentioned are James Lawder and William Martin, chaplains, Stephen Yong, John Pennicuke, John Martyn, John Leslie and William Scherar.
[4] Harrison, *Life in a Medieval College*, p. 291.

care, who was to instruct them in grammar learning and singing', and left in his will two pence to each of the four choristers of his cathedral.[1] Bishop John Morgan added two more choristers in 1501, and in 1504 there were sixteen vicars and seven choristers in the cathedral, and a master and six fellows, three of whom were also vicars, in the college. According to an account of the history of St. David's written in the eighteenth century, 'Mr. John Norman, a skilful and learned musician, was organist and Master of the Choristers' in the time of Bishop Edward Vaughan (1509–22).[2] This is probably the composer John Norman, who was later a clerk at Eton.

In 1152, eighteen years before the Norman conquest of Ireland, the Synod of Kells established the four archiepiscopal sees of Ireland at Armagh, the seat of the Primate, Dublin, Cashel and Tuam. Two years after the Norman occupation a council of the Irish bishops summoned by Henry II at Cashel decreed that the liturgical use of England, that is, of Salisbury, should be observed in Ireland.[3] The episcopal seat of Dublin was the cathedral priory of the Holy Trinity, later called Christ Church, where St. Laurence O'Toole (Archbishop, 1161–80), the last Irish-born occupant of the see until the seventeenth century, brought the canons, who had been seculars, under a form of the Augustinian rule. John Comyn, the first Anglo-Norman Archbishop of Dublin (1180–1212), moved his palace from the precincts of the priory to a new palace of St. Sepulchre outside the city wall, beside the ancient church of St. Patrick, which he rebuilt and founded as a collegiate church with thirteen canonries. His successor Henry de Loundres, who had experienced the unfortunate results of the Bishop of Coventry's attempt to replace monks by secular canons, gave St. Patrick's in 1220 a constitution modelled on that of Salisbury, and thus brought about a unique solution of the conflict between the secular and regular foundations by providing the city of his see with two cathedrals, one of each kind. Thereafter the Archbishop of Dublin was both 'Regular

[1] Yardley, *Minevia Sacra*, pp. 371–2.
[2] Ibid., pp. 383, 86. William Warryn received payments as organist from 1490–3. Jones and Freeman, *History and Antiquities of St. David's*, pp. 326, 377, 380.
[3] Wilkins, *Concilia*, i, p. 473.

Abbot of the Cathedral Church of the Holy Trinity and Bishop of St. Patrick's'. Under Henry's foundation the Cathedral and Collegiate Church of St. Patrick had twenty-two canons and a college of vicars.[1] The further development of the choir of St. Patrick's was due to Richard Talbot (Precentor of Hereford, 1407; Dean of Chichester, 1415; Archbishop of Dublin, 1418–49), who founded in 1431 a college of four minor canons (*parvi canonici*), intermediate in rank between the canons and vicars, and six choristers.[2]

Collegiate Churches and Household Chapels

A collegiate church was similar to a cathedral in its constitution, being a *collegium* or brotherhood of priests presided over by a warden, dean or provost, but was distinct from a cathedral in having no necessary connection with a bishop. Among the oldest of such churches were the three great northern minsters (the term was used in Anglo-Saxon times) of Ripon, Beverley and Southwell. The titular head of all three was the Archbishop of York, while the working head of Beverley was a provost, and Ripon and Southwell were in the curious position of having no designated head, the president of their chapter being the senior residentiary canon. In Archbishop Kemp's injunctions to Ripon in 1439 the number of members is given as seven canons (*personae*), one of whom acted as precentor (*rector chori*), six vicars, six deacons, six thurifers and six choristers. All were to be competent in reading and singing. Archbishop Corbridge had ordered in 1303 that each canon should pay an annual stipend to his vicar, but neither this order nor that of Archbishop Melton (1317–40) that the vicars should be paid out of the common fund can have worked well, for Archbishop Kemp (1426–52) directed that they should be paid under the Archbishop's supervision and not by the chapter.[3]

The foundation at Beverley consisted of nine canons, a precentor and seven singing clerks who rejoiced in the name of *berefellarii* or *clerici berfell*, probably because they wore bearskin

[1] Stokes, *Ireland and the Anglo-Norman Church*, pp. 272, 266.
[2] Mason, *History and Antiquities of St. Patrick's*, pp. 84, xxxiii.
[3] *Memorials of Ripon*, pp. 44, 110, 149.

collars. In 1320 the chapter added an indefinite number of 'clerks of the second form', eight boys 'apt in singing and filling the office of choristers' and two thurifers. Archbishop Arundel's statutes of 1391 observed that no proper provision had been made for the maintenance of these people, so that many of them went elsewhere and others were reduced to begging, which brought 'disrepute to the clergy and dishonour to the church'. He decreed that the Archbishop and canons should each pay his own clerk, and that the clerks of the precentor and of the *clerici berfell*, with the choristers and thurifers, should be paid out of the canons' revenues.[1] The existence of a song school at Beverley is recorded in 1423-4. At Southwell there were sixteen vicars, who received their statutes in 1248, six choristers and two thurifers. Attached to the minster were schools of song and grammar, each with a vicar as its master.[2]

The church of the Holy Cross at Crediton, which had been the episcopal see before *c.* 1050 and became a collegiate church in 1304, was enlarged in 1334 by Bishop John Grandisson of Exeter, who added four young clerks with changed voices (*virilem vocem habentes*) and four boy-clerks to the foundation. The boys, who were to occupy themselves alternately in school and in choir, were to be trained in singing by one of the clerks.[3] Grandisson's own foundation, the raising in 1337 of the parish church of Ottery St. Mary near Exeter to the status of a collegiate church, is one of the most interesting of the century from the musical point of view because of the detailed nature of his statutes.[4] The establishment included a warden, minister, precentor, sacristan and four other canons, eight priest-vicars, eight clerks called 'secondaries' as at Exeter, eight choristers and a grammar master. The choristers were to be admitted as secondaries when their voices changed (*cum ad virilem vocem pervenerint*), and secondaries, if competent, were to be promoted to vicars in preference to outsiders. The qualification for admission as a vicar or secondary was ability to read and sing the *Tonale* with the differences and the *Venitarium*, and vicars were then required to memorize the melodies of the *Commune*

---

[1] *Memorials of Beverley*, i, pp. 380, 277, lxv.
[2] *Visitations and Memorials of Southwell*, p. lxv.
[3] *Monasticon Diocesis Exoniensis*, pp. 415, 81.
[4] Printed in Dalton, *The Collegiate Church of Ottery St. Mary*.

Sanctorum. Secondaries and choristers had to memorize the *Venitarium* and all the usual melodies for the *Benedicamus* within a month after admission or lose half of their stipend. A separate statute on the teaching of polyphonic music decreed that the precentor and the 'Chaplain of the Blessed Mary', that is, of the Lady-chapel, should see that the boys and secondaries who were sufficiently musical were taught to sing and play polyphonic music (*in cantu organico et organicis instrumentis*) and that they attended the daily Mass of the Virgin. Among the other matters which Grandisson, with characteristic thoroughness, dealt with in his statutes were the proceedings at the annual feast on the festival of the Assumption, the parts of the services which were to be sung without books (*extra librum*), the numbers of each kind of service book and of candles to be provided for each side of the choir, and the proper way to handle books and turn pages.[1]

The same period saw the incorporation by royal charter of two important collegiate churches of royal foundation, the chapels of St. Stephen at Westminster (1348) and of St. George at Windsor (1352).[2] The building of a royal chapel at Westminster was begun under Edward I in 1292, perhaps in rivalry with Sainte Chapelle, the private chapel of the French kings, and was completed by Edward III in 1347. Sainte Chapelle had thirteen canons, one being treasurer and head of the chapel and another precentor, thirteen priest-chaplains, thirteen clerk-deacons and six boys under a master.[3] Edward III's foundation of St. Stephen's provided for a dean and twelve canons, thirteen priest-vicars, four clerks and six choristers. In 1396 the vicars, clerks and choristers were given the right, for the purpose of owning property, to style themselves 'the college of vicars, clerks and choristers of the chapel royal of St. Stephen in the palace of Westminster' and to elect their own warden. In the first year of Edward VI (1547-8) the chapel of St. Stephen was handed over to the Commons for their use, and in 1834 it

---

[1] '. . . non cum digitis sputo tinctis, ut sutores, nec plicando quasi per aures caperent, set cum digitis incipiendo in superiore parte, descendendo vertant'. Ibid., p. 162.

[2] The letters patent for both foundations are dated August 6, 1348. *Calendar of Patent Rolls, 1348–50*, pp. 144–7.

[3] Brenet. *Les Musiciens de la Sainte-Chapelle*, p. 13.

was destroyed by fire.[1] It has been established that the composer Nicholas Ludford was a member of the chapel at its dissolution.[2]

The chapel in Windsor Castle goes back to the reign of Henry I, when it was dedicated to St. Edward and endowed with eight canonries. With the rise of the cultivation of chivalric pageantry under Edward III it was refounded as the chapel of the order of the Knights of St. George, with a warden and twelve other canons, thirteen priest-vicars, four clerks and six choristers. The statutes provided that one of the vicars was to instruct the choristers in grammar and singing,[3] and the Treasurer's rolls show that his usual title was Master of the Choristers. The composers Thomas Damett (d. 1437) and Nicholas Sturgeon (d. 1454) were both granted prebends in Windsor after serving as clerks in the Royal Household Chapel, Damett in 1431 and Sturgeon in 1442.[4] In 1474–5 Edward IV began the building of his new chapel of St. George, and in 1483 his 'new' foundation was incorporated by an Act of Parliament, which noted that the King had 'now greatly encresed the noumbre of Ministres daily serving Almighty God in the said Chapell'.[5] This increase can be traced month by month in an attendance book of the chapel which runs from June 1468 to July 1479. Two clerks were added in 1475–6, and in 1477–8 we find four clerks, described as 'of the first foundation', being paid four pounds each, plus an extra payment of two pounds thirteen shillings and four pence *ex gratia superadditione domini regis Edwardi quarti fundatoris nostri*,[6] while three others, described as 'of the new foundation', were paid eight pounds each. In 1479–80 there were twelve clerks receiving ten pounds each and eleven boys, and by 1482–3 the complement was the 'symmetrical' one of the new foundation, which matched the original thirteen canons and thirteen vicars with thirteen clerks and thirteen choristers. While previously the musical instruction of the choristers had sometimes been

[1] *Calendar of Patent Rolls, 1391–96*, p. 669; Hastings, *St. Stephen's Chapel*, pp. 2, 41, 44.
[2] According to a broadcast talk by Hugh Baillie.
[3] Fellowes, *Windsor Organists*, p. xiii.
[4] Ollard, *Fasti Wyndesorienses*, pp. 91, 117.
[5] Fellowes, *Vicars and Minor Canons of Windsor*, p. 7.
[6] Treasurer's Roll No. XV.34.54.

entrusted to one of the clerks instead of to a vicar, this now
became the regular practice, and at the same time the post of
'supervisor' of the choristers, held by a vicar, was instituted.
The composer Walter Lambe was *informator* in 1479–80 jointly
with William Edmunds, later (1490) a gentleman of the Royal
Household Chapel,[1] and Lambe was sole *informator* in 1483–4.
Other composers who filled this post were Richard Hampshire
in 1492 and from 1496 to 1499,[2] and John Marbeck, whose
name first appears in 1541–2 as an organ player, in 1558–9.[3]

Besides these two permanently endowed royal foundations
there was also a chapel of the Royal Household which has not
always been clearly distinguished from them by writers on
English medieval music. In the twelfth and thirteenth centuries
the royal 'chapel' consisted of the chaplains and clerks of the
household whose duties included ministering to the king's
private devotions and attending him at special ceremonies
outside the court. Henry III's extreme piety caused him to
hear Mass several times a day and his love of liturgical ceremony to have the royal Laudes (*Christus vincit*, etc.) sung before
him on all important festivals. Three, and sometimes four,
clerks of his chapel were paid twenty-five shillings each for
chanting the Laudes, and later were granted five pounds a
year each.[4] It may have been Edward III (r. 1327–77) who
first put the household chapel on a more formal basis, for in
1349 John Wodeford was 'a king's clerk and dean of his
chapel'.[5] The Wardrobe Account of 1393 gives the names of
eleven chaplains and clerks, among them William Excestre,[6]
and six clerks who appear in that list, together with the dean
(John Boor), went to Ireland with Richard II in the following
year.[7] The music by Excestre in the early fifteenth-century
choirbook of the Household Chapel, now known as the Old Hall
manuscript, has been credited to William Excestre, but one

---

[1] *Calendar of Patent Rolls 1488–94*, p. 309.   [2] Treasurer's Rolls.

[3] Fellowes, *Windsor Organists*, p. 14.

[4] Harvey, *The Plantagenets*, pp. 25, 29, 56; Kantorowicz, *Laudes Regiae*,
pp. 98, 175–6. The period covered by these payments for the Laudes is
1227 to 1241.

[5] *Calendar of Patent Rolls 1348–50*, p. 285.

[6] I owe this information to John Harvey, who has kindly allowed me to
use his lists of chapel members from the Wardrobe Books of 1393–1450.

[7] *Calendar of Patent Rolls 1391–6*, p. 473.

of the three pieces is marked J. Excetre, and all three are probably by a clerk of that name who was in the king's retinue going to Ireland, and who was connected with the chapel from *c.* 1374 to *c.* 1396.[1]

Under the Lancastrian kings the Household Chapel began to play a more important part in the musical life of the kingdom. Two years after his reign began Henry IV engaged a chaplain[2] to teach grammar to the boys of the chapel. In 1402 there were eighteen chaplains and clerks under Richard Prentys, formerly one of the clerks, as dean, while in the first year of Henry V's reign (1413) there were some twenty-seven. Four of these, John Burell, John Cooke, Thomas Damett and Nicholas Sturgeon, were composers, as was Robert Chirbury, who had joined the chapel by 1421. In 1420 the composer John Pyamour, who may have acted as master of the choristers, though he is called merely 'one of the clerks of the chapel of the household', was commissioned to impress boy choristers and bring them to the King in Normandy,[3] where his chapel had been with him since 1417. The excellence of Henry V's chapel music was thus celebrated in a contemporary poem:[4]

> Psallit plena Deo cantoribus ampla capella:
> Carmine sidereo laudabilis est ea cella.

In his will Henry left two hundred pounds to the clerks of his chapel, and steps were taken in 1432 to distribute this sum 'to the clerks of the chapel of the household before they separate' and in the following year to decide the proportion to be paid to each.[5]

In the last complete year of Henry V's reign (1421–2) there were sixteen choristers in the chapel, but within a year their number had fallen to six,[6] and it is likely that the numbers in the chapel were reduced during Henry VI's minority. In 1437

---

[1] Calendars of Patent Rolls, passim.

[2] John Bugby, who 'had to wait at least three years before he got a penny of his salary'. Wylie, *England Under Henry IV*, ii, p. 487.

[3] *Calendar of Patent Rolls 1416–22*, pp. 127, 272.

[4] *De Honestate hospitii domini Regis et ministrorum eius*, printed in *Memorials of Henry V*, p. 68.

[5] *Calendar of Patent Rolls 1429–36*, pp. 205, 349.

[6] *Acts of the Privy Council*, iii, p. 104. The date is June 15, 1423, and the names are given.

Henry assumed the rule of his kingdom and household, and in 1440 the dean was commissioned to impress choristers.[1] The Wardrobe Accounts show seven members of the chapel in 1436, twenty-six in 1441, in which year the composer John Plummer was granted ten pounds, perhaps for instructing and supervising the choristers.[2] The first definite evidence of the appointment of a master is the grant in 1444 of forty marks a year to Plummer for the 'exhibition' of eight boys of the chapel and for his reward.[3] Subsequent masters of the children who are known as composers were Gilbert Banester (1478–86), William Newark (1486–1509) and William Cornysh (1509–23). A complete list of the King's 'honeurable household' in 1454 gives the numbers in the chapel as twenty chaplains and clerks and seven children,[4] while ten children are mentioned in the grant of the mastership to Henry Abyngdon from Michaelmas of the following year.[5] In August of that year the priests and clerks petitioned the Privy Council 'to consider their great labour because their number was less than formerly', to authorize that there should be at least twenty-four singing men, to retain the 'poor priest' William Stevyns to say the daily Mass of Our Lady, keep the vestry and read the Gospel, and to provide a man to read the Epistle. Stevyns was confirmed in his post and an epistoler was provided, but there was no response to the other part of the petition.[6]

In 1483 Edward IV incorporated the Royal Free Chapel of the Household with a dean and three canons who were to act as sub-dean, treasurer and precentor, and gave it the endowments of the chapel of St. Peter in the Tower of London.[7] Under Edward's ordinances for his household the chapel comprised twenty-four chaplains and clerks, the latter being referred to as 'gentylmen clerkes'. While the terms 'gentleman' and 'yeoman' were used in other branches of the household, and defined the rank of the singers among its members, they seem also to have implied that the clerks of the Household Chapel

[1] *Calendar of Patent Rolls 1436–41*, p. 452.   [2] Ibid., p. 519.
[3] *Calendar of Patent Rolls 1441–6*, p. 311.
[4] *Acts of the Privy Council*, vi, p. 223.
[5] *Calendar of Patent Rolls 1452–61*, p. 279.
[6] *Acts of the Privy Council*, vi, p. 256.
[7] *Calendar of Patent Rolls 1476–85*, p. 341.

could be lay-clerks, and were no longer required to be in orders. They should be 'endowed with vertuuse morall and speculatiff as of theyre musike, shewing in descant, clene voysed, well releesed and pronouncynge, eloquent in reding, sufficiaunt in organes pleyyng'. There were also two yeomen of the chapel 'called pistellers groweing from the children of the chappell by succession of age and after that theire voices change', and eight children under a master chosen by the dean from the members of the chapel to teach them 'as well in the schoole of facett as in songe, organes and such other vertuous thinges'. If no preferment were found in the chapel for a chorister when he reached eighteen and his voice had changed, then 'the King assigneth every suche child to a college of Oxenford or Cambrige of the King's foundation, there to be in finding and study sufficiauntly, tyll the Kinge otherwise list to advaunce him'.[1]

The number of gentlemen in some lists of between 1504 and 1548 varies between eighteen and twenty-one. A list for 1525-6 has nine priest-chaplains and nineteen gentlemen besides the master, whose grant was raised in that year to forty pounds, Henry VIII having increased the number of children to twelve.[2] Besides the masters of the children already mentioned, the following composers were members of the Royal Household Chapel: John Fowler, Robert Fayrfax, John Cornysh, Henry Prentyce, Robert Jones, John Lloyd, Thomas Farthyng, Avery Burton, Richard Pygot, Richard Sampson (Dean of St. Stephen's, Westminster, 1520; Dean of the Household Chapel, 1523), Robert Okeland, Thomas Tallis and Thomas Wryght.

Household chapels were also maintained from time to time by great lords and prelates, though these chapels did not have the continuity of the royal chapel, for obvious reasons. The chapel of John of Gaunt, Henry IV's father, who was created Duke of Lancaster in 1362, had four chaplains and two clerks between 1371 and 1374,[3] and by 1380-1 it was under the control of John Grantham as dean,[4] and had been increased

---

[1] *A Collection of Ordinances*, pp. 50-1.

[2] Roper, 'The Chapels Royal', p. 25; Lafontaine, *The King's Musick*, pp. 2-5.

[3] *John of Gaunt's Register, 1372-1376*, pp. 88, 132, 231, 327.

[4] In 1353 the principal chaplain of the household of Henry, Duke of Lancaster, John of Gaunt's father-in-law, is referred to as 'dean' of his chapel. *Calendar of Papal Registers, Petitions*, i, p. 238.

by three choristers. The chapel was normally at Leicester, but moved with the Duke for extended stays elsewhere, as in 1381, when the dean and one of the clerks were ordered to pack the jewels, vestments and ornaments ready to be carried to Pontefract Castle, and to go there with all the chapel clerks and ministers. In 1383 William Excestre, who may well be identical with the William Excestre of the royal chapel in 1393, was one of the clerks of the Duke's chapel.[1] During the reign of Henry VI his uncle Duke Humphrey of Gloucester (d. 1447) maintained a chapel, for at his death Eton and King's Colleges petitioned the King that they should have 'the ferste choise . . . of all maner bokes, ornementes, and other necessaries as nowe late were perteynyng to the Duke of Gloucestre'.[2] In 1445 the Duke gave a grant of eight pounds a year for life to 'his servitor' Henry Abyngdon, who may therefore have been in charge of his chapel,[3] and who became a clerk at Eton in the year of the Duke's death. Gloucester's brother John, Duke of Bedford, had his chapel, of which John Dunstable was a member, in Paris as Regent of France from 1423 to 1429 and in Rouen as Governor of Normandy from 1429 to 1435. William Courtenay, Archbishop of Canterbury (d. 1396), left sums of money in his will to two clerks and the boys of his chapel,[4] and there is evidence that Queen Catherine, Henry V's widow, and Cardinal Beaufort also kept private chapels during this period.[5]

Edward IV maintained a household and chapel for his elder son Edward (b. 1470), who was murdered in the Tower after his accession in 1483.[6] There are indications of a chapel in the household of Henry VII's mother Margaret Beaufort, Countess of Richmond and Derby (d. 1509), to which the composer Thomas Farthyng probably belonged,[7] and in that of Henry VIII's illegitimate son Henry Fitzroy, Duke of

---

[1] *John of Gaunt's Register, 1379–83*, pp. 41, 90, 177, 278.

[2] Lyte, *History of Eton*, p. 27.

[3] *Calendar of Patent Rolls 1446–52*, p. 21; *Calendar of Patent Rolls 1461–67*, p. 94.

[4] The clerks were Salesbury and William Motte. Duncan, 'The Will of William Courtenay', p. 63.

[5] *Calendar of Papal Registers, Letters*, viii, p. 486, and see below, p. 173.

[6] See below, p. 170.

[7] Henry VIII granted him an annuity in 1511 'in consideration of his services' to the Countess. *Letters and Papers of Henry VIII*, i, p. 443.

Richmond (1519–36).[1] An account begun in 1512 of the chapel of Henry Percy, fifth Earl of Northumberland, at his castles of Wresile and Lekingfield in Yorkshire shows that it had a dean, sub-dean, Lady-Mass priest, gospeller, a number of gentlemen varying from eight to eleven and five or six children.[2] Cardinal Wolsey's private chapel comprised a dean, gospeller and epistoler, ten chaplains, twelve clerks and ten choristers, whose master was Richard Pygot, later of the royal chapel.[3]

The history of the chapel of the Scottish kings goes back to 1120, when Alexander I founded a chapel in Stirling Castle dedicated to his mother, Queen Margaret. Its establishment was enlarged by James III (r. 1460–88), and there are records of payments to the clerks of James IV's chapel between 1488 and 1490. In 1501 the 'Chapel Royal of St. Mary and St. Michael within the palace of the castle of Stirling' was made a collegiate church, with a dean, sub-dean, sacristan, sixteen canons, sixteen prebends 'skilled in singing' and six boy clerks 'competently trained in singing or fit to be instructed therein'.[4]

Ottery St. Mary was an example of a collegiate church founded by raising a parish church to collegiate status. Similarly, Manchester parish church was made the collegiate church of St. Mary the Virgin, with a warden, four fellows, four priests and six choristers, by Thomas Delawarr in 1421.[5] After re-establishments under Mary, Elizabeth I and Charles I it eventually became a cathedral in 1847. In other cases collegiate churches had a close connection with the family and estates of the founder, like the college founded at Arundel (Sussex) in 1386 by Richard, Earl of Arundel, which consisted of a master, twelve canons or priest-fellows, six clerks, two acolytes, two sacrists and seven choristers. Arundel replaced the parish church of St. Nicholas by a new building, the nave and transepts of which were for the use of the parishioners while the east end was the collegiate chapel.[6] The college of Fotheringhay Castle (Northants), which was endowed in 1410–11 by

[1] See below, p. 173.
[2] *Regulations and Establishment of the Household of the Fifth Earl of Northumberland*, pp. 254, 256.
[3] Hawkins, *History of Music*, iii, p. 67.
[4] Rogers, *The Chapel Royal of Scotland*, p. xxvi.
[5] *Monasticon*, vi, p. 1423.
[6] *Monasticon*, vi, p. 1377.

Henry IV and Edward, Duke of York, as the burial place and chantry college of the house of York, took over the site of the parish church in 1415. It had a master, twelve chaplain-fellows, eight clerks, four of whom are described as gentleman-clerk (*clericus generosus*) and four as yeoman-clerk (*clericus valetus*), and thirteen choristers. The statutes provided that the precentor and three senior fellows should choose a skilled instructor to train the choristers. When Bishop Alnwick visited the college in 1438 the precentor was William Typpe, who is probably the composer W. Typp who contributed seven pieces to the Old Hall manuscript. At the visitation of 1442 it was reported that, contrary to statute, there were only six clerks and ten choristers in the college.[1] The record of the visitation of 1530, however, gives the names of the full complement of fellows, clerks and choristers.[2]

When Ralph, Baron Cromwell, the king's treasurer, completed his castle of Tattershall in Lincolnshire, he raised the parish church there to the status of a collegiate church, with a warden, six chaplains, six clerks and six choristers, and joined to it an almshouse for thirteen poor persons.[3] In the record of the visitation by Bishop Longland's chancellor in May, 1525,[4] John Taverner is listed as a clerk-fellow (*clericus socius*); his submission to the Visitor was: 'est quedam camera magistri Clercke ruinosa'. In the following year Taverner went, at the instance of Longland, to be the first *informator* at Wolsey's Cardinal College in Oxford, though at first, as Longland reported to Wolsey, he was reluctant 'to give up his living at Tattessall, and the prospect of a good marriage which he would lose by removal'.[5]

Charity was an element in some collegiate foundations, for Fotheringhay, like Tattershall, included an almshouse. Newarke

---

[1] Thompson, 'The Statutes of the College of St. Mary and All Saints, Fotheringhay', pp. 244–6, 268 sqq.; *Visitations in the Diocese of Lincoln*, ii, pp. 94, 108.

[2] Ibid., pp. 147–8.

[3] *Monasticon*, vi, p. 1432 (patent for the foundation granted in 1439); *Lincoln Statutes*, iii, pp. 447–8 (foundation sanctioned by the Bishop and Chapter of Lincoln in 1441).

[4] *Visitations in the Diocese of Lincoln*, iii, p. 112.

[5] *Letters and Papers of Henry VIII*, B, iv, 2, No. 2604, quoted in *Tudor Church Music*, i, p. xlviii.

College, Leicester, is an example of a collegiate chapel combined with a family chantry in a foundation of which charity was the chief object. It was originally founded in 1330-1 by Henry, Earl of Leicester and Lancaster, as a hospital dedicated to the Assumption of the Virgin, and was enlarged, probably in emulation of Edward III's colleges at Westminster and Windsor, by his son Henry, Duke of Lancaster, in 1355 as the Hospital and College of the Annunciation of St. Mary in the Newarke, Leicester. The hospital made provision for fifty poor men and fifty poor women, and the college consisted of a dean, twelve canons, thirteen vicars, three clerks and six choristers. The canon who acted as sacrist was in charge of the choir and received annual payments for the food and clothing of the choristers, who were to serve in the chapel 'after the manner of the choristers of the Church of Salisbury', while the clerks were to ring the bells and assist in the celebration of Masses at the altars.[1] A revision of the statutes which was made in 1491 seems to imply a development of the music, for the sacrist became precentor, the clerks came under his charge, and a fourth clerk was added to help in choir on Sundays and festivals.[2] At Bishop Longland's visitation in 1525 one of the canons gave evidence that the dean had nominated a fourth clerk who was incompetent and two choristers who could neither read nor sing, while two vicars said that the boys were ignorant of and unfit to learn plainsong and polyphony (*in cantu plano et diviso*).[3]

For some time there had been disturbances and quarrels in the college arising out of the residence there of Mary, Lady Hungerford, and her second husband, Sir Richard Sacheverell. There was ill-feeling between the dean, Lord George Grey, grandson of Edward IV's queen Elizabeth Wydville, and Lady Hungerford, who proposed to be a patroness of the college and was said to have given an endowment to add a chorister to the foundation. The evidence at the Bishop's enquiry shows that even the services in choir were interrupted by disputes. One of the charges brought by the dean against one Thomas Cawardyn and other servants of Sacheverell was that they 'dyd fface the

[1] Thompson, *Newarke Hospital and College*, Chaps. I, II; pp. 45, 52.
[2] Ibid., pp. 121, 124.
[3] *Visitations in the Diocese of Lincoln*, iii, pp. 138, 141-2.

PLATE III

New College and its members *c.* 1463, showing the Warden and seventy scholars (twenty-five
nior members, thirty-one fellows, fourteen probationary fellows), ten chaplains, three clerks
and sixteen choristers—one hundred members in all

PLATE IV

7. Illumination of the Consolidation Charter of Eton College (March, 1446): the Commons, led by the Speaker ('Prient lez comunes') and the Lords, led by the Chancellor, Archbishop Stafford, and Cardinals Beaufort and Kemp ('Et nous le prioms auxi') petition Henry VI ('Henricus sextus rex et fundator huius regalis collegii'), who addresses the Virgin ('Fiat ad laudem gloriam et cultum tuum') represented in her Assumption, to which the College was dedicated

deane at his own stall within the queer dore of the seyd collyge, laying hondis on theyr swordis and daggers, seyeng they wold stand their without the deane his leve'. Canon John Dale's evidence was that

'upon Relique Sonday last at even song oon Thomas Cawardyn stood in the porche at the chauncell doore in the college, saing his even song; and this deponent was sensying the highe awter. And when he cam down, the dean said to this deponent, Master Dale, I pray you have thies fellowes away: they stand here facyng and bracyng. And then this deponent cam thudder, and founde Thomas Cawardyn standyng leanyng on the porch syde, saying his even song; and he bad hym goo bak, and that the dean was not content that ye shall stand here. And then the said Cawardyn said noo worde, but went his waie. And then oon Wilmer stode behynde the said Cawardyn, and said, We stand here neyther to face nor brace, but to serve God as other men have been wonte to doo, and so went their waye. And after that oon John Haryngton, gentilman, came into the said porche and stode ther, and then the dean called this deponent and bad hym goo with hym; and so they went both they to my lady Hungreford, and sir Weatewod with them, she then beyng in the lower end off a chapell. And the dean said to hyr, Madame, is this a fare ruell that your servantis shall comme into the qwer, and face and brace. And she said agayn to him, I have seen men comme into the kingis chapell and other greate chapells, and noo matter made off yt. And aswell may they doo this, as you to be from service hunting, and comme home at mydnyght.'[1]

Among those who gave evidence at this enquiry was 'Hugo Asseton, *magister chorustarum*'. This is undoubtedly the composer Hugh Aston, about whose identity there has hitherto been some confusion. His evidence was about the boast of George Villiers, a Sacheverell man, that he would release a clerk of the college whom the dean had put in the stocks.[2] In the year following this enquiry Longland proposed to send a master of the choristers, presumably Aston, from Newarke College to the post of

[1] Ibid., pp. 143, 153-4. There is an extended account of the enquiry in Thompson, *Newark Hospital and College*, pp. 143-82.
[2] *Visitations in the Diocese of Lincoln*, iii, p. 222.

informator at Wolsey's new college which Taverner assumed in November of that year.[1] Aston remained at Leicester until the dissolution of the college in 1548, and was still alive at Michaelmas 1549, when he is noted as receiving the annuity of twelve pounds a year which the dean and canons had granted him in 1544.[2]

Colleges

At the time when the vicars-choral of the secular cathedrals were beginning to form colleges and organize their corporate life, a collegiate community of a different kind was brought into being by Walter de Merton, Bishop of Rochester. His statutes of 1274 for Merton College, Oxford, which he had founded ten years before, created the pattern of the collegiate life of the English universities. The scholars of his college were to be seculars living a corporate life for the purpose of study, forming a self-governing body, subject only to the visitation of the Archbishop of Canterbury, of a warden (*custos*) and fellows (*socii*), and having their own chapel, hall and library. The statutes provided that there should be three or four chaplains to celebrate the Hours services and Masses.[3] At this time University College existed only as an endowment to support scholars, becoming a college 'after the pattern of the nephews and scholars of Walter de Merton' in 1280. Balliol became a corporate community in 1282, though John de Balliol had given money to support poor scholars between 1260 and 1269.

The statutes of Exeter College in 1314, of Oriel in 1326, and Sir Philip Somerville's statutes of 1340 for Balliol were more specific than Merton's about the chapel duties of their members, but as yet no separate provision was made for a chapel choir. At Oriel Masses were to be said by two priest-scholars or by two chaplains provided by the college,[4] while at Balliol they were to be celebrated by those of the fellows who were in orders (*capellani intrinseci*).[5] On the other hand the statutes of

[1] *Letters and Papers of Henry VIII*, iv, p. 1097.
[2] Thompson, *Newarke Hospital and College*, p. 224.
[3] Brodrick, *Memorials of Merton College*, p. 322.
[4] *Statutes of Oriel College*, p. 12.
[5] *Statutes of Balliol College*, p. xvi.

Robert de Eglesfield for The Queen's College, Oxford, drawn up in 1340, provided for thirteen chaplains, and for two clerks skilled in plainsong and polyphony to serve under the chaplains and teach the 'poor boys' singing. The number of boys was to be half that of the scholars, and they were to 'minister in the chapel as choristers'.[1] John Wyllyot, Fellow of Merton from 1334 and later Chancellor of Exeter, left money to Merton to support nine 'poor scholars', called *portionistae* (later 'post-masters') because they had a portion of the common goods. They were required to wait on the fellows in hall, and those who had good voices were to serve as choristers in chapel.[2]

Almost exactly a century after Walter de Merton had established his college, William of Wykeham (Bishop of Winchester, 1367–1404) took the first steps in a plan which was to have equally fruitful results. In the words of the preamble to the statutes (1400) of Winchester College,[3] this was the foundation and endowment of

'two perpetual Colleges, viz., one perpetual College of poor and indigent scholars in the *studium* of the University of Oxford in the diocese of Lincoln, bound to study and pursue the various sciences and faculties, commonly called "Saint Mary College of Winchester in Oxford", and another perpetual College for other poor and indigent scholars bound to learn grammar, similarly called "Saint Mary College of Winchester", to the praise, glory and honour of the Crucified one and of the most glorious Mary his mother, and to the exaltation of the faith of the Holy Christian Church, the advancing of the divine ritual, and the increase of the liberal arts, sciences and faculties'.

This idea of the close union of grammar school and university college was followed in some of the most important foundations of the next century, and the elaborate statutes of Wykeham for his twin colleges find many echoes in those of later founders. It was particularly significant for the musical history of the colleges that Wykeham counted 'the advancing of the divine ritual' among his objects.

---

[1] *Statutes of The Queen's College*, pp. 29–30.
[2] *Registrum Collegii Mertonensis*, p. 515.
[3] Kirby, *Annals of Winchester College*, pp. 455 sqq.

The statutes of Winchester College provided for a warden, ten priest-fellows, seventy scholars, three chaplains, three clerks, and sixteen boy choristers 'bound to serve in the divine offices'. A knowledge of plainsong was one of the requirements for election as a scholar, and skill in reading and chant for election as a fellow or nomination as a chaplain. The choristers were to be less than twelve years old and 'competent in reading and singing', and were required to help the servants in hall and make the beds of the fellows and chaplains. One of the fellows was to be appointed sacrist, to take charge of the books and ornaments of the chapel and to fill the office of precentor. Though the statutes made no definite provision for an instructor of the choristers, the college accounts show that in 1396–7 this duty was carried out by 'Edmund, a clerk of the chapel', in the next year by an anonymous *informator choristarum* and from 1398 to 1400 by one of the chaplains. As far as can be ascertained from the muniments of the college there was no separate payment for this office again until 1541, when Robert Barber, who is known as a composer, was paid five pounds as *informator*. In the following year Robert Godwin (Fellow, 1541–50) acted as *informator* and Robert Mos or Moose as organist; from 1555–6 onwards the two offices were held by one person.

In Wykeham's university foundation of New College, Oxford, which consisted of a warden and seventy scholars, there were ten chaplains, one of whom acted as precentor and another as sacrist, while the three clerks and sixteen choristers had serving as well as chapel duties. The chaplains and clerks were *conductitii et remotivi*, that is, hired and removable, and not life members of the foundation like the *presbyteri socii perpetui*. This was the first college which required the scholars to attend Mass every day, Merton's scholars being bound to do so only on festivals. From 1394–5 the Bursar's Rolls show payments to an *informator choristarum*, who apparently taught both singing and grammar. The names which are recorded do not include any known composers, though there are many payments for writing or copying polyphonic music.[1]

Wykeham's concern was equally for scholarship and for devotion, and led him to give both the boyhood study of grammar and the university study of the arts and sciences a

[1] See below, pp. 157–9.

setting in a collegiate community with a permanent chapel foundation. The effects of his vision became manifest in the fifteenth century in the lives and work of Winchester and New College men, and in the new foundations which were modelled on his ideals. Henry Chichele (Fellow of New College, 1387–93; Bishop of St. David's, 1408; Archbishop of Canterbury, 1414) was the founder of a grammar school at his birthplace Higham Ferrers (Northants) in 1422, of St. Bernard's College, Oxford, on the site of which St. John's College was founded in 1555, in 1436, and of All Souls College, Oxford, in 1438. Henry VI's tutor and secretary of state Thomas Bekynton (Fellow of New College, 1406; of Winchester, 1408–20; Bishop of Bath and Wells, 1443) played an important part in the founding of Eton and King's, built the bridge leading to the chapter house from the vicars' hall at Wells, and was a benefactor of New College, Lincoln College, and Winchester College. Another of the great churchmen of the century, William of Wayneflete (Headmaster of Winchester, 1429; of Eton, 1442; Provost of Eton, 1443; Bishop of Winchester, 1447), founded Magdalen College, Oxford, and was mainly responsible for the completion of Eton College chapel.

Chichele joined to his grammar school at Higham Ferrers a collegiate chapel with a master and seven other chaplains, four clerks, one of whom was grammar master and another singing master, and six choristers.[1] At Lincoln College, Oxford, founded in 1429 by Richard Fleming (Bishop of Lincoln, 1419–31) with a rector and seven scholars, no special provision was made for a choir, but there were two chaplains on the foundation, and two of the fellows were to act as *rectores chori* when the rector officiated at a service.[2] All Souls, where the chapel had two chaplains, three clerks and six choristers, was conceived as both a Lancastrian war memorial and a centre of study, though Chichele put more emphasis on the former aspect. Its members were

'constantly bounden not so much to ply therein the various sciences and faculties as with all devotion to pray for the souls of glorious memory of Henry V lately King of England and France, the Lord Thomas Duke of Clarence, and the other

[1] *Monasticon*, vi, p. 1424.　　[2] *Statutes of Lincoln College*, p. 27.

lords and lieges of the realm of England whom . . . the havoc of that warfare so long prevailing between the two said realms have drenched with the bowl of bitter death, and also for the souls of all the faithful departed'.[1]

When Henry VI founded in 1440–1 his 'two colleges Roiall, one called the College Roiall of our Ladie of Eton beside Windesor, and the other called the College Roiall of our Ladie and St. Nicholas of Cambridge',[2] he followed Wykeham in many respects, but made more ample provision for the chapel services and establishment. Both Eton and King's had a provost, ten fellows, ten chaplains, ten clerks and sixteen choristers. The choristers, unlike the Winchester choristers, had no duties apart from the chapel services. Seven of the clerks at Eton were to be skilled in polyphonic music, and one at least of the seven in playing the organ. Two others acted as parish clerk and clerk of the vestry, and the complement was made up by the instructor of the choristers, a clerk or priest qualified in polyphonic and other kinds of music (*in cantu organico et aliis*), whose appointment was in the hands of the provost. The fellows were required to have some skill in plainsong, and the chaplains, who were *remotivi*, to be graduates in some faculty or else know plainsong and have good voices.[3]

Under the King's authority choristers were drafted to Eton from Salisbury and Norwich, and in 1447–8 the college had its full number of clerks and choristers. With the deposition of Henry VI and accession of Edward IV in 1461 both Eton and King's entered on a critical period. At the King's request the Pope issued a Bull in 1463 abolishing Eton and annexing its possessions to St. George's, Windsor, and in 1465 the Provost was compelled to deliver to St. George's the vestments, images, jewels, relics, books and furniture of the chapel. The Audit Rolls show that between 1467 and 1472 there were only four or five clerks in the choir. Eventually the King relented, and in 1476 Cardinal Bourchier gave a judgement, with papal authority and the King's approval, which reversed the Bull of 1463 and returned to the college its goods and most of its endow-

---

[1] *Statutes of All Souls College*, p. 2.
[2] *A Collection of Wills*, p. 293.
[3] *The Ancient Laws for King's and Eton*, pp. 513 sqq.

ments.[1] However, the number of clerks was reduced to seven and of choristers to ten. It is not without interest that the King's decision was given in the year after he had begun to build the new chapel of Windsor and to augment its foundation. The names of the instructors of the choristers at Eton, one of whom was the composer Robert Wylkynson, can be traced with but few gaps through the first century of its history. Other composers who were members of the college at some time during this period are John Sutton, William Brygeman, Henry Rysby, Robert Okeland and John Norman. Oliver Stonyng, who was precentor from 1533 to 1535, may be the composer Stonings or Stenings, whose first name is not known.[2]

At King's the crisis resulting from the deposition of the founder was reflected, as far as the musical establishment was concerned, in the dropping of clerks altogether in the years between *c.* 1460 and 1481, when the chapel was served by about seven chaplains and the choristers. Eight clerks were paid for the memorial services for Queen Catherine and Henry V in 1466–7, and four clerks for these services and for the memorial service for the benefactors in 1468–9, but it is likely that they were engaged specially for these services. In 1481–2 clerks were engaged again on a regular basis, and the record of their names has survived with almost complete continuity during the rest of our period. The earliest recorded instructor of the choristers was John Halywell, who was paid from 1449 to 1451 *pro doctrina chorustarum*. Halywell became a clerk at Eton at the beginning of 1453 and was *informator choristarum* there in 1454–5. During the period when there were no clerks the choristers were taught by a chaplain, and later the posts of instructor and supervisor seem to have been separate, for in 1502–3 John Parker, a clerk, is referred to as *informator* and in the following year Master Hobbys and Master Stalys, who were chaplains, received a joint payment *pro supervisione choristarum*. The roll of composers who were members of King's includes the names of Thomas Farthyng, Richard Hampshire, Robert Cowper, William Rasor, John Sygar,

---

[1] Lyte, *History of Eton*, p. 75.

[2] Names from the Audit Rolls and Books in the College Muniments. Compositions by Stonings are in the British Museum MSS. Add. 17802–5 and Add. 31390.

Robert Hacomblene or Hacomplaynt (Provost, 1509–28) and Christopher Tye.[1]

Wayneflete's *collegium beatae Mariae Magdalenae vulgariter dictum* Maudeleyne College *in Universitate Oxon*[2] had a grammar school joined to it, which did not, however, have a separate chapel choir. The college consisted of a president, forty scholars, thirty poor scholars called 'demys', four chaplain-conducts, eight clerks, sixteen choristers and their instructor. Both scholars and demys were required to have a knowledge of plainsong, while the clerks were to be good singers and competent in plainsong and reading. The president was to appoint one of the chaplains as sacrist or cantor and a chaplain or clerk to instruct the choristers in plainsong and other kinds of music (*in plano cantu et alio cantu*). If no one in the college were competent to be *informator* he was to appoint one from outside.[3] One of the clerks was paid for this duty from the time of the completion of the chapel *c.* 1480, and from 1490 to 1492 the post and that of organ player were divided between two or three clerks, one of whom was the composer Richard Davy.[4] John Sheppard was *informator* at various times between 1542 and 1556 but was not a Fellow of the college from 1549 to 1551, as has been stated.[5] This spelling of his name is the one most often used in contemporary documents (including the Magdalen accounts) and musical manuscripts, and will be used here rather than the later form Shepherd, which has been adopted in modern writings.

Wolsey's Cardinal College at Oxford (1525) was the most splendid and comprehensive of this succession of college foundations of the later Middle Ages. It was planned on a vast scale, having a dean and sixty canons 'of the first rank', forty canons 'of the second rank', thirteen priest-conducts, twelve clerk-

---

[1] Information in this paragraph, except that on Hacomblene, from the Mundum Books, and F. L. Clarke's lists of names from them, in the College Library.

[2] *Instrumentum Fundationis* of June 12, 1458, printed in Chandler, *Life of Wayneflete*, p. 391.

[3] *Statutes of Magdalen College*, pp. 18, 23–4.

[4] Bloxam, *Register of Magdalen*, ii, pp. 258–62.

[5] Following Bloxam, *Register of Magdalen*, ii, pp. 187–90, due to confusion of Sheppard with Shepprey, corrected in Macray, *Register of Magdalen*, i, p. 121.

conducts, sixteen boy choristers and a 'very skilled' (*peritissimus*) *informator* to instruct them. This was the post which John Taverner filled from 1526 to 1530. A companion foundation of a grammar school at Ipswich, Wolsey's birthplace, was planned at the same time. Following Wolsey's fall and death both colleges were dissolved, and in 1532 the King established a new college on the same site, called 'King Henry VIII's College in Oxford', with a dean and twelve canons, priest-vicars (presumably thirteen) and clerks and choristers the number of which is not given in the statutes. One of the vicars was to be precentor, another sacristan, and a third was to instruct the choristers in grammar and music. In 1546 the chapel of the college became the cathedral of the new diocese of Oxford, under the title *Ecclesia Christi Cathedralis Oxon: ex fundatione Regis Henrici Octavi.*[1]

Jesus College at Rotherham (Yorkshire), founded in 1483 by Thomas Rotherham (Archbishop of York, 1480–1500), is an example of a collegiate chantry associated with a grammar and song school. It had a provost, three fellows who acted as masters of grammar, song and writing, and four choristers.[2]

The first college of a Scottish university to have an endowed chapel and choir was the College of St. Salvator, founded in 1450 by Bishop James Kennedy in the University of St. Andrew's, which had been chartered in 1412. The foundation comprised thirteen persons, of whom three, including the provost, were graduates in theology, four were priest-chaplains, being Masters of Arts who were maintained until they became Bachelors of Theology, and six were poor clerk-scholars who were maintained until they were Masters and who served as singers in the chapel. The number of chaplains, who were expected to be skilled in plainsong, increased as new prebends and chantries were founded, and they became a distinct body electing their own proctor. By 1534 there was a song school under the control of one of the chaplains.[3] St. Leonard's, the second college of St. Andrew's University, was founded in 1513 by James Hepburn, prior of the Augustinian Priory of St.

[1] *Statutes of Cardinal College and King Henry VIII's College*, pp. 185, 192, 194.
[2] *Educational Charters*, pp. 424–5.
[3] Cant, *The College of St. Salvator*, pp. 1–12, 27–8, 79.

Andrew's, primarily for the training of clergy for the priory. It was styled the 'College of poor clerks of the Church of St. Andrew's', and consisted of a principal, four chaplains and twenty students. Those of the students who were sufficiently musical were required to 'sustain and adorn the divine office with singing, at least with plainsong and if possible also with descant'.[1] The third and largest college at St. Andrew's, Archbishop James Beaton's College of the Assumption of the Virgin, was founded in 1538 but did not assume its final form until the charter of Archbishop Hamilton in 1553–4.[2]

In 1495 Bishop William Elphinstone founded the College of St. Mary at Old Aberdeen, later known as King's College, with a chapel establishment of eight priest-chaplains skilled in plainsong and polyphony and four choristers (*juvenes seu pueri pauperes*) trained at least in plainsong. The senior chaplain was to be precentor and teach the boys, the second chaplain was to act as sacrist, and one of the chaplains was to be a skilled organist (*in ludo organorum peritus*). In his charter of 1529 Bishop Gavin Dunbar added six further members, including two choristers, to the foundation.[3]

Monasteries

The Benedictine houses in medieval England included, besides the nine cathedrals which were under their rule, many of the larger abbeys in the kingdom. Among these were Westminster, Chester, St. Alban's in Hertfordshire, St. Edmund's at Bury in Suffolk, Evesham in Worcestershire, Glastonbury in Somerset, Hyde in Hampshire, Peterborough in Northants, Gloucester and Tewkesbury in Gloucestershire, St. Mary's at York, Whitby and Selby in Yorkshire, Reading and Abingdon in Berkshire and Ramsey in Huntingdonshire. Some of the more important houses of other orders were the Cistercian abbeys of Meaux, Rievaulx and Fountains, all in Yorkshire, and Waverley in Surrey, and the Augustinian abbeys of Waltham Holy Cross in Essex and Oseney in Oxfordshire. The community of a monastery was under the direct rule of the

---

[1] Herkless and Hannay, *The College of St. Leonard's*, p. 117.
[2] Cant, *The College of St. Salvator*, p. 38.
[3] *Fasti Aberdonenses*, pp. 60, 80 sqq.

abbot or, in the case of a cathedral, where the bishop was titular abbot, of the prior. Benedictine houses were subject to the
visitation of the bishop of the diocese. Cistercian houses were
independent of the bishop, but were kept in close touch with
the parent house at Cîteaux through annual General Chapters,
so that such matters as church design and ritual music were
kept in almost complete uniformity.

The officers ('obedientiaries') under the abbot or prior who
were responsible for the work of the choir were the precentor,
the succentor and the sacrist (*secretarius, sacrista*). The precentor
took charge of the choir on festivals, and was responsible for
the chant books, while the succentor ruled the choir on ordinary days, taught the younger monks singing and reading, and
rehearsed them in the reading of lessons. The duties of the
sacrist, as far as they related to the choir, were similar to those
of the treasurer of a secular cathedral, involving the care of
non-musical books and the provision of vestments, candles,
incense and other necessaries for the altar and choir.[1] Naturally,
the monastic rules made no provision for non-residence or for
'vicars'. The entire community, save the sick and those with
special permission to be absent, formed the choir throughout
the daily observance of the liturgy. Plainsong was an essential
part of the training of a novice. According to a statute of the
General Chapter of the Benedictines for the province of Canterbury in 1277, novices were required to learn by heart the
Psalter, Hymnal and canticles, the rule of the order, all the
Invitatories, the verses of all the responds, antiphons and canticles at Lauds, and the complete *Commune Sanctorum*.[2] At St.
Augustine's, Canterbury, a young monk who showed special
ability might be given dispensation from his duties in the
monastery and be sent to the university (*ad studium*), provided
he knew by heart the Psalter, Hymnal and canticles, the
Commune Sanctorum, the week-day antiphons and short responds,
and the verses of the Antiphonal.[3]

The monastic liturgies, unlike the secular uses, gave no part
to boys. The parts given to them in the secular ritual, and such

[1] *Customary of St. Augustine's, Canterbury, and St. Peter's, Westminster*, i,
pp. 90 sqq.
[2] Pantin, *Chapters of the Black Monks*, i, pp. 73–4.
[3] *Customary of St. Augustine's, Canterbury, and St. Peter's, Westminster*, i, p. 157.

duties as censing and carrying candles, were carried out by junior monks. In the Norwich Customary of *c.* 1250, however, boys are mentioned as taking part in the services on the Eve of St. John the Baptist, on All Saints, and on All Souls, and also, accompanied by their masters, in the procession on Palm Sunday.[1] Many of the monasteries maintained a grammar school, employing a secular clerk as schoolmaster,[2] though song schools, which were usual in secular cathedrals, seem not to have been a part of the monastic scheme of things until the later Middle Ages. Norwich may have been an exception in this respect.

The establishing of song schools by the greater monasteries was connected with the late medieval custom of maintaining a choir to sing services which took place outside the monastic choir, in the nave or Lady-chapel, and independently of the monastic liturgy. What may be an early instance of this practice occurs at Glastonbury, where four 'clerks of the church' and a 'clerk in the chapel of Our Lady' named William *le Organistre* were attached to the monastery in 1322.[3] A separate Lady-chapel establishment, with a monk as warden (*custos capellae Beatae Mariae*), secular clerks and boy choristers was maintained at Worcester from some time in the fourteenth century. The account rolls of the *custos* show a payment in 1392 to one clerk, and payments in the following year to three clerks as well as to 'outside clerks' (*clerici extranei*) who stayed in the hostelry and sang polyphonic music in the Lady-chapel. In 1394–5 there were two *pueri de capella* and John Ylleway was given a courtesy payment for teaching them, in addition to his stipend as clerk. The account for the following year records a payment of four pence for 'parchment bought for a book of polyphony made in the form of a roll'. The choir of the Lady-chapel was endowed in 1478 by John Alcock (Bishop, 1476–86), who gave the Prior and Community one hundred pounds for the singing of services in the chapel by the master, clerks and choristers. The composer John Hampton was appointed in 1486 to instruct the eight choristers of Alcock's foundation in plainsong and polyphonic music, to direct the

[1] *Customary of Norwich*, pp. 135, 187, 76.
[2] See Moorman, *Church Life in England*, p. 362.
[3] Palmer, *Collectanea I*, p. 28.

services in the new Lady-chapel which Alcock had built, and to officiate at certain services in the monastic choir. Two years before this appointment Hampton had succeeded Richard Grene as *organista* in the Lady-chapel.[1]

At Durham Bishop Thomas Langley founded in 1414 a chantry of two chaplains to sing services at the altar of St. Mary, until another altar or chapel should be provided by the Bishop or his executors. The chaplains were to be competent to keep schools, one in grammar and the other in song, and the chaplain who kept the song school was to sing the Lady-Mass[2] with some of his scholars.[3] About 1430–5 Langley made extensive alterations to the Lady-chapel at the west end which was called the 'Gallilee', and erected a new altar of the Virgin where the great west door had been. According to a late sixteenth-century description of the monastery and its services, the function of the song school was 'to teach vi children for to learne to sing for the maintenance of God's Divine service in the abbey church, which children had there meat and there drink of the house coste amonge the children of thalmarie', that is, with the poor children of the almonry.[4] In 1447 the monastery appointed John Stele as 'cantor', to teach plainsong and polyphony to some monks and eight 'secular boys' and to sing and play at the services in the Gallilee and, when requested, in the monastic choir. The indenture of the appointment sets out these duties in detail, and similar indentures exist for the appointments to this post of Thomas Foderley in 1496, of John Tildesley in 1502 and of the composer Thomas Ashewell (here Hashewell), formerly of Lincoln, in 1513.[5] John Brimley was cantor in 1536–7[6] and remained to be organist and choirmaster under the New Foundation. Three pieces by Brimley for the Anglican service have survived.

The chronicles and registers of St. Alban's Abbey record in

---

[1] Atkins, *Early Occupants of the Office of Organist of Worcester*, pp. 6–13.

[2] The Votive Mass of the Blessed Virgin, see below, pp. 77 sqq.

[3] *Calendar of Patent Rolls 1413–16*, pp. 206–7.

[4] *Rites of Durham*, p. 62.

[5] *Historiae Dunelmensis Scriptores Tres*, pp. cccxv, ccclxxxvi, cccxcviii, ccccxiii. An account of 'Liberatura Specialis' for 1510 has under *Generosi*: 'Roberto Langforth, cantori, 3[ulnae] et 1 ultra 2s. 8d.   In stipendio'; and under *Valecti*: 'Roberto Langforth, janitori, 3'. *Rites of Durham*, pp. 144–5.

[6] *Durham Account Rolls*, p. 703.

some detail the gifts and good works of John Wheathamstead, who was Abbot from 1420 to 1440 and again from 1451 to 1464. During his first abbacy he had the Lady-chapel painted and provided with new ornaments, and instituted the daily singing in polyphony of the Lady-Mass by singers from outside the community. He decreed in 1423 that since the community could not provide qualified singers from its own members at least two stipendiary singers of polyphony (*organistae*) should be engaged, and should sing at the Lady-Mass and at Vespers and High Mass in choir on Sundays and festivals. In addition the Master of the Lady-chapel, who was probably one of the community, should have a clerk skilled in ministering at the altar and in singing to assist him.[1] Robert Fayrfax may have been master of a choir of stipendiary singers at St. Alban's, though the nature of his connection with the Abbey has not been clearly established.

The records of Christ Church, Canterbury, show that Leonel Power, undoubtedly the composer, was received into the fraternity of the monastery in 1423 and died on June 5, 1445.[2] He was not employed by the Priory during all of this period, however, for his name appears only in the livery lists (which were made out yearly at Easter) covering the years 1441–5.[3] It is among the *armigeri* or esquires, called *generosi* in most of the later lists, who were laymen of relatively high status, such as the master mason, who worked for the Priory and received an annual allowance of livery. The chronicle of events at Christ Church written by John Stone, who was a monk there from 1415 to 1471, records Power's death in 'the guest-house facing the court' and his burial 'next to the gate of the cemetery' on June 6, 1445.[4] Stone makes no reference to Power's musical fame, though he elsewhere pays tribute to the musical ability

[1] Amundesham, *Chronicle*, i, p. 106.

[2] British Museum, MS. Arundel 68 (lists of persons received into fraternity 1290–1526, and obit days of priors, brethren and benefactors; see *The Chronicle of John Stone*, p. xxix), fos. 62v., 29v. (obit date June 6). The rediscovery of this reference, which was apparently known to Johannes Wolf (see Moser, *Musik Lexikon*, p. 979) is due to Prof. Manfred Bukofzer, and was kindly communicated to me by John Harvey.

[3] Bodleian Library, MS. Tanner 165 (Christ Church Livery Lists, 1413–60), fos. 121–176v.

[4] *The Chronicle of John Stone*, p. 37.

of two precentors of the monastery and gives interesting details about the music sung there, including the names of composers.[1] The first Lady-chapel at Christ Church was built early in the fifteenth century by Thomas Chillenden (Prior, 1391–1411), and a new Lady-chapel beside the site of the martyrdom of St. Thomas was built by the first Thomas Goldston (Prior, 1449–68) and was finished by 1455.[2] Stone mentions 'boys of the church' in 1446, when Queen Margaret visited the monastery and heard them sing Mass at the altar of the Virgin in the crypt.[3] They were not provided for in the livery lists until 1454, after which they appear regularly as *octo pueri cantoris*. Though the cantor is not identified in the lists, it is possible that the post was held by John de Frenyngham (d. 1470), whose name first appears among the *generosi* in 1455[4] and who composed polyphony for a special occasion in 1470.[5] He seems to have joined the order in the meantime, for Stone describes him as a monk of the Priory in deacon's orders. He also tells us that the singers at Mass when the 'great nave of the Trinity' was dedicated by the Archbishop of York in 1469 were three monks and 'all the boys of the church'.[6] At the foot of an inventory of the books of the monastery of *c.* 1530 John Wood is referred to as 'Master off the chyldren in crist's church'.[7]

The first recorded master of the choristers at Westminster Abbey was William Cornysh the elder, who filled the office from 1479–80 to 1490–1, and whose appointment may mark the establishment of a group of singing men and boys. There were ten choristers at the dissolution of the Abbey in 1540, and the same number under the new secular foundation which followed the dissolution.[8] At the Benedictine Abbey of Muchelney in Somerset Ralph Drake was made cantor *c.* 1500, and was required to be at the daily Lady-Mass and at High Mass and Vespers on festivals, and to teach four boys and one of the monks to play the organ (*pulsare organa*), as well as any other monks who might wish to learn.[9] Winchester Cathedral Priory

---

[1] See below, pp. 189-90. [2] *The Chronicle of John Stone*, p. 65.
[3] Ibid., p. 39. [4] MS. Tanner 165, fo. 171v.
[5] See below, p. 190. [6] *The Chronicle of John Stone*, p. 110.
[7] Legg and Hope, *Inventories of Christ Church, Canterbury*, p. 164.
[8] Pine, 'Westminster Abbey: Some Early Masters of the Choristers', p. 258.
[9] *Muchelney Memoranda*, p. 42.

appointed Edmund Pynbrygge in 1510 to officiate at services in the Lady-chapel, nave and choir, and to instruct the boys, up to ten in number, in plainsong and polyphony. Thomas Goodman was appointed to the same duties in the following year, and Matthew Fuller, 'syngyng-man', in 1538, when there were eight boys. A grant of the headmastership of the priory school to John Potingere in 1538 shows that the 'chyldren of the Chapell' were taught there, as well as the 'chyldren of the almery' and the junior monks.[1]

In 1515 John Tucke, B.A., who was a fellow of New College from 1500 to 1507[2] and wrote a treatise on musical theory dated 1500 which still exists,[3] was appointed by Gloucester Abbey to teach grammar to the young monks and thirteen boys, to train five or six boys who had aptitude in plainsong and polyphony and direct the services in which they sang, and to participate in the more important services in the monks' choir. The boys are referred to as *pueri de camera clericorum*, and apparently lived in a common house (*domus capellae*) with the singing clerks.[4] Thomas Tallis may have been master of a group of stipendiary singers at Waltham Abbey, which had five choristers at its dissolution.[5] In 1534 the Abbey of Glastonbury appointed James Renynger to teach polyphony to six children and to sing and play the organ in the Lady-chapel and choir.[6] Christ Church Cathedral, Dublin, was given an endowment to maintain four choristers in 1480, and its song school was founded in 1493 by Prior David Winchester.[7]

The size and balance of the choirs of collegiate churches and colleges in the later Middle Ages, as well as what the statutes reveal about the qualifications and training of their members, show that the performance of polyphonic music was an essential part of their function. In their establishment of similar choirs the monasteries followed in the footsteps of the secular institutions, and at the same time took advantage of the presence of a qualified master for their stipendiary singers to

[1] Winchester Cathedral Library, Enrolment Register 2, fo. 44–44v; Enrolment Register 3, fos. 73, 83v.
[2] See below, p. 158.   [3] British Museum, MS. Add. 10336.
[4] *Historia et Cartularium Monasterii Sancti Petri Gloucestriae*, iii, pp. 290–1.
[5] *Tudor Church Music*, vi, pp. xii–xiii.
[6] *Letters and Papers of Henry VIII*, vii, p. 411.
[7] Lewis-Crosby, *The Annals of Christ Church Cathedral*, p. 41.

employ him for some of their own services. The institution and development of balanced groups of singers was the most significant feature of the musical history of the later Middle Ages, and was comparable in importance to the rise of the orchestra in the eighteenth and nineteenth centuries. It was closely related to the origin and growth of choral polyphony, as distinct from the polyphony of soloists practised in the larger secular and monastic choirs in earlier centuries. Like the rise of the orchestra, it was accompanied by the adoption and gradual expansion of new musical forms, for the earlier of the two main phases in the history of medieval music was the era of the motet and conductus, the later that of the festal and votive Masses, the votive Antiphon and the Magnificat. These changes in the forms of polyphony correspond, in their turn, to new trends in the expression of devotion and new movements in the festal treatment of the ritual which took place within the established framework of the medieval liturgies.

II
THE LITURGY AND ITS
PLAINSONG

THE English secular cathedrals derived their liturgies, as they derived their constitutions, from Norman models. At the same time, there was some continuity with earlier Irish and Anglo-Saxon liturgical traditions, and this may in part account for local differences.[1] The variations of detail, both in constitutions and liturgy, which existed between the Norman cathedrals are also reflected to some degree in England. Salisbury and York, for example, show a relation, not by any means exact, to Bayeux,[2] Lichfield and Hereford to Rouen.[3] Some English monasteries had maintained an earlier form of their ritual, and they too felt the impact of the Norman conquest. At Glastonbury in 1083 the abbot Turstin, who had been transferred from Caen, attempted to introduce the use of Fécamp, a revised version of the use of Cluny, which was itself a 'reformed' Benedictine use brought to Fécamp by William of Volpiano in 1001.[4] Turstin's action met with violent opposition and led to a bloody struggle in the abbey choir.[5] Before the

[1] For an example, see Frere, 'The Newly-found York Gradual', pp. 24–5.
[2] Frere, 'The Connexion between English and Norman Rites', pp. 32–40; Bishop, *Liturgica Historica*, p. 300, n. 1.
[3] Savage, *The Great Register of Lichfield*, p. xxvi; Bishop, 'Holy Week Rites of Sarum, Hereford and Rouen'.
[4] *Customary of Norwich*, p. xiii.   [5] *Worcester Antiphonary*, i, p. 106.

46

end of the century, however, Archbishop Lanfranc settled such differences by issuing his *Decreta pro Ordine S. Benedicti*, which began with the rules for the regulation of the liturgy (*Ordinarium totius anni*).[1]

Ordinal and Customary

The Use of Salisbury was the most important of the secular liturgies of medieval Britain. The earliest version of the Sarum Customary (*Consuetudinarium, Custumarium*), which was drawn up by Richard Poore about 1210,[2] begins with an expanded form of St. Osmund's Institutes[3] and continues with the arrangement of seating in the choir-stalls, the rules of deportment in choir, and the duties and procedures of those who carry out the services throughout the year. A Customary presupposes an Ordinal, since 'the Ordinal defines the character, contents, and method of the Services, while the Consuetudinary defines the persons who are to conduct them: in other words, the Ordinal deals with the Rite, and the Consuetudinary with the Ceremonial'.[4] In practice Ordinal and Customary could be combined to give a running commentary on the ceremonial as well as the opening words of the chants and lessons, and could be prefaced by the Statutes, as in Grandisson's Exeter Ordinal.

Perhaps the earliest reference to the existence of a secular Ordinal in England is in Bishop Nonant's Lichfield Statutes (1188–98), which begin by explaining the need for and function of constitutions and customs, and soon afterwards refer to the Ordinal and the Customary.[5] The Sarum Ordinal is in fact mentioned in Poore's *Consuetudinarium*, was revised and added to during the thirteenth century, and was superseded by a 'New Ordinal' about the middle of the fourteenth century. This in turn was added to and clarified, and eventually the substance of the part concerned with the ceremonial of particular days and seasons was incorporated in the service books as 'rubrics', and of that concerned with the cycle of feasts and observances

---

[1] Printed in Migne, *Patrologia*, cl, cols. 446–82.
[2] *Use of Sarum*, ii, p. xx.   [3] Ibid., pp. 1–12.
[4] Ibid., p. vii.   [5] *Lincoln Statutes*, ii, p. 12.

47

in a digest or handbook called the *Directorium Sacerdotum*.[1] In
the meantime the influence of the Salisbury customs and ritual
had been widespread. They were adopted, with variations in
the observances of local saints, in secular cathedrals (except
York, Hereford and London), in houses of Augustinian canons,
in collegiate churches and colleges, and in all the dioceses of
England, Scotland and Ireland.[2] The dioceses which had
monks in their cathedrals turned naturally to the Sarum use,
since the rites of their cathedral churches were those of a
monastic order.

The term 'use' was occasionally applied to a book adapted
from Sarum use to the minor peculiarities of another diocese,
as in the cases of a fifteenth-century Missal *secundum usum Lincoln*[3] and an 'antiphonare some tyme of Lyncoln use and now
of the use of Sarum' which belonged to the town of Louth in
Lincolnshire in 1486.[4] For Exeter Cathedral Bishop Grandisson
in 1337 'made and extracted from the uses of Exeter and
Sarum'[5] an Ordinal-cum-Customary to which he prefixed the
Statutes (*status et personarum numerus situatio et officia*).[6] At the
request of Bishop Brantyngham the Dean and Chapter agreed
to accept the Sarum Ordinal in so far as it was compatible with
their statutory rights and duties. This was not, apparently, far
enough, as the request was renewed by Bishop Oldham in
1505.[7]

In their travels abroad in the early fifteenth century the
English royal and ducal chapels naturally observed their own
Sarum rites, and the impact of their liturgical customs, as well
as of the style of their polyphonic music, on French composers of
that time had important consequences. The Sarum liturgy was

[1] *Use of Sarum*, ii, pp. x–xxvii. *Clement Maydestone's Directorium Sacerdotum*
has been edited by Cooke and Wordsworth.

[2] *Use of Sarum*, ii, pp. xxvii–xxxii. When the Archbishop of Canterbury
celebrated Mass in the presence of the college of Bishops, the Bishop of
Salisbury was precentor, 'by ancient observance and custom'. *Lincoln
Statutes*, iii, p. 844.

[3] *York Missal*, pp. 343–8.

[4] *Lincoln Statutes*, iii, p. 848. A Sarum Missal used at Lincoln had as later
additions the votive Mass of St. Hugh and some sequences. Ibid., p. 842.

[5] 'Que eis fecimus et extraximus ex Exonie et Sarum usibus', in his statutes
for Ottery St. Mary. Dalton, *The Collegiate Church of Ottery St. Mary*, p. 136.

[6] Edited by Dalton as *Ordinale Exon*.

[7] *Lincoln Statutes*, iii, pp. 842, 850.

carried still further afield when Philippa of Lancaster, daughter
of John of Gaunt and queen of John I of Portugal, introduced
its use in Braga in 1385.[1] Some elements of the English rite,
notably certain chants used at the ceremony of the Deposition
on Good Friday, remained in the Portuguese service-books.[2]
St. Ferdinand Confessor, son of John and Philippa, recited
daily from his fourteenth year (1415) until his death in 1443
'all the canonical hours according to the use of the Church
of Salisbury. . . . His chapel was fully equipped with vestments and all other necessaries and he had chaplains and
singers competent to carry out the services of the Salisbury
rite.'[3]

The rites of York and Hereford maintained their standing
as more or less independent uses until the Reformation. York
adopted elements of the Sarum Customary from time to time,
but remained distinct in its Calendar of observances, in the
antiphons and responds of the Breviary, and conspicuously in
its greater number of sequences, many peculiar to itself.[4] The
differences between the Sarum and Hereford uses were of the
same kind,[5] though less extensive since the Ordinal and service-
books of Hereford borrowed considerably from the New
Ordinal of Salisbury in the later Middle Ages. From the preferment of a Savoyard, Peter de Egeblank (or Pierre d'Aigue-
blanche, or de Aqua blanca, or de Aqua bella), to the bishopric
of Hereford in 1240 arose the curious fact that the use of Hereford was observed in a collegiate church in Savoy until 1580.
During an absence from Hereford in 1258–62 Egeblank founded
the Collegiate Church of St. Katharine at Aiguebelle in the
diocese of Maurienne with a provost, precentor, treasurer and
ten other canons, four deacons and four sub-deacons. All the
services were to be carried out 'according to the use of the
Church of Hereford', including the graduals and tropes, and

---

[1] Ibid., p. 841.

[2] Corbin, *Essai sur la musique religieuse portugaise*, pp. 302–15.

[3] *Lincoln Statutes*, iii, p. 843.

[4] Frere, 'York Service Books', p. 162; 'The Newly-found York Gradual',
pp. 27–9. See also the list of 'Sequences of the English Church' in *Breviarium
Sarum*, iii, pp. xcii–xcix; York had one hundred and seventy-two sequences,
Salisbury ninety-four and Hereford eighty-one.

[5] The Breviaries of Salisbury, York and Hereford are compared in
Hereford Breviary, iii, Introduction.

the services of the Virgin and for the Dead.[1] In 1413 Richard Kyngeston, Dean of St. George's, Windsor, who had been Archdeacon of Hereford from 1379 to 1404, was granted permission by Pope John XXIII to continue to say the canonical Hours according to the Hereford use rather than that of Salisbury, which was followed at Windsor.[2]

Some elements of the statutes and customs of Salisbury were adopted by St. Paul's during the fourteenth century.[3] The *usus Sancti Pauli* was discontinued in 1414 in favour of the Sarum use, but the choir apparently retained something of their older methods of singing and reading.[4] Though Elgin Cathedral had followed Lincoln in some features of its constitution, it adopted the liturgical use of Salisbury in 1242.[5] Bishop Gervase of St. David's ordered in 1223 that certain parts of the use of Salisbury should be adopted in his cathedral, which in other respects may have maintained an older ordinal.[6] Two thirteenth-century collegiate foundations, Chester-le-Street and Bishop Auckland, both in Durham, were ordered to adopt the *modus psallendi* of York or Salisbury.[7] This may not have been a real alternative since the rules for the singing of psalms, traditionally ascribed to St. Bernard,[8] were common to all rites, and were widely copied.[9] Mixtures of use were possible, however, for the use of the nunnery of St. Mary and St. Ethelburga in Barking (Essex)[10] combined the Hours of St. Benedict, the Psalter sequence of the Roman use, and the Mass of the *usus Sancti Pauli*.[11]

Having dealt with the dignities and duties of the chief officers of the church, the Sarum Customary went on to the arrangement of the stalls and general rules for deportment and procedure in choir.[12] The ministers of the church occupied in

[1] *Lincoln Statutes*, ii, pp. 40–2.

[2] *Calendar of Papal Registers, Letters*, vi, p. 377.

[3] *Use of Sarum*, ii, pp. xxxi–xxxii.

[4] *Lincoln Statutes*, iii, p. 843, where the date is given as ? 1415. *Registrum Statutorum et Consuetudinum*, p. lix, gives 1414.

[5] *Lincoln Statutes*, iii, p. 835.   [6] Ibid., p. 833.

[7] Ibid., p. 837.

[8] E.g., 'teste Barnardo qui ait . . .' *Use of Sarum*, i. p. 36.

[9] Van Dijk, 'Saint Bernard and the *Instituta Patrum* of St. Gall', pp. 103–9.

[10] *The Ordinale of the Nuns of Barking*.   [11] *Lincoln Statutes*, iii, p. 841.

[12] *Use of Sarum*, i, pp. 13–40. Frere suggests the heading 'De Consuetudine Chori'.

order of precedence the three rows of seats: a highest row (*gradus superior*), a second row (*secunda forma*) and a lowest row (*prima forma*). In large choirs, including all the secular cathedrals except Lichfield, there were 'return-stalls' at the western end of the choir against the choir-screen and facing towards the altar. In the nearest stalls to the choir-doors on the south side sat the Dean and on the north side the Precentor; hence the south side of the choir (called *decani*) had precedence over the north (called *cantoris*). In the corners at the east end were the stalls of the Chancellor and Treasurer. Next to the four 'principal persons' were the stalls of Archdeacons, whose functions were mainly diocesan, and of Abbots of monasteries if, as at Wells, they held prebends.[1] After these dignitaries came the sub-dean on the *decani* side and the succentor on the *cantoris* side, and then the canons, priest-vicars and (at Salisbury) a few older deacons *ex dispensatione*. Since comparatively few canons were in residence at any one time, the greater number of stalls in the highest row were in practice occupied by priest-vicars. In the second form were the places of deacons and 'other clerks', and in the first row of the choristers (*canonici pueri*) and probationary choristers in order (*ceteri pueri secundum aetatis exigentium*).

For the weekly assignment of certain duties of singing and reading the sides of the choir alternated in being the 'duty' or leading (*principalis*) side, so that one week was *decani* week, the next *cantoris* week. This alternation was a daily one from the Sunday before Christmas[2] to the Sunday after Epiphany, from Maundy Thursday to the Sunday after Easter, and from Whitsunday to Trinity Sunday.

From this general body of singers (*chorus*) smaller groups were taken out at various times to act as 'rulers of the choir' (*rectores chori*) or to sing certain parts of the services. The rulers either assisted the precentor or acted in his place, according to the festal rank of the day. They carried staves, often elaborately carved and decorated, such as that described in the Lincoln inventory of 1536: 'Imprimis a staffe covered with sylver and gylte with one Image of owr lady graven yn sylver of one end and an Image of seynt hugh yn the other end

---

[1] See the choir-seating plans in *Lincoln Statutes*, i, pp. 105, 136–8.
[2] If a *decani* week began on that day; otherwise from Christmas Day.

havyng a bose vi squared with xii Imagies enamelled havyng vi botteresses wantyng one pynnacle and ii topes of the gyft of Mr. Alex. Prowell'.[1] The rulers sat on short forms on each side of the middle of the choir with benches in front on which to place their books. Two rulers (*canonici hebdomadarii*) functioned each fortnight, one from each side, taking 'principal' duty for one week each with their side of the choir. The singers of special parts of the service went to a lectern at one of three places, depending on the rank of the day and on the ritual situation, as laid down in the Customary: at the choir-step (*gradus chori*), in the middle of the choir (*medius chori*), or at the lectern on the choir-screen (*ad lectrinum in pulpito*).

The assigning of singing duties was done by the precentor or his deputy, of reading duties as a rule by the chancellor or his deputy. The names were written on a board which was normally filled out on Sunday for the following week (*tabula hebdomadaria*), or, when the choir alternated daily, on each day (*tabula communis*).[2] The table was read out each day, in Salisbury by a boy, when the community assembled in the chapter-house for readings, announcement of obits and prayers.[3]

The main part of the Customary and all of the Ordinal were based on the division of the year into (1) seasons or periods, and (2) saints' days, and on the division of the day into the two principal kinds of service, the canonical Hours and the Mass. The church year began on the first Sunday in Advent, and its seasons were: (1) Advent, comprising the four Sundays and odd week-days, if any, to Christmas Eve; (2) Christmas to the Sunday after the octave[4] of the Epiphany (January 6); (3) that Sunday, called the Sunday *Domine ne in ira* from the opening words of the first respond at Matins, to Septuagesima, i.e., the third Sunday before Ash Wednesday,[5] a period which varied in length according to the date of Easter; (4) Septuagesima to

---

[1] Under the heading 'Baculi pro chori regentibus'. Alexander Prowett was Precentor from 1448 to 1471. Wordsworth, 'Lincoln Inventories', p. 21.

[2] *Use of Sarum*, i, pp. 105–11.

[3] Ibid. p. 51. For an example of the methods of making out a monastic *tabula*, see *Ordinale of St. Mary's, York*, i, pp. 58–67. There the two rulers were called *cantaria* and *subcantaria*.

[4] I.e., the day itself and the seven days following.

[5] Which was called 'caput jejunii'.

the Saturday of Holy Week, i.e., Easter Eve, being nine weeks; (5) Easter Sunday to Pentecost (Whitsunday), being seven weeks; and (6) the first Sunday after Trinity, called the Sunday *Deus omnium* from the beginning of the first respond at Matins, to Advent, again of varying length according to the date of Easter. The section of an ordinal or service-book dealing with these seasons, which was called the *Temporale*, included also the anniversary of the dedication of the church.[1] The section dealing with the saints' days, including, of course, the feasts of the Virgin, naturally all fixed in date, began with St. Andrew's day (November 30), and was called the *Sanctorale*.

The ranking of festivals varied somewhat in the various uses, most frequently as it concerned patronal saints and saints specially venerated in a church, region or diocese. The main categories were *duplex* and *simplex*. Doubles were further subdivided into four ranks: *principale*, *maius*, *minus* and *inferius*.[2] The services on principal and greater double feasts were distinguished by having a procession, two canons and two vicars to rule the choir, elaborate censing at Matins and Vespers, and other marks of their dignity. The lesser and inferior doubles had no procession (unless they fell on a Sunday), two canons and two clerks of the second form to rule the choir, and less elaborate ceremonial in other respects. Simple feasts, on which the choir was ruled by the two *canonici hebdomadarii*, were subdivided at Salisbury into three kinds according as the *Invitatorium* at Matins was sung by three or two persons, or by one.[3] Sundays on which no special observance fell (*dominicae simplices*) were ranked as simple, with the regular addition of a procession before High Mass and certain other ceremonial. A week-day on which no feast occurred was called a *feria*, though the term

[1] The 'Festum Dedicationis Ecclesiae', varying with the church, as distinct from the 'Festum Sancti Loci', the feast of its patron saint.

[2] So in Salisbury; Exeter had *maius* (including *principale*), *medium*, *minus*, *semi-duplex*; Hereford had *principale* (including the Salisbury *maius*), *duplex*, *semi-duplex*. Monastic foundations used the terms *in capis* (in copes) and *in albis* (in albs) for feasts corresponding in general to the Salisbury *minus* and *inferius*.

[3] At Hereford two kinds, with nine or three lessons at Matins; at Exeter two kinds, one called *simplex* and having two rulers, the other *profestum* with no rulers (*sine regimine chori*) and three lessons; in monasteries two kinds, with twelve or three lessons at Matins.

might occasionally be used to distinguish a week-day, festal or not, from a Sunday. The three days after Easter and after Whitsunday were double feasts. In the octaves of certain feasts the choir was ruled and the ritual of the Sunday and week-days was related to that of the feast.[1] In all uses, whatever the differences of terminology, the character of seasons and the ranking of festal and ferial days were expressed by differences in ceremonial, e.g., lights, bells, vestments, processions, the ruling of the choir, the number singing certain chants, and in ritual, e.g., the number of lessons at Matins, the singing or not of *Te Deum* at Matins and of *Credo* and *Gloria*, Sequence, *Alleluia* and Tract at Mass.

It was the object of the Customary to give specific directions for the adaptation of the ceremonial to, and the consequent making out of the *tabula* of duties for, the various degrees of feasts and ferias, giving references when necessary to the texts of the ritual contained in the Ordinal.

In setting out the ritual of the services, with the opening words of chants, lessons, psalms and prayers, the Ordinal adopted the following sequence: (1) the offices, i.e., canonical hours, of the Temporale; (2) the offices of the Sanctorale, divided into (*a*) those for specific saints' days, and (*b*) those for groups of saints (*Commune Sanctorum*), e.g., apostles, martyrs, bishop-martyrs, bishop-confessors, doctor-confessors, etc., and, here or elsewhere, those for the dead;[2] (3) Masses of the Temporale (*Proprium de Tempore*); and (4) Masses of the Sanctorale (*Proprium de Sanctis* and *Commune Sanctorum*) and votive Masses, i.e., occasional and recurring Masses such as those for the Christian community,[3] for peace, the nuptial Mass, and the Mass for the dead.[4]

For 'festal' purposes the liturgical day was conceived as beginning with Vespers followed by Compline, and the offices continued with the 'night-hours' of Matins and Lauds and the 'day-hours' of Prime, Terce, Sext, None, Vespers and Compline.

[1] E.g., in the octaves of the Epiphany (*Use of Sarum*, ii, pp. 45–6) and the Ascension (ibid., p. 82); cf. *Ordinale Exon*, i, pp. 162–6.

[2] Vespers in *vigilia mortuorum* were called *Placebo* from the opening of the first antiphon; Matins of the Dead were called *Dirige* (whence 'dirge') for the same reason.

[3] Called *Salus populi* from the opening of the Introit.

[4] Called *Requiem* from the opening of the Introit.

On Sundays and greater doubles both first and second Vespers (*utraeque vesperae*) were related to the day, first Vespers being more important, while on lesser feasts Vespers on the evening before, and not those on the day, were proper to the feast. The most important of the offices, musically and otherwise, were Vespers, Matins and Lauds. The choir was not ruled at the other hours,[1] which were called 'little'.[2]

The ringing of the bells which signalled the times of the hours and of the principal Masses was just as carefully ordered to conform with the dignity of the day and the service as was every other detail of custom and ritual.[3] Bells were also rung during processions, during the singing of the Sequence and of the *Te Deum* on feasts, in the last case with a clashing (*classicum*) of all the bells from the verse *per singulos dies* until the beginning of Lauds. The instructions to the ringers show that the time of Matins varied with the seasons and feasts, beginning immediately after midnight on doubles in winter and summer until August, and otherwise at midnight in winter and at such a time as to end at dawn in summer.[4] The exceptions were Christmas, when Matins was finished before midnight, Easter Day and the following week, when it was begun at first daylight, and certain festivals in midsummer, when it was allowed to be sung in the evening (*in sero*) after Vespers and Compline.[5] When Matins was sung in the evening, Lauds, which normally followed it, was sung on the following morning. There was no significant variation in the times of the other offices. Prime was about nine, Terce about ten, Sext and None about eleven, Vespers and Compline about three.[6]

[1] *Use of Sarum*, i, p. 188.

[2] At Lincoln Prime was counted among the *horae majores*. *Lincoln Statutes*, i, p. 376.

[3] *Use of Sarum*, i, p. 220; *Lincoln Statutes*, i, pp. 364–88, passim; *Ordinale Exon*, ii, pp. 535 sqq.

[4] *Ordinale Exon*, ii, p. 539. In Benedictine communities the bell for Matins was rung at midnight all the year round and that for Prime at seven a.m. *Ordinale of St. Mary's, York*, iii, pp. vi sqq.

[5] *Use of Sarum*, i, p. 221; *Ordinale Exon*, ii, p. 539. At Ottery St. Mary Grandisson ordered Matins on the three days before Easter (*Tenebrae*) to be sung 'de sero, propter parochianos'. Dalton, *The Collegiate Church of Ottery St. Mary*, p. 135.

[6] Though the Hours services were not necessarily sung at the 'true' times of first hour, third hour, etc., they represented the times at which

The elements common to all the offices, which may be seen in their simplest form in the 'little' hours, consisted of opening sentences, a hymn, psalms with an antiphon, a lesson and prayers. At Compline the order was psalms, lesson, hymn and canticle (*Nunc dimittis*) with antiphon. At Prime the Athanasian Creed (*Quicumque vult*) was added as a 'canticle' before the final prayers. Lauds and Vespers contained sentences, psalms with antiphons, a lesson, a hymn, a gospel canticle (*Benedictus* at Lauds, *Magnificat* at Vespers) with antiphon, and prayers. All of the Hours services normally ended with the versicle *Benedicamus Domino* and the response[1] *Deo gratias*. Matins was the most variable in length of the offices, and even in its shortest form was longer than any other. It consisted of sentences, *Invitatorium* (a respond with the *Venite*), the *Venite* (Psalm 94[2]), a hymn,[3] and one or three Nocturns, each consisting of psalms with antiphons and three lessons each followed by a respond. The *Te Deum* was sung at the end of Matins on Sundays and most feasts, except in Advent and Lent. One of the convenient marks of the ranking of a feast was the number of lessons in its Matins, three (one nocturn) or nine[4] (three nocturns).

Each of the canonical hours was celebrated once a day. Mass, on the other hand, was celebrated several or many times, according to the size of the church and the number of its altars and chantries,[5] between dawn and eleven o'clock. The most

the events of Christ's Passion took place. See *De Horis Canonicis Hymnus* from the Primer of 1532 in *Breviarium Sarum*, iii, p. cxxxii.

[1] A response (*responsio*) to a short versicle (*versiculus*) is to be distinguished from a respond (*responsorium*), which is a comparatively lengthy text, alternating with a verse (*versus*), normally sung after a lesson.

[2] The numbering of the medieval Latin Psalter is used here. It corresponds to the Anglican numbering (after the Hebrew Psalter) thus: Pss. 1–9 and 148–50 are the same; Ps. 10 (Latin) is Pss. 10 and 11 (Anglican); Pss. 11–145 are numbered one higher in the Anglican; Pss. 146 and 147 (Latin) are Ps. 147 (Anglican). In medieval Ordinals and service-books psalms are given by their opening words, with a number in cases of identical openings, e.g., *Domine ne in furore i* is Ps. 6.

[3] Except in the Easter Octave.

[4] Twelve in the monastic liturgies, each nocturn having four lessons on the festivals concerned. In both secular and monastic uses Matins on Easter Day and Whitsunday had three lessons only.

[5] In Lincoln, for example, there were thirty-eight Masses daily in 1506, forty-four in 1531. *Lincoln Statutes*, ii, p. cclxv.

important of these celebrations was that of Mass of the day, which normally took place immediately after Terce. All the others were votive Masses of various kinds.

In setting out the ritual of the Mass of the day through the year, and of the votive Masses, the Ordinal gave the opening words of the following variable items: the Introit (called *Officium*[1]) and its psalm-verse, the prayer or collect (*Oratio*), the Epistle (i.e., a reading from the Epistles, or on certain days from the Acts of the Apostles), the Gradual, the *Alleluia* and its verse (or, from Septuagesima to Easter, the Tract), the Sequence (on Sundays during Advent and on most festivals except during Lent), the Gospel (*Evangelium*), the Offertory and the Communion. These form the Proper of the Mass, though the term is generally used, and will be used here, of the chanted parts of the Proper, excluding the collect and lessons.

As to the invariable parts of the Mass which formed the Ordinary, the Ordinal referred to them only in connection with the omission of some of them on certain days or with festive additions to their texts in the form of tropes. A trope consisted of words set syllabically to that part (called a *neuma*) of a melody which had previously been sung to one syllable, or of new words and music inserted into certain parts of the ritual. The *Gloria in excelsis* was omitted in Advent and from Septuagesima to Easter, and the *Credo* was omitted on ferias and lesser festivals.[2] Mass ended with *Ite missa est* and its response *Deo gratias* when the *Gloria* was sung, and with *Benedicamus Domino* and the same response when the *Gloria* was omitted. On days when the *Kyrie* was troped *Ite missa est* was sung to the music of the first *Christe* of the particular *Kyrie* trope which had been sung at the beginning of the Mass. In the celebration of Mass the items of the Proper and Ordinary succeeded one another in the following order: Introit, *Kyrie*, *Gloria*, Epistle, Gradual, *Alleluia*, Sequence, Gospel, *Credo*, Offertory, *Sanctus* with *Benedictus*, *Agnus Dei*, Communion and *Ite missa est* or *Benedicamus*.

[1] It had this title in the Mozarabic rite also; see Anglès, 'Latin Chant before St. Gregory', p. 75.

[2] *Use of Sarum*, i, p. 91; ii, p. 150.

57

Psalm and Canticle

For liturgical purposes the one hundred and fifty psalms were divided into eight sections,[1] sometimes called 'nocturns', in order that the complete course would be sung once in the Matins and Vespers of each week, assuming that all the week-days were ferias. In practice, however, the course was virtually never an uninterrupted one, since festivals had special psalms. On ferias the *Gloria patri* was sung after a group of psalms, other-wise after each psalm. When sung in choir the psalms were chanted verse by verse 'antiphonally', i.e., with the two sides alternating. When a Canon died, the choir kept watch over the bier through the night, singing the whole of the psalter. At Lincoln the *decani* side kept the vigil before Matins and the *cantoris* side continued it after Matins.[2] At Norwich the community sang the psalter in the cloister on the morning of the anniversary (July 23) of Bishop Herbert Losinga, under whom the building of the Cathedral was begun in 1096.[3]

In addition to the Gospel canticles, there were seven can-ticles from the Old Testament which were sung daily in turn at Lauds.[4] All of these were sung *alternatim*, in the same fashion as psalms.

Antiphon

The term *antiphona* was not used in the ordinals for singing in alternation, which was expressed by *alternatim* or *alternis vicibus*, but to indicate a chant sung with a psalm, group of psalms or canticle at the Hours, or without a psalm in proces-sions and memorials. In the early centuries of the Christian liturgy the antiphon was sung before and after the psalm and also between each verse.[5] This practice survived to later times only in such special cases as the antiphon *Asperges me Domine*, sung with two verses of Psalm 50 (*Miserere mei*) and the *Gloria patri* at the sprinkling with holy water before the procession

---

[1] Wordsworth and Littlehales, *Old Service Books*, p. 110.
[2] *Lincoln Statutes*, iii, p. 343.
[3] *Customary of Norwich*, pp. xiv, 152.
[4] Wordsworth and Littlehales, *Old Service Books*, p. 109.
[5] Wagner, *Introduction to the Gregorian Melodies*, pp. 141–2.

on Sundays,[1] and the antiphon *Lumen ad revelationem* to the *Nunc dimittis* at the distribution of candles before the procession on the Purification (February 2).[2] Normally only the opening notes of an antiphon were sung before the psalm, and the person who was 'tabled' to do this continued to the end of the first half-verse of the psalm (*usque ad metrum*), the choir on his side taking up the chanting from the second half of the verse.[3] A different treatment of the beginning was needed when the antiphon used the same words as the opening of the psalm. In such cases these words were not repeated at the beginning of the psalm,[4] and the Ordinal and Antiphonal showed the psalm as *Ipsum*. After the *Gloria patri* the antiphon was again announced and then continued to the end by the choir. At the end of the last antiphon at Vespers and Lauds and in each nocturn of Matins, and of all antiphons to the *Magnificat*, *Benedictus* and *Quicumque vult*, the neuma[5] of the mode was added as a sort of *jubilus* on the last vowel, except from Passion Sunday (the fifth Sunday in Lent) to the Sunday after Easter and in services for the dead.[6] On the more important double feasts the antiphon to the *Magnificat* was 'doubled', that is, sung complete both before and after the canticle.[7]

A small group of antiphons had an exceptional form resembling that of a respond, for they included a verse which was sung after the psalm, before the antiphon was sung complete. This was true of all the antiphons at Matins on the feasts of St. Paul and St. Laurence.[8] A further development of this form is seen in the antiphons to the *Nunc dimittis* for the last four weeks of Lent, *Media vita*, which a tradition originating in the seventeenth century has credited to Notker Balbulus of St.

[1] Replaced by the antiphon *Vidi aquam egredientem* with one verse of the psalm *Confitemini Domino* from Easter to Trinity. *Missale Sarum*, col. 33**.

[2] *Ordinale Exon*, i, p. 342. Other examples are the psalms during the procession to the Font after Eastertide Vespers, and the psalm at the Adoration of the Cross on Good Friday. See below, pp. 94–7.

[3] *Use of Sarum*, i, p. 36; ii, p. 209. See also Van Dijk, 'Saint Bernard and the *Instituta Patrum* of Saint Gall', p. 109, and the texts printed there, p. 105.

[4] *Use of Sarum*, ii, pp. 208–9.

[5] A short piece of vocalized melody; there was one for each mode, given in the Tonale. See below, p. 102.

[6] *Use of Sarum*, ii, p. 209.

[7] Ibid., i, p. 31; *Ordinale of St. Mary's, York*, ii, p. 199.

[8] *Ordinale Exon*, i, pp. 209, 247.

Gall,[1] and *O rex gloriose*, each of which had three verses. *Media vita* was used during the two weeks before Passion Sunday, and its complete form, with the verses, on the Saturdays, Sundays and festivals within that period. After the complete antiphon was sung by the choir the verses were sung as solos, each being followed by one of the three phrases of the second half of the antiphon in order, thus: ℣. *Ne proicias nos . . .* Choir *Sancte Deus;*[2] ℣. *Noli claudere . . .* Choir *Sancte fortis;* ℣. *Qui cognoscis . . .* Choir *Sancte et misericors salvator amarae morti ne tradas nos.*[3] The verses of *O rex gloriose*, which was used from Passion Sunday to the Wednesday in Holy Week, were likewise sung on Saturdays, Sundays and feasts. In this case, however, the partial repetitions were carried to the end of the antiphon each time.[4]

The Introit of the Mass was originally a complete psalm with antiphon.[5] In the English uses the term *introitus missae* was applied to the entrance of the clergy rather than to the chant which accompanied it, which was called *officium*. It consisted of an antiphon, one psalm-verse and the *Gloria patri*, sung in the order antiphon, verse, antiphon, *Gloria patri*, antiphon. The rulers began the antiphon and the *Gloria*, which were then taken up by the choir, the verse being sung by the rulers only.[6] In the threefold singing of the antiphon of the Introit the English rite held to an earlier practice; elsewhere the antiphon after the verse had either been dropped or shortened by half.[7]

Like the Introit, the Offertory and Communion had each originally been a complete psalm with antiphon, and although by the Middle Ages they were independent melodies, they still kept some traces of their earliest form.[8] In some Offertories, for

---

[1] See Clark, *Abbey of St. Gall*, p. 191.

[2] *Ordinale Exon*, i, p. 120, adds 'et non ulterius'. In Hereford the choir sang to the end of the antiphon each time ('semper repetitiones post versus usque ad finem dicuntur'). *Hereford Breviary*, i, p. 274.

[3] Music in *Antiphonale Sarisburiense*, pl. 170.

[4] *Ordinale Exon*, i, pp. 125–6; *Hereford Breviary*, i, pp. 289–90; *Breviarium Sarum*, i, col. dccxvi. Music in *Antiphonale Sarisburiense*, pl. 190. Neither of these antiphons appears in the monastic liturgies.

[5] Wagner, *Introduction to the Gregorian Melodies*, pp. 54 sqq.

[6] *Use of Sarum*, i, p. 38; ii, p. 149; the *Gloria patri* was not sung between Passion Sunday and Easter, except on Holy Thursday if the Bishop celebrated. Ibid., ii, p. 161.

[7] Wagner, *Introduction to the Gregorian Melodies*, pp. 59–60.

[8] Ibid., pp. 93–9, 102–5; Smits van Waesberghe, *Gregorian Chant*, pp. 23–6.

PLATE V

8. Lincoln Cathedral: the choir in 1819. The carved stalls were the gift of John de Welbourne, Treasurer, 1350-1380

PLATE VI

9. Henry VI and a Bishop at service in the King's Chapel

example, the first sentence was repeated.[1] Since repetition of words, unless as a part of the liturgical text, was otherwise unknown, this suggests that the original antiphon and psalm-verses had been fused into one continuous chant. The only Communion chant which kept the form of antiphon and verse was that in the Mass for the dead.[2]

Respond

Though the antiphon and the respond both had their origin in the early forms of psalmody, they had, in general, distinct forms and ritual functions in the Middle Ages. While the antiphons were choral chants sung with a psalm the responds were more elaborate chants sung after lessons. Hence Matins with nine lessons had also nine responds. In its normal form a respond was begun by one or a few singers and continued by the choir; then the verse was sung by the soloist or soloists and the respond was repeated from mid-point by the chorus. The third, sixth and ninth responds at Matins, i.e., the third respond of each nocturn, were distinguished by the singing of the first half of the *Gloria patri* (to the same music as the verse) after the repeat, followed by the same or a still shorter repeat.[3] On Trinity Sunday all the responds at Matins were sung with the *Gloria*. The first respond at Matins on the first Sunday in Advent, *Aspiciens a longe*, which began the liturgical year, had a still more extended form, with three verses and the *Gloria*, each answered by successively shorter portions of the respond.[4] The ninth respond, *Libera me*, in Matins for the dead had also on occasions three verses: *Dies illa*, *Quid ergo* and *Nunc Christe te petimus*.[5]

The *Invitatorium*, with which the office of Matins began, kept

[1] E.g., *Jubilate Deo omnis terra* (First Sunday after Epiphany), *Jubilate Deo universa terra* (Second Sunday after Epiphany), *Benedictus es Domine* (Quinquagesima), *Precatus est Moyses* (Thursday after the Second Sunday in Lent and Twelfth Sunday after Trinity).

[2] See *Missale Sarum*, col. 868*.

[3] When *Te Deum* was sung the last repeat was omitted from the ninth respond.

[4] Music in Grove, *Dictionary*, vii, p. 131.

[5] *Breviarium Sarum*, iii, col. 983.

the ancient form of a responsorial chant[1] sung between each of the verses of a psalm, in this case the *Venite*. Depending on the rank of the day the *Invitatorium* was sung by one to four singers, and this was one of the ways of indicating rank in the calendar. The entry in the calendar for January 2, for example, was: *Octava S. Stephani, invitatorium duplex, iii lectiones cum regimine chori*. On feasts of highest rank it was sung by four canons and repeated complete by the choir. The *Venite* was then sung *alternatim* by the two canons of each side, the choir, led by the precentor, singing the whole Invitatory after the odd-numbered verses and its second half after the even-numbered verses. When the Invitatory was sung by two or three its first part was sung by the rulers and its second part by the choir, both before and after the psalm. The psalm was sung throughout by the rulers, the choir interposing the Invitatory in the same fashion as before.[2]

A respond was sung after the lesson at Vespers on double feasts (with some exceptions) and on week-days in Advent and Lent.[3] Compline had a respond only in Lent, *In pace in idipsum* with *Gloria patri* being sung from the first Sunday in Lent to Passion Sunday, and *In manus tuas Domine* from Passion Sunday to Maundy Thursday. The respond *Jesu Christe fili Dei* with a varying chant and verses changing with the seasons was sung at Prime, except from Passion Sunday to 'Low' Sunday.[4]

The responsorial chants of the Mass, the Gradual and the *Alleluia*, were sung between the Epistle and the Gospel. The performance of the Gradual was carried out in the same way as that of the responds at Matins, except that the repeat was complete and, like the opening, was begun by soloists.[5] The repeat of the Gradual was omitted on double feasts, except at the second Mass of Christmas Day, and on a few other occasions.[6] The *Alleluia* was sung from the beginning by the choir

[1] See Grove, *Dictionary*, iv, p. 527. Wagner, however, regards it as an antiphonal chant; *Introduction to the Gregorian Melodies*, p. 23, n. 5.

[2] *Use of Sarum*, i, pp. 212–13; *Ordinale Exon*, i, p. 30.

[3] *Ordinale Exon*, i, pp. 45, 117, 147.

[4] The Sunday after Easter, called *Dominica in albis*. The respond was, however, sung on the Annunciation. *Use of Sarum*, ii, pp. 222–4; *Ordinale Exon*, i, p. 219.

[5] In the Gradual, the ending of the verse, i.e., usually the last word or two, was sung by the choir.   [6] *Missale Sarum*, col. 8.

after it had been begun by the soloists,[1] and the neuma at the end of the verse was also sung by the chorus. Then the repeat of the *Alleluia* was begun by the soloists and its neuma, which was the same melody as the neuma of the verse, was sung by the choir.[2] Neuma in this case means the melody of the last vowel of *Alleluia,* which was also called, and is now generally called, the *jubilus.*[3]

On Easter Day and during its octave the Gradual and *Alleluia* of the Mass of the day were sung at the day hours in place of the hymn.[4] At Vespers the Gradual was sung with a verse and without neuma, at the other hours without verse or neuma.[5] Here again neuma means the melody of the last syllable of the text, which in the Gradual of Easter Day was (*laetamur in e*)*a*.[6] The Gradual was omitted and two *Alleluias,* each with verse, were sung at Mass from the octave of Easter to the day before Trinity Sunday.[7] From Septuagesima to the Saturday of Holy Week the *Alleluia* was not sung; the repeat of the Gradual was omitted, and its verse was followed by a Tract. The two feasts of the Virgin which might fall between Septuagesima and Easter, the Purification and the Annunciation (March 25), were special cases. Whether *infra Septuagesima* or not, each had a Sequence; between Septuagesima and Easter the Sequence was sung after the Gradual, and the Tract was then said *privatim* by the celebrant and his ministers.[8]

[1] It seems to be the only chant in which this was done; see *Use of Sarum,* i, p. 36.

[2] *Missale Sarum,* col. 10; *Ordinale of St. Mary's, York,* p. 132.

[3] In the secular Ordinals it was always called *neuma.* Grandisson uses the verb *jubilare* in the sense of singing in a festive manner, i.e., in polyphony; *Ordinale Exon,* i, p. 19. The Ordinal of St. Mary's, York, discusses 'neuma seu jubilus quod idem est' as exemplified 'in e ut in Kyrieleyson vel in a ut in Alleluia'. *Ordinale of St. Mary's, York,* i, pp. 14–15.

[4] Not in the Benedictine use; see *Ordinale of St. Mary's, York,* ii, pp. 299–301; *Customary of Norwich,* pp. 94–7.

[5] *Ordinale Exon,* i, pp. 140–1.

[6] As may be seen by comparing the Gradual as written in the chant books for Mass and for Vespers in *Graduale Sarisburiense,* pl. 117, and *Antiphonale Sarisburiense,* pl. 238.

[7] *Ordinale Exon,* i, p. 342; *Missale Sarum,* cols, 381–418, with the direction (col. 379): 'Nunquam enim repetatur primum Alleluya post suum Versum quando duo Alleluya habentur'.

[8] *Use of Sarum,* i, pp. 132–3; *Ordinale Exon,* i, p. 342.

Tract

A Tract was sung in the Mass for the dead, on Ember Saturdays,[1] on the Vigil of Whitsunday and on Mondays, Wednesdays and Fridays in Lent, as well as on Sundays and feasts of
nine lessons between Septuagesima and the end of Holy Week.
In form it was a varying number of verses from a psalm, sung
alternatim without antiphon. Four singers from the senior row of
stalls, standing two at each end of the choir-step, began the first
verse, which was completed by the two from the 'duty' side.
The rest was sung *alternatim* by these four, all singing the last
verse. In the two longest Tracts, those for the First Sunday in
Lent and for Palm Sunday, the choir on the 'duty' side took up
the Tract after its beginning, and it was sung *alternatim* throughout by all.[2]

Hymn, Sequence and Prose

A hymn was sung at each of the hours, except from Maundy
Thursday to the Saturday after Easter.[3] The words of the
hymns sung at the 'lesser' Hours remained constant throughout
the year,[4] and were: *Jam lucis orto sidere* at Prime, *Nunc sancte
nobis Spiritus* at Terce, *Rector potens verax Deus* at Sext and
Rerum Deus tenax vigor at None. The tunes, however, varied with
the season, *Jam lucis*, for example, being sung to the tune of the
Christmas hymn *Christe redemptor omnium* at Christmas, to *Hostis
Herodes impie* at Epiphany, and so on. For this reason *Jam lucis*
was sung to about twenty different tunes during the year, *Nunc
sancte* to four, and the others to three each.

The hymn at Compline changed with the season. In Advent,
from the Octave of Epiphany to Lent and from Trinity to

[1] Ember days, called *Quatuor Tempora* because they occurred four times
in the year, were days of special penitence.

[2] *Use of Sarum*, i, pp. 72, 92. For the early history of the Tract, see Wagner,
Introduction to the Gregorian Melodies, pp. 86–8; Wellesz, *Eastern Elements*,
pp. 127–40.

[3] For the processional hymn (or prose) *Salve festa dies* and the hymn
Crux fidelis see below, pp. 90, 97. Lists of hymns in the secular uses are given
in *Breviarium Sarum*, iii, pp. c–cxx.

[4] The only exception was the hymn at Terce on Whitsunday, which was
Veni creator Spiritus.

Advent it was *Te lucis ante terminum*, which had two tunes, its *cantus festivus* being the tune of the Easter season hymn *Jesu salvator saeculi*. From Christmas to the Octave of the Epiphany, and on double feasts and through their octaves from Epiphany to the First Sunday in Lent and from Whitsuntide[1] to Christmas Eve, it was *Salvator mundi Domine*, which in the English secular uses was sung to the tune of *Veni creator Spiritus*. There was a special Compline hymn during each of the periods from Passion Sunday to the Wednesday in Holy Week (*Cultor Dei momento*), from the Octave of Easter to the Ascension (*Jesu salvator saeculi*) and from Ascension to Whitsunday (*Jesu nostra redemptio*).

The hymns at first Vespers, Matins and Lauds were proper to a day, *de Tempore* or *de Sanctis*, or to a season, e.g., Advent, the post-Trinity period, or to a group of saints, e.g., Apostles, Martyrs, Confessors, Virgins. Some of the hymns in this last division which were used quite frequently had two or more tunes so as to provide simpler settings for use in octaves or commemorations. Thus *Exsultet caelum laudibus* for Apostles at Lauds had five tunes.

A hymn was begun by the two *decani* rulers, 'turning towards the vicars on that side', when there were four rulers, by the principal ruler when there were two, and by one from the senior stalls when the choir was not ruled.[2] The beginners sang the first line, and the hymn was continued *alternatim*, verse by verse, by the choir. The last verse, or 'doxology', was sung by all.

The *Te Deum*, on account of its venerable age, its curious combination of various textual and musical elements and its extra-liturgical use and associations, has a special place among hymns.[3] The first thirteen verses, a hymn to the Trinity (in prose, as is the whole text), are set in psalm-tone style in the fourth mode ending on G; verses fourteen to twenty are in praise of Christ, with a different melody in the fourth mode

---

[1] Except that on Whitsunday and the three days following the sequence *Alma chorus Domini* was sung in place of the hymn.

[2] *Use of Sarum*, i, pp. 35–6; *Ordinale Exon*, i, pp. 42, 63.

[3] For a discussion of the earliest versions, see Julian, *Dictionary of Hymnology*, pp. 1119–27, 1547–8. Besides its ritual use, the *Te Deum* was sung at coronations, at the enthronement of a bishop, immediately after the election of a bishop, dean or abbot, and on occasions of national or communal rejoicing.

ending on E; verse twenty-one (*Aeterna fac*) is a short antiphon, also in the fourth mode, and was probably the ending of the *Te Deum* in one of its earlier forms. The rest is a series of five verses to the same melody as the second part, preceded by two antiphons (*Salvum fac* and *Et rege eos*) and followed by a more extended antiphon (*In te Domine speravi*), all set to melodies similar to that of verse twenty-one:[1]

[1] Chant from the Sarum noted Breviary, Oxford, Bodleian Library, MS.

The *Te Deum* was always begun by the senior person present, who sang from his stall *Te Deum laudamus*; the two rulers on the 'duty' side completed the first verse (*te Dominum confitemur*), and the rest was sung by the choir *alternatim*.[1] Since it was not sung on ferias, its performance always ended with the neuma of the fourth mode.

A hymn used the same melody for every verse; the melody of a sequence changed with each pair of verses. In the early medieval sequences the verses of each pair had the same number of lines and syllables, but the pairs did not necessarily correspond to each other, and in many cases the first and last verses were unpaired. In the twelfth century the sequence became regular in rhythm and rhyme; the established metre of the later medieval sequence is exemplified in *Stabat mater dolorosa*.[2]

The sequence had developed from the troping of the neuma of the *Alleluia* of the Mass,[3] and when it was sung the neuma of the repeat of the *Alleluia* after its verse was omitted.[4] The rulers, standing in mid-choir, sang the opening phrase, and the choir continued *alternatim*.[5] In the Sarum use a sequence was sung on double feasts, on saints' days on which the choir was ruled (except from Septuagesima to Easter) and on Sundays in Advent and from Easter to the Ascension.

The term *prosa* was used in France in the early Middle Ages as a synonym for sequence.[6] It was occasionally used in that sense in England,[7] but as a rule the two terms were kept distinct. A prose was in the same form as a sequence, and was sung at Vespers on certain feasts, at Matins on St. Nicholas's Day, and in some processions. If the church had an altar

---

Laud misc. 299 (XV cent., first half); neuma from *Use of Sarum*, ii, p. lxix. The plainsong symbol ⌐ has been transcribed as a tied note. In polyphonic settings it is normally treated as a note of double length.

[1] *Ordinale Exon*, i, p. 66.

[2] See Raby, *History of Christian Latin Poetry*, Chapter XI.

[3] For a discussion of its early history, see Handschin, 'Trope, Sequence and Conductus'; for a summary of the literature of the subject up to 1944, see Apel, *Harvard Dictionary*, p. 674.

[4] *Missale Sarum*, col. 10.   [5] *Ordinale Exon*, i, pp. 296, 71.

[6] It may be an abbreviation for 'pro sequentia'; the eleventh-century Gradual of St. Yrieux (*Paléographie musicale*, xiii) has *prosula*.

[7] E.g., *Use of Sarum*, i, p. 92 ('prosa ad missam'); *Ordinale Exon*, i, p. 19.

dedicated to the saint concerned, the prose was sung there on the arrival of the procession after first Vespers.[1] If not, it was sung in choir, as an interpolation in the respond after the lesson. St. Nicholas's feast was unique in having two proses, one (*Oportet devota mente*) with the respond *Beatus Nicholaus* at first Vespers, and the other (*Sospitati dedit aegros*) with the ninth respond (*Ex ejus tumba*), at Matins. Some of the proses, possibly the oldest group, are clearly tropes, being either the addition of words to the last neuma of the respond or of new music and words towards the end of the respond. They are interesting survivals in the English secular uses of the early practice of troping a respond.[2]

An example of the former kind of addition is the prose *Aeternae virgo memoriae* in the respond *O mater nostra* at first Vespers on the feast of St. Katherine, where the words of the prose are set to the neuma of the word *suscipe* of the respond. The complete scheme of the respond, verse, prose and *Gloria patri* is as follows:[3]

Ex 2

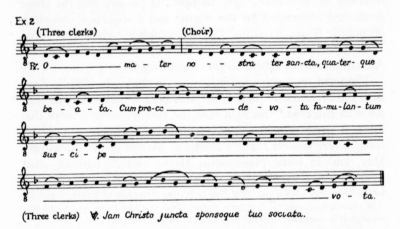

(Three clerks) ℣. *Jam Christo juncta sponsoque tuo sociata.*

---

[1] At Sarum, but not at Exeter, the prose *O morum doctor* was sung in choir at second Vespers on St. Andrew's day. *Breviarium Sarum*, iii, col. 18.

[2] See Handschin, 'Trope, Sequence and Conductus', pp. 133–5. Proses were rare in the monastic rites; the Worcester Antiphonal (*Paléographie musicale*, xii) has two: *Inviolata*, and *Hodie prodit virga Jesse* for the Nativity of the Virgin, which is not in Sarum.

[3] Bodleian Library, MS. Rawl. liturg. d. 4 (fourteenth-century Sarum Processional), fo. 187.

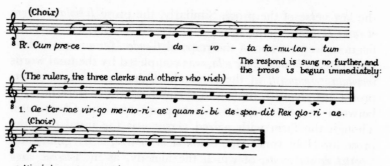

(Choir)

℟. Cum pre-ce _____ de - vo - ta fa - mu-lan - tum

The respond is sung no further, and
the prose is begun immediately:

(The rulers, the three clerks and others who wish)

1. Ae - ter-nae vir-go me-mo-ri - ae quam si-bi de-spon-dit Rex gio-ri - ae.

(Choir)

Æ.

2. Virginis proles egregiae sponsusque virginis ecclesiae (same music).(Choir)Æ ___

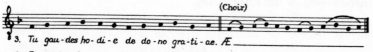

(Choir)

3. Tu gau-des ho-di-e de do-no gra-ti-ae. Æ _____

4. Et cantas in caelo carmen laetitiae (same music).(Choir)Æ ___

5. Te laudantes in terra respice (to the music of verse 6).(Choir)Æ ___

(Choir)

6. At-que no-stra cle-men-ter sus-ci-pe vo - ta

Gloria patri et filio et spiritui sancto.(Three clerks, to the music of the Verse, Jam Christo)
(Choir) ℟. Cum prece .... vota (as at first).

The choir repeated the melody of each verse of a prose to its
final vowel in this way whether or not the melodies were paired
as they are in *Aeternae virgo memoriae*, which was normal in both
sequence and prose.[1] *Sospitati dedit aegros*[2] seems to be the only
exception to this rule, for both the verse (*Catervatim ruunt
populi*) of the respond and the prose were sung by the whole
choir, the prose being sung *alternatim*.[3] *Sospitati* is an example
of the second kind of prose, in which the music is not based on
the neuma it replaces. The words are an insertion between
Et debilis quisque (*sospes*) and (*sospes*) *regreditur*, and as in *Aeternae
virgo memoriae* the ending of the respond completes the sense of

[1] At Exeter the verse of the respond and the prose were sung 'ab omnibus
qui voluerint'. *Ordinale Exon*, i, p. 196. For the Sarum method of announcing
the prose to each member of the choir, see *Breviarium Sarum*, iii, col. 17.

[2] *Antiphonale Sarisburiense*, pl. 360; *Breviarium Sarum*, iii, col. 36.

[3] *Ordinale Exon*, i, p. 201; the Sarum Ordinal (*Use of Sarum*, ii, p. 105) does
not give the details. This seems to have been the practice with other proses
in Hereford; see *Hereford Breviary*, i, p. 145, and compare *Ordinale Exon*,
i, p. 201.

the last verse of the prose. Similarly, the prose *Inviolata integra et casta es Maria*, sung in choir at second Vespers on the Purification, was a trope of the respond *Gaude Maria virgo*, and its last verse, *O benigna quae sola*, was completed by the final words *inviolata permansisti* of the respond.[1] Other, presumably later, proses are poems complete in themselves which were inserted between the first repeat of a respond and the *Gloria patri*. Though the form with paired verses was the usual one, the prose for Holy Innocents, *Sedentem in superne*, is irregular, and *Oportet devota mente*, of which the melody, as in *Aeternae virgo memoriae*, is exactly that of the neuma of its respond, has only three verses in the form AAB.

Lesson

Lessons at Matins were normally chanted to a simple reading tone. The lessons at 'Tenebrae', known as the 'Lamentations', since they were from the Lamentations of Jeremiah, in the first nocturn on Maundy Thursday, Good Friday and Holy Saturday, were sung to a simple reciting tone with inflections. The introductory formula *Incipit* (or *De*) *Lamentatio Jeremiae Prophetae* of the group of three lessons and the closing sentence *Jerusalem Jerusalem convertere ad Dominum Deum tuum* of each lesson were also sung to this tone. The Hebrew letters *Aleph, Beth, Gimel*, etc. at the beginning of each section of each lesson were sung to a simple melodic cadence, and each lesson was followed by a respond and verse in the normal way. In Sarum use the Lamentations were sung by a boy.[2]

Immediately before the Epistle at the Mass of Christmas Eve and at each of the three Masses of Christmas Day[3] there was a lesson from the book of Isaiah, chanted on one note with a fall of a fifth at the end of each verse.[4] Where there were com-

[1] *Antiphonale Sarisburiense*, pl. 403; *Breviarium Sarum*, iii, col. 145.

[2] *Use of Sarum*, ii, p. 66 ('a tribus pueris'); *Hereford Breviary*, i, p. 309 ('a tribus pueris singulis per se cantando').

[3] Midnight Mass (*Missa in gallicantu*), Mass at Dawn (*Missa in aurora*) and the 'Third Mass'.

[4] *Use of Sarum*, i, p. 272. This tone was used for all lessons sung at Mass, e.g., during Holy Week, when lessons from the Old Testament replaced the Epistle.

petent singers the lesson at Midnight Mass was sung to a special chant, and was also troped.[1] Two singers took part alternately, one singing the words of the prophet and the other the text of the trope. Before the lesson they sang together *Laudes Deo dicam per saecula*, etc., and after it they sang *Ab ortu solis usque occiduos*, etc. The chant of the trope is quite varied in style and contains at least two quotations of words and music; one is a verse (*Fulserunt*) from the sequence *Nato canunt omnia* of the same Mass, the other a verse (*Messias . . . Adonay*) from the sequence *Alma chorus Domini* for the Thursday after Whitsunday.[2]

The Epistle was chanted to a less simple tone than was a lesson, and the usual Gospel tone was similar, with a slight change on double feasts.[3] On Palm Sunday and on the Tuesday, Wednesday and Friday of Holy Week the Gospel was the story of the Passion of Our Lord according to St. Matthew, St. Mark, St. Luke and St. John respectively. The Passions were sung to the Gospel tone for simple feasts, with special formulae added for two other ranges of voice, at a high pitch for the words of the Jews and the disciples and a low pitch for the words of Christ. The three parts were distinguished in the Missal by the letters *a(lta)*, *b(assa)* and *m(edia)*, the last being the part of the Evangelist-narrator.[4]

Between the ninth respond and the *Te Deum* at Matins of Christmas Day and of the Epiphany was sung the Genealogy of Christ. On Christmas Day the text (beginning *Liber generationis*) was taken from St. Matthew; the text for the Epiphany (*Factum est autem*) was from St. Luke. These were the most elaborate of the Gospel chants. The *Liber generationis* was set to eight recurring melodies for forty verses and two other melodies

---

[1] The untroped form is given after the troped form, and is headed 'Ubi non habetur cantus legitur Lectio Esaiae Prophetae'. *Missale Sarum*, col. 51.

[2] *Missale Sarum*, col. 439. It was also the sequence for the votive Mass of the Trinity. Ibid., col. 837*.

[3] The tones are printed in *Use of Sarum*, i, p. 265.

[4] 'Et est notandum quod triplici voce debet cantari aut pronunciari; scilicet voce alta, bassa, et media'. *Missale Sarum*, col. 264, where it is noted by the editor that in the printed Missals of 1494 and 1497 the words of Christ were marked with a cross. In other cases, e.g., the Gospel Lectionary in Chetham's Library, Manchester (MS.A.6.1), one finds C for Chronista and S for Synagoga. In the printed Gradual of 1527 the voices are distinguished by numbers.

for the announcement and the last verse, and the Epiphany Genealogy was made on similar lines.[1]

Ordinary of the Mass; Tropes

The only invariable chant in the Ordinary was that of the Creed, which was a plain and almost entirely syllabic setting using a limited number of recurring phrases and motives.[2] There were a number of settings of the *Agnus Dei*, which were allotted, with some alternatives *pro dispositione cantoris*, to the various ranks of festival.[3] The music followed the tripartite form of the words by using the scheme AaBaAa or the simpler plan AAA. The chants of the *Sanctus* were more varied in form, though the same music was almost invariably used for the two *Hosanna* endings. Neither the Creed nor the *Agnus Dei* was troped. The only trope of the Sanctus consisted of the two words (*Benedictus*) *Mariae filius* (*qui venit*); this was sung at the Saturday Lady-Mass in the Lady-Chapel and on four occasions in choir, viz., at the last Lady-Mass before Advent and before Lent, and at the Masses on the octave of the Assumption (August 15) and of the Nativity (September 8) of the Virgin. At the same Masses the *Gloria in excelsis* from the words *Jesu Christe* to the end was troped with a series of insertions beginning *Spiritus et alme orphanorum*. In the octaves of the Assumption and Nativity of the Virgin this trope was sung at the choir-step by three from the senior stalls.[4]

The *Kyrie* was sung in one of three forms, in accordance with the rank of the day: (1) 'with verses' (*cum versibus*), i.e., with the complete words and music of a trope; (2) 'without verses' (*absque versibus*), i.e., with the same music as that of a trope but without its words, though referred to by its name; or (3) in

---

[1] *Antiphonale Sarisburiense*, pls. 51, 88.

[2] Music from the Sarum Ordinal in *Use of Sarum*, i, p. 267.

[3] The chants of the *Kyrie, Gloria, Sanctus, Agnus Dei, Benedicamus* and *Ite missa est* are in *Graduale Sarisburiense*, pls. 1*–19*.

[4] *Missale Sarum*, col. 768*, which uses the words *prosa* and *farsura* in referring to this trope (cols. 585, 796). As Frere notes in his Introduction to *Graduale Sariburiense*, p. xlix, the *Gloria* trope *Regnum tuum solidum* is not included there. It was common in early Graduals and is met with in polyphonic settings before 1400, but seems not to have been in common use in the secular rites later.

simple form without name or trope. In Sarum use there were ten of the first kind,[1] of which three, *Deus creator*, *Rex genitor* and *Fons bonitatis*, were never used without verses: on the other hand four of the *Kyrie* chants with a name, *Rex semper*,[2] *Rex summe*,[3] *Deus sempiterne* and *Rex clemens*,[4] were no longer used with the verses of the tropes from which they derived their names.[5] The chants of the *Kyrie*, like those of the *Agnus Dei*, reflected the tripartite form of the words. Several, both troped and plain, have the plan AaaBbbCcc, e.g., *Deus creator omnium*; other schemes used are ABA CDC EFE, e.g., *Omnipotens pater* and *Rex semper*; and ABA CBC DCD, e.g., *Conditor*. The last *Kyrie* is usually extended, as in *Conditor*, where the last D is actually in the form DDC, and the endings of phrases frequently correspond though the rest of their music differs.

The secular uses exercised a stricter control over the use of tropes than was customary in the monastic uses. The old use of St. Paul's may have been an exception to this, for an inventory of the books of St. Paul's in 1295 includes a Missal and a Troper both containing *Epistolae farcitae*, and a Troper containing an *Agnus cum versibus In Egiptum*.[6]

---

[1] In his Introduction to *Graduale Sarisburiense*, p. xxxiii, Frere says nine, but this does not include *Rex virginum* (which was sung to the melody of *Cunctipotens genitor*) for feasts of the Virgin. See *Use of Sarum*, ii, p. 207. *Ordinale Exon*, pp. 463–71, gives a complete scheme for the Ordinary throughout the year, which differs considerably from the Sarum Ordinal and from *Graduale Sarisburiense*, which are not identical. The last has been used as the basis of this discussion. The Exeter Ordinal also gives the opening notes of a *Kyrie* ('quod non est in libris Sarum') and of an *Agnus Dei* which were special to Exeter. The beginning of the *Agnus* corresponds to that in the modern Roman Mass XVII (*Liber Usualis*, p. 59).

[2] Not in Exeter.

[3] *Ordinale Exon* (ii, p. 468) expresses a strong objection to one of the *Kyrie* tropes which Sarum used for simple feasts: 'Et dimmitatur penitus illud dissonans Kyrie quod habet unum longum nimis, et aliud curtum nimis, quia non valet, licet inter cetera soleat dici Sarum.' This was probably *Rex summe*, which has very short phrases in the second *Christe* and fifth *Kyrie*.

[4] See *Graduale Sarisburiense*, p. xlix; *Ordinale Exon* (ii, p. 463) has *O Rex clemens*, which is not in Sarum.

[5] For a discussion of York tropes of the Ordinary, see Frere, 'The Newly-found York Gradual', pp. 23–7. For the texts of Hereford *Kyrie* tropes, of which there were sixteen, see *Missale Herfordensis*, pp. xxxviii sqq.

[6] Dugdale, *History of St. Paul's*, p. 324.

Benedicamus Domino

The melody of the *Benedicamus Domino* at the end of Vespers and Lauds on a feast day was drawn from a neuma of one of the responds of the feast. This procedure is an interesting parallel to the use of the melody of the *Christe eleison* trope for the *Ite missa est* at the end of Mass, but for the latter a complete phrase was used while for the *Benedicamus* a neuma was taken out of its melodic context and given a separate existence. The Sarum Customary gives a very simple melody for the *Benedicamus* on ferias and a less simple one, ending with *Alleluia*, for the second *Benedicamus*[1] during the weeks after Easter. Either of these, the former with *Alleluia* added, could be used for the first *Benedicamus* during the Easter season. On important feasts at other times of the year the *Benedicamus* could be taken from a respond of the day, or else replaced by some piece appropriate to the occasion.[2] As might be expected, the selection of melodies varied considerably, even as late as the time of the printed service-books,[3] and they soon lost any indication of their original source. A rare instance of such indications in a thirteenth-century Gradual from the diocese of Exeter[4] enables us to establish the source of many of the *Benedicamus* melodies, for all but two of the seventeen given for double feasts and feasts when the Invitatory was sung by three singers show the words of the neuma to which they originally belonged. The melody marked *in perenni*, for example, was taken from the neuma on those words in the Trinity respond *Honor virtus*:[5]

Ex. 3.

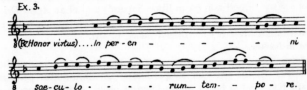

1 The first *Benedicamus* was sung at the end of the service, the second after the *memoria* which followed the service.

2 'Dicitur aliquod proprium Benedicamus de historia festi de quo agitur vel aliquod aliud quod festo conveniat.' *Use of Sarum*, i, p. 254. *Historia* was used of the lessons and responds at a particular Matins, as well as of a single lesson or cycle of lessons; see ibid., p. 135.

3 See *Missale Sarum*, col. 636, n.

4 Manchester, John Rylands Library, MS. Lat. 24.

5 *Antiphonale Sarisburiense*, pl. 290; Rylands Library, MS. Lat. 24, fo. 14.

Other *Benedicamus* melodies the source of which is indicated in the Exeter Gradual[1] are *in saecula,* from the Trinity respond *Benedicamus patrem; hodie processit, flos filius* and *Judea Mariam,* from the responds for the Nativity of the Virgin *Solem justitiae, Stirps Jesse* and *Ad nutum Domini* respectively; *praeconia,* from the Assumption respond *Candida virginitas; clementiam,* from the respond of St. Nicholas *Qui cum audissent; gladio* and *et egrediens,* from the responds *Misit impius Herodes*[2] and *Dixit angelus ad Petrum* for the feast of St. Peter ad Vincula; *contra inimici jacula,* from the antiphon *Crux fidelis,*[3] sung in the procession to the Rood on Saturdays in summer; *Eructavit,* from the respond *Regnum mundi* for feasts of a Virgin; *commutans lutea* and *vel carnis opera,* from the responds *Jacet granum* and *Christe Jesu* at Matins of St. Thomas of Canterbury; and *in odorem,* from the respond *Beatus Laurentius dixit* at Matins on the feasts of St. Laurence.

A fourteenth-century Ordinal in Salisbury Cathedral Library contains twelve melodies for *Benedicamus* and twelve for *Ite missa est,* for days on which the *Kyrie* was not troped, eight melodies being common to both sets.[4] Salisbury and Exeter had six *Benedicamus* melodies in common, while the Hereford *Benedicamus* for the Purification, which was based on the neumae at the beginning and end of the verse *Haec speciosum* of the respond *Videte miraculum* at Matins on that feast, does not appear in Salisbury or Exeter.[5] The Customary of *c.* 1260 in the Black Book of Lincoln gives not only the names of the *Benedicamus* melodies for double feasts but also the name of the respond

---

[1] The manuscript gives the word(s) of the neuma, but not its original source in a respond, which must be searched for. The only neuma I have not traced to its respond is marked *quem suscita.*

[2] The word 'Benedicamus' has the music of 'Misit', and 'domino' of 'gladio', the last word of the respond.

[3] *Antiphonale Sarisburiense,* pl. 535 (not in the Index).

[4] MS. 175, fos. 135, 173.

[5] It is printed in *Missale Herfordensis,* p. 138.

from which each was drawn. The *In perenni* melody was sung at first Vespers, the *flos filius* melody at Lauds, and the *clementiam* melody at second Vespers.[1]

Commemorations and Memorials

In addition to the canonical hours, the Hours of the Virgin (*Commemorationes beatae Mariae Virginis*), which were invariable, were said daily. Originally monastic, they were widely observed by secular communities and, from the late thirteenth century, by individuals.[2] It was for this devotion that the medieval Books of Hours, the finest examples of which were adorned with the most beautiful work of the illuminators of the age, were written, though the later Books of Hours also contained other votive offices. From the earliest period of the English uses a special office of the Virgin was sung instead of the ferial office on Saturday. Its ritual had three sets of texts, one for Advent, one for Christmas to the Purification, and one for the Purification to Advent, with some changes during the Easter season.[3] By the later Middle Ages the offices of one or two other days were replaced by commemorations devoted to a saint, normally the patron saint of the church. This second commemoration was devoted to St. Thomas of Canterbury in Salisbury, to SS. Peter and Paul in Exeter, to St. Andrew in Wells, to St. Ethelbert in Hereford, and to St. Chad in Lichfield.[4]

Commemorations were complete offices in the usual forms. Memorials, on the other hand, were miniature services added at the end of Lauds and Vespers, and consisted of an antiphon without psalm followed by versicle, response and collect.[5] Some memorials, for example those of the Virgin, of All Saints

---

[1] 'In secundis vesperis cantetur *Benedicamus* a regentibus chorum principalibus in loco ubi stant sicut canitur *clemenciam* in fine quinti Responsorii hystorie beati Nicholai.' *Lincoln Statutes*, i, p. 381. For the other passages, see below, p. 111.

[2] Their origins and early history are discussed in Bishop, 'The Prymer', pp. 224–37.

[3] *Ordinale Exon*, i, pp. 49, 85–7, 155.

[4] Ibid., pp. 46–7; *Breviarium Sarum*, iii, pp. lxix–lxxvi; *Hereford Breviary*, ii, pp. 22–39; iii, pp. 82–3.

[5] For their early history, see Batiffol, *History of the Roman Breviary*, pp. 147–9. Memorials at Mass consisted of collects only.

PLATE VII

10. Melodies for *Agnus Dei, Ite missa est* and *Benedicamus Domino* in an Exeter Gradual of the thirteenth century

PLATE VIII

11. Page from a Book of Hours of *c.* 1350-60, showing choristers singing at the Lady-Mass

and of the patron saint of the church, were observed throughout the year,[1] and were called *memoriae consuetae*. Others, which
might be described as 'short-term' memorials, were sung during
their appropriate season or week, for example those of Advent,
of the Resurrection, of the Trinity, of the Cross, or of a particular saint or day. The special musical interest of memorials
is that, like processions, they provided a liturgical situation in
which an antiphon was sung without a psalm, thus establishing
itself as a separate item of the ritual.

Votive Mass

The Mass of the Virgin was commonly celebrated weekly as
part of her commemorative office on Saturday. From the early
Middle Ages this celebration was treated as one of special importance, and from the thirteenth century onwards it became
a daily observance in many places. At Salisbury the daily celebration of the Lady-Mass[2] in her chapel by four clerks and
choristers (in addition to the Saturday Mass in choir) was instituted by Bishop Poore on the completion of the Lady-chapel
in 1225.[3] Bishop Brewer of Exeter (1224–44) gave the choir
an endowment so that five vicars, five clerks of the second form
and four choristers, on a weekly roster, should celebrate the
Mass of the Virgin daily in her chapel.[4] These examples were
followed by most of the secular cathedrals and new collegiate
foundations, for example by St. Elizabeth's, Winchester, in
1300,[5] by The Queen's College, Oxford, in 1340,[6] and by Clare

---

[1] Except from Ash Wednesday to Low Sunday; *Ordinale Exon*, i, p. 27.

[2] This term will be used for the votive Mass of the Virgin, as distinct
from Mary-Mass, a Mass sung on one of the festivals of the Virgin. This
corresponds to the usage of the period, and is also a useful distinction for
musical purposes.

[3] *Valor Ecclesiasticus*, ii, p. 85. Bishop Mortival's statutes of 1319 required
the attendance of a sufficient number of vicars at the weekly Mass of the
Virgin at the altar of the Holy Trinity. Dayman and Jones, *Statutes of
Sarum*, p. 69. The altar in the 'Lady-chapel' was dedicated to the Trinity
and All Saints, the cathedral itself, and therefore the high altar, being
dedicated to the Virgin.

[4] Oliver, *Lives of the Bishops of Exeter*, p. 417.

[5] 'Cum nota et solempnitate decenti secundum usum et consuetudinem
Sarisburiensis ecclesie.' *Monasticon*, viii, p. 1340.

[6] *Statutes of The Queen's College*, p. 27.

Hall, Cambridge, in 1359 (*cum nota* on Saturdays, Sundays and feast-days).[1] If there was a separate Lady-chapel, as was usually the case in cathedrals and larger collegiate churches, the daily Lady-Mass was celebrated there. In his Exeter Ordinal, Grandisson gave a more than usually comprehensive order for the daily Mass in the Lady-chapel[2] which he had reconstituted 1336.[3] He sanctioned the singing in polyphony of at least part of the Ordinary, and in setting down the distribution of the various chants of the *Gloria* through the week he ordered that the 'simple chant in ferial style with few notes should never be sung at the Mass of the Virgin'.[4] In his college of Ottery St. Mary the 'clerk of the chapel of the Virgin' played the organ at the daily Lady-Mass (*sollemnis missa de beata Maria*), which was celebrated by all the clerks and choristers with at least one canon and two vicars.[5]

The daily Lady-Mass may have been customary in some other places before its institution in the new building at Salisbury. At St. Paul's, for example, provision was made by Bishop Eustace de Fauconbrigge *c.* 1210 for one priest, probably a minor canon, and six clerks to be at the Lady-Mass and hours every day,[6] and Abbot William de Trumpington of St. Alban's (1214–35) ordered the celebration of the Mass by six monks, observing that 'in all the noble churches of England a Mass of the Blessed Mary is solemnly sung by note daily'.[7]

In 1439 Archbishop Kemp of York decreed that the *missa sollemnis de beata Maria virgine* should be celebrated at Ripon at least on Saturdays, Sundays and feasts, since it was the 'laudable custom' to celebrate it daily in York Minster and in the collegiate churches throughout the province.[8]

At Westminster the daily celebration in the Lady-chapel was established by *c.* 1260, and the Customary of St. Augustine's,

---

[1] Heywood, *Early Cambridge Statutes*, pp. 138–9.

[2] The Saturday Mass of the Virgin was sung in choir. *Ordinale Exon*, ii, p. 464.

[3] Ibid., pp. 465, 472–5.

[4] 'Ita quod illud simplex et quasi feriale paucarum notarum nunquam dicitur ad Missam beate Marie.' Ibid., p. 465.

[5] Dalton, *Collegiate Church of Ottery St. Mary*, p. 142.

[6] Dugdale, *History of St. Paul's*, p. 13.

[7] *Gesta Abbatum S. Albani*, i, pp. 284–5.

[8] *Memorials of Ripon*, ii, pp. 148–9.

Canterbury, speaks of it as an 'old' observance, *sollemniter per notam*, at the altar of the Virgin in the crypt. The Customary notes that it was moved to the altar of St. Stephen and St. Mary Magdalene in the north aisle of the nave in the time of Abbot Nicholas Thorne (1273–83).[1] At St. Mary's, York, the Lady-Mass at her altar was also the daily *Missa familiaris*, the Mass for the friends of the community.[2]

The ritual of the Sarum Lady-Mass changed with the principal periods of the year. In the longest of these, from the Purification to Advent, the Introit was *Salve sancta parens*, and the Mass was often referred to by this title, or simply as *Missa Salve*. Similarly the Lady-Mass of Advent was called *Missa Rorate* and that of Christmas to the Purification *Missa Vultum tuum*.[3] Since it was treated as a festival Mass a troped *Kyrie* was always sung, though *absque versibus*, in a given order throughout the week, and the *Alleluia* and Sequence were always sung, even in Lent; consequently a Tract was never sung in the Lady-Mass. For the *Missa Salve* a different *Alleluia* was sung on each day of the week. Eleven sequences were provided for the Lady-Mass, three for Advent, one for Sundays at other times, and seven from which a free choice could be made on week-days outside of Advent. In addition, the printed Missal mentions that another chant or piece of music could be sung in the Lady-Mass instead of the sequence.[4] As in other masses, the *Gloria* was omitted in Advent and Lent and the Creed was omitted on days on which it was not sung at the principal Mass.

In the secular cathedrals the number of perpetual votive Masses for the dead provided by private endowment grew constantly. They were said at lower altars or in their particular chantry chapels by chantry priests or by vicars-choral who held chantry chaplaincies. Another Mass celebrated daily was the Chapter-Mass (*missa in capitulo*) or Mass of the community, which was said at one of the side altars for the departed members of the chapter after the daily meeting in the chapter-house.

---

[1] *Customary of St. Augustine's, Canterbury, and St. Peter's, Westminster*, ii, p. 91; i, p. 144.

[2] *Ordinal of St. Mary's, York*, i, p. 56. The date of this Ordinal is *c.* 1400.

[3] *Missale Sarum*, cols. 759*–82*.

[4] 'In missis vero quotidianis de sancta Maria sufficit quod habeatur Cantus loco Sequentiae, scilicet in Capella ejusdem.' Ibid., col. 9.

Most of the new collegiate foundations of the fourteenth and fifteenth centuries had no chantry obligations, or rather, were themselves single chantries on a larger scale; hence their daily Masses, apart from the Mass of the day, were votive Masses of various kinds. At Eton, for example, seven Masses were sung daily, beginning with the Lady-Mass *per notam et cum cantu*. Then came Mass for the Safety of the Realm (*Missa Salus populi*), the Mass of the day, and a different votive Mass for each day of the week in the order (beginning with Sunday) *de Trinitate, de Angelis, de S. Thoma martyre, de Sancto Spiritu, de Corpore Christi, de Cruce* and *de Nomine Jesu*.[1] The last three were the Chapter-Mass, the Mass of the Assumption of the Virgin, being the dedication of the college, and a Mass to be decided by the celebrant. The third, sixth and seventh Masses were celebrated by a fellow, the others by a chaplain, and the clerks and choristers tabled for the day attended the first three.[2]

By the terms of Bishop John Alcock's grant to the Priory of Worcester in 1478 one of the monks was to celebrate a Mass daily in the Lady-chapel in the nave: on Easter Day, Whitsunday, Christmas Day or a feast of the Virgin falling on Sunday the Mass of that day, otherwise the Mass of the Trinity or of the day; on Monday the Mass of the Holy Spirit; on Tuesday the Mass *Salus populi*; on Wednesday *Requiem aeternam*; on Thursday the Mass of Corpus Christi; on Friday the Mass of the Name of Jesus, of the Five Wounds, or of the Holy Cross; and on Saturday the Mass of the Virgin. In addition, the Master, clerks and boys of the chapel were to sing every day, after Vespers had been sung in choir, the respond *O Maria et Johannes* with its verse and *Gloria patri*, or the antiphon *Stellae claritatis*[3] with certain prayers.[4]

In prescribing the Mass of the Name of Jesus for Saturday the Eton statutes observed that it was to be celebrated in the form specially written into the Missals of the college. At that time the Jesus-Mass, which was either *de Nomine Jesu* or *de*

---

[1] The printed Sarum Missals have the same plan, except on Thursday (*Salus populi*) and Saturday (*de nostra Domina*). See *Missale Sarum*, col. 735*.

[2] *Ancient Laws of King's and Eton*, pp. 562–5.

[3] These texts are not in the Worcester Antiphonal (*Paléographie musicale*, xii), nor in the Sarum liturgy.

[4] Atkins, *Early Occupants of the Office of Organist of Worcester*, pp. 6–7.

Quinque vulneribus,[1] was beginning to assume a new importance, and from the latter part of the fifteenth century was celebrated in many places on Friday of every week. It was not celebrated in choir but, like the Lady-Mass, in a place where a congregation could attend to the ritual; in larger churches this was usually at the altar before the crucifix which was at the east end of the nave.[2] William Booth (Archbishop of York, 1452–64) made provision for a daily Jesus-Mass at Southwell for the repose of his soul, and at Lichfield Dean Heywood (1457–92) endowed a Jesus-Mass and Antiphon to be sung by eight choristers for his obit.[3] The Jesus-Mass became an object of popular devotion, as had the Lady-Mass, not only in cathedrals and abbeys but also in parish churches.[4]

Votive Antiphon

The singing of antiphons without psalms has been noted in connection with memorials. In the Roman rite an antiphon to the Virgin (*Regina caeli, Alma redemptoris mater, Ave regina caelorum* or *Salve regina* according to the season) has been sung at the end of Compline since the Middle Ages.[5] According to a letter written in 1254 by John of Parma, Minister-General of the Franciscan order, the Franciscans had adopted these four antiphons by then.[6] In most of the English monastic uses an antiphon was sung after Compline, though not necessarily according to the modern arrangement of a different one for each season. The General Chapter of the Benedictines held at Northampton in 1343 ordered the saying of an antiphon and collect in honour of the Virgin daily immediately after

[1] See Bishop Smyth's will of 1513 establishing it at Lincoln in *Lincoln Statutes*, ii, p. lxxii. The texts are printed in *Missale Sarum*, cols. 846 and 751*.

[2] In Lincoln 'on the south side of the church'. Loc. cit.

[3] Cited from *Valor Ecclesiasticus* in Rock, *Church of Our Fathers*, iii, p. 92.

[4] Some examples in *Rites of Durham*, pp. 220–1. See also Duncan and Hussey, *Testamenta Cantiana*, passim.

[5] All four were originally attached to psalms in the Office. Wagner, *Introduction to the Gregorian Melodies*, pp. 140–1.

[6] S. J. P. Van Dijk, review of J. Maier, *Beiträge ur Geschichte der Marien-antiphon Salve Regina* (Regensburg, 1939), in *Ephemerides Liturgicae*, lv, 1941, p. 99.

Compline,[1] though as early as *c.* 1260 the singing of *Salve regina* at the end of Compline was customary at Westminster, being described as *ex moderno et non ex veteri usu.*[2]

At St. Mary's, York, *Salve regina* was sung immediately after Compline of the Virgin with the trope of three verses,[3] one before each of the exclamations *O clemens, O pia* and *O dulcis Maria.* The singing was begun by the precentor and continued by the choir, and the verses were sung by single members of the community in ascending order of rank.[4] In the Dominican rite *Salve regina* was sung in procession after Compline,[5] and in the English house of the Briggitine nuns at Syon, Middlesex, founded by Henry V in 1414, *Salve regina, Regina caeli* and *O mitissime,*[6] the last in Lent, are mentioned in the directions for singing the 'antem of our lady'. In each antiphon the verses of the trope were sung by a single sister standing at the lectern, while the others knelt.[7] In the use of the Premonstratensians *Salve regina* was sung in procession on leaving the Chapter-house each morning after Chapter.[8]

In the English secular uses the evening antiphon, though sung after Compline, did not become a part of the office, but was treated as a separate devotion. It is not mentioned in the Sarum Ordinal. The Exeter Ordinal directed that the psalm *De profundis,* the *Kyrie eleison,* and some versicles, responses and prayers were to be said by all, standing at the choir-step and around the presbytery, at the end of Compline. Then follows: 'Afterwards those who are assigned to the Office of the Virgin for the week shall go to her altar and there sing her Vespers and Compline, as they are contained in the Ordinal of Bishop John Grandisson. Meanwhile the boys shall go to the altar of St. Paul and there sing the antiphon of the Virgin with the other things which are customary'.[9] At Lincoln Bishop John de Bokingham appropriated to the choristers in 1380 the income

---

[1] *Monastic Breviary of Hyde Abbey,* vi, p. 131.

[2] *Customary of St. Augustine's, Canterbury, and St. Peter's, Westminster,* ii, p. 201.

[3] See below, p. 301.   [4] *Ordinale of St. Mary's, York,* i, p. 27.

[5] Bonniwell, *History of the Dominican Liturgy,* p. 161.

[6] An antiphon of Jesus.

[7] Aungier, *History of Syon Monastery,* pp. 333-4. This order was founded by the Swedish saint Birgitta (1303-73).

[8] *Customs of Augustinian Canons,* p. cii.   [9] *Ordinale Exon,* i, p. 29.

of a church, ordering that they should gather 'at the place of our tomb in the choir of our church of Lincoln every day, Compline being finished', and sing 'to the praise and honour of God and of the glorious Virgin his mother and in our perpetual memory both in life and after death' the antiphon *Nesciens mater* from Christmas to the Purification, *Mater ora filium* from the Purification to Easter and from Trinity to Christmas, and *Regina caeli* from Easter to Trinity. Then they should say Psalm 129 (*De profundis*) and prayers for the souls of the Bishop, of Edward III, of the Bishop's parents, of the benefactors of the cathedral and of other faithful departed.[1] The gathering of the singers at an altar, before an image or in some other designated place was the regular manner of singing the evening votive antiphon from the mid-fourteenth century to the Reformation.

The choristers of St. Paul's were bequeathed ten shillings by Sir John Pulteney (d. 1349) so that every evening after Compline they should go into the chapel he had built and sing an anthem of the Virgin 'solemnly with note' before her image. At St. Paul's a votive antiphon was also sung 'after mattens celebrated in the quire every day, and those present thereat gone out', for it was ordered in 1365 that at that time 'an anthem of Our Lady, *scil. Nesciens mater*, or some other solemn one suitable to the time should be sung before the said image'. This observance was endowed with property given by John Barnet, Bishop of Bath and Wells,[2] and the image was at the second pillar on the south side of the nave, close to the tomb of Sir John Beauchamp.[3] Richard Martin, Bishop of St. David's (1482–3), who was buried before the crucifix near the north door of St. Paul's, settled an annual sum on the choristers in 1482–3 for singing before the crucifix *Sancte Deus, [sancte] fortis*, which was commonly used as an antiphon of Jesus.[4]

In 1395 William Courtenay (Archbishop of Canterbury, 1381–96) decreed that the choristers of Salisbury should gather before the high altar each day after Compline, 'and there kneeling should sing in a loud voice (*alta voce*) the antiphon *Sancta*

---

[1] *Lincoln Statutes*, iii, p. 177.
[2] Dugdale, *History of St. Paul's*, pp. 22, 14.
[3] Milman, *Annals of St. Paul's*, p. 150.
[4] Vallance, *Greater English Church Screens*, p. 176; Yardley, *Minevia Sacra*, p. 77.

Maria virgo' with a versicle and prayer, to show their gratitude for a bequest of money left to them by Bishop John Waltham of Salisbury (d. 1395).[1] After 1540 this bequest to the choristers, which had been made over to the monastery of Edington in return for an annual payment, appears as a payment by the King for 'the singing of an antiphon *Sancte Deus* before the Great Cross in the Nave of the Cathedral'. In this case Henry VIII changed the terms of an endowment for a Mary-antiphon into one for a Jesus-antiphon.[2] In 1396 property in York was given to the support of the vicars-choral of the Minster by letters patent of Richard II. In return, the vicars undertook to sing daily after Compline an antiphon and collect of St. John Baptist, the King's patron saint, before his image in the church of St. Sampson, which had been given to them by the King two years before.[3] It appears that at some time later the choristers began to take part in the singing of an antiphon, for the accounts of the vicars for 1474 record a payment of six shillings and eight pence to them 'for the antiphon', and the same payment appears in 1506-7 and 1518-19.[4] At Chichester Bishop John Arundel (1459-78) founded an altar of the Virgin 'at the choir door', i.e., against the stone screen which he is said to have built at the east end of the nave,[5] and probably at its south side, at which an antiphon was sung every evening.[6] At his visitation in 1481 Bishop Storey ordered that the antiphon should be sung 'before the image of the Virgin next to the choir-door at the accustomed times' by the vicar most recently installed during his first year, and then by the hebdomadary vicar until another new one was appointed.[7]

The votive antiphon of the Virgin was an almost invariable observance in colleges and collegiate churches. Under Robert de Eglesfield's statutes the chaplains of The Queen's College, Oxford, were to sing the antiphon *Ave regina caelorum, ave domina angelorum* immediately after High Mass. A *canticum de beate Virgine* was also sung *alternatim* by the chaplains, clerks and 'poor boys' immediately after Compline every day. *Gaude virgo*

[1] Salisbury Muniments.   [2] Robertson, *Sarum Close*, pp. 60-1, 68.
[3] Harrison, *Life in a Medieval College*, pp. 32, 98.
[4] York Minster Archives.   [5] Bond, *Screens and Galleries*, p. 156.
[6] *Early Statutes of Chichester*, p. 28.
[7] *Statutes and Constitutions of Chichester*, p. 21.

salutata was sung from Monday to Thursday, *Salve regina* (*cum versibus*, that is, with the trope) on Friday, and *Benedicta es caelorum regina* 'solemnly' in the presence of the fellows on Saturday. The antiphon was followed by prayers for Edward III and for Queen Philippa, foundress and patroness of the college.[1] Sir Philip Somerville's Balliol College statutes mention the singing of an antiphon on Fridays, and the statutes of 1507 required that all the members of the college should sing *Benedicta es regina caelorum* (*sic*) in chapel at five o'clock on that day.[2] The students who lived in the Oxford Halls, the houses of scholars who were not in colleges, were bound to go to the University Church of St. Mary the Virgin on the vigils of the five feasts of the Virgin, immediately at the ringing of the curfew, for the singing of the Mary-antiphon.[3] The antiphons mentioned in the statute are *Ave regina* [*caelorum, mater regis angelorum*],[4] *Benedicta* [*es caelorum regina*], *Stella caeli* and *Sancta Maria* [*virgo intercede*].

The whole community of Magdalen College, Oxford, was ordered by the statutes to assemble in hall after Compline on Saturdays and on vigils of the Virgin, and sing *devote per notam* some antiphon in honour of the Virgin.[5] For this purpose the college had two antiphons written out on a board by John Wymark, a fellow, and the capital letters written and painted by John Lylly in 1485-6. Two more boards on which were written the notes of *Stella caeli* were bought in the following year, and in 1538 the 'boards hanging on the wall with antiphons' were repaired and Thomas Lees was paid *pro modulatione duarum antiphonarum*.[6] At a visitation by the Bishop in 1520 five bachelors of arts were deprived of commons for a day for monotoning instead of singing, and four for being absent from the singing of the antiphon.[7] On the same days as at Magdalen the members of Corpus Christi College, Oxford, sang a

---

[1] *Statutes of The Queen's College*, pp. 27, 33.

[2] *Statutes of Balliol College*, pp. xvi, 9.

[3] Fifteenth-century statutes in Gibson, *Statuta Antiqua Universitatis Oxoniensis*, p. 575.

[4] The context, in which a fine of a farthing was imposed for late arrival, in this case 'post inceptionem clausulae *Funde preces* etc.', shows that it was this antiphon and not *Ave regina caelorum, ave domina*.

[5] *Statutes of Magdalen College*, p. 54.

[6] Macray, *Register of Magdalen*, i, p. 6; ii, p. 18.   [7] Ibid., i, pp. 71, 74.

Mary-antiphon in chapel.[1] The members of Brasenose College sang two antiphons, one (*Te Deum patrem*) to the Trinity and one to the Virgin, after the Mass which the members attended daily.[2] The latest instance of the prescribing of the evening antiphon in a college statute occurs in Sir Thomas White's statutes of 1555 for St. John's College, Oxford, where it was to be sung by the whole college on Saturdays and vigils of Our Lady.[3]

The singing of a Mary-antiphon after Compline is mentioned in the statutes of Grandisson's Collegiate Church of Ottery St. Mary. In addition, the two clerk-watchmen who slept in the building were to sing each night after curfew a short antiphon of the Virgin before her altar, and *Mater ora filium* was suggested.[4] At the chantry colleges of Sibthorpe, Notts (1342–3), and Cotterstock, Northants (1343–4), *Mater ora filium* was sung nightly; at Cotterstock it was replaced by *Regina caeli* during the Easter season.[5] *Salve regina* was sung every evening at Thomas Elys's chantry of St. Thomas of Canterbury at Sandwich (1392)[6] and at seven every evening at Fotheringhay.[7] The chaplains, clerks and choristers of Whitington College, London, sang an antiphon of the Virgin at nightfall, 'when the poor artisans and neighbours living around the church came from their work and duties'.[8]

At Jesus College, Rotherham, the music master and the six choristers sang a Mass and antiphon of Jesus daily; they sang an antiphon of the Virgin on Saturdays at her altar in the parish church, and on the vigils of her feasts at her altar in the chantry chapel on the bridge in the town.[9] In making provision for the master and choristers the founder of the college expressed the hope that the parishioners of the church and 'people from the hills' would be led to 'love Christ's religion the better, and the more often visit, pay honour and cleave in affection

---

[1] *Statutes of Corpus Christi College*, p. 45.
[2] Sir Richard Sutton's Statutes of 1521; *Statutes of Brasenose College*, p. 19.
[3] *Statutes of St. John's College*, p. 48.
[4] Dalton, *Collegiate Church of Ottery St. Mary*, pp. 235, 238.
[5] *Visitations in the Diocese of Lincoln*, ii, p. 135, n.
[6] Boys, *History of Sandwich*, p. 192.
[7] Thompson, 'The Statutes of the College of St. Mary and All Saints, Fotheringhay', p. 241.
[8] *Monasticon*, vii, p. 741.
[9] On bridge-chapels, see Cook, *Medieval Chantries*, pp. 44–5.

to His church'.[1] In 1532 Thomas Magnus directed that the schoolmaster and six children of his new free school of grammar and song at Newark (Notts) should recite every night the antiphon of the Virgin and the antiphon of Jesus in front of the Rood, 'kneleyng in the manner and forme as . . . hath and ys used before the Roode of the north dore in . . . Seynt Paule in London'.[2]

In the later Middle Ages the corporate devotion of parishes and communities was expressed through fraternities and guilds, many of which supported the singing of votive Masses and antiphons. An early example is the Mary-guild of St. Magnus the Martyr, London Bridge, which was founded in 1343 by 'the better folk of the parish', who 'caused to be made a chantry to sing an anthem of Our Lady called *Salve regina* every evening' to which they each paid a halfpenny a week.[3] From the mid-fifteenth century onwards craft guilds in many places built chapels in the larger churches and supported priests to sing votive Masses and antiphons.[4] The merchants' guild of Chichester, for example, was refounded in 1446 as a fraternity of St. George and sang an antiphon on St. George's day in the cathedral, where a Mass of St. George was celebrated daily.[5]

It is clear that there was a wide range, and sometimes complete freedom, of choice of text for a votive antiphon, and considerable variety of time and place in its observance. When

---

[1] *Educational Charters*, pp. 425, 432.

[2] Quoted in Vallance, *Greater English Church Screens*, p. 76. Thomas Damett's will has: 'Also I will that a priest of virtuous repute shall celebrate before the Crucifix called "le Roode at the Northdore" for my soul for three years if my goods bequeathed shall be sufficient for this.' Harvey, *Gothic England*, p. 183.

[3] Cook, *Medieval Chantries*, pp. 40–1. The author suggests (p. 136) that 'Pewe' in the term 'St. Mary of the Pewe' for a Lady-chapel may mean enclosure. It is likely that it refers to the antiphon *Salve regina*, which was probably written by Aimar, Bishop of Le Puy (b. *c.* 1050), and not, as was formerly believed, by Hermannus Contractus; see H. Leclerq's article 'Salve Regina' in *Dictionnaire d'Archéologie chrétienne*. It was called 'the antiphon of Le Puy' (Raby, *History of Christian Latin Poetry*, p. 227), so that a chapel 'of the Pewe' may be the equivalent of the frequent term '*Salve* chapel', which could, however, be derived equally from the Lady-Mass *Salve sancta parens* and the Mary-antiphon *Salve regina*.

[4] Cook, *Medieval Chantries*, pp. 22–4.

[5] *Statutes and Constitutions of Chichester*, p. 67.

there was a specific direction it was contained in a statute and not, except in the comparatively late instance of the Brigittine nuns, in an Ordinal. Of the eleven antiphons so far mentioned four (*Nesciens mater, Sancta Maria, Te Deum patrem* and *O mitissime*[1]) were psalm-antiphons sung out of their normal context in the ritual, four (*Salve regina, Regina caeli, Mater ora filium* and *Ave regina*) were processional antiphons, two (*Gaude virgo salutata* and *Stella caeli*) were devotional poems not found in liturgical books but in Books of Hours for private devotion, and one (*Benedicta es*) was a sequence.[2]

Processions

Processions of great splendour and elaborate ceremonial were a characteristic element in the customs of the English secular churches.[3] Departing from and returning to the choir, they always had some definite object or station, whether an altar, the rood, the font, a designated point outside the church where a distinguished visitor was to be received, or a neighbouring church where Mass was to be celebrated. They used no distinct ritual forms but adapted to their purposes such forms as the respond with verse, the antiphon, generally without psalm but sometimes with verses, and the hymn with refrain. The procession before Mass on an ordinary Sunday went out of the choir through the north door, around the presbytery on the outside, along the south aisle and around the font, and up the centre of the nave to the rood. During Advent, from Septuagesima to the fourth Sunday in Lent and on the five Sundays after Easter an antiphon was sung during this part of the procession, and at other times a respond and verse. At the rood a station was made, where, from the first Sunday after Trinity to Advent, there was an antiphon of the Cross, and during Advent and from Septuagesima to Passion Sunday, a

[1] In the Brigittine use only, where it was the antiphon to the *Nunc dimittis* on Fridays. When sung as an antiphon after Compline in Lent it was combined with verses beginning *O benigne creator*, which follow it in a manuscript of Brigittine Masses and Offices in Trinity College, Dublin (MS. L.1.13).

[2] Of York and Hereford use, not of Sarum.

[3] For the processions in a Benedictine house, see *Ordinale of St. Mary's, York*, i, pp. 91–5.

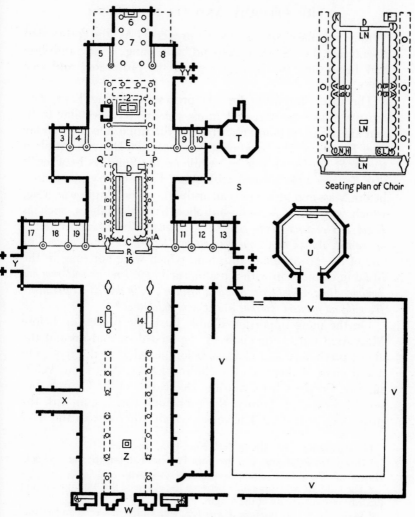

SALISBURY CATHEDRAL

Seating plan of Choir

KEY

A. Tomb of Bishop Simon of Ghent (d. March 31, 1315)
B. Tomb of Bishop Roger de Mortival (d. March 14, 1330)
C. Choir-screen
D. Choir-step
E. Presbytery-step
F. Bishop's Throne
G. Dean
H. Precentor
J. Chancellor
K. Treasurer
L. Archdeacon of Dorset
N. Lectern

M. Subdean
N. Archdeacon of Berkshire
O. Succentor
P. South Choir-door
Q. North Choir-door
R. Rood
S. Canons' Cemetery
T. Sacristy (Muniment Room over)
U. Chapter House
V. Cloister
W. West Door (the Blue Porch)
X. The Beautiful Gate (*Speciosa*) (1443)
Y. St. Thomas's Porch
YY. St. Stephen's Porch
Z. Font

AA. Senior Stalls
BB. Second Form
CC. Third Form (Choristers)

ALTARS

1. High Altar
2. St. Osmund (1456)
3. St. Martin
4. St. Katherine
5. St. Peter and the Apostles
6. *Salve*, All Saints (Trinity)
7. All Saints (*c.* 1460)
8. St. Stephen

9. St. Mary Magdalene
10. St. Nicholas
11. St. Margaret
12. St. Laurence
13. St. Michael
14. St. Andrew
15. St. Denis
16. Parochial (Holy Cross) (on the screen, or at the north side of the choir-door)
17. St. Thomas of Canterbury
18. St. Edmund, Archbishop and Confessor
19. St. John Baptist (Relics)

THE LITURGY AND ITS PLAINSONG

sermon in place of the usual prayers.[1] As the procession re-entered the choir a respond was sung if an antiphon had been sung in the first part of the procession, and vice versa.

The three antiphons for the procession during Lent, *Ecce carissimi*, *Cum venerimus* and *In die quando*, were peculiar to it, and are not to be found elsewhere in the ritual. On the Sunday after Easter and the Sunday before Ascension Day the antiphon was *Sedit angelus* with verse,[2] while on the Sundays between it was *Ego sum alpha et omega* with verse. For ordinary processions before Mass and at Vespers an antiphon of the Virgin was sung, which was either a psalm-antiphon from the offices, such as *Beata Dei genitrix*, *Tota pulchra es*, *Ascendit Christus super caelos et preparavit*, *Anima mea liquefacta est* or *Descendi in ortum meum*,[3] or one of the processional antiphons which were not sung in the ritual in connection with a psalm, such as *Ave regina caelorum ave domina*, *Alma redemptoris*, *Speciosa facta es . . . in deliciis virginitatis*,[4] *Ibo mihi ad montem myrrhae* and *Quam pulchra es*.[5]

On the more important double feasts the procession before Mass went out of the choir by the west door and around the choir, presbytery and cloisters before arriving at the rood. On about eight of these days, including Easter, Ascension, Whit-sunday, Corpus Christi and the Dedication of the Church, but not Christmas or Trinity, the procession was begun with the prose *Salve festa dies*.[6] The verses, which differed with the day[7]

---

[1] *Use of Sarum*, ii, p. 148; *Ordinale Exon*, i, pp. 293–4.

[2] It is called *Responsorium* in the York Processional, but the Sarum books always call the Easter processional chants antiphons.

[3] The last four were sung only between the octave of the Assumption and the feast of the Nativity of the Virgin.

[4] *Speciosa facta es et suavis in deliciis tuis*, with different words and music, was the third antiphon at Matins in the weekly commemorative Office of the Virgin.

[5] *Use of Sarum*, i, p. 179; *Ordinale Exon*, i, p. 177.

[6] The form is processional hymn with refrain (see Raby, *Christian Latin Poetry*, pp. 92–3), but the ordinals and service-books are unanimous in calling it *prosa*.

[7] *Breviarium Sarum*, iii, p. xcviii, lists eight sets of verses for Sarum and one peculiar to York; Frere (*Hymns Ancient and Modern*, p. 205) mentions seven feasts, including the late medieval additions of the Visitation and the Name of Jesus. Local saints also had their versions of the processional *Salve*, for example Hereford for St. Ethelbert (*Hereford Breviary*, iii, p. 76) and

though the music was invariable, were sung by the rulers, and the refrain *Salve festa dies*, with a varying second line, by the choir. The procession was completed to the singing of two responds, or two antiphons (on Easter Day *Sedit angelus* with the verse *Crucifixum in carne*[1] and *Christus resurgens* with the verse *Dicant nunc Judei*), or a respond and antiphon (on Corpus Christi).

The procession on Christmas Day was begun to the respond *Descendit de caelis*, and as it proceeded around the cloisters to the font and rood three proses were inserted into the respond. This resulted in the following scheme, the respond and its partial repeats being sung by the choir, and the verse, *Gloria patri* and proses by two or three *clerici*,[2] with the chorus repeating each line to its final vowel: R͡/. *Descendit*; Prose *Felix Maria*; R͡/. from *fabrice*; V͡. *Tanquam*; R͡/. from *Et exivit*; Prose *Familiam custodi*; R͡/. from *fabrice*; *Gloria patri*; R͡/. from *Lux et decus*; Prose *Te laudant alme*; R͡/. from *fabrice*.[3] For re-entering the choir the antiphon *Hodie Christus natus est* was sung, and was repeated from *Hodie in terra* if necessary. Two or more responds were sung during the procession on certain other feasts, for example on the Circumcision (with the prose *Quam aethera*), on the Epiphany (three responds), on Passion Sunday, on the Sunday after the Ascension and on Trinity Sunday.

The procession on Palm Sunday had special features of its own.[4] The palms were first distributed to the singing of two antiphons. At Salisbury the procession then went through the west door of the choir and around the cloisters to the first station near the south-east corner of the church,[5] one or more antiphons being sung on the way. Meanwhile two clerks of the second form had carried the relics and the Blessed Sacrament

Lichfield for St. Chad (Shrewsbury School MS. Mus. iii. 42, fo. 23v; see below, p. 99, n. 1).

[1] *Crucifixum in carne* was sung in the *pulpitum* by three from the senior stalls, turning towards the people. *Use of Sarum*, ii, p. 168.

[2] *Use of Sarum*, ii, p. 53; *Ordinale Exon*, i, p. 65.

[3] This as in *Ordinale Exon*; the Sarum plan differs slightly. See also *Hereford Breviary*, i, p. 145; iii, p. 68. These proses do not appear in the Benedictine rite; cf. *Ordinal of St. Mary's, York*, ii, p. 90.

[4] *Use of Sarum*, i, pp. 59–61; ii, pp. 161–2. On Holy Week ceremonies, see also Bishop, 'Holy Week Rites of Sarum, Hereford and Rouen'.

[5] 'In extrema orientali parte cimiterii laicorum.'

to the first station. There a lesson from the Gospels was read, and the antiphon[1] *En rex venit* was sung for the adoration of the Sacrament.[2] The form of this antiphon was: *En rex venit* sung by three *clerici* turning to the people; *Salve quem Jesum* sung by the principal officiant turning to the relics; the continuation *Testatur plebs* sung by the choir, with a genuflection to the relics; and the verses *Hic est qui de Edom* and *Hic est ille* by the clerks, each being followed similarly by another *Salve* sung by the officiant and continued by the choir. Two antiphons and, if needed, two responds accompanied the procession to the next station at the door of the north transept where seven boys in a high place (*in eminentiori loco*) sang the prose *Gloria laus et honor*.[3] This refrain was repeated by the choir below, and also after each verse of the prose had been sung by the boys. Then with the antiphon *Collegerunt* the procession continued along the north side of the church to the third station before the north-west door, where the verse *Unus autem ex ipsis* was sung by three from the senior stalls turning to the people.[4] From there a respond brought the procession through the west door to the fourth station at the rood. The cross, which had been covered since the first Monday in Lent, was uncovered,[5] and the officiant began the antiphon *Ave*, the choir singing *rex noster*, with a genuflection to the rood. These three words were sung

[1] So called in *Missale Sarum*, col. 261; it is actually a set of antiphons, as in *Missale Herfordensis*, p. 80.

[2] Among the monastic uses this appears only in the Norwich form of the Benedictine rite, which was derived from Fécamp and has other similarities to the secular uses. See *Customary of Norwich*, pp. xiv–xvi, 77; the distribution of the parts of the chant differs from Sarum.

[3] At Lincoln the church servants prepared seats for the canons at the first station, and hung a pall at the 'Bail Gate' or wherever the boys were to sing *Gloria laus* (*Lincoln Statutes*, i, p. 292). At York the boys sang from a temporary gallery over the church door (*York Missal*, i, p. 87). At Hereford (as at Rouen) this ceremony took place at the closed gate of the town, the boys being on top of the gate (Bishop, 'Holy Week Rites of Sarum, Hereford and Rouen', p. 284).

[4] *Use of Sarum*, i, p. 61; ii, p. 162.

[5] At St. Mary's, York, this was done during the singing of the antiphon: 'Cum autem pronuntiari ceperit *Ave*, unus serventium ecclesie in absconso trahet per longam cordulam velum crucifixi usque ad genua eius; in secunda pronuntione usque ad latus; et in tercia totaliter denudetur, et sic nuda maneat illa et magna crux super altare usque post Vesperas hujus diei.' *Ordinale of St. Mary's, York*, ii, pp. 265–6.

twice more at a higher pitch each time, and at the third time the antiphon was continued and completed by the choir. Then the crucifix on the high altar was uncovered, and the procession entered the choir to the singing of a respond.

During Mass on Maundy Thursday the Bishop blessed the oil for the sick and the oil for the chrism, for consecrations, ordinations and baptism. The chrism was carried in solemn procession from the sacristy to the high altar, and before it went three choristers singing the hymn *O redemptor sume carmen* and its verses, while the choir responded with *O redemptor* after each verse.[1] On the afternoon of Holy Saturday all went in procession through the west door of the choir to a column on the south side of the church for the blessing of the New Fire, saying the psalm *Dominus illuminatio mea* (Ps. 26) as they went, and singing as they returned the hymn *Inventor rutili*.[2] Then followed the blessing of the Paschal Candle and the lighting of the other candles from it, to the singing of the ancient prose *Exsultet jam angelica turba*, which consisted of six verses to the same melody with considerable variations, and the long preface *Vere quia dignum et justum est* by a deacon.[3] After several lessons separated by tracts, and the singing of the sevenfold Litany *Kyrie eleison, Christe eleison, Christe audi nos*, etc. by seven choristers, the procession went by the north door of the choir to the font, to the singing of the fivefold Litany by five deacons of the second form. The font was blessed, and as the procession returned the metrical Litany *Rex sanctorum angelorum*[4] was sung by three from the senior stalls, the choir repeating *Rex sanctorum* after each verse.[5] Then followed Mass and Vespers in succession, as on the previous two days of the week.

A procession to the font in the same order as that on Easter Eve but with different ritual took place after Vespers from

[1] *Use of Sarum*, i, pp. 203–4.

[2] In Salisbury two of the second form sang the verses, in Exeter two boys, the chorus always responding with *Inventor*. *Use of Sarum*, i, p. 146; *Ordinale Exon*, i, p. 322.

[3] *Use of Sarum*, i, pp. 146–7; *Ordinale of St. Mary's, York*, ii, p. 293. For a discussion of the chants of *Exsultet*, see the article in *Die Musik in Geschichte und Gegenwart*.

[4] 'A doggerel which hardly deserves the name of litany or hymn.' Bishop, 'Holy Week Rites of Sarum, Hereford and Rouen', p. 296.

[5] *Use of Sarum*, i, pp. 149–51.

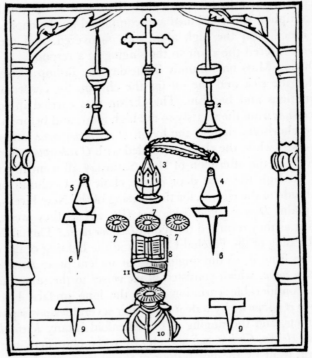

Station at the Font at Vespers in Easter Week, from the printed
Sarum Processional

1. Cross-bearer. 2, 2. Taperers. 3. Thurifer. 4, 5. Oil and Chrism. 6, 6. Subsidiary rulers
(*rectores secundarii*). 7, 7, 7. Three boys singing *Alleluia*. 8. Boy carrying book. 9, 9. Principal
rulers. 10. Officiant. 11. Font.

Easter Day to the Friday of Easter week.[1] On Easter Day, as
the procession began, a senior person began the antiphon
Alleluia Alleluia Alleluia Alleluia and the rulers on the *decani* side
began the psalm *Laudate pueri Dominum* (Ps. 112), the choir on
that side completing the first verse *Laudate nomen Domini* and
repeating the first *Alleluia* of the antiphon. This single *Alleluia*
was joined similarly to the end of each verse of the psalm, being
sung by the side singing the verse, not by the whole choir.[2]

[1] *Use of Sarum*, i, pp. 157–9; ii, p. 72; *Ordinale Exon*, i, pp. 142–3. The
chants are in *Antiphonale Sarisburiense*, pl. 239; the chant of the psalm only
in *Use of Sarum*, ii, p. lxxv.

[2] 'Alius versus ex alia parte chori dicatur cum *Alleluya* in fine versus,
quasi *Alleluva* esset de eodem textu versus cuiuslibet.' *Ordinale Exon*, i, p. 142.

After the *Gloria patri* all the rulers began the antiphon again and it was completed by the choir. At the font three boys, turning to the east, sang an *Alleluia*, which was repeated, with the neuma, by the choir. The boys then sang the verse *Laudate pueri Dominum* as far as the last word *domini*, which was sung by the choir with the neuma, and then the *Alleluia* was repeated by all without the neuma.[1] Going to the rood the psalm *In exitu Israel* (Ps. 113) was sung, its antiphon *Alleluia* being treated in the same way as that of the psalm *Laudate pueri*,[2] and the procession re-entered the choir to an antiphon of the Virgin.[3] During the week the ritual was changed, the antiphons *Sedit angelus* and *Christus resurgens*, without their verses, being used for going to and returning from the font. The Easter Eve ritual, with litanies and procession to the blessing of the Font, was also carried out before Mass on the vigil of Whitsunday.

On Easter Saturday and every Saturday thereafter until Advent (except on the vigils of Whitsunday and Trinity) and on the feasts of the Holy Cross (the Finding, May 3; the Exaltation, September 14), the procession to the rood took place after Vespers. Until Ascension week the ritual consisted of the antiphons *Christus resurgens* and *Regina caeli*;[4] the verse *Dicant nunc* was sung before the rood by three from the senior stalls on Easter Saturday and the Saturday before the Ascension and by two priests of the second form on the other Saturdays. After Trinity an antiphon of the Holy Cross, *Crux fidelis*, *O crux gloriosa* or *O crux splendidior*, and on the feasts of the Holy Cross the antiphon *O crux gloriosa* with verse, accompanied the

[1] This *Alleluia* was also sung, with two verses, *Laudate pueri* and *Sit nomen Domini*, at Mass on the Saturday after Easter and on the feast of the Seven Martyr Brothers (July 10). *Antiphonale Sarisburiense* gives the two verses with the Easter Eve procession, but the ordinals give only *Laudate pueri*. *Ordinale of St. Mary's, York* (ii. p. 301), has no procession at this point; the *Customary of St. Augustine's, Canterbury* (i, p. 38), mentions processions, not described, at both Vespers of Easter. The *Alleluia* was not sung at Hereford, which used *Christus resurgens*, its verse being sung at the Font, and *Sedit angelus*, its verse being sung in the *pulpitum* (*Hereford Breviary*, i, p. 331). Norwich (*Customary*, p. 96) agrees with Hereford, not with the other Benedictine ordinals.

[2] 'Quasi *Alleluya* foret de textu versus in fine cuiuslibet versus.' *Ordinale Exon*, i, p. 143.

[3] *Use of Sarum*, i, p. 158. Exeter specifies *Regina caeli*, the special Mary-antiphon of the Easter season.

[4] *Ordinale Exon*, i, p. 148; *Use of Sarum* (i, pp. 163-4) does not specify.

procession to the rood, and an antiphon of the Virgin was sung while re-entering the choir.[1]

A procession took place after first Vespers of a saint's day if the church had an altar dedicated to that saint. On the way a respond was sung, and for the return an antiphon of the Virgin, except in Advent, when the All Saints antiphon *Salvator mundi salva nos omnes* was used. On some of these days a prose was sung before the altar of the saint. In the secular uses the rites of St. Stephen's day were carried out by the deacons, headed by an 'archdeacon', on St. John's day by the priests, under a 'dean', and on Holy Innocents' day by the boy choristers,[2] ruled by a 'bishop'.[3] In each case the ceremonies began with the procession after first Vespers. On St. Stephen's eve the 'archdeacon' began the respond *Sancte Dei pretiose* for the procession and all the deacons sang *sollemniter et concorditer* the verse *Ut tuo propitiatus*. At the altar the prose *Te mundi climata* was sung by the deacons, the choir responding on the vowels. The boys began their day with ceremonies which included a procession to one of the altars and the singing of the prose *Sedentem in superne*, and ended it with the blessing of the people by the boy-bishop after second Vespers.

Processions on days of intercession or penitence were accompanied by antiphons, psalms and responds as they proceeded to a neighbouring church for the celebration of Mass. On the way back one or several litanies were sung by two singers with the choir responding. Processions of this kind with the 'greater Litany' took place on the three Rogation days, which were the Monday, Tuesday and Wednesday before the Ascension,[4]

---

[1] The antiphon was chosen from those given above, p. 90. *Use of Sarum*, i, p. 179.

[2] At Eton and King's College the boy bishop's day was the feast of St. Nicholas, December 6; *Ancient Laws of King's and Eton*, pp. 112, 560.

[3] Grandisson was careful to point out that the leaders signified respectively St. Stephen, St. John and 'Christum puerum verum et eternum pontificem'. *Ordinale Exon*, i, pp. 68–74. See also the Sarum text in Chambers, *Mediaeval Stage*, ii, pp. 282–7.

[4] For a full account of the order on these days, see *Ordinale of St. Mary's, York*, ii, pp. 318–21. The community went to the Minster on Monday, to the Hospital of St. Leonard on Tuesday and to St. Mary's Chapel 'juxta portam' on Wednesday.

on St. Mark's day,[1] which was observed on April 25 (unless that day fell in Easter week or on a Sunday), and in times of trouble.[2]

Ceremonies of Holy Week and Easter

Nine antiphons were sung during the ceremonial washing of feet on Maundy Thursday in the Sarum rite, beginning with *Mandatum novum*, from which the day has taken its name, and ending with *Venit ad Petrum*.[3] The monastic uses differed considerably from that of Sarum in the number and order of the antiphons.[4] The ceremonies of the Adoration of the Cross and the Deposition into a symbolic *sepulchrum* of the Cross and Holy Sacrament during the combined Mass and Vespers of Good Friday, and of their Elevation before Matins on Easter morning, were virtually the same in all the secular and monastic uses.[5] After the St. John Passion and prayers two priests, holding the cross and standing at the south side of the high altar, began the *Improperia* ('Reproaches') with the words *Popule meus*, etc. After each verse two deacons standing at the choir-step sang *Agios O Theos*, and the choir continued with *Sanctus Deus . . . miserere nobis*. Then, as they unveiled the cross, the priests sang the antiphon *Ecce lignum*. While the community made their adoration the choir sang the psalm *Deus misereatur* (Ps. 66), interposing the antiphon *Crucem tuam adoramus* after each verse, and the two priests, sitting on the altar step one on each side of the cross, sang the hymn *Crux fidelis*, the choir repeating the refrain *Crux fidelis* after each verse. As the cross was carried to another altar for the adoration of the people the choir sang the antiphon *Dum fabricator* with its verse.

[1] St. Mark's Day 'was commonly fasted thorowe all the countrie & no flesh eten upon it'; *Rites of Durham*, p. 104. For descriptions of some of the processions of the year as carried out at Durham, see ibid., pp. 104–8.

[2] *Use of Sarum*, i, pp. 172–4; *Ordinale Exon*, i, pp. 11–12, 327–8.

[3] The last four were optional, 'si necesse fuit'.

[4] See Bukofzer, *Studies in Medieval Music*, pp. 230–8, for some comparisons. At St. Mary's, York (*Ordinale*, ii, pp. 280–3), *Ante diem festum* was sung slowly immediately before the entrance of the Abbot and *Venit ad Petrum* does not appear.

[5] For their history, see Chambers, *Mediaeval Stage*, ii, Chap. XVIII; for a description by one who had probably seen them, see *Rites of Durham*, pp. 11–13, which is reprinted in Chambers, op. cit., pp. 310–11.

After further ceremonies at the high altar and the saying *privatim* of Vespers came the Deposition of the Cross and Sacrament in the *sepulchrum*, with the responds *Estimatus sum* and *Sepulto Domino*, in both of which the choir sang the verse. Finally, with the closing of the *sepulchrum* the choir sang three antiphons, *In pace in idipsum*, *In pace factus est* and *Caro mea*.[1] At dawn on Easter morning all gathered in choir for the opening of the *sepulchrum*, and the two senior dignitaries present placed the Sacrament on the altar and carried the Cross in procession 'to the place provided'. As they did so, they began the antiphon *Christus resurgens* and the choir sang both the antiphon and the verse *Dicant nunc*.[2] The Ordinals make no mention of the Visitation, but it is contained, with the music, in two fourteenth-century Processionals of Sarum use which belonged to the church of St. John the Evangelist, Dublin.[3] This is the famous play of the three Maries, the Angel and SS. John and Peter, which takes its name from the first words of the Angel (*Quem queritis ad sepulchrum, O christicolae?*).[4] It included the singing of the sequence *Victimae paschali laudes*, divided between the Maries and the saints and accompanying their actions, the last verse being sung by the choir. The Visitation began after the third (and last) respond of Easter Matins, *Dum transisset sabbatum*, the words of which introduced the story, and ended with the singing of the *Te Deum*.

The Lichfield statutes of c. 1190 contain references to the Easter play, a Christmas play and a play on the Monday of Easter week.[5] In the library of Shrewsbury School there is an

---

[1] The Sarum directions are printed in Chambers, op. cit., pp. 312–15. See also *Missale Sarum*, cols. 328–33, and (for the Good Friday music) *Graduale Sarisburiense*, pls. 101–3; *Ordinale Exon*, i, pp. 138–9, 320–1; *Ordinale of St. Mary's, York*, ii, pp. 286–9, 296–8 (where the *Elevatio* was after Matins). For the directions for the Adoration in the York Gradual, see Frere, 'The Newly-found York Gradual', p. 29.

[2] *Use of Sarum*, i. 153. *Ordinale Exon*, i, p. 139. On the following three days the procession took place after Lauds, the verse was sung by two clerks of the second form (three from the senior stalls in Exeter) at the station before the cross from the *sepulchrum*, and a Mary-antiphon was sung in returning. On the last three days of the week the verse was omitted. *Use of Sarum*, i, pp. 160–1; *Ordinale Exon*, i. p. 144.

[3] Dublin, Archbishop Marsh's Library, MS. Z4.2.20, fos. 59–61; Oxford, Bodleian Library, MS. Rawl. liturg. d.4, fos. 130–2.

[4] Text in Chambers, *Mediaeval Stage*, ii, pp. 315–8.   [5] Ibid., p. 36.

actor's part in the vernacular, with some music to Latin words, for each of these plays.[1] At Rouen the Christmas *Officium pastorum* was played after the *Te Deum* of Christmas Matins, and included the singing of *Gloria in excelsis* by boys from the vaults of the church.[2] It is possible that the manner of singing the first respond of Christmas Matins in the English secular uses is a relic of this drama.[3] The Easter Monday play (*Peregrini*) of the meeting with the risen Christ on the road to Emmaus was acted during the procession to the font at Vespers.

In some places a dove was made to descend from the roof of the church at the beginning of the hymn *Veni creator Spiritis* at Terce on Whitsunday. An eye-witness of this curious piece of liturgical symbolism at St. Paul's has described the descent of a white pigeon and of a censer that 'reached at one sweep almost to the West gate of the church and with the other to the choir stairs'.[4] A description of the reception of Henry VII at St. Paul's tells how 'at his entrie into the Chirche his Grace was senserde with the great Senser of Powles by an Angell commyng oute of the Roof, During which Tyme the Quere sange a solempne Antyme and after *Te Deum Laudamus* for Joy of his late Victory and prosperous Comyng to his saide Citie'.[5]

Plainsong Books; the Tonale

The plainsong of the liturgy was written in a number of separate books, the contents of each kind of book being directly related to the function of its user. By the early thirteenth century the ritual of the hours services, in their order during the

---

[1] In the same manuscript as the *Salve festa dies* of St. Chad mentioned above, p. 90, n. 7. See ibid., p. 90; Smoldon, 'Liturgical Drama', p. 189; Young, *The Drama of the Medieval Church*, ii, pp. 514–20.

[2] Chambers, *Mediaeval Stage*, ii, p. 41.   [3] See below, p. 107.

[4] Simpson, *History of Old St. Paul's*, p. 79. The Lichfield Statutes of *c.* 1190 have: 'Die vero Pentecostes et tribus diebus sequentibus dum cantatur sequencia nebule consueverunt dispergi' (*Lincoln Statutes*, ii, p. 15), while at St. Mary's, York (*Ordinale*, ii, p. 332): 'Si ad representandum adventum Spiritus Sancti alba columba sive viva, sive ymaginaria, in inceptione ympni *Veni creator* cum nebulis descendat, et septem cerei in signum septem donorum ejus cum beata Virgine et apostolis intendentibus in celum accendantur, bene licet.'

[5] Leland, *Collectanea*, iv, p. 218, with 'sensende' for 'senserde'.

day and in the divisions of the Temporale and Sanctorale, was organized into a collection known as the Breviary. Though voluminous, it was, as its name indicates, an abbreviation, because such parts as the psalms with their ferial antiphons and the hymns, which all knew by heart, were not included, but could be found in the separate Psalter and Hymnal. Nevertheless, the Breviary with music, or 'noted' Breviary, of the later Middle Ages attained a very large size. The Antiphonal, also a large volume, was particularly for the use of singers, and contained the antiphons, responds, invitatories,[1] proses, genealogies and some hymns of the Breviary, while the lessons were written in separate Lectionaries.[2] The Missal was for the use of the celebrant, and normally included music only for the items which were sung at the altar, such as the opening of the *Gloria*, the Prefaces, and the *Ite missa est* and *Benedicamus domino*. The choir's chants of the Mass were written in the Gradual, the Epistles in the *Epistolarium* and the Gospels in the *Evangelarium*. A separate *Troparium* (Troper) was necessary for rites which had many tropes, but in the secular uses the tropes of the Ordinary of the Mass were generally put at the end of the Gradual with the other chants of the Ordinary. Sequences were sometimes written into the Gradual and sometimes into a separate *Sequentiarium*. From the fourteenth century onwards the chants for processions were written in a Processional, which usually included also the music for votive Masses. The Manual of occasional services and the Pontifical containing services carried out by the bishop were of minor musical importance.

The Tonale served as a handbook and directory of the ritual music, as the Ordinal and Customary did of the rites and customs.[3] Its chief function was to show the beginner of an antiphon and psalm how much of the antiphon he should sing before the psalm, and to indicate which intonation (*intonatio*, now generally called psalm-tone) and variety of ending (*differentia*) should be used for chanting the psalm. The antiphons

---

[1] These were sometimes written, with the corresponding chants for the *Venite*, in a separate *Invitatorium*, also called *Venitarium*.

[2] The whole body of Lessons was called *Legenda*, and was subdivided into separate volumes, e.g., the *Homilarium* with patristic homilies and expositions, the *Legendarium* with acts of the saints, and the *Passionarium* or Martyrology with sufferings of the martyrs.

[3] The Sarum Tonale is printed in *Use of Sarum*, ii, Appendix.

were grouped initially according to the eight modes[1] (*toni*), or melodic types, and there was one psalm-intonation in each mode. The Tonale explained the grouping of the antiphons into their modes by the practical criteria of their last note[2] or 'final' and their range.[3] Naturally an antiphon and psalm sung together had to be in the same mode, but since the antiphon was sung after the psalm a further subdivision (called *variatio*) of the antiphons was made, according to the note and type of melodic idiom with which they began.[4] Each psalm-intonation was provided with a suitable number of differences, so that a smooth connection could be made between the ending of the psalm and the beginning of the antiphon.

In the Sarum Tonale the psalm-intonation of the fourth mode, for example, is provided with nine differences, and the variation of the particular group of antiphons with which the second of these differences must be used is described in the following terms: 'Every antiphon of the fourth mode which begins on C and immediately or gradually rises through D to F, or repeats the C before thus rising to F, has the second difference, in this way':[5]

Ex. 4.

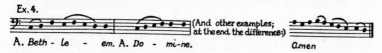

A. *Beth - le - em*. A. *Do - mi-ne*.   (And other examples; at the end the difference:)   *Amen*

The actual procedure may be illustrated in the case of the antiphon *Lucem tuam*, which was sung with the *Nunc dimittis* at Compline on double feasts from Trinity to Advent and from

---

[1] A mode may be defined as a set of melodic idioms which formed the 'raw material' of composition.

[2] D in Modes I and II; E in modes III and IV; F in modes V and VI; and G in modes VII and VIII.

[3] This and other criteria could be used to correct errors in chant books, e.g., in the first mode: 'Si autem inferius quam quartam vocem descenderit vel superius quam decimam vocem ascenderit, tunc cantus falsus erit.' *Use of Sarum*, ii, Appendix, p. i.

[4] E.g., in the first mode: 'In quatuor autem locis regulariter incipit: id est in cefaut Desolre Efaut gravibus [i.e., C, D or F in the bass clef], et in alamire acuta [i.e., A below middle C]. In elami vero gravi [i.e., E in the bass clef] non inveniemus in antiphonis, sed in missarum officiis sicut patebit inferius'. Loc. cit. 'Variacio' is called 'inceptio' in the Hereford Tonale. *Hereford Breviary*, iii, p. li.

[5] *Use of Sarum*, ii, p. xxvii.

Epiphany to Lent. It is in the fourth mode and its beginning shows that it has the variation which our quotation from the Tonale describes. Hence it will be sung with the second difference of the psalm-intonation, and its performance with the canticle will proceed thus:[1]

Ex.5.

Besides arranging the antiphons according to mode and variation, the Sarum Tonale gave for each mode a complete verse of its psalm-intonation and of its intonations for the *Benedictus* and *Magnificat*, its neuma, its chants for the *Venite*, its *Gloria patri* for ferial responds, and its Introits with their psalm-intonations, differences and chants for the Eastertide *Alleluia*.

In the earlier Middle Ages much of the ritual music was sung from memory. At St. Alban's Abbey, for example, before Abbot John de Marinis (1302–8) ordered sconces to be placed in front of those who wished to sing the night office from books, the only books used in the choir were the Lectionary and the Collectar, the book of special prayers.[2] Grandisson's statutes

---

[1] Antiphon and difference in *Antiphonale Sarisburiense*, pl. 287.

[2] 'Quod prius non erat usitatum praeter Legendam et Collectarium; unde multi minus bene reddere servitium curaverunt, et minus sciverunt.' *Gesta Abbatum Monasterii S. Albani*, ii, p. 106.

for Ottery St. Mary give more than usually detailed information on this point. Three was to be the usual number to sing from one book,[1] and the statutes provided for three Antiphonals, three Psalters and three Graduals on each side of the choir, a book at the choir-step with the music to be sung there, and one in mid-choir for the rulers at Mass. Every canon and vicar was to have a Processional, so that they should not be inconvenienced by having to share a book when singing in procession. At Matins there were to be three candles on each side (the canons being obliged to supply their own), but on simple feasts and ferias the boys and secondaries were to sing the Invitatory and the *Venite* and the boys were to sing the beginning of the respond and its verse 'without book or light'.[2]

The entrance test for the vicars and secondaries of Ottery St. Mary, requiring that they should be able to read and sing the Tonale with the differences and the melodies of the *Venite*, marks a change from the memorizing by rote laid down by the cathedral and monastic statutes and rules to a test of actual musical ability. In later foundations the requirement to memorize was dropped in favour of a general qualification in reading and singing. The few inventories of the later period which give the place of books in choir as well as the number of each type[3] suggest that Grandisson's ideas became accepted practice in colleges and collegiate churches during the fifteenth century.

[1] In 1484 Thomas Beylby of Southwell complained that 'Dom. Nicholaus Knolles ad antiphonare coram eodem et Domino Thoma Beylby et Domino Thoma Tykhyll jacens non permittit dictos suos consocios habere libri aspectum ut ceteri, sed se totaliter divertit ad illud alios impediendo ne videant'. *Visitations and Memorials of Southwell*, p. 51.

[2] Dalton, *Collegiate Church of Ottery St. Mary*, pp. 158, 160, 140.

[3] See the Winchester College Inventory printed as Appendix V, p. 434 below.

III
THE POLYPHONY OF THE
LITURGY FROM 1100 TO 1400

PLAINSONG was an integral part of the Christian liturgies from the beginning of their history. Polyphony, on the other hand, gained a place in the liturgy by its ability to lend ceremonial distinction to the performance of the established plainsong. Its function, therefore, was analogous to that of the many other forms of ceremonial by which the more significant parts of the ritual were distinguished from the less significant, the more important services of the day from the less important, and the services of the various ranks of festival from each other and from ferias. The earliest period in the history of polyphony, from *c.* 900 to the twelfth century, was also the period of extensive troping of the ritual. While polyphony often went hand in hand with ritual tropes, it also had the faculty, which verbal additions could not match, of incorporating the plainsong as the basis of its design without changing the ritual text or music. It was in these two forms, the setting of ritual plainsong and the setting of tropes, that polyphony became accepted as an additional element in ceremonial, and as a further means of festive adornment and elaboration of the ritual.

Ceremonial in Choir

As far as the musical ceremonial was concerned, the most important means of distinguishing festivals was the method of ruling the choir. On double feasts there were four rulers.[1] On the most important festivals all four were chosen from the senior stalls, while on other doubles the two principal rulers (*principales*) were from the senior stalls, and were canons if two canons were present, and their assistants (*secundarii*) were from the second form.[2] The precentor took part in ruling the choir on principal and greater double feasts, at least at Mass, and rehearsed the rulers in the chants they had to begin, or to 'intimate' (*injungere*) to the beginners, on other doubles. On greater doubles the precentor began the repeat of the Invitatory and of the antiphons after the psalm was sung (Exeter), the first chant in processions (York and Hereford), the sequence at Mass and the prose at Vespers (Hereford), and the Introit at Mass (York). He also intimated to the Bishop any chants which the Bishop began.[3] *Injungere* meant to set the pitch of a chant by singing quietly its opening (its *variatio* in the case of an antiphon) to the beginner. The two hebdomadary priests acted as rulers on ordinary Sundays and on simple feasts; on ferias and feasts without ruling of the choir (*sine regimine chori*) the beginning of chants and the singing of solo parts were done by the vicars, clerks and two boys who were tabled for the week.

The beginning and singing of solo parts in the series of responds at Matins was carried out according to the understood principles that the sides of the choir alternated, beginning with the 'duty' side, and that the order of persons went from lower rank to higher.[4] The chief function of a ruler, besides beginning or singing certain parts of the ritual as laid down in the Customary, was to ascertain from the precentor or his deputy the beginnings of antiphons and responds and in what rank they were to be begun, and to intimate the beginning to the person concerned on his side. The following table shows by whom and where the principal chants were begun and sung on double feasts when there were four rulers, according to the Sarum use.

[1] At Exeter there were five for Mass on Whitsunday. *Ordinale Exon*, i, p. 168.

[2] *Use of Sarum*, i, pp. 29–33.

[3] *Use of Sarum*, i, p. 3; *Ordinale Exon*, i, p. 3; see also *Lincoln Statutes*, ii, pp. 17, 63, 94.

[4] *Use of Sarum*, i, pp. 93–107.

SERVICE	PART OF RITUAL	BEGUN BY[1]	WHERE
Vespers	Antiphons	One from senior stalls in descending rank	Stalls
	Antiphon to Magnificat	Person of highest rank on duty side	Stall
	Respond after Lesson	Three from senior stalls, two from duty side	Choir-step
	Hymn	Two rulers	Mid-choir
	Versicle after Hymn	Two boys	Choir-step
	Benedicamus I	Two of second form, being rulers; Deo gratias by two rulers from senior stalls	Before altar
	Benedicamus II, after memorials	Two boys	,, ,,
Matins	Invitatory and Venite	Rulers	Mid-choir
	Hymn and Versicle	As at Vespers	
	Antiphons	One from senior stalls in descending rank	Stalls
	Versicle before the first Lesson of each Nocturn	Two boys	Choir-step
	Lessons	In ascending rank from a clerk of second form	Pulpitum
	Responds 1, 2	Two clerks of second form	Choir-step
	,, 3, 6, 9	In ascending rank from three of second form to three from senior stalls	,,
	,, 4, 5, 7, 8	Two from senior stalls in ascending rank	,,
	Te Deum	Senior person present	Stall
Lauds	Antiphons	One from senior stalls in descending rank	Stalls
	Hymn and Versicle	As at Vespers	
	Antiphon to Benedictus	Person of highest rank on duty side	Stall
	Benedicamus I and II	As at Vespers	
Mass	Introit	Two rulers	Mid-choir
	Kyrie	,, ,,	,,
	Gloria	Officiant	Mid-altar
	Epistle	A sub-deacon	Pulpitum
	Gradual	Three of second form, two from duty side	,,
	Alleluia	Three from senior stalls	,,
	Sequence	Two rulers	Mid-choir
	Tract	Four from senior stalls	Choir-step
	Gospel	A deacon	Pulpitum
	Creed	Officiant	Mid-altar
	Offertory	Two rulers	Mid-choir
	Sanctus	,, ,,	,,
	Communion	,, ,,	,,
	Agnus Dei	,, ,,	
	Ite missa est or Benedicamus	Officiant	Mid-altar
	Deo gratias	Choir	

[1] In responsorial chants the beginners also sang the verse. The Epistle, Gospel, Versicles, Ite missa est, Benedicamus and Deo gratias were sung throughout by those indicated.

On some of the principal feasts certain chants were distinguished by unusual treatment; thus the respond at first Vespers on Christmas Day, *Judea et Jerusalem* with the verse *Constantes estote*, was sung by four from the senior stalls.[1] Another special event of Christmas was the singing of the first respond at Matins, *Hodie nobis caelorum rex de virgine nasci dignatus est.* The Sarum Ordinal directed that the verse of this respond, *Gloria in excelsis*, should be sung by five boys standing in a high place above the altar and holding lighted candles,[2] while at Exeter this was extended into a little play carried out in mime. There the first eight words of the respond were sung by a boy with 'a good and clear voice', who came from behind the altar holding a lighted torch (*torticium*) in his left hand. At the words *caelorum rex* he pointed with his right hand to heaven, at *de virgine* he turned to the altar and held out his hand towards the image of the Virgin, and at *dignatus est* he genuflected. While the choir sang the rest of the respond, three boys came from the south door of the choir and three from the north door and stood at the choir-step. The solo boy joined them and all sang the verse, turning towards the choir, and then walked slowly through the choir and out by the main choir-door.[3]

At Matins of All Saints the general rule of ascending rank in the singing of the responds was reversed—*servatur ordo preposterus*, as the Customary expresses it. The first respond was begun by a person of high rank and the others were begun in descending order of precedence until the eighth respond, *Audivi vocem* ... ℣. *Media nocte.* This was begun and its verse was sung by five boys at the choir-step facing towards the altar, each holding a lighted candle, and turning towards the choir when they came to the words *Ecce sponsus.*[4]

The Benedicamus at the end of first and second Vespers and of Lauds on Christmas Day, and at the end of Vespers of the

---

[1] *Use of Sarum*, ii, p. 28; *Ordinale Exon*, i, p. 61 (by four canons).

[2] *Use of Sarum*, ii, p. 30. The Audit Roll of Eton College for 1479–80 (the chapel had just been completed) has: 'Et xviiid solutis Thos Hall pro quinque hopis ponis summi altari pro candelis fusendis in mane Nativitatis Domini ubi pueri cantant Gloria in excelsis deo.'

[3] *Ordinale Exon*, i, p. 64.

[4] *Use of Sarum*, i, pp. 120–1. *Ordinale Exon*, i, p. 270, has: 'Tunc conveniant quinque pueri in superpelliciis, capitibus velatis amictis albis ad modum virginum feminarum tenentes cereos ardentes in manibus.'

three following days, was also specially treated.[1] On Christmas Eve it was sung by four boys standing at the farthest end of the choir (*in extrema parte chori*). The first Benedicamus of Lauds on Christmas Day was replaced by the Benedicamus trope[2] beginning *Verbum patris hodie*. The first two verses, which ended with *cum canoro jubilo benedicant Domino*, were sung by two[3] from the senior stalls at the choir-step, instead of at the usual place before the altar, and the other two verses, with the ending *redemptori debitas jubilando gratias*, by two from the senior stalls of the other side of the choir.[4] After the memorial of the Virgin,[5] the second Benedicamus[6] was sung by two boys[7] in mid-choir. *Verbum patris* was also sung instead of the first Benedicamus at second Vespers on Christmas Day by the four rulers or four other singers at the choir-step, and again at Lauds and Vespers on the following three days—on St. Stephen's day by the deacons, on St. John's day by the priests, in this case before the altar, and on Holy Innocents' day by the boys. After the first Benedicamus at Vespers on Christmas Day the deacons formed in procession to begin their services of St. Stephen,[8] and after their procession they sang the second Benedicamus 'solemnly' at the altar-step in whatever kind of musical setting they might choose.[9] Similarly the priests sang 'any Benedicamus solemnly at will'[10] after their procession on the eve of St. John, and the boys likewise on the eve of Holy Innocents.[11] The last Benedicamus on Holy Innocents' day, after the procession to St. Thomas's altar on the eve of his feast, which was the day after Holy Innocents, was sung by three singers of the second form, since the boys, as Grandisson's Ordinal observes, would very likely

[1] *Ordinale Exon*, i, pp. 63–77.

[2] The Exeter Ordinal calls it an antiphon, the Hereford Breviary (i, p. 148) a prose.

[3] By four in Exeter. *Ordinale Exon*, i, p. 67.

[4] By the whole choir in Exeter.

[5] Which was sung 'excelsa et clamorosa voce, ad consummacionem tocius misterii Incarnacionis'.

[6] Its melody (*Antiphonale Sarisburiense*, pl. 54) was *In perenni*.

[7] Four in Exeter. *Ordinale Exon*, i, p. 67.

[8] In Exeter they were attended by nine boys. *Ordinale Exon*, i, p. 68.

[9] 'Prout eis placuerit.' Ibid., p. 69.

[10] '*Benedicamus* aliquod solempne ad placitum.' Ibid, p. 72.

[11] 'Aliquod *Benedicamus* solempniter prout eis placuerit, sed non *Verbum patris*.' Ibid., p. 74.

be in bed.[1] The Benedicamus substitutes sung at Hereford at Lauds on the Circumcision (the prose *Mirabile misterium*) and on the Epiphany (the prose *Puer natus in Bethlehem*) seem to have been peculiar to the use of Hereford.[2]

Polyphony and the Ritual

The Sarum Customary notes that on Christmas Day and the four following days the Benedicamus was always sung *dupliciter*. Although the usual meaning of *duplex* is 'sung by two persons', there seems no doubt that in this case it means 'sung in two-part music'. The other feasts on which polyphonic singing of the Benedicamus was usual are given as the Circumcision, the Annunciation when it fell after Easter, and the Finding of the Holy Cross. But the Customary points out that the setting on those days must always be based on the plainsong of the Benedicamus, and at Eastertide must include the Alleluia.[3]

The most comprehensive directions for the use of polyphony in a secular liturgy are contained in Bishop Grandisson's Exeter Ordinal.[4] Like all Grandisson's liturgical provisions they are detailed and specific, but the surprising thing about them in this case is their liberality, for they include several parts of the ritual of which there are no known polyphonic settings either in the fourteenth century or later. The ranks of festivals and the parts of the ritual for which Grandisson permitted the singing of polyphony may most conveniently be seen in the table on page 110.

This section of the Exeter statutes also provided that in processions plainsong and polyphony should be employed (*cantent et discantent*) according to the rank of the festival and the nature of the chant. In addition, if those in authority approved, polyphony could be performed by voices or the organ in place of the Benedicamus at Vespers and Matins (i.e., Lauds), and after

[1] 'Propter absenciam forte puerorum tunc in dormitorio.' Ibid., p. 77.

[2] The former consisted of three verses ending with *Benedicamus domino* to which the choir responded *Deo gratias*. Hereford Breviary, i, pp. 183, 197.

[3] 'Et semper cum tali cantu *Benedicamus domino:* et in tempore paschali cum *Alleluya.*' *Use of Sarum*, i, p. 255.

[4] 'De modo psallendi et modulandi discantandi aut organizandi.' *Ordinale Exon*, i, pp. 19–20. Besides *discantare* and *organizare*, the term *jubilare* is used here for polyphonic singing.

SERVICE	GREATER DOUBLES	LESSER DOUBLES	SEMI-DOUBLES	ORDINARY SUNDAYS AND FEASTS WITH RULING OF CHOIR	FERIAS AND FEASTS OF THREE LESSONS
Vespers	Antiphon Respond, but not verse or Gloria Hymn Magnificat and its antiphon Benedicamus substitute 'ex licencia' Deo gratias	As for Greater Doubles except that at Matins only the ninth respond (and the ninth antiphon?) could be sung in polyphony	Antiphon Hymn Antiphon to Magnificat	Hymn Antiphon to Magnificat	Nothing, except at memorials of the Virgin or of Saints Peter and Paul
Compline	Hymn Nunc dimitis and its antiphon		Hymn		
Matins	Hymn Antiphons 3, 6, 9 Responds 3, 6, 9 but not verses or Gloria Te Deum 'solempniter'		Ninth antiphon Ninth respond	Ninth respond	
Lauds	Hymn Benedictus and its antiphon Benedicamus substitute 'ex licencia' Deo gratias		Antiphon to Benedictus	Hymn 'si placet' Antiphon to Benedictus 'si placet'	
Prime	Hymn Antiphon to Quicumque vult		Antiphon to Quicumque vult		
Terce, Sext, None	'Nichil nisi ad placitum ex devocione'				
Mass	Introit when sung third time Kyrie Gloria Sequence ('Prosa') Credo Offertory Sanctus Post Sanctus 'ex licencia' Agnus Dei Deo gratias		Kyrie Sequence Sanctus Agnus Dei	Kyrie Sequence Sanctus Agnus Dei	

the Sanctus at Mass.[1] The singing of a polyphonic substitute for the Benedicamus was also specifically allowed in the body of the Ordinal at Lauds and Vespers on Easter Day and at first Vespers of Trinity Sunday.[2] Curiously, the Ordinal allowed the polyphonic singing of a respond but not of its verse and Gloria, though it is clear from surviving examples that it was the normal practice to set the opening, verse and Gloria in polyphony. In the later Middle Ages it was usual to set the sequence in the Lady-Mass, on which Grandisson wrote a special section in the Ordinal, but settings of the sequence for other occasions are very rare. At the Lady-Mass in the Exeter Lady-chapel the Kyrie could be sung either in polyphony or to a chant, with or without trope, proper to the Lady-Mass, and the Gloria could be sung if desired in plainsong and polyphony *alternatim*.[3]

The Customary contained in the Black Book of Lincoln Cathedral explained the procedure to be adopted if the Benedicamus were replaced by a polyphonic piece at the end of first Vespers and Lauds on greater doubles, when it was sung by some of the vicars, and on lesser doubles, when it was sung by boys. At Vespers the duty side of the choir, and at Lauds the rulers, responded with *Deo dicamus gratias* sung to the melody of the Benedicamus which had been replaced, which was *in perenni* at Vespers and *flos filius* at Lauds.[4] The Lincoln Customary makes no mention of polyphony in the Mass, but

[1] 'Ex licencia, si placet senioribus, loco *Benedicamus* ad Vesperas et ad Matutinas et ad Missam post *Sanctus*, poterunt organizare cum vocibus vel organis.'

[2] 'Vel aliquis cantus organicus in pulpito, loco *Benedicamus*, cantetur'; 'Vel in pulpito cantetur aliquod canticum, si placet, organicum, loco *Benedicamus*. Et respondeatur a choro *Deo gracias. Alleluya*'; '*Benedicamus* a tribus more solito vel organicum loco *Benedicamus*.' Ibid., pp. 140, 142, 171.

[3] 'Dicantur *Kyrie* organici vel proprii si habeantur de sancta Maria cum versibus vel sine ad placitum . . . Potest semper a clericis responderi aliquod organicum vel quod magis placet.' Ibid, ii, p. 465.

[4] 'Unde oracione finita eant aliqui bene cantantes cum premunicione *magistri* scolarum cantus et organizent ad lectrinam predictam. . . . Cantu finito debent illi qua parte chorus est respondere cantando et stando *Deo dicamus*, et cantatur eodem modo sicut *In perhenni seculorum tempore* in fine vi responsorii sancte trinitatis et illo modo cantantur omnes *Benedicamus* in duplicibus et semiduplicibus in primis vesperis excepto tempore paschali'. And: 'Unde organizent vicarii sive pueri de choro disposicione succentoris et respondent regentes chorum cantando sicut canitur *flos filius* in fine versus qui vocatur *virga* [recte *virgo*] *dei*.' Lincoln Statutes, i, pp. 369, 373.

another part of the Black Book records an order of the Dean and Canons in 1322 that certain payments should be made out of the offerings of the worshippers at the tomb of Robert Grosseteste (Bishop of Lincoln, 1235–53) on his annual commemoration on the eighth of October to those who took part in the Mass on that day, including three pence to each singer of the *organum*. The same order provided payments to the organ blower (*trahens organa*) of six shillings and eight pence from the offerings at the shrine of St. Hugh and of the same sum from the offerings at Grosseteste's commemoration.[1]

An inventory of the books of Exeter Cathedral in 1327 mentions a *liber pro gradu chori et pulpiti*, which may have been a book of polyphonic music, among later additions of books and ornaments, most of which were given by Bishop Grandisson.[2] The practice of polyphonic singing at York is recorded in a somewhat negative way by the refusal of the vicars in 1375 to sing polyphonic music in the *pulpitum* on festivals unless the canons recompensed them with wine, which they justified by an appeal to the custom of the church.[3] Surviving inventories show that in 1384 St. George's, Windsor, possessed a roll of polyphonic music bequeathed by John Aleyn,[4] who became a canon in 1362 and died in 1373,[5] and who may have been the composer of a notable motet which has been preserved in a continental manuscript,[6] and that Lichfield Cathedral had a book of polyphonic *cantilenae* in 1345.[7] The musical life of both places owed something to the work of Adam Pentrich who, as a vicar of St. George's, went to Salisbury in 1362–3 to copy music,[8] and who taught the choristers of St. George's for the first six

[1] A payment was also provided 'capellano custodi inferiori excitanti populum'. Ibid., p. 337.

[2] Oliver, *Lives of the Bishops of Exeter*, p. 301.

[3] 'Vicarii in diebus solempnibus nolunt organum cantare in pulpito nisi canonici dicte Ecclesie eis conferant vinum, quod vendicant ex consuetudine.' *York Fabric Rolls*, p. 243.

[4] 'Item unus rotulus de cantu music' ex legato Johannis Aleyn'; and in 1409–10 the same 'ex legacione domini Johannis Aleyn'. Bond, *Inventories of St. George's*, pp. 34, 103.

[5] Ollard, *Fasti Wyndesorienses*, pp. 65, 136.

[6] See below, pp. 224 sqq.

[7] 'i liber organicus de cantilenis'. 'The Sacrist's Roll of 1345' in *Catalogue of Muniments of the Lichfield Vicars*, p. 204.

[8] Fellowes, *Vicars and Minor Canons of Windsor*, p. 17.

months of 1366.[1] He was Succentor of Lichfield from *c.* 1370 and died in that office in 1378.[2] The practice of polyphony at St. Paul's is attested by an inventory of the books of the choir made in 1295[3] and by the fact that Richard Cotell, one of the minor canons at the end of the fourteenth century, wrote a brief summary of the new method of teaching elementary polyphony.[4]

The most active centres of the cultivation of polyphony until the mid-fourteenth century were undoubtedly the greater Benedictine abbeys. There are actual musical remains from Reading, Worcester and Bury St. Edmund's, while the Customaries of Westminster Abbey and St. Augustine's, Canterbury, both mention, in identical terms, that the sequence (*prosa*), Benedictus and Magnificat were sung in two-part polyphony (*sollemniter in duplum*) on principal feasts.[5] The Westminster Customary, which was written during the abbacy of Richard de Ware (1259–83), gives detailed instructions to the precentor about the performance of the hymn *Aeterna Christi munera*, which was sung in three parts (*sollemniter in triplum*) by both sides of the choir together, and not apparently *alternatim*, on the two feasts of St. Peter,[6] the patron saint of the Abbey, and on the feast of Relics. It also observes that the verse of the respond at Vespers on Christmas Eve, that is, the verse *Constantes estote* of the respond *Judea et Jerusalem*, was sung in three-part polyphony (*in triplis sollemniter*).[7] References to polyphony in the Norwich Customary (*c.* 1260) occur in connection with the verse *Vidit beatus Stephanus* of the respond *Ecce jam coram*[8] for the procession to St. Stephen's altar after Vespers on Christmas Day, and the verse *Stephanus Dei gratia* of the respond *Impetum fecerunt* at Vespers on St. Stephen's day. The former was sung in three

---

[1] Fellowes, *Windsor Organists*, p. 1.

[2] According to a document of 1361 he was sub-chanter at Lichfield then; see *Catalogue of Muniments of the Lichfield Vicars*, p. 168. John Codyngham was succentor in the following year, however. Ibid., p. 178.

[3] See below, p. 132.

[4] See below, pp. 149 sqq.

[5] *Customary of St. Augustine's, Canterbury, and St. Peter's, Westminster*, i, p. 94; ii, p. 32.

[6] Cathedra S. Petri (February 22) and Ad vincula S. Petri (August 1).

[7] Op. cit., ii, pp. 33–4.

[8] This is not in the Worcester Antiphonal nor the Ordinal of St. Mary's, York, nor in the secular uses.

parts by the whole choir (*triplici cantu ab omnibus*) and the latter by several singers, also in three parts (*triplici cantu*). The Alleluia *Angelus Domini* on the Sunday after Easter might also be sung *triplici cantu* at the discretion of the cantor.[1]

The practice of a large Benedictine community in the fourteenth century, as far as it concerns the Temporale, may be gathered from the Ordinal and Customary of St. Mary's, York, written *c.* 1400. Polyphony was expressly permitted for the beginning and verse of *Judea et Jerusalem*,[2] for the hymn *Nunc sancte nobis Spiritus* at Terce on principal feasts,[3] and for the verse *In principio* of the respond *Verbum caro factum est*, which was sung before the rood in the procession before the third Mass on Christmas Day.[4] The two-part setting of *Nunc sancte* is given in the Ordinal.[5] It uses the same music four times, with a short extension of the upper part at the end, and the parts exchange in *rondellus* fashion with each line.[6] Some parts of the Ordinary of the Mass, and the Gradual, the verse of the Alleluia, the Sequence, the Offertory and the Communion might also be sung in polyphony on high festivals.[7] Durham Cathedral paid three

[1] *Customary of Norwich*, pp. 34–5, 99.

[2] This beginning and verse and the Benedicamus were sung at the choir-step if in plainsong, at the lectern in mid-choir in front of the rulers' form if in polyphony (*cantu organi*). *Ordinale of St. Mary's, York*, p. 179.

[3] 'Canatur secundum duplicem melodiam et incipitur a duobus in medio chori.' Ibid., p. 189.

[4] 'Coram cruce ℞. *Verbum caro*. Quinque fratres de medio conventus cantant versum aut certe organiste, si sint, triplici melodia.' *Ordinale of St. Mary's, York*, p. 190.

[5] Cambridge, St. John's College, MS. D.27, fo. 141. The music is not printed in the Henry Bradshaw Society's edition.

[6] See also a setting in this style in a Hymnal of the early fourteenth century written for Coldingham Priory, Berwick, a dependency of Durham (British Museum, MS. Harley 4664; facsimile of the page in *Early English Harmony*, pl. 39). For transcriptions and discussion of these and similar examples, see Handschin in *Zeitschrift für Musikwissenschaft*, xvi, p. 119, and *Acta Musicologica*, vii, pp. 67–71; also *Monumenta Monodica Medii Aevi*, i, pp. 532–8.

[7] 'Ad *Kyrieleyson, Gloria in excelsis, Credo*, Offertorium et Communionem, preterquam ad *Adoramus Te, Suscipe deprecationem nostram* [these when the Gloria was sung in alternating plainsong and polyphony], et cetera hujusmodi, quando ab organistis cantantur. Ad Gradale etiam et versus de *Alleluia* et Sequentiam dum sic cantantur chorus sedet'. And under Christmas Day: 'Talibus diebus quando Abbas celebrat Missam, solet mittere Capellanum suum custodibus ordinis ad ostium refectorii pro ministrantibus

shillings and four pence for a *liber organi* in 1387–8, and in the same year there were payments 'to the singers at Christmas' and to 'Nicholas the singer'.[1] At a visitation of Durham made *c.* 1390 it was observed that it had been the custom to have clerks who sang polyphony (*cantantes organum*) to help the monks by singing the treble part (*adjuvantes monachos in cantu qui dicitur trebill*), but there were now none, and the singing of the brethren in choir was much hampered.[2]

The musical theorist and astronomer Walter Odington came to Oxford from the Benedictine monastery of St. Mary's, Evesham. Two treatises on astronomy under the name Walter Evesham now in the Bodleian Library are dated 1316, and his important treatise *De Speculatione Musicae*[3] was probably written about this time. This Walter Odington, monk of Evesham, has been incorrectly identified with Walter de Evesham, fellow of Merton.[4] The Franciscans also pursued musical studies at Oxford, for the treatise *Quatuor Principalia Musicae*[5] was written in 1351 by a friar while Simon Tunsted, 'skilled in music and also in the seven liberal arts', was Regent of the Franciscans there. The section on polyphony in the *Quatuor Principalia* discusses the simpler kinds of polyphonic technique, while Odington's treatise deals more fully with the chief polyphonic forms of his time.

Polyphony in the Twelfth and Thirteenth Centuries

The only collection of pre-Norman polyphony which survives in England is contained in one of the two Tropers from Winchester which were written in the first half of the eleventh century.[6] It comprises more than one hundred and fifty two-part settings of Invitatories, antiphons and responds for the

sibi in Missa, pro Precentore et Organistis si qui sint, ut prandeant secum in aula, vel in camera sua,' *Ordinale of St. Mary's, York*, pp. 134, 191.

[1] *Durham Account Rolls*, i, p. 134.
[2] Pantin, *Chapters of the English Black Monks*, ii, p. 84.
[3] Printed in Coussemaker, *Scriptores*, i, pp. 182 sqq.
[4] In 1330; he was still fellow in 1346.
[5] Printed in Coussemaker, *Scriptores*, i, pp. 182 sqq.
[6] Cambridge, Corpus Christi College MS. 473; the companion book in Oxford, Bodleian Library, MS. Bodl. 775, contains only monophonic music.

offices, of troped Introits, of Kyries and Glorias both with and without tropes, and of Alleluias, Graduals, Sequences and Tracts.[1] Unfortunately, the music cannot be reliably transcribed since it is written in neumes without lines. Between this Winchester Troper and the Old Hall manuscript of the early fifteenth century no collection of English part-music has survived in anything like complete form. Here we except the St. Andrew's manuscript, a collection of French music, with local additions, made in the thirteenth century. What remains consists of fly-leaves and paste-downs, often cut and otherwise mutilated, short pieces written into plainsong service-books, examples in the writings of theorists, and a few pieces preserved in non-musical manuscripts. The oldest of these fragments, which is decipherable because it was written in letter notation, is a two-part setting of the verse *Ut tuo propitiatus* of the respond *Sancte Dei pretiose* for the feast of St. Stephen.[2] It was written *c.* 1100, probably at Canterbury for the monastery of St. Augustine, on a page at the end of a school book, together with some lines in honour of St. Augustine, a Benedicamus with neumes, a rhymed antiphon, and a prose for the Dedication of a Church.[3] A two-part piece of something less than a century later, the verse *Dicant nunc* of the antiphon *Christus resurgens*,[4] is found in a less unexpected place, namely in its liturgical position in a Gradual,[5] which otherwise contains only plainsong, and which came from a cathedral in Ireland.[6] In these pieces the parts have an approximately equal range and

[1] Texts and some facsimiles in Frere, *Winchester Troper*; other facsimiles in *Early English Harmony*, pls. 2–6. See also Ludwig, *Repertorium*, pp. 268–9; Handschin, 'The Two Winchester Tropers'; Wellesz, *Eastern Elements*, pp. 192–201.

[2] In the later secular rites this respond was sung by the deacons in their procession to St. Stephen's altar; it is not in the Worcester Antiphonal, nor is it mentioned in the English Benedictine Ordinals or customaries.

[3] Bodleian Library, MS. Bodl. 572, fo. 49v; facsimile in *Early English Harmony*, pl. 1, and *Early Bodleian Music*, ii, pl. xvi; transcriptions in *Historical Anthology*, i, p. 22; *New Oxford History of Music*, ii, pp. 308–9.

[4] Which had an important place in the monastic as well as the secular rites of Eastertide. See *Ordinale of St. Mary's, York*, ii, p. 300; *Customary of Norwich*, p. 96.

[5] Bodleian Library, MS. Rawl. c. 892, fo. 67v; facsimile in *Early Bodleian Music*, iii, pl. lxiv.

[6] Van Dijk, *Liturgical Manuscripts*, p. 19.

cross quite frequently, the added voice going higher in both
cases:[1]

Ex.6.

Plainsong

Di - cant nunc—— Ju - de - i quo - mo - do mi - li - tes.....

Di - cant nunc—— Ju - de - i quo - mo - do mi - li - tes

During the twelfth century a new and large repertory of
polyphonic music for the liturgy was created in France, largely
at two centres, the Benedictine monastery of St. Martial at
Limoges and the secular cathedral of Notre Dame in Paris.
The four manuscripts from St. Martial which have survived[2]
are mainly concerned with music for the great winter feasts of
St. Nicholas (December 6), Christmas, Holy Innocents, the
Circumcision (January 1) and the Epiphany. Some of the pieces
appear to be intended for the plays which were inserted into the
services on those days, and which, like the Visitation and
Peregrini plays at Easter, were dramatic tropes which expanded
and illustrated a particular point in the story unfolded by an
office or, less frequently, by a Mass. Parts of the ritual itself,
including the Christmas Gradual *Viderunt omnes fines terrae*[3] and
the Benedicamus, were also troped and set in polyphony.

The earliest of the polyphonic Benedicamus tropes in these
manuscripts is a poem of five verses beginning *Jubilemus exsultemus* and ending *Benedicamus Domino*,[4] and is thus, like *Verbum*

[1] 'Bar-lines' as in manuscript; plainsong from *Antiphonale Sarisburiense*,
pl. 242. This piece also appears, with variants, in Chartres, Bibl. de la Ville,
MS. 109, of *c.* 1100.

[2] Paris, Bibliothèque Nationale, MSS. lat. 1139, 3719 and 3549; British
Museum, MS. Add. 36881. See Adler, *Handbuch der Musikgeschichte*, i, pp.
177–80; Reese, *Music in the Middle Ages*, pp. 266–7.

[3] Facsimile in Apel, *Notation of Polyphonic Music*, p. 211; transcriptions in
Adler, op. cit., pp. 179–80, and *Historical Anthology*, i, p. 23.

[4] Transcription in Handschin, 'Die mittelalterliche Aufführungen', pp.
13–14. The first verse of a similar trope from the St. Martial music, *Prima
mundi seducta sobole*, is transcribed in *New Oxford History of Music*, ii, p. 297.

patris hodie, practically a substitute for the Benedicamus rather than a trope of it. Another setting of the Benedicamus, which is not troped and is based on the *flos filius* melody, has a very florid upper part with as many as twenty or so notes to one note of the tenor.[1] As in all polyphony until the late twelfth century, both parts are free in rhythm, and must therefore have been mutually adjusted in performance. The singing of *Viderunt* apparently called not only for the accommodation of a single note to a group of notes, but of group to group in such combinations as two or four notes against three. Both kinds of movement were *organum* as defined by the theory of the period,[2] and the method of performance must have been well understood at the time. On the other hand, when the words are in regular metre the music of the *Viderunt* trope has basically note-to-note movement, a style which was termed *discantus*. The piece ends with a neuma on the penultimate syllable.

Between the St. Martial music and the Notre Dame corpus comes the Codex Calixtinus, a collection of plainsong and polyphony for the services on the feasts and octaves of St. James at his shrine at Santiago de Compostela,[3] then as later the object of innumerable pilgrimages. The manuscript is called after Pope Calixtus II (1119–24), who before his elevation was Guy of Burgundy, Archbishop of Vienne. His name appears as the compiler of the ritual of the services, and that of Bishop Fulbert of Chartres (d. 1028) as the writer of tropes for the Mass. There are clear affiliations with the French style of St. Martial in the polyphonic music, and the ascriptions show that some of the composers were French. It is here that we first meet the word *conductus* (actually *conductum* in the manuscript) applied to polyphonic music. The second of the four pieces for which the name is used, *In hac die laudes cum gaudio*, is set in two parts, and three of these pieces end with the words *Lector lege et de rege qui regit omne dic Jube domne*, sung in plainsong. These pieces are clearly intended to precede the reading of a lesson or Gospel

---

[1] The beginning is printed by Adler (i, p. 179) and Reese (p. 266).

[2] Handschin, 'Zur Geschichte der Lehre von Organum', p. 321.

[3] Compostela, Cathedral Library, Codex Calixtinus, written (?) *c.* 1140. Transcriptions in *Liber Sancti Jacobi*, a complete edition of the manuscript, and Wagner, *Die Gesänge der Jakobusliturgie*, an edition with commentary of the liturgical part.

and to be sung before the reader asks the blessing of the officiant with the usual words *Jube domne benedicere* and receives it in the words *Domine sit in corde tuo*, etc. They probably accompanied the procession of the reader and his ministers to the lectern. Under the words of the last verse of the first piece is written *Quapropter regi regum benedicamus domino*, presumably as an alternative to the 'Lector lege' ending, so that it could also serve as a troped Benedicamus.

The polyphonic pieces in the Codex Calixtinus comprise a group of eight Benedicamus tropes and substitutes, five responds for Matins, a prose for one of the responds, two troped Kyries,[1] a Gradual, an Alleluia and three untroped settings of the Benedicamus. Five of the first group end, like the *Jubilemus exsultemus* in the St. Martial collection, with some form of the words *benedicamus* (or *benedicat*) *domino* or of its response *Deo gratias. Congaudeant catholici*,[2] for example, has *benedicamus domino die ista* at the end of the sixth verse, and *solvamus laudes gratias die ista* at the end of the seventh (and last). The others do not contain these words, but take advantage of the licence by which a piece suitable to the day could be sung instead of the Bene-dicamus. The prose *Portum in ultimo da nobis judicio*, which seems to be the earliest surviving polyphonic setting of this ritual form, is an expansion of the last word (*duc nos ad salutis*) *portum* of the twelfth respond, *O adjutor omnium saeculorum*, at Matins of St. James. Its three verses were set, with one syllable to each note, to each of the three sections into which the neuma on the word *portum* was divided, and are thus a trope of the same type as *Aeterna virgo memoriae*, discussed in the previous chapter. As usual, the plainsong is in the lower part. The untroped Bene-dicamus settings were written with several notes, or rather neumes,[3] to one note or neume of the plainsong, that is, in organum. The upper part of the first, which is by *Magister Gauterius de Castello Rainardo* (of Chateaurenard) and is based

[1] *Cunctipotens genitor* is transcribed in *Historical Anthology*, i, p. 23; the opening of *Rex immense* is printed in *New Oxford History of Music*, ii, p. 300.

[2] A middle part was added later to *Congaudeant catholici*; see the trans-criptions in ibid., p. 305.

[3] The term neume (i.e., sign; Latin, *figura*), meaning a symbol in musical notation for a note or group of notes, is to be distinguished from neuma, a passage of melody on one syllable, for which the term *melisma* is commonly used in modern writings.

on the *flos filius* melody, shows a very sensitive feeling for melodic design and contour.[1] Of the other two, both by *Magister Droardus Trecensis* (of Trèves), one is on the *clementiam* melody and the other on one of the simplest of the plainsongs of the Benedicamus.

In these continental collections fewer parts of the actual ritual were set in polyphony than in the Winchester Troper. If the Codex Calixtinus may be taken as representative of the general practice of French churches for the feasts of their patronal saints, that practice was to set chiefly the responsorial chants of the office and the Mass, treating only the beginning and the verse, the Benedicamus both with and without trope, and the conductus. The composition of polyphonic responds for two voices for the ritual of all the great feasts of the year was the achievement of *Magister Leoninus* of Notre Dame, who worked there from *c*. 1160 to *c*. 1180. The responds which are generally attributed to him were laid out on a larger scale than hitherto, and he treated some of the neumae in a slightly elaborated descant style in measured rhythm (perhaps for the first time), and other parts of the chant in organum fashion.[2] The Easter Gradual *Haec dies*, for example, was composed on the following scheme; the words sung in organum style are underlined, those in descant style are in capitals, and those not included in the polyphonic setting, because sung by the choir in plainsong, are in brackets:[3]

Haec dies (quam fecit Dominus: exsultemus et laetemur in ea). ℣. Confitemini DOMINO quoniam bonus: quoniam IN SAECULUM (misericordia ejus).

The sections in the new kind of descant, which was ordered in continuously recurring rhythmic patterns or 'modes',[4] occur more frequently in the responds of the Mass than in those of the office. Among the responds of the office which contain descant

---

[1] It is transcribed in *Historical Anthology*, i, p. 24.

[2] On the rhythmic interpretation of these sections, see Apel, 'From St. Martial to Notre Dame', and Waite, *Rhythm of Twelfth-Century Polyphony*. The latter contains transcriptions in modal rhythm of the two-part responds in the St. Andrew's manuscript (see below, p. 130).

[3] Music in *Historical Anthology*, i, p. 27.

[4] See Reese, *Music in the Middle Ages*, pp. 207–10.

sections are the two responds for Christmas *Judea et Jerusalem* and *Descendit de caelis*.[1] Of the settings of the Benedicamus which were composed by Léonin or in his style, some are entirely in organum and others, in which the word *Domino* is in descant, have the same division of method as the responds.[2]

According to an English student, probably from Bury St. Edmund's, who was at Paris in the thirteenth century,[3] Léonin's collection of polyphony, the *Magnus Liber Organi de Gradali et Antiphonario pro servitio divino multiplicando*, was used at Notre Dame until the time of *Magister Perotinus*, who was there from *c*. 1180 to *c*. 1220. Pérotin, according to Anonymous IV, 'abbreviated' the Magnus Liber and 'composed many better *clausulae* or *puncta*, since he was *optimus discantor* and better than Léonin', whom he calls *optimus organista*. He also tells us that Pérotin wrote many very fine Tripla, or pieces for three parts, and excellent Quadrupla such as *Viderunt* and *Sederunt*, composed '*cum abundantia colorum harmonicae artis*'.[4]

It is not unlikely that the occasion of the composition of these four-part pieces of Pérotin was a new set of statutes for the services of the days after Christmas which were laid down by Odo de Sully, Bishop of Paris, in 1198. The Bishop had decided that something must be done to restrain the excesses (*enormitates et opera flagitiosa*) indulged in by the sub-deacons in the church on the day, traditionally the feast of the Circumcision, known as the 'Feast of Fools', on which they took charge of the services. He ordered that the *dominus festi* should begin his rule with the singing of a prose before Vespers and that the services should be carried out with the normal ceremonial of a feast. He allowed that the respond and the Benedicamus at Vespers, the third and sixth responds at Matins, and the Gradual (*Viderunt*, as at High Mass on Christmas Day) and Alleluia at Mass could be sung *in triplo vel quadruplo vel organo*. In the following year an order was made along the same lines for St. Stephen's day, the day of the deacons, and payments were provided on both days for

---

[1] See Ludwig, *Repertorium*, pp. 17–21, 65–7.

[2] Ibid., pp. 40, 67. For an example, see *Historical Anthology*, i, p. 24.

[3] He is known as Anonymous IV, since his treatise beginning 'Cognita modulatione melorum' was printed fourth among the anonymous treatises in Coussemaker, *Scriptores*, i, pp. 327 sqq.

[4] Ibid., p. 342.

the clerks and boys who attended, and for the clerks who sang the Gradual (*Sederunt principes* on St. Stephen's day) and Alleluia at Mass. Similar provision was later made for St. John's day, when the priests took charge of the services.[1]

Benedicamus and Conductus; Clausula and Motet

Pérotin's *Viderunt* and *Sederunt* are the only surviving four-part responds of his period,[2] and may in fact have been the only ones composed until the mid-fifteenth century. Besides these compositions, the English Anonymous mentions by name two three-part Alleluias (*Nativitas* and *Posui adjutorium*[3]) and three conductus, for one (*Beata viscera*), two (*Dum sigillum*[4]) and three voices (*Salvatoris hodie*[5]), all by Pérotin. In each of a group of five three-part Benedicamus settings which can probably be attributed to Pérotin[6] the word *Benedicamus* is set in a long section of organum and *Domino* in descant. Both styles, as in all his music, were definitely in measured rhythm, to be sung in conformity with the practice of the rhythmic modes. It has been generally assumed, from the reference of Anonymous IV to Pérotin's 'abbreviation' of the Magnus Liber, that his new treatments of the neumae (i.e., his clausulae or puncta)[7] were sung in place of the corresponding sections of Léonin's music

[1] Handschin, 'Zur Geschichte der Notre Dame'.

[2] For published transcriptions, see Reese, *Music in the Middle Ages*, p. 302. Pérotin's other four-part work, *Mors*, is a clausula on a neuma from the Easter Alleluia *Christus resurgens*; transcription in *Die Mittelalterliche Mehrstimmigkeit*, p. 24.

[3] Transcriptions from the Montpellier MS. in *Polyphonies du XIIIᵉ siècle*, ii, pp. 16, 31.

[4] Transcription in *El Còdex musical de Las Huelgas*, iii, p. 337.

[5] Facsimile of one page and transcription of the whole in Wooldridge, *Oxford History of Music*, 1st. ed., i, pp. 292 sqq.

[6] Ludwig, *Repertorium*, p. 43.

[7] A clausula is a short phrase; a punctum is a single note, and hence a passage of organum written on a single note. Punctum was also used of each section in the *estampie*, a medieval dance similar in form to the liturgical sequence. Anonymous IV observes that instrumentalists used punctum for a phrase: '. . . et hoc plane patet in *Alleluia, Posui adiutorium*, in loco post primam longam pausationem. Et quidam dicerent post primam clausulam notarum, quod alii nominant proprie loquendo, secundum operatores instrumentorum, punctum.' Coussemaker, *Scriptores*, i, p. 347.

and that Léonin's organum sections were eventually dropped. There are, for example, among the two cycles of clausulae, both arranged in the order of seasons as used in the Ordinal, which were written by Pérotin or in his style, a *Haec dies*, a *Domino*, a *Quoniam* and three *In saeculum* settings for the gradual *Haec dies*. If these clausulae were to be inserted in Léonin's setting of the gradual it would be performed thus, the words over a broken line being sung in plainsong, or in Léonin's organum, if it were still used:

HAEC DIES (quam fecit, etc.) ℣. Confitemini DOMINO QUONIAM bonus: quoniam IN SAECULUM (misericordia ejus).

This 'replacement' theory of the use of the clausulae[1] is far from convincing, for if the words not set as clausulae reverted to plainsong the organum parts of the responds, which were written in the same manuscripts as the clausulae, would have been put out of use. This is unlikely, since compilers of manuscripts for use in choir were not given to including items which had only an antiquarian interest. Alternatively, if the organum sections were retained and the clausulae substituted for the descant sections musical difficulties would arise. From the musical point of view the responds form a continuous texture, in spite of the juxtaposition of organum and descant styles, and almost every attempt at replacement raises some problem of detail in actual fitting. The clausulae, in fact, are not really capable of being inserted in this way. Finally, there is no definite evidence, apart from the pieces of Pérotin cited by name by the English Anonymous, about the composers of any of the 'Notre Dame' pieces. Pérotin's three-part responds do not differ essentially in form from the two-part responds in the manuscripts, though in rhythmic and melodic style the upper parts of his three-part organum are necessarily closer to descant than is organum in two parts. Whatever share in the composition of this music

---

[1] Ludwig, who was the first to outline this theory, called them *Ersatzstücken*; see his 'Über die Entstehung der Motette', p. 516. In an article 'Zur Melodiebildung Leonins und Perotins', H. Schmidt suggested that Pérotin composed the descant sections of the two-part responds as we have them to replace parts of hypothetical settings in continuous organum by Léonin. See also Handschin, 'Zur Leonin-Perotin Frage'.

may have been taken by these or other composers, it must be assumed that it constitutes a coherent body of ritual polyphony, written in the forms of respond, clausula, Benedicamus and conductus, each with its own function in the adornment of the services.

The adoption of a neuma from a respond of a feast-day as the melody of the Benedicamus on that day, whereby the melody of the neuma achieved an independent place in the ritual, has already been noticed. In addition, troped settings of the Benedicamus not based on plainsong, as well as substitutes which omitted the ritual words entirely, had won admission to the ritual of certain feasts before the period of the Notre Dame music. Its corpus includes a relatively small number of untroped Benedicamus settings on the plainsong, a few descant-style pieces which include the ritual words,[1] and a large number of conductus, none of which contain the *Jube domne* formula. It seems clear that the chief liturgical function of a conductus was now to act as a substitute for the Benedicamus, and that the term was applied to these substitutes because their metrical form and musical style, which was descant, though not their ceremonial function, were the same as those of the earlier *Jube domne* conductus. As an element in the ritual the conductus should almost certainly be grouped with the Benedicamus and the Benedicamus tropes and be regarded as a Benedicamus substitute.[2]

There is a striking parallel between the use of the neumae of the office responds for the melodies of the Benedicamus and the use of neumae from the responds of the Mass as the plainsong basis of the clausulae. If the 'replacement' theory of the function of the clausulae be rejected, it must follow that they

---

[1] E.g., *Deus creator omnium, Naturas Deus regulis, Ista dies celebrari* (also in the fly-leaves of the printed book Wood 591 in the Bodleian Library), *Serena virginum* (actually a conductus derived from a motet by omitting the tenor, the motet in turn having been derived from a set of clausulae; see *New Oxford History of Music*, ii, pp. 365–7). *Leniter ex merito a Columbae simplicitas* and *Relegata vetustate* end with 'Benedicamus Domino'; see also Bukofzer, 'Interrelations between Conductus and Clausula'.

[2] The subject matter of the conductus covers a very wide range; see Schrade, 'Political Compositions in French Music'. What is suggested here is the probable ritual position of those conductus which are related to the seasons and feasts of the church.

PLATE IX

12. Exeter Cathedral c. 1820, showing the choir-screen before openings were made in the side-arches by Sir Gilbert Scott in 1877. The 'Minstrels' Gallery', which was probably used for music for Masses celebrated in the nave, has fourteen figures of angels playing instruments. Behind it is a large room, reached by a spiral stairway from the north aisle

PLATE X

13. Rondellus sections of *Salve mater misericordiae*

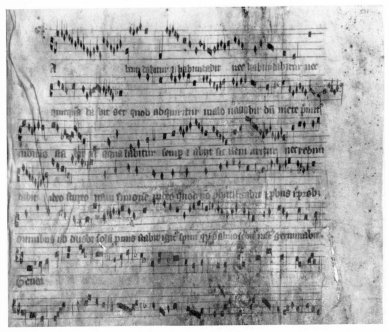

14. Countertenor and tenor parts of *Omnis terra—Habenti dabitur*

were from their origin self-sufficient compositions, either descant sections detached from existing responds (a comparatively small number, perhaps representing the earliest procedure)[1] or new pieces composed on the same and other neumae. As extra-ritual items, their performance during the Mass would have been permitted by a licence analogous to that which allowed Benedicamus substitutes at the end of the office. The most likely place in the ceremonial of the Mass to be open to such a licence was the period during the officiant's ritual of the Canon. Since the Sanctus and Benedictus, which preceded the Canon, were sung in plainsong, the time was available and could be filled in with music appropriate to the day.[2]

Clausulae were written down as one piece or set of pieces on each neuma, and hence their performance could easily have been adjusted to the length of time the ritual allowed.[3] The syllable or word(s) of the neuma were written at the beginning of each clausula under its tenor, which consisted of one, or occasionally two, statements of the neuma disposed in a regu-larly recurring rhythm. The upper part or parts moved in a quicker rhythm ordered, like the tenor, according to one of the rhythmic modes. Both the dance-like rhythm of the clausulae, which was their most noticeable characteristic, and the fact that the term *puncta* was applied to them by the English Anony-mous suggest a relationship to the instrumental estampies of the period. A suite of clausulae performed in succession were, in fact, virtually a set of *puncta* rendered liturgically relevant by being based on one or more of the plainsong neumae of the day. They could be played on instruments, most likely with the

[1] The second *Potentem* clausula on fo. 61v of the St. Andrew's manuscript, for example, was taken out of the Alleluia verse *Posui adjutorium super potentem* on fo. 47.

[2] 'Pour la messe célébrée avec chant, on a rénoncé complètement au silence du canon et libre carrière a été donnée, non pas sans doute à la voix du prêtre, mais au chant du choeur': Jungmann, *Missarum Sollemnia*, p. 47. The later separation of the Sanctus from the Benedictus came about, according to Jungmann, because the greater length of the polyphonic Sanctus caused it to last until the Consecration, the Benedictus being sung during the rest of the Canon.

[3] There are over five hundred extant, all in two parts except about twelve, which are in three. The most comprehensive anthology of sacred music of the period (Florence, Biblioteca Laurenziana, Pluteus 29, Codex 1) con-tains four hundred and sixty-two.

tenor part played on an organ, or vocalized to the syllable of the neuma, or performed by a combination of voices and instruments. The choice would no doubt depend on the resources and customs of the particular church.

This theory of the 'independent' origin and use of the clausulae and of the place of their performance in the ritual makes it unnecessary to assume that at some later time the clausula and its successor the motet ceased to be inserted in the responds and entered on a separate existence. Having established its musical method and style and its position in the liturgy, the clausula could pass quite naturally to the next stage in its history, in which it became a motet by the addition of words to its upper part or parts. This development presented no new problem to the inheritors of the technique of writing sequences, proses and tropes to pre-existing neumae. The effect was to give a clausula closer relevance to the feast by enlarging on some aspect of its subject in poetic form. The Notre Dame corpus includes examples of the motet in this first period of its history, when it was a two-part clausula rewritten with words added to the upper part (*duplum*), or a three-part clausula with words added to the duplum or different words to both duplum and triplum. The simultaneous singing of two sets of words[1] became a characteristic of the motet of the thirteenth and fourteenth centuries, and this, together with the fact that it was based on a plainsong neuma which was rhythmically contrasted with the upper parts, distinguished it from the conductus, which always held to the descant style. In the course of the thirteenth century the use of both genres was extended to extra-liturgical and to secular spheres.

The manuscripts of the second half of the thirteenth century on the continent contain many new motets, but no new clausulae, unless one includes in that category an interesting group of apparently instrumental 'motets',[2] one of which bears the title '*In saeculum* veillatoris'.[3] On the assumption that the sacred motet inherited directly the place in the ritual which has been

---

[1] The idea had been anticipated in a Benedicamus in the St. Martial music in which the upper part was given its own words. See Reese, *Music in the Middle Ages*, p. 266.

[2] *Cent Motets du XIIIᵉ Siècle*, Nos. CIII–CVIII.

[3] I.e., 'of the viol-player'.

proposed for the clausula, the place of the various forms of polyphony sung on festivals in the thirteenth century could be tabulated thus:

SERVICE	FORM OF POLYPHONY	PLACE IN RITUAL
Vespers	Respond	After Lesson
	Benedicamus, or Benedicamus trope, or Benedicamus substitute, i.e., Conductus	At end of service
Matins	Third or Ninth respond	
Lauds	Benedicamus, etc., as at Vespers	As at Vespers
Mass	Gradual	Between Epistle and Gospel
	Alleluia	„ „ „
	Clausulae and/or Motets	After Sanctus

Although this scheme may be valid as a general framework, it is almost certainly too rigid to comprise the diversities of actual practice. For example, a certain number of clausulae and motets were composed on neumae from the responds of the office. The clausulae on office responds form a comparatively small proportion of the clausula repertory, amounting to about sixty of the four hundred and sixty-two in the Florence manuscript.[1] The neumae of these 'office' clausulae could have been derived either from the neumae of responds of the office, or from those Benedicamus melodies which had earlier been derived from the same neumae.[2] The clausulae, and later the motets, whose tenors were taken from office responds were probably sung as Benedicamus substitutes on feasts to which they were appropriate. It is remarkable that no clausulae were derived from the office responds of the three days after Christmas, of the Circumcision or of the week after Easter, perhaps

[1] Ludwig, *Repertorium*, pp. 79, 83, 84, 90, 92. In the two cycles attributed to Pérotin or his time only one office respond appears as a source of a neuma. This is the Christmas respond *Descendit de caelis*, and it may be noted that Midnight Mass followed directly after Matins, separating it from Lauds, and that the Notre Dame corpus has no settings of the Gradual or Alleluia for that Mass.

[2] Clausulae on the *flos filius* melody did, in fact, arise in both of these ways; in the Florence manuscript there is one *flos filius* clausula in a series derived from the *Stirps Jesse* respond, grouped in the manuscript with the Mass clausulae (Ludwig, p. 83), and eight, which are cued *Domino*, in a group of Benedicamus settings (ibid., p. 67). See also the transcriptions in *Historical Anthology*, i, pp. 24–7.

because the services on these days were already well provided with Benedicamus tropes or substitutes.

The extent of the interchange of Benedicamus substitutes of the offices with clausulae and motets of the Mass hinges in part on the practical difference, which is bound up with the stylistic difference, between a conductus and a clausula or motet. A conductus was primarily intended for vocal performance and was therefore better adapted to singing in choir, which was normal, though not invariable, for the Benedicamus. All the parts of a clausula or motet could also be sung, the parts without words being vocalized, but the style was better suited to performance by instruments in the case of a clausula, and by voices and an instrument, normally an organ, in the case of a motet. It may be assumed that instruments would not be introduced into the actual choir, and that music which included instruments would be performed in a gallery or pulpitum. In England, and possibly also in France,[1] the most important musical items of the Mass, the Gradual and Alleluia, were sung in the pulpitum, and this would naturally follow for the motet also. Grandisson's licence to the musicians of Exeter to perform polyphony in place of the Benedicamus at Vespers and after the Sanctus at Mass lends support to our table. On the other hand, references in the body of his Ordinal show that polyphony in place of the Benedicamus on Easter Day was performed in the pulpitum.[2]

Characteristics of English Polyphony

Remains of English polyphonic music during the period of these important developments in France are extremely scant. Apart from the setting of *Dicant nunc* already mentioned, the only twelfth-century polyphony is a group of pieces[3] whose musical style and liturgical types seem to belong to a stage of

---

[1] The use of the pulpitum at Bayeux was similar to that in the English secular rites. See Frere, 'The Connexion between English and Norman Rites', p. 36.

[2] See above, p. 111, n. 2.

[3] On fly-leaves in Cambridge, University Library, MS. Ff. 1.17; facsimiles in *Early English Harmony*, pls. 25–30. The contents are described in Ludwig, *Repertorium*, pp. 328 sqq.

development between the St. Martial music and that of the Notre Dame corpus, and to derive from the French tradition rather than the earlier English one of the Winchester tropes. It includes three conductus to precede a lesson,[1] a three-part *Verbum patris humanatur O O*[2] which would make a particularly joyful substitute for the second Benedicamus when *Verbum patris hodie* was sung for the first, and three Benedicamus tropes, one of which, *Regis civis potentia*, is for St. Stephen's day. Another is remarkable for the breaking of the word *Domino* by the trope, thus: *Benedicamus domi Spiritus almi gratia renovati Spiritus alme illustrator omnino*, while the third is a very curious experiment in the form of a *quodlibet* in which a number of plainsong extracts, with their words, are quoted in the course of an upper part to the *flos filius* melody of the Benedicamus. The quotations are so arranged that each syllable of *Benedicamus Domino* is matched by the same syllable occurring at the same time in the upper part.[3] The same pages also contain the earliest known version of the Christmas song *Ad cantus laetitiae*, which was widely known throughout the Middle Ages. It is an early example of exchange of parts, for the melody of the lower part is the same for two lines and the parts exchange for the third line.[4]

There are many indications that French and English polyphony in the thirteenth century were closely associated, and that some English churches adopted French music of the time. The secular motet, however, found no place in England, and there is no trace of any anthologies corresponding to the great Montpellier manuscript in France, in which secular motets are greatly in the majority.[5] The chief surviving evidence of the wholesale adoption of French music is a collection made for

[1] *Exsultemus et laetemur Nicholaum* (which is transcribed in *Oxford History of Music*, 1st ed., i, p. 313) has the words 'iube domne dicat lector' and a refrain with French words; *In natali novi regis* ends with 'Data benedictione lectionem incipe'; and *Hoc in sollemnio* ends with 'dic iube domne'.

[2] The beginning is transcribed in *New Oxford History of Music*, ii, p. 304.

[3] They include *Amborum sacrum spiramen* . . . (from the Kyrie *Cunctipotens genitor*), *Lux et decus* . . . (from the respond *Descendit de caelis*), *O crux ave* (from the hymn *Vexilla regis*), the opening of the hymn *Veni creator Spiritus*, and the beginning of *Verbum patris hodie*.

[4] As in the sixteenth-century version, printed in *Piae Cantiones*, No. XIII.

[5] Facsimile, transcriptions and commentary in *Polyphonies du XIIIe siècle*.

the Augustinian Priory of St. Andrew's,[1] which contains a considerable proportion of the Notre Dame corpus but no motets.[2] This exclusion of motets may well have been deliberate, because the writer included six motets without their tenors, thus effectively turning them into conductus capable of purely vocal performance.[3] At the end of the office responds there are domestic items in the form of two responds of St. Andrew, *Vir perfecte* and *Vir iste*, and at the end of the manuscript there is an indigenous section of music for Masses of the Virgin, comprising Alleluias (but no Graduals),[4] Sequences, Offertories, and settings of troped parts of the Ordinary. These pieces are of great interest as the first comprehensive scheme, and the only surviving scheme until some two centuries afterwards, of part-music for the Lady-Mass.[5] Elsewhere in the manuscript there are other settings of the Sanctus and Agnus Dei which are probably also 'insular', since there is nothing to correspond to them in the French music of the period.

The St. Andrew's music for the Lady-Mass, which is all for two voices with the plainsong in the lower part, may be illustrated by the Alleluia *Post partum*[6] (see facing page). The style is modelled on that of the French responds in the earlier part of the manuscript, though it is less elaborate, while the treatment of the neuma on *genitrix* shows the same impulse towards rhythmic order in the tenor as did the descant sections

[1] Now in Wolfenbüttel, Ducal Library, MS. 677; facsimile in *An Old St. Andrew's Music Book*. Catalogue of its conductus in Gröninger, *Repertoire-Untersuchungen*, pp. 64–87.

[2] Anonymous IV, writing *c.* 1275, did not mention motets, though he cited several clausulae by name; Walter Odington, writing *c.* 1316, discussed the motet with an example.

[3] Ludwig, *Repertorium*, p. 35; *New Oxford History of Music*, ii, p. 359.

[4] Cf. page 286, n. 3, below.

[5] It does not agree with the later Sarum ritual for the Lady-Mass, though there are features in common. Only one of the Kyrie tropes, *Rex virginum* (which is transcribed in *Historical Anthology*, No. 37), is also in Sarum, but the melodies of four others correspond thus: St. Andrew's No. 3, *Lux et gloria*, to the Sarum *Lux et origo*; St. Andrew's No. 4, *Kyrie virginei lux*, to the Sarum *Rex genitor*; St. Andrew's No. 6, *Kyrie virginitatis amor*, to the Sarum *Fons bonitatis*; and St. Andrew's No. 7, *Conditor Mariae*, to the Sarum *Conditor Kyrie*. Four of the nine St. Andrew's Alleluias are in the Sarum Lady-Mass cycle, while seven of the fifteen sequences are also in Sarum, and two others are in the York use.

[6] *An Old St. Andrew's Music Book*, fo. 181, which also gives the plainsong.

Ex. 7.

of the French responds. This manner of disposing a neuma in a recurring rhythmic pattern was adopted in the clausula and continued in the motet, and thereafter until the mid-fifteenth century one of the distinguishing features of a motet was a form based on the rhythm and proportion of the tenor.

Other evidence of the importation of French music in the thirteenth century includes a few leaves containing known French pieces which have chanced to survive,[1] and inventories of the service-books belonging to St. Paul's Cathedral and to the chapel of Edward I. The St. Paul's list, which was made in 1295, contains four books of polyphonic music and gives a word-cue from the beginning and end of each by which it could be identified.[2] One of the four began with *Viderunt*, which was the first of the responds of the Mass in the French series, and another began with *Austro terris* and ended with *Transgressus legem Domini*, two conductus in the French corpus, both of which are in the St. Andrew's manuscript. A note of the contents of Edward I's chapel in 1299–1300 has two books of polyphonic music (*de cantu organi*), one of which began with *Viderunt* and the other with *Alleluya*.[3]

In one instance the adoption of French music took the form of the incorporation of a French motet in an *Alleluia* written by an English composer. In a setting of the Alleluia *Nativitas* which is presumed to be the Pérotin setting mentioned by Anonymous IV there is a descant section on the words *ex semine*, which was abstracted and made into a motet by adding a text beginning *Ex semine Abrahae divino moderamine* to the duplum and one beginning *Ex semine rosa prodit spine* to the triplum. When the English composer of a setting of the same Alleluia, which is in the surviving fragments of a collection of polyphony associated with Worcester Cathedral,[4] came to the words *ex semine*, having worked independently of Pérotin's setting up to that point, he copied the music of the motet and put the *Ex semine Abrahae* text under his score, intending it to be sung to the duplum or, more probably, to both of the upper parts. It has been suggested that he was the first to put words to the

---

[1] Two leaves bound in at the front of the printed book Wood 591 in the Bodleian Library contain two conductus and portions of a third which are also in the St. Andrew's manuscript. Two leaves bound in at the back of the book contain English music; see below, p. 139, n. 3.

[2] Printed in Dugdale, *History of St. Paul's*, pp. 310–35. A St. Paul's inventory of 1245, printed in Simpson, 'Two Inventories of St. Paul's', contains no books of polyphony.

[3] Cited from the Wardrobe Book in Stevens, *The Mulliner Book*, p. 12, n. 7.

[4] See *Worcester Mediaeval Harmony*, pp. 80–1. The complete page is reproduced in *Cent Motets du XIIIe Siècle*, ii, pl. II.

ex semine passage,[1] but in view of the date (*c.* 1275–1300 or later) and style of the Worcester music this does not seem likely. The case is rather one of quotation from the point of view of the music[2] and of troping with an existing text from the point of view of the ritual.

In his discussion of contemporary methods of musical notation Anonymous IV gave the names of the foremost composers and teachers in France, including among them an Englishman (*alius ANGLICUS*) who 'used the English method of notation and also, to a certain extent, of teaching'.[3] After mentioning other French masters he went on to say that 'there were good singers in England, and they sang exceeding sweetly, among them Master *Johannes filius Dei*, Makeblite at Winchester and Blaksmit at the court of the last King Henry'.[4] The name of *Johannes filius Dei* appears in the St. Paul's inventory, where one of the Tropers was noted as having been willed by him.[5]

Although England took so much from France in the thirteenth century, the cross-channel traffic in music was not altogether a one-way affair. The Montpellier manuscript contains a pair of motets[6] which were almost certainly written by an English composer, and which have survived in part in the remains of an English manuscript.[7] They are based on a tenor from the sequence *Epiphaniam Domino canamus gloriosam*[8] for the Epiphany, the words of the part from which the melody was taken being *Balaam de quo vaticinans* . . . and, continuing for the

---

[1] Aubry (op. cit., ii, p. 15, n. 2) cited the Worcester piece as confirmation of Wilhelm Mayer's thesis of the origin of the motet from the neumae of organum. It cannot, however, be considered as evidence for the replacement of sections in organum by clausulae (or motets) written later.

[2] Instances of quotation in the composition of conductus have been discussed in Schrade, 'Political Compositions in French Music', and in Bukofzer, 'Interrelations between Conductus and Clausula'.

[3] Coussemaker, *Scriptores*, i, p. 344.   [4] Henry III (d. 1272).

[5] 'Item Troperium bonum quod legavit Johannes filius Dei.' (His 'ligavit' amended to 'legavit' by Bodleian MS. Ashmole 845.) Dugdale, *History of St. Paul's*, p. 324.

[6] Transcriptions in *Polyphonies du XIIIᵉ siècle*, iii, pp. 258–62.

[7] Oxford, New College, MS. 362 has the duplum part of the two motets written as for a single piece. See *El Còdex de Las Huelgas*, i, pp. 229–31; *Polyphonies du XIIIᵉ siècle*, iv, p. 90, n. 4. For a discussion of the contents of this manuscript, see *New Oxford History of Music*, iii, Chap. 4.

[8] Music in Handschin, 'Trope, Sequence and Conductus', pp. 156–7.

second motet, *Huic magi munera.* . . . . It was quite unusual to use the chant of a sequence for the tenor of a motet,[1] but the reason in this case may be that the melody of the *Balaam* verse from this sequence was used for the singing of the Benedicamus with Alleluia at both Vespers and at Matins of the Epiphany in the Sarum use.[2] Hence the motets were probably used as Benedicamus substitutes at those services. For their musical design both pieces make use of the *rondellus* technique in the upper parts, whereby one singer repeats the words and melody of the other.[3] Thus one poem served for both singers, which was abnormal in the motet. This kind of continuous interchange between parts has long been recognized as an English trait. It is found also in another Montpellier piece, *Alle psallite cum luya*,[4] which occurs in the Worcester collection with words beginning *Ave magnifica Maria.*[5] The tenor is not a plainsong neuma, though it has a rather vague connection with the Alleluia *Post partum* for the Vigil of the Annunciation.[6] The

---

[1] Other cases are the Easter sequences *Mane prima sabbati* (Montpellier No. 51; the text of its triplum is in the Worcester music at fo. 27v) and *Victimae paschali laudes* (Montpellier No. 174). There may be some connection between these choices and the fact that there was a Balaam episode in the Epiphany *Prophetae* play (Chambers, *Mediaeval Stage*, ii, pp. 54–5) and that the two Easter sequences were sung in some forms of the Easter Visitation play (*Polyphonies du XIII*ᵉ *siècle*, iv, p. 186, n. 3).

[2] 'Et cantus hujus versus Balaam dicatur super *Benedicamus* cum *Alleluya* ad utrasque vesperas et ad matutinas secundum usum Sarum Ecclesiae.' *Missale Sarum*, cols. 85–6, n. The melody appears as Benedicamus No. 21 in Rylands Library, MS. Lat. 24. The words of an earlier motet on this tenor, the opening of which is transcribed in Besseler, *Musik des Mittelalters*, p. 122, are a satire on English ways; the text of the duplum begins: 'Balaam! Goudalier ont bien auran Lour tuns pour la goudale Ke chascuns embale Ke en sont engliskeman.' Raynaud, *Receuil de Motets*, ii, p. 68.

[3] Odington defined rondellus thus: 'Et si quod unus cantat omnes per ordinem recitent vocatur hic cantus Rondellus, id est, rotabilis vel circumductus; et hoc vel cum littera vel sine littera sit'. Coussemaker, *Scriptores*, i, p. 245. Odington's example may be seen in the facsimile in *Early English Harmony*, pl. 41.

[4] Montpellier No. 339; transcription also in *Historical Anthology*, i, p. 35.

[5] Facsimile in *Worcester Mediaeval Harmony*, p. 71. A descriptive catalogue and complete transcriptions of the Worcester music have recently been printed in *The Worcester Fragments*.

[6] Dittmer, 'An English Discantuum Volumen', p. 31. See also Handschin, 'The Summer Canon', for a discussion of these pieces and of a number of English 'suspects' in Montpellier.

piece is followed in the manuscript by a setting of a troped form of that verse, and was most probably written as a 'prelude trope' to the Alleluia. As we shall see, there are other examples in the Worcester music of this treatment of the beginning of the Alleluia.

An index to a lost collection of polyphonic music which belonged to Reading Abbey, contained in the same manuscript as the famous canon 'Sumer is icumen in', is a further indication that English composers were creating their own liturgical polyphony in the second half of the thirteenth century.[1] The heading of the index contains the name W. de Winton, who in 1276 was a monk of the Priory of Leominster (Herefordshire), a dependency of Reading Abbey, and was later (1284) at Reading. He was probably the composer of the first group of pieces, with the exception of the initial item, a setting of the Gloria trope *Spiritus et alme* which has the name of R. de Burg[ate], Abbot of Reading from 1268 to 1290, as its composer.[2] The other pieces in the group are two settings of the Gloria trope *Regnum tuum solidum*, one of a trope of *Virgo Dei genitrix* (probably the verse of the Gradual *Benedicta et venerabilis es* for the Vigil of the Assumption), and four troped Alleluias for Commemorations of the Virgin. The second group of pieces consisted of Alleluias for various feasts and for Commemorations of the Virgin, at the head of which is the name W. de Wicumbe. William de Wicumbe, or de Winchecumbe,[3] was a monk of Reading who spent four years at Leominster, where he was precentor for part of that time, and where he wrote a number of manuscripts for the library and choir, including a treatise on music, a book of Lady-Masses, and two rolls, one containing polyphony in three parts, the other containing two-part music.[4] The third section of the Reading index lists the

[1] Printed with commentary in Ludwig, *Repertorium*, pp. 267–78. The provenance and date of the manuscript (British Museum, Harl. 978) were further discussed in Bukofzer, 'Sumer is icumen in'; Schofield, 'The Provenance and Date of "Sumer is Icumen in"'; and Handschin, 'The Summer Canon'.

[2] Schofield, 'The Provenance and Date of "Sumer is Icumen in"', p. 83.

[3] See Dittmer, 'An English Discantuum Volumen', p. 37. At Winchcombe (Gloucestershire) there was a small Benedictine Abbey.

[4] 'Scripsit eciam librum ad Missam de Sancta Maria super proprium pergamenum suum. Scripsit eciam compotum optimum cum quodam

conductus,[1] and the last four sections the motets, which are divided into *Moteti cum una littera et duplici nota*, presumably for tenor and a duplum with words, and *Moteti cum duplici littera*, for tenor and both duplum and triplum with words. As far as can be judged from their titles, the conductus and motets in this lost manuscript were indigenous compositions, and had little or no connection with the French repertory of the period.

The surviving music of the Worcester collection comes into the same general categories as those of the Reading index. For the Ordinary of the Mass there are settings of troped forms of the Kyrie, Gloria (*Regnum tuum* is the only one remaining) and Sanctus, and of the Gloria and Agnus Dei without tropes. Music for the Proper includes troped settings of the Introit *Salve sancta parens*, of the Gradual verse *Virgo Dei genitrix*, and of a number of Alleluias. From the evidence of the Worcester and other fragments[2] and the Reading index it is possible to distinguish three stages in the elaboration of the polyphonic Alleluia. William de Wicumbe's Alleluias in the Reading list were apparently settings of the soloists' parts of the chants, as in the earlier French examples and the St. Andrew's Lady-Masses. The Worcester fragments have several Alleluias in which words are added to the upper parts, a procedure which may be termed 'parallel' troping since the words of the trope are sung simultaneously with the words of the ritual.[3] An example is the Easter Day Alleluia *Pascha nostrum*, where the plainsong of the verse is set out motet-wise in the tenor in

tractatu de musica. . . . Scripsit eciam duas rotulas unam continentem triplices cantus organ' numero. Aliam continentem duplices cantus numero.' Schofield, 'The Provenance and Date of "Sumer is Icumen in" ', p. 84.

[1] This section does not contain the titles of the conductus which have survived in the fly-leaves of a Reading manuscript (Bodley 257) in the Bodleian Library.

[2] E.g., Bodleian Library, MS. Rawl. c.400*. For the most recent discussion of possible concordances between these and other contemporary sources, see Dittmer, 'An English Discantuum Volumen', pp. 36–45.

[3] The beginning of a Sanctus set in this way is printed in Walker, *History of Music in England*, p. 12. Another example in the Worcester collection is a setting of the prose *Inviolata*, itself a trope of the respond *Gaude Maria virgo*; transcription in *Worcester Mediaeval Harmony*, p. 95.

the same pattern as was the neuma *genitrix* in our previous example:[1]

Ex.8.

It was this practice, which may be viewed as the application of the method of the mid-thirteenth century motet to the early thirteenth century respond, which gave the composer of the Worcester Alleluia *Nativitas* the opportunity of quoting the French *Ex semine* motet in the course of his setting. While the quoting seems to be unique the method of troping is a special case, and perhaps an earlier stage, of this English practice.

The final stage of troping elaboration, which like the 'motet' stage seems to be a peculiarly English and monastic practice, involved the composition of prelude tropes to the soloists' beginning of the Alleluia, prelude and parallel tropes for the verse, and sometimes a 'substitute' trope for the soloists' repeat of the Alleluia.[2] The prelude trope to the Alleluia commonly

---

[1] Bodleian Library, MS. Lat. liturg. d.20, fos. 13v–14; transcription in *Worcester Mediaeval Harmony*, p. 73. I have treated the rhythm as first mode.

[2] In the only case of a substitute trope noted so far, the trope is a rondellus,

used rondellus technique, as in *Ave magnifica Maria*, the tenor of which has the cue *Alle*. Another instance is the rondellus *Alleluia psallat*,[1] also in the Worcester fragments, which appears to be a prelude trope to the Alleluia *Virga Jesse floruit virgo*, for it leads into a setting of the opening notes of that Alleluia, which would be followed in turn by the choir's singing of the complete Alleluia in plainsong. The prelude trope to the verse was usually brief, though it could be somewhat extended and also take the form of a rondellus.[2] In the tenor of the verse the plainsong could be treated in a freely-conceived rhythm, rather than in a repeated pattern as in *Pascha nostrum*. While the most elaborate forms of troping seem to have been reserved for the Alleluia, parallel troping was applied to the Introit *Salve sancta parens*, to the Gradual *Benedicta et venerabilis*, possibly to the Offertory *Felix namque*,[3] to the Gloria and Sanctus, and in one surviving case to the Christmas respond *Descendit de caelis*.[4]

Motets are the largest single group in the Worcester collection, and the orthodox method of composition may be exemplified in *Virginis Mariae laudemus praeconia—Salve gemma virginum —Veritatem*:[5]

Ex.9.

The rhythmic pattern (*ordo*) of the tenor, which is the neuma

and an alternative setting of the Alleluia 'In Fine' is provided, marked 'vel si brevitas ipsare deposcit dicatur sic'. The piece, the Christmas Alleluia *Dies sanctificatus*, is transcribed in Dittmer, 'An English Discantuum Volumen', where a number of Alleluias of this kind in MS. Rawl. c.400* are reconstructed and discussed.

[1] Transcribed in *Worcester Mediaeval Harmony*, p. 83, and in *Historical Anthology*, p. 61.

[2] As in the Alleluia *Assumpta est*, transcribed in Dittmer, 'An English Discantuum Volumen', p. 53.

[3] See *Worcester Mediaeval Harmony*, p. 86.

[4] Transcription in Dittmer, 'An English Discantuum Volumen', p. 55.

[5] Worcester, Chapter Library, MS. Add. 68, No. xiii; transcription in *Worcester Mediaeval Harmony*, p. 107.

veritatem from the Gradual *Propter veritatem* for the feast of the
Assumption, is the same as in the two previous examples, and
was one of the commonest *ordines* of the period. There are some
four-part motets; either two or three parts have words, and in
the former case the *quartus cantus*, without words, is structurally
an auxiliary part to the tenor. Among the Worcester conductus
are some in simple descant style[1] and others in more extended
form and less simple style, usually with vocalized sections. Rondellus technique was commonly used in vocalized sections, and
might also be applied to the setting of a verse.[2] *Salve mater
misericordiae*, a conductus of the second half of the thirteenth
century,[3] shows a variety of treatments of this kind. The first
verse is set in normal conductus style, without extension,
beginning:

Ex. 10.

Sal - ve ma - ter mi-se - ri - - cor - di - ae, _____

while the second begins with an introductory rondellus on the
first syllable:

Ex. 11.

Quae _____

[1] See below, p. 150.   [2] As in *De supernis sedibus*, ibid., p. 135.
[3] On end-leaves in the binding of the printed book Bodleian Library
Wood 591, a copy of William Painter's *The Pallace of Pleasure Beautified*
(London, Thomas Marsh, 1569), which belonged to Anthony Wood. The
piece is incomplete at the beginning, but fortunately the missing opening
is in Oxford, Corpus Christi College, MS. 489, No. 22.

Each of its first two lines is a rondellus:

the second ending with a short *cauda*, and the other two lines are a rondellus of two phrases ending with a longer rondellus-*cauda*:

PLATE XI

15. Ottery St. Mary: pulpitum in the Lady-chapel

16. Positive organ of the early fourteenth century

17. Plymtree Parish Church, Devon: chancel screen and loft

PLATE XII

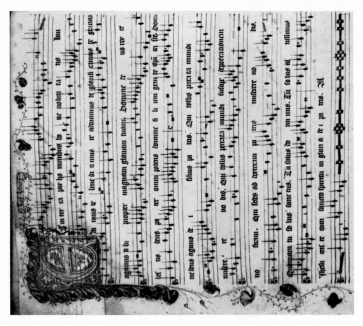

19. Cantus part of Roy Henry's *Gloria in excelsis*

18. King Henry IV (1367-1413)

Although its texture is continuous this last section is, in fact, designed as a *rota* (canon),[1] since the parts enter successively with a melody which overlaps in rota fashion.[2]

Rondellus-motet and Rondellus-conductus

The persistence of rondellus technique is one of the most characteristic features of English polyphony of the thirteenth and early fourteenth centuries, and the variety of its applications led to composition in forms which lie on the border-line between motet and conductus. In such cases it seems to have acted as a catalyst which broke down the traditional distinctions and brought about new combinations of technical and formal methods. Its origins may possibly have some connection with the form of troping common to both sequence and prose, in which each phrase of a melody was repeated to supply the music for paired verses. It may well be that it became customary for the singers to exchange parts in the paired verses when

[1] This term does not appear in extant treatises, but was used in the manuscript of 'Sumer is icumen in'; see below, p. 142.

[2] Compare the opening section of *Fulget caelestis curiae*, an extended rondellus-conductus, transcribed and discussed in Bukofzer, 'Sumer is icumen in', pp. 98 sqq.

such forms were set in two-part polyphony, but at present this can only be surmise. Examples of interchange of parts within the verse of a hymn have been referred to in the cases of *Nunc sancte nobis spiritus* and *Ad cantus laetitiae*. In the pair of pieces on the tenor *Balaam* rondellus technique was applied to the composition of a motet. The tenor of such a piece must be set out in the form of repeated phrases *a a b b c c* . . . in order to allow for the interchanging of the upper parts. The *Balaam* melody was in that form as it stood, being part of a sequence,[1] but in such Worcester examples as *Ave magnifica Maria* the tenor is generally in shorter phrases, and must either have been adapted from plainsong or composed for its purpose, as in a conductus.

The most famous piece of English thirteenth-century music, 'Sumer is icumen in',[2] is written in the form of a four-part rota superimposed on a two-part rondellus. Its composition involved, in effect, the writing of twelve separate melodies over the 'ground' sung by the two-part *pes*.[3] When the canon is sung by four singers, as the manuscript suggests, these melodies form nine successive two-bar phrases from the time all the singers have entered until they begin to drop out. Hence the first four melodies must be independent, while the others may be variations or combinations of these four provided that two close variants of the same melody do not fall in the same group of four. In addition, each melody and variation must be a good counterpoint to the lower part of the *pes*, and the variations must be so ordered that their performance makes a satisfactory melody as a whole.[4] It is a measure of the composer's artistry that he succeeded in realizing these technical requirements in a piece of such enduring charm and attractiveness.

The 'Summer Canon' is the only known six-part piece earlier than the fifteenth century and the only known example of the combination of rota and rondellus. Though long regarded as

---

[1] The composer used the melody of each verse four times, rather than the twice of the sequence itself.

[2] Facsimile as frontispiece to Grove, *Dictionary of Music*, vii.

[3] This term is sometimes used in the Worcester music for the tenor.

[4] No part makes parallel octaves or unisons with the lower part of the *pes*. The form of the melody is $4 + 4 + 2 + 4 + 4 + 6 = 24$ bars; with three two-bar sections for entering the length of the complete piece is 30 bars.

something of a miracle, its position is rather that of a special case of a peculiarly English technique. The manuscript has a sacred poem celebrating the Resurrection, *Perspice christicola*,[1]

Ex. 14.

[1] The Easter Day sequence *Fulgens praeclara* contains the verse 'Perspice christicolas, qualiter laeti canunt inclyta redemptori carmina'. *Missale Sarum*, col. 361.

written in red ink below the secular words, which are written
in black ink. It has generally been assumed that the secular
text is the original one, though there is no trace of any established art of secular composition to which such a piece could
have belonged. It has not, however, been noticed before that
the lower part of the *pes* is the first five notes of *Regina caeli*,
the special Mary-antiphon of the Easter season, in the same
notation as they are written in the plainsong. This cannot easily
be coincidence, for it is safe to say that no medieval musician
hearing or seeing these notes under an Eastertide poem would
fail to connect them with the beginning of the antiphon. From
the points of view of its technique and its character as a sacred
piece the 'Summer Canon' could properly be described as the
rota-rondellus-motet *Perspice christicola*—Pes duplex *Regina caeli*
(see Ex. 14).

Thomas gemma Cantuariae—Thomas caesus in Doveria,[1] a somewhat later work (*c.* 1300), written in praise of St. Thomas of
Canterbury and Thomas de la Hale (d. 1295) of Dover Priory,
has an ingenious combination of rondellus and variation techniques. In its general style it is a motet, but it is not based on
plainsong. In form it consists of twenty-seven sections, each a
variant of a basic phrase, with an introduction and a coda.
The phrase is varied by interchange between the two tenors and
between the two upper parts, by simple ornamentation, and
by the writing of new melodies:[2]

Ex. 15.

[1] In Princeton University, MS. Garrett 119, and, in part, on leaves which
have been considered to belong to the Worcester collection; see Hughes,
Medieval Polyphony, p. 38. Discussion and transcription in Levy, 'New
Material on the Early Motet in England'.

[2] Transcription from ibid., pp. 234–6; a few notes in the parts on the
second staff have been supplied by the transcriber.

145

A more extended use of the method of rondellus may be seen in one of a pair of pieces of the early fourteenth century, presumably from the Abbey of St. Edmund at Bury, both of which are based on the antiphon of St. Edmund *Ave rex gentis Anglorum*.[1] One of the pair is in the normal form of a motet, having two parts with different texts, *Deus tuorum militum* (not identical with the hymn which has that beginning) and *De flore martyrum*, over the first two phrases of the antiphon sung twice in the same rhythm.[2] The other, which is for four voices, is a Benedicamus substitute[3] written in a form which may be called rondellus-motet since it is based on plainsong, though it has the equalized rhythm of all the parts and the single set of words which are characteristic of a conductus. The two tenor parts sing in rondellus fashion the successive phrases of the antiphon, which has the same melody as the Mary-antiphon *Ave regina caelorum, mater regis angelorum*, while the upper parts alternate with the sections of the poem *Ave miles*, set in sequence fashion. The joins between the sections are most cleverly managed, and the piece ends with an 'Amen' based on the first difference of the first mode.[4]

This application of rondellus technique to the design of a piece based on plainsong arrives at a style which is virtually indistinguishable from that of the extended conductus of the same period. In *Ovet mundus laetabundus*,[5] for example, the rondellus idea is applied to each verse of the poem by means of an interchanged repeat of each verse in the upper parts, while the lower parts repeat their music, indicated by *recita* in the manuscript, without interchange. Here it is evident that the principle of composition based on the lowest part no longer holds, for the setting of the words must have preceded the writing of the other parts:

---

[1] Discussion and transcriptions in Bukofzer, *Studies in Medieval Music*, Chap. I.

[2] The tenor part 'is noteworthy for the incipient isorhythmic structure'. Ibid., p. 22.

[3] The penultimate verse ends 'Benedicamus devote Domino', and the last verse ends 'dignas laudes referre Domino'.

[4] Written in the manuscript as Euouae, the vowels of *saeculorum Amen*, which were used as an abbreviation under the notes of a difference.

[5] Bodleian Library, MS. Hatton 81, fos. IV, 44.

Ex. 16.

In contrast to the cultivation of border-line forms in England, the motet in France pursued a consistent course from its origins in the thirteenth century to the adoption of isorhythm in the early fourteenth and the full mastery of isorhythmic design in the motets of Guillaume de Machaut (d. 1377) and his successors. The appearance of isorhythmic motets in England in the second half of the fourteenth century is sure evidence of renewed contact with French music, and from the early fifteenth century to the death of Dunstable in 1453 forms based on isorhythm were constantly practised by English composers. The main features of the isorhythmic motet were the use in the upper parts of a wide range of note-lengths (large, long, breve, semibreve and minim) and the development and expansion of the lay-out of the tenor, which was now a phrase of plainsong rather than a neuma. It was disposed in a correspondingly

147

longer rhythmic scheme (*talea*) which was repeated once or
more in shorter notes of the same relative lengths as those of the
first statement, that is, in isorhythm with diminution. While in
the thirteenth century the rhythmic order of the tenor had been
the basis of a single section in which one or more statements of a
neuma were set out in short patterns of equal rhythm, it now
became the basis of a form in which the several sections, each
based on a plainsong phrase (*color*), were of proportionate
lengths, governed by its progressive diminution. The former
principle might still operate within the latter, the lesser
rhythmic order continuing to exist within the greater, as may be
seen in the first section of *Omnis terra—Habenti dabitur*—Tenor
(unidentified):[1]

Ex.17.

(Tenor continues)

[1] In a group of leaves in the same binding as *Ave miles*, Bodleian Library,
MS. e Mus. 7, pp. 530-1. The music in this second group of leaves may

The tenor is divided into nine phrases which use three rhythmic patterns arranged in the order *a b a b a b c b c*. In the second section the tenor is repeated in the same rhythms diminished by half, so that the lengths of the sections are in the proportion two to one. The upper parts move throughout with clearly defined rhythms in notes ranging from semibreves to quaver triplets, and in the second section they enhance the quicker movement of the tenor with the mutual stop-and-go device known as hocket,[1] which was commonly used in the final section of a motet:[2]

Ex.18.

Descant in the Fourteenth Century

Richard Cotell ended his summary of the rules for improvising a descant on a plainsong[3] with the observation that it was

be of French origin, for several of the texts are French and one of the pieces appears with different words in manuscripts in Ivrea and Cambrai; see Hughes, *Medieval Polyphony*, p. 29.

[1] Or *truncatio*; 'ita quod dum unus pauset, alius non pauset, vel e contrario . . .; unde truncatio idem est quod hoketus'. *Quatuor Principalia*, in Coussemaker, *Scriptores*, iv, p. 296.

[2] I have discussed some other examples of rondellus and isorhythm in 'English Church Music in the Fourteenth Century', *New Oxford History of Music*, iii, Chap. 4.

[3] Printed in Bukofzer, *Geschichte des englischen Diskants*, pp. 141–3.

'feyr singing to syng many imperfite acordis togedyr descending or ascending with the playnsong and a perfite acorde folnande, as for to synge 3, 4 or 5 thyrdis togedyr with a 5 foln ande'. When composers used this recipe for making the simplest kind of two-part setting of a melody they used sixths ending with an octave rather than thirds followed by a fifth, and for a third part completed the sixths with a third and the octaves with a fifth. This method is found in a setting of the last verse *In te Domine* and final neuma of the *Te Deum*, in which the plainsong is in the lowest part.[1] Until the late fourteenth century, however, writing in simple descant style normally used parallel fifths and thirds as well as parallel sixths and thirds. The Worcester music contains examples of this method in a Gloria (beginning *Et in terra* since the celebrant began the Gloria)[2] and a conductus *Beata viscera* (not the same text as the Communion *Beata viscera*),[3] neither of which is based on plainsong, while the composer of a setting of the hymn *O lux beata Trinitas* of the second half of the fourteenth century put the plainsong in the highest part, slightly changed and ornamented:[4]

Ex. 19.

[1] *Geschichte des englishen Diskants*, Ex. 18, and Reese, *Music in the Middle Ages*, p. 399, dated thirteenth century, but fourteenth is more likely. The previous verse has the plainsong in the middle voice.

[2] *Worcester Mediaeval Harmony*, pp. 39–40, and *Historical Anthology*, i, p. 62.

[3] *Worcester Mediaeval Harmony*, p. 108.

[4] British Museum, MS. Sloane 1210, fo. 140.

Jam___ sol re - ce-dit___ ig - ne - us

In - fun - de lu - men cor - di - - bus.

In the late fourteenth century this technique was also being used in a less obvious way, in which the melodic line of the plainsong was shared by all the parts. This setting of the hymn *Conditor alme siderum* includes the neuma of the fourth mode:[1]

Ex. 20.

Plainsong

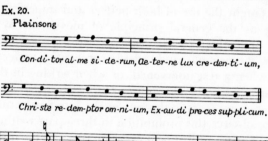

Con-di-tor al-me si-de-rum, Ae-ter-ne lux cre-den-ti-um,

Chri-ste re-dem-ptor om-ni-um, Ex-au-di pre-ces sup-pli-cum.

Con - di - tor al - me si - de-rum, Ae-ter - ne lux cre -

den - ti - um, Chri-ste re - dem-ptor om-ni-um, Ex - au - di

[1] Written *c.* 1400 in a Psalter, Collectar and Hymnal of *c.* 1200, Bodleian Library, MS. Laud lat. 95, fo. 133v. The book was probably of secular use, since the hymn *Salvator mundi* has the tune of *Veni creator.*

pre - ces sup - pli - cum.

Cotell remarked that 'the old techyng was that a man shal never take none imperfite acord bot if he hade a perfite after him, as after a 3 a 5 and after an 8 [*recte* 10] a 12 and after a 13 a 15, bot now it is levyd the techers of descant that after a 3 a man may take a 6 or after a 6 a man may take a 10'. Here Cotell was recalling a commonplace of the teaching of the thirteenth century, the working of which in composition may be seen in the Alleluia *Post partum* from the St. Andrew's manuscript quoted above (p. 131). The writer of *Quatuor Principalia* (1351) taught the use of both perfect and imperfect intervals, so long as the general principle of movement by contrary motion was observed (*ita quod quando tenor ascendit discantus descendet, et e contrario*), and forbade consecutive perfect intervals except when a rest intervened, or when writing in three parts (*nisi pausa intervenit, aut quando tres cantus simul modulantur*).[1] However, composers of descant in the late fourteenth century began to observe this prohibition in three-part writing, though consecutive fifths still appear occasionally until the mid-fifteenth century. The method of setting a plainsong in three-part descant during this period was to write a lower part ('counter') to the melody, using contrary motion in mixed intervals and parallel motion in imperfect intervals, the latter particularly at the approach to a cadence, and then to add the highest part.[2] An example of this technique is a late fourteenth-century setting, now incomplete, of the verse *Eructavit cor* and

[1] Coussemaker, *Scriptores*, iv, p. 281.
[2] The view that English descant was characterized by the use of plainsong in the lowest part (while continental *fauxbourdon* used it as the *cantus*), which was proposed by Bukofzer in his *Geschichte des englischen Diskants*, is not tenable. The musical evidence shows conclusively that the plainsong in English descant was normally the middle part. The descant treatises deal only with the teaching of extempore descanting by a single singer above or below the *cantus prius factus* according to his voice.

the *Gloria patri* of the respond *Regnum mundi* for feasts of a Virgin:[1]

Ex.21.

This method was also adopted for treating the ritual chants of the Mass. A group of settings of the Sanctus and Agnus Dei which have survived, in curious circumstances, on the back of a document in the Public Record Office shows that the rhythmic style could be quite simple, as in *Eructavit cor*, or moderately ornamental, with occasional groups of three quavers.[2] The adoption of the new descant style for the Ordinary of the Mass was an important development in the history of that form, which leads directly to the descant Mass settings of the Old Hall manuscript, to be discussed in the following chapter.

Polyphony to English Words

The few examples of early polyphony in the vernacular which have survived use elementary forms of motet and descant techniques. 'Worldes blisse have god day'[3] is a two-part motet in which the poem, a meditation on the Passion, is set

[1] From leaves in the fifteenth-century binding of an early fourteenth-century Psalter from Peterborough Abbey, Bodleian Library, MS. Barlow 22.

[2] See Stevens, 'A Recently Discovered English Source of the 14th Century'.

[3] Transcription in Bukofzer, 'The First Motet with English Words' pp. 232–3.

as a duplum over the *clementiam* melody of the Benedicamus, disposed in a recurring rhythmic pattern in the usual way, while 'Edi beo thu hevene quene'[1] and 'Jesu Cristes milde moder'[2] are simple two-part descants. The words of the last are a free translation of the York sequence *Stabat juxta Christi crucem*, which was later used with the Latin text as a votive antiphon. In all three pieces the parts are in the same range and cross frequently, and in 'Jesu Cristes milde moder' they keep very close company and cross continually, so that their movement is chiefly by alternation of thirds and unisons.

This method of composing a simple descant has usually been called 'gymel' (*gemellus*).[3] The word does not appear in English manuscripts until the late fifteenth century, where it marks the division of a part into two in a 'solo' section; nor was it explained by a theorist until the same period, when the Italian Guilielmus Monachus wrote of it (*c.* 1475) as a *modus Anglicorum*. What Guilielmus actually describes is the setting of a melody in continuous parallel thirds beginning and ending on a unison and crossing just before the cadence, or in parallel sixths beginning and ending on an octave. In either case a third part (*contra*) might be added using the third, fifth, octave or tenth below the melody, avoiding parallel movement and ending with a fifth going to the octave.[4] On the evidence of English sources, however, gymel means a pair of voices of equal range, and therefore written in the same clef. It may be applied to such early examples as *Dicant nunc Judei*[5] as well as to the three pieces under discussion, and had the same significance in the later manuscripts, such as the Eton choirbook, where the term 'semel' is also used in this sense. Our definition also holds for two instances in which the term is used in continental manuscripts. One is a two-part setting of the troping section of a *Sanctus* by Roullet in a manuscript at Munich.[6] In the other

[1] Transcription in Walker, *History of Music in England*, p. 10.

[2] Partial transcription in Reese, *Music in the Middle Ages*, p. 389.

[3] See ibid., pp. 388–90.

[4] Coussemaker, *Scriptores*, iii, pp. 289, 292–3; emendations in Bukofzer, *Geschichte des englischen Diskants*, pp. 153–4; facsimile in *Die Musik in Geschichte und Gegenwart*, v, Tafel 49.

[5] See above, p. 117.

[6] Quoted in Bukofzer, article 'Gymel' in *Die Musik in Geschichte und Gegenwart*.

an anonymous composer added two alternative parts to Dunstable's *O rosa bella*. They are marked 'Gimel' and 'alius Gimel', and each makes a gymel with the original cantus part.[1]

The normal method of three-part descant with the melody in the middle voice is used in a fourteenth-century setting of *Angelus ad virginem*,[2] which is mentioned by Chaucer in 'The Miller's Tale'. The same melody also exists in a thirteenth-century manuscript with both the Latin words and an English version beginning 'Gabriel from evene king'.[3]

The appearance of simple polyphony in the vernacular may well be connected with the early period (1224–*c*. 1300) of the ministry of the Franciscans in England. By the end of the thirteenth century the friars had largely turned from preaching to university studies and the founding of houses.[4] There are no surviving examples of polyphony to English words between the pieces we have mentioned and the polyphonic carols of the early fifteenth century.

---

[1] Transcription in *Denkmäler der Tonkunst in Österreich*, vii, p. 229. There seems no point in extending the term gymel to a duet of two parts in different clefs or to the normal English descant of the Old Hall manuscript, as Bukofzer did in *Studies in Mediaeval Music*, pp. 49, 135, etc.

[2] Transcription in Walker, *History of Music in England*, p. 14.

[3] Facsimile in *Early English Harmony*, pl. 34.

[4] Moorman, *Church Life in England*, Chaps. XXV–XXVI; Knowles, *The Religious Orders*, i, Chap. XVIII.

IV

THE INSTITUTIONS AND THE CULTIVATION OF POLYPHONY FROM 1400 TO THE REFORMATION

Polyphonic music in the early Middle Ages, and until the late fourteenth century, was sung by solo voices. The respond, Benedicamus and conductus were ceremonial elaborations or replacements of soloists' chants in the ritual, while the motet originated as a troping elaboration of a neuma from the soloists' part of a respond. The later Middle Ages saw the development of forms of polyphony in which the whole choir took part, as in the Mass and the votive antiphon, and of others in which polyphony sung by one side of the choir alternated with plainsong sung by the other side, as in the Magnificat and Hymn. The leaders of this movement towards choral polyphony were the more important colleges and collegiate churches, and the royal and aristocratic household chapels. The singers in these institutions formed a balanced choir, and there is good reason to assume that all of them were expected to be competent in polyphonic music. Though this was not a statutory or usual requirement in secular cathedrals, it became customary to support the singing of polyphonic antiphons and votive Masses by the more expert of the vicars and choristers in rotation. The greater monasteries also adopted this idea, instituting choirs of monks or clerks and choristers, under a secular or lay master, to sing votive polyphony in parts of the building which were open to the laity. In the older foundations, therefore, a balanced choir and choral music in the modern sense came into being in connection with the new forms of polyphony which were sung 'out of choir' in the ritual and physical sense. Late in the period polyphony on the chief festivals and in votive forms was cultivated in the larger parish churches, with singers hired either for the occasion or on an annual basis. During this period too the organ entered on a new phase in its history, taking an increasingly important part in the ritual music. More elaborate instruments were developed, and the performance of ritual polyphony on the organ became an established custom.

The musical remains of this period are fortunately more substantial than those of the preceding period, and include a fair number of complete, or almost complete, manuscripts. Their appearance reflects the growth of choral polyphony, for the more important manuscripts are increasingly larger until the early sixteenth century, when the Caius College manuscript, the largest surviving choirbook, measures twenty-eight and a quarter inches by nineteen inches. Separate part-books began to be adopted *c.* 1500–10, and became the normal way of writing and printing polyphonic music in the sixteenth century. Though the number of surviving manuscripts and fragments is not inconsiderable, the losses have been very great. Some idea of their nature and extent can be gained from inventories and accounts, while these and other documents help to reveal the part played by institutions of various kinds in the music of the time. Such sources also throw light on the place of the new forms of choral polyphony in the ritual and on the liturgical use of the organ, and in other ways help to fill some of the gaps in the musical history of the period.

Colleges

The statutes of New College, Oxford, did not expressly require the singing or teaching of polyphonic music, nor did the chapel books given by the founder include books of polyphony.[1]

[1] They included eleven noted Antiphonals, nineteen Graduals and thirteen

In preparation for Henry VI's visit to the college in 1442–3 certain Masses, probably for the King's good estate, were added to the Graduals in the choir, and in the same year the *informator* (John Francis) received for the first time an additional payment for teaching the antiphon of the Virgin, which was followed by prayers for the King.[1] In 4–5 Edward IV (1464–5) the 'King's Mass' was again 'noted',[2] and the Bursars' Roll for 1494–5 also has a payment *pro missa Domini Regis*. The first definite mention of polyphonic music is in 1470–1, when three books of *cantus fractus* were repaired, and later entries in the Rolls show the building up of a considerable repertory. They include payments to 'Andrew' for noting a Mass and antiphon in 1479–80; to the *informator* for noting books of antiphons, proses and responds in 1496–7; to John Tucke (of London; Fellow, 1499–1507, when he left to teach at Higham Ferrers;[3] later at Gloucester Abbey)[4] for writing and noting a Mass (*pro scriptura et notatione unius missae*) in 1505–6; to Richard Cloterboke for noting a five-part antiphon and some music for Christmas in 1509–10;[5] to the *informator* for setting Masses and antiphons in 1511–12;[6] to Nicholas Hoker for noting the Mass 'popularly called God Save Kynge Harry'[7] in 1518–19; to the precentor for noting *Stella caeli* in 1527–8; to the *informator* for four books of sequences for the Lady-

Processionals. Register I (1400–80), fo. 1 in the College Muniments. The list is printed, without the second folio identifications, in Walcott, *William of Wykeham*, p. 285, where 'Antiphonaria, ii' should read 'Antiphonaria, xi'.

[1] 'Et pro diversis quaternis pergameni emptis pro missis scribendis et notandis in diversis Gradalibus erga Adventum Domini Regis. . . . Et solutum informatoris Chorustarum per annum una cum vis. viiid. eidem pro informatione Antiphone beate Marie Virginis xxvis. viiid.'. And in 1444–5: 'Et in stipendio Informatoris Chorustarum ad xxs. per annum una cum vis. viiid. Allocatis eidem pro supervisione Antiphone beate Marie cum precibus adiunctis pro bono et salubri statu domini Regis xxvis. viiid.'

[2] 'Et solutum pro Notacione Misse Domini Regis ixd.'

[3] 'Assumpto opere docendi in Collegio de Higham Ferrers'. MS. Register of Wardens, Fellows and Scholars in New College Library.

[4] See above, p. 44.

[5] 'Et solutum Ricardo Cloterboke pro notatione unius Antiphone quinque partium et quorumdam aliorum cantuum erga festum natalis Christi xxd.' *Notatio* may mean composing or merely copying.

[6] 'Et solutum ad manus Informatoris Choristarum pro modulatione diversorum missarum et antiphonarum hoc anno viis. viiid.'

[7] Two voices of a Mass by Thomas Ashewell with this title are extant.

Mass and some books of *cantilenae* in 1529–30;[1] to *dominus* Myllyng[2] in the same year and the precentor in 1532–3 for noting *cantilenae*; to Henry Brether for the same on three occasions during 1534–6; to a 'bibliophile' in 1538–9 for making a large book of antiphons;[3] and to *dominus* Segary in 1540–1 for twenty-two books of polyphony containing antiphons, Masses and other music needed for the choir.[4] Other entries concerning the provision and repair of musical books occur in 1509–10, when *magister* Gober was paid for some quartos *de cantico* which he had bought, the *informator* for the materials and binding for a large book and five other books of *cantus fractus*,[5] John Cornysh and his son for repairing books in the choir and mending the board in the nave from which the antiphon was sung,[6] and Richard Cornysh and his father for mending the books of the chaplains on the precentor's side.

The deed which lists the books given to the choir in 1458 by William Porte, former Fellow,[7] also records that he gave *Orgona [sic] magna pro choro*.[8] This organ was most probably in a gallery over the north side of the choir, as at Winchester College, which has since been removed. Entries referring to the pulpitum occur for the first time in 1460–1, when John Smith, 'lokyer', supplied various materials *pro hostiis ascensorii ad pulpitum*, and *le pavyng introitus chori* was also paid for. Repairs were carried out in 1484–5 on both the organ *in choro* and the

---

[1] 'In primis solutum Informatori choristarum pro 4or libris sequentiarum pro missa beate marie xs. . . . Et solutum Informatori choristarum pro libris cantilenarum per eum confectis xiiiis. . . . Et solutum Informatori pro quatuor libris cantilenarum iiis.'

[2] Thomas Myllyng, Fellow 1488–1509.

[3] 'Et solutum bibliophole pro constructione unius magni libri antiphonarii iii mensas vs.'

[4] 'Solutum Domino Segary per 22 libris simphoniaris habentibus antiphonas, missas et alia necessaria ad cantum divinum in choro xliiis. iiiid.' John Segar was a Fellow 1537–49.

[5] 'Et solutum ad manus Informatoris choristarum pro ligatura unius magni libri cantici fracti et aliorum quinque librorum cantici fracti una cum pergameno et paupiro deservientibus eisdem libris xxvo aprilis iiis. iid.'

[6] 'Et solutum Joanni Cornenysch et filio eiusdem laborantibus pro xliiii dies circa reparacione librorum jacentum in choro et emendacione tabule deservientis Antiphone cantate in navi ecclesie in toto xlixs.'

[7] From 1418 to 1423, when he joined the household of Bishop Beaufort (MS. Register); in 1417–18 Porte was paid 6s. 8d. 'pro notatione novorum Antiphonariorum'.

[8] Register I, fo. 8.

organ in the pulpitum, and in 1488–9 on the 'smaller organs' by William Wotton. Others who worked on the organs were Thurlby in 1496–7, Nicholas Kendall and Richard Borrow in 1500–1, and Robert Horne in 1524–5. In 1536–7 the sum of twenty-five pounds six shillings and ten pence halfpenny was paid for organs made over a two-year period, and three years later the college possessed four organs, one of which was in a Jesus-chapel.[1] In 1542–3 Gustinian *clericus* was paid for playing the organ during two terms.[2]

The chapel inventories of Winchester College between 1404 and 1432 list a book of polyphonic music beginning with a setting of the Kyrie,[3] which may have been the *liber de cantu organico* which was among the books given by the founder (d. 1404).[4] In 1451–2 a book of polyphony given by Richard Glyn (Scholar, 1434; Fellow of New College, 1440–1)[5] was repaired, and in 1466–7 material for new books of *cantici* was bought. Payments which may concern polyphonic music were made to *dominus* John Cote (Chaplain, 1469–72) in 1470–1 for noting a Mass and some antiphons; to Harris in 1474–5 for noting Masses, antiphons and other *cantici* in the choristers' books; to Richard Crow (Scholar, 1466; Fellow of New College, 1473–6) for noting Masses and antiphons and to Edward Clerke for noting *cantus* in 1476–7; and to *dominus* Laurence (? William Laurance, admitted Fellow, 1478) for noting Masses and antiphons and Crow for noting *cantus* in the year following. In 1490–1 John Cornysh supplied 'six new quires of a book for the choristers arranged for singing responds and antiphons'.[6]

---

[1] In 1527–8: 'Et solutum pro reparacione organorum in capella Jhesu viis. vid.'; in 1539–40: 'et solutum confectori organorum pro emendatione 4or organorum xxvis. viiid.'

[2] 'Solutum gustinian clerico pulsanti organa primo et secundo termino vis. viiid.'

[3] Inventories of 1404–5, 1412–13 and 1432; in 1412–13 it is described as 'i liber de cantu organico iio folio e-e-leyson et est ligatus cum tabulis cum ii clapsulis'.

[4] The Founder's book was valued at 6s. 8d.; he also gave seven Antiphonals each valued at over nine pounds; Kirby, *Annals of Winchester*, p. 152.

[5] Kirby, *Winchester Scholars*, p. 56.

[6] 'Et in solutis Johannes Cornyshe pro vi quaternis novis unius libri pro choristis ad cantandum Responsoria et antiphonas ordinati cum xs. vid. pro Reparacione et notacione antiquorum quaternorum ligacione et cooperture eiusdem libri xxiiis. viiid.'

The chapel inventory made in 1531[1] shows the number and place in choir of each kind of service-book, and includes a book of polyphonic music containing Masses, another with antiphons, and a book with the Bass part of hymns. One of the Antiphonals is noted as being for the use of the *organista*, the term used at Winchester for the organ-player.

The college had an organ in 1399, when it was borrowed by Wykeham and carried by six scholars to Bishop's Waltham. Bishop Beaufort borrowed an organ to go to Farnham Castle in 1415, and again to go to Highclere, one of his houses, in 1420.[2] Robert Derby, clerk of the Prior of Winchester Cathedral, was brought to the college to play the organ in chapel for the visit on St. Cecilia's day (November 21–2) in 1444 of Henry VI, who was present at both Vespers and at Mass.[3] On Sunday, January 19, 1449, the King attended the installation of Wayneflete as Bishop at the time of Mass at the Cathedral, and heard both Vespers in the college chapel. On that occasion John Payne and Henry Abyngdon took part in the services, and Abyngdon, then a clerk at Eton, was rewarded by the college with a pair of gloves.[4] By 1476–7 there was an organ in the pulpitum, which was repaired in that year by Robert Joyner, coming from Salisbury. John Massyngham and William Dutton repaired an organ in the following year;[5] Walter, organmaker, worked on two organs in 1498; and in 1542 further work was carried out by Edmund Popingay, Nicholas 'joiner' and his family, and William Dore, the *organista*.[6] The 1531 inventory shows that there were then three organs in the college. One, given by John Webbe (Fellow, admitted 1494), was in the gallery at the north side of the choir, which is the position of the present organ and was probably that of the original organ, as at New College. There was another in the pulpitum and the third was in the Fromond chantry chapel, built in the cloister under the will of John Fromond (d. 1420), and consecrated in 1437.[7]

---

[1] Printed below, p. 434.   [2] Kirby, *Annals of Winchester*, pp. 56–7.

[3] H. Chitty, 'The Basins given by Henry VI to Winchester College', reprinted from *Notes and Queries*, 12S.i, pp. (of reprint) 7–8.

[4] H. Chitty, 'The Visits of Henry VI to Winchester College', reprinted from op. cit., pp. 16–18.

[5] These two items from the Bursars' Rolls.

[6] Kirby, *Annals of Winchester*, p. 57.   [7] Ibid., pp. 164–8.

The books of All Souls College, as listed in an inventory of 1490–1500 and in two earlier inventories, included a 'book of prykked song' the second folio of which began with *descendi in,* certainly the Mary-antiphon *Descendi in ortum,* and a *liber pro Organo 2 fo habens in utero,* words which occur in the antiphon *Spiritus sanctus* at Lauds on the first Sunday in Advent. The latter was probably a plainsong Antiphonal. Two All Souls lists of 1556 have 'a great prickesong book of velame covered with a shepes skynne', evidently a large choirbook, and 'fyve other pricksonge bokes', most likely a set of part-books.[1]

Eton College is the only foundation of the period which has managed to preserve its own late medieval choirbook, which is listed in a chapel inventory of *c.* 1531 as 'a grete ledger of prick song ii folio *tum cuncta*',[2] a description which identifies it with the large manuscript of polyphonic antiphons and Magnificats now in the college library.[3] Though about half of its pages have unfortunately been lost, the Eton choirbook is outstanding among the surviving manuscripts of medieval music in Britain in the value of its contents and the beauty of its writing and illumination. The daily singing of a polyphonic antiphon was required by the statutes of the college, which said that every evening the choir, accompanied by the *informator,* should process two by two into chapel, say a *Pater noster* before the crucifix, and then sing *meliori modo quo sciverint* a Mary-antiphon before the image of the Virgin. *Salve regina* with the trope (*cum suis versiculis*) was to be sung during Lent, and any other antiphon on feast-days in Lent and during the rest of the year.[4] In its original state[5] the choirbook contained sixty-seven antiphons for from four to nine voices, of which fifteen were settings of *Salve regina,* twenty-four Magnificats for from four to seven voices, a four-part setting by Richard Davy of the Passion according to St. Matthew, and a setting of the Apostles' Creed in the form of a thirteen-part rota by Robert Wylkynson, who was *informator* from 1500 to 1515.[6]

[1] Unpublished Inventories.
[2] The Eton inventories are printed in James, 'Chapel Inventories'.
[3] MS. 178.
[4] *The Ancient Laws of King's and Eton,* p. 552; the relevant part of the statute is reprinted in Harrison, 'The Eton Choirbook', pp. 158–9.
[5] Detailed catalogue in ibid., pp. 169–75, and in *The Eton Choirbook,* iii.
[6] Unpublished Audit Rolls.

Earlier the college had owned two 'bokes of prikked song', one of which began *illud et* and the other *beata Dei*[1] on the second folio, and also a 'boke for organys' beginning *laris qui*[2] on the second folio, which was still in use in 1531. The inventory containing these items is endorsed in a later hand: 'Roll of what things the Provost was forced to deliver to the Dean of Windsor in 1465', that is, when the college was threatened with dissolution. The college accounts show that there were one or more organs in the chapel from 1496–7 onwards, and that payments were made in 1498–9 for regulating the *magna organa in choro*, for making a lectern near the organ, and for a door at the foot of the steps leading to the great organ.[3] In 1506–7 John Howe, a famous name in organ-building in the sixteenth century, was paid forty shillings for the carriage of a new organ and for erecting it in the chapel.[4] The college had 'iiii peare of organs, iii lytyl lectorns for orgayns' and 'iii formys to the orgayns' in 1531, and in 1549 there were 'one little paire of orgaynes in the Scholars Chamber and one other greate in the quyar'.[5]

The choir of King's College also sang a polyphonic antiphon every evening. The wording of the statute is similar to that for Eton, though *Salve regina* was not specified for Lent.[6] King's had a book of *cantus fractus* in 1448–9,[7] and three in 1452.[8] In 1495–6 the composer Thomas Farthyng, then a clerk in the choir, was paid for writing music for the feast of St. Nicholas,[9] and in

---

[1] Probably the antiphon *Beata Dei genitrix Maria*.

[2] The words *singularis que* occur in the sequence *Ave mundi spes Maria*.

[3] Unpublished Account Rolls.

[4] James, 'Organs and Organists in the College Accounts', p. 369. For the work of the Howe family, see Sumner, *The Organ*, pp. 104–7.

[5] James, 'Chapel Inventories'.

[6] *The Ancient Laws of King's and Eton*, p. 107.

[7] 'It pro emend' unius libri de cantu fracto Et pro pellibus pro eadem vs.' College Mundum Book.

[8] These are described as: 'duo libri de cantu fracto quorum 2m fo unius incipit *Kirieleyson*, It' 2m fo alius incipit *Nos autem populus*, It' alius liber de cantu fracto emptus de Boston cuius 2m fo incipit *fa sol la*' (unpublished inventory). The words *Nos autem populus* occur in the *Venite*. The last item, which is also in the 1529 inventory, may have been a book for teaching descant.

[9] 'Thome ffarthyng pro notacione diversorum cantuum erga festa Sancti Nicholai iis. Et eidem pro notacione diversorum librorum pro

1499–1500 payment was made to John Sygar, a chaplain and the composer of a Magnificat (now incomplete) in the Eton manuscript, for writing two Masses.[1] These entries probably refer to polyphonic music, and three among later entries certainly do so: they are payments in 1502–3 for binding and covering a book of *cantus fractus*,[2] in the next year to Jaxson, a chaplain, for noting Masses called *Regali ex progenie* and *Lux aeterna*,[3] and in 1508–9 to Sygar for noting two Masses, one of which was called *Per signum crucis*, seven sequences composed by Fayrfax and Cornysh and three sequences for Advent.[4] *Regali ex progenie* is certainly the Mass by Fayrfax which has survived elsewhere, and this entry is the first evidence concerning its date to be discovered; no Masses *Lux aeterna* or *Per signum crucis* are extant. Comparison with the 'Inventarye of the pryke songys longynge to the Kyngys College in Cambryge' made in 1529[5] shows that Jaxson copied the two Masses named in the entry towards the end of a set of six part-books on parchment. The lost sequences by Fayrfax and Cornysh were almost certainly the seven sequences for the daily Lady-Mass and the others the three sequences for the Lady-Mass in Advent. The books in which Sygar copied them may have been the 'iiii bokys of papyr havynge Sequenses and Taverners Kyries' which appear in the same inventory. There are no identified survivals of this rich array of polyphonic books, which contained Masses, antiphons, responds, settings of the Magnificat and Nunc dimittis and some ritual items which, like many of the Masses, reflect the dedication of the college to St. Nicholas.

In 1467–8 William Boston was paid for repairing both the

choristis viis viiid' and 'Thome ffarthyng pro notacione diversorum cantuum viis.'

[1] 'Domino Johanni Sygar pro notacione duarum missarum pro qualibet missa xiis. iid.'

[2] 'Waltero Hatley pro ligacione unius libri fracti cantus et pro coopertorio ad eundem vs.'

[3] 'Dno Jaxson pro annotacione duarum missarum unius vocat' Regali ex progenie et alterius lux eterna viiis.' The same year has also: 'Dno Jaxson pro Annotacione Misse pro utraque parte chori iis. vid.'

[4] 'Dno Sygar notatione duarum missarum in librum collegii quarum una vocat' per signum crucis et cum notacione vii sequentiarum ex compositione ffayrfax et Cornysshe et iii sequentiarum pro adventu iis iiiid. . . . iiiis. viiid.'

[5] Printed below, p. 432.

great and small organs at King's,[1] and payments for the maintenance of organs occur at intervals thereafter. There is an entry in 1507–8 for mending the new organ, and Thomas Browne, organmaker, was paid two years later for mending the great organ.[2] The chapel inventories of 1506 and 1529 show an Antiphonal *pro organis* beginning at the second folio with *Qui mittendus est*. These words occur in *Non auferetur*, the third respond at Matins on the fourth Sunday in Advent.

The surviving music of Davy and Sheppard testifies to the great accomplishments of the choir of Magdalen during the first half-century of its history, while the accounts of that period[3] show how generous was the provision made by the college for the chapel and its services. Among the early payments referring to polyphonic books are one in 1484–5 to the instructor of the choristers for parchment to make books of 'set song' and one in 1490–1 to William Barnard, who shared the post of instructor with Davy, for new books *de cantu fracto*. John Cornysh worked at Magdalen at various times as scribe and binder of chapel books,[4] and in 1502–3 John Shevane was paid for two books of *cantus fractus*. Some books *de cantu crispo* were bound and repaired in 1505–6, and in 1515–16 Dom Newman received a payment for various books *de cantu diviso* which he had bought and given into the care of Robert Perrott, the *informator*. Further entries in the accounts record payments in 1519–20 to George Roper for a Mass *de cantu fracto* which he got from Master Skokysley;[5] to Master Burges[6] in 1530–1 '*pro rescriptione le* pryck-

---

[1] 'Pro reparacione organorum parvorum viis. iiiid.' and 'pro reparacione magnorum organorum xxs.'

[2] 'Uno emendanti nova organa vis. viiid.' and 'pro emendacione magnorum organorum xls.'

[3] Printed in Bloxam, *Register of Magdalen*, ii, pp. 258 sqq.; Macray, *Register of Magdalen*, ii, pp. 3 sqq.

[4] In 1488–9: 'Sol Johanni Cornyshe pro scriptura officii Visitationis B. Mariae tam in gradalibus quam in Antiphonariis viis. viiid'; in 1502–3: 'Cornysshe pro hymnali xxviis. viid.' The latter entry may refer to Thomas Cornysh, who received 6s. 2d. in 1508–9 for writing three *tabulae* for the hall, and, with his son, a number of payments for repairing chapel books in 1511–12. A man who brought some songs from Edward Martyn (Fellow, 1495–1504) in 1506–7 was paid eight pence, and in 1509–10 Turton was paid three shillings and four pence 'pro notacione diversorum cantuum'.

[5] John Stoksley, Fellow from *c.* 1495 and later Bishop of London.

[6] John Burgess, a Fellow in 1505.

song bokys'; to the clerk Wells in 1532 '*pro le* prykkyng *quatuor missas 8 partium*' and '*pro le* prykkyng *duas missas quatuor partium*'; to the clerk Noland in the same year '*pro le* prykkyng *unam missam*'; to Sheppard for books of music in 1547 (twelve books) and 1548; and to a priest in 1540 for noting the Passion and some antiphons. The payment made to one or more of the clerks for playing the organ is described as *pro organis* or *pulsanti organa* or, as in 1530–1 to Perrott, *pro pulsatione organorum diebus festis per totum annum.*

It appears from some entries in the accounts that the Jesus-Mass on Fridays during Lent was sung by the clerks only, the daily Lady-Mass being sung by the choristers. These entries concern rewards in the form of breakfasts (*jantaculi*), oysters, bread and drink which were given to the clerks for their singing of the Jesus-Mass, and also of the Lady-Mass while the choristers were away during the plague, when most of the members of the college migrated to one of its properties in the country.

The inventories of the chapel books made in 1486 and in 1495[1] give no details about the polyphonic music, merely noting that the *libri de cantu diviso* were in the custody of the *informator*, but the numbers of plainsong service-books are worth noticing. In 1495 there were fifteen Antiphonals on each side, besides three other Antiphonals, one of which was for the organ; thirteen Graduals on the president's side and sixteen on the vice-president's, of which one was for the rulers and another for the organ, besides six other Graduals; sixty-seven Processionals; nineteen Missals; and one or two each of the other necessary books, including two noted Hymnals and an Ordinal. In the inventory of 1522–4 the polyphonic music is described in unusually informative detail in a section which is reprinted here in full.[2] Except for one book called *le Base* all the music was in choirbooks, and the nine 'most beautiful' books among these contained the main items in the choir's repertory, consisting of Masses, antiphons, and settings of the Magnificat and Nunc dimittis for five to seven parts. The music of the Lady-Mass, which included settings of the Kyrie, Alleluia and Sequence, was sung in four parts, apparently by boys or men only,

[1] The Magdalen Inventories are printed in Macray, *Register of Magdalen*, ii, pp. 198 sqq.

[2] Ibid., pp. 209 sqq.; reprinted below, p. 431.

and antiphons in four parts were also provided. A printed Missal and six printed Hymnals 'chained in the choir' were added to this inventory during the following years.

Payments for organ repairs appear in the Magdalen accounts in 1481–2 and in 1486–7. The great organ was built by William Wotton, who was paid fourteen pounds in part payment in 1486–7 and the balance of fourteen pounds in the following year. There are many entries concerning organs in subsequent years. Those named in payments for working at the organs are Wotton in 1488–9, for mending the small organ; John Chamberlayn in 1508–9 and the following year; Vicarye, a clerk, in 1509–10; Simon in 1519–20; *magister* Barbbye in 1522, for mending the small organ; John Hanson and John Showt, the latter for working on the new organ, in 1529–30; John Sarte (= Showt ?) in 1530–1; *magister* Whyte, for mending three organs, and John Carpenter, for mending the wood (*teca*) of the organ in the choir and for work on the small organ, in 1531–2; Whyte, for mending two organs, John Kever, for mending the bellows of the new organ, and Richard Benton, for mending the bellows of the organ in the choir, in 1532–3; Benton (Beynton) in 1535, for mending two organs; Whyte in 1539, 1542 and 1545; and Butson in 1543, for repairing the organ in the choir.

In 1486 Warden Richard Fitzjames, afterwards Bishop of London, and the Fellows of Merton decided to build a new rood-loft,[1] and when it was finished in 1488 they signed a contract for a new organ to be installed in it. In the contract it was agreed that 'Wylliam Wotton off the seyde Town off Oxefforde organmaker . . . schall make or cawse to be made a goode and suffycyent payr of organs lyke on to the new payr off organs wych he promysyd to make and sett up withyn Maudelene College off Oxfforde aforesayde', the cost to be twenty-eight pounds.[2] It was decided in the following year that one of the chaplains *in cantu doctior* should act as precentor, and John Davres was appointed to the office.[3] During the following years the chapel services were elaborated, new choir-stalls were made, and vestments, ornaments, books and an image and reliquary for the high altar were given to the chapel by the Warden and

---

[1] See below, p. 209. [2] *Registrum Collegii Mertonensis*, p. 109.
[3] Ibid., p. 121.

other donors. All the postmasters at this time had to be able to sing so that they could act as a choir, and in 1507 it was decided that the eight senior Masters should not accept scholars unless they could sing plainsong, and that the scholars of the other Masters and the commoners must be able to sing polyphonic music ('*cantum fractum scilicet* pryckdsong', with a few notes in the margin of the Register for illustration).[1] The Fellows also agreed to provide the stipend for a cantor, presumably to direct the polyphonic music. However, this attempt to create a polyphonic choir within the framework of an existing foundation did not meet with success. It proved to be difficult to find enough scholars with these qualifications and to prevent them going elsewhere after they were found, and in 1519 the decree was modified to allow Masters to accept philosophy as an alternative qualification.[2]

Under Wolsey's statutes for Cardinal College, three antiphons, one to the Trinity, one to St. William of York[3] and one to the Virgin, were sung daily *intorto cantu aut diviso*, after the chaplains and clerks had sung Vespers and Compline some time after four o'clock. At seven o'clock all the choristers and their instructor, with the chaplains and clerks who had been assigned by the precentor, went into chapel again and sang a polyphonic setting of *Salve regina*; then a chorister sang the versicle *Ave Maria* and a prayer, and all knelt and sang *solemniter* the antiphon *Ave Maria*, which was divided into three sections by the ringing of a bell. The *informator* and the choristers then went into the nave of the chapel and, kneeling before the Crucifix, sang the antiphon *Sancte Deus, sancte fortis* in polyphony.[4] In Henry VIII's statutes the order of the evening antiphons was changed, and *Sancte Deus, sancte fortis* was sung in the nave after the Mary-antiphon had been sung in the choir; then three bells were rung three times, and in the intervals the choristers sang '*intorto cantu quem* pricked *appellant*' the 'salutation of Gabriel', with *Ave Maria* in the first two intervals and *Ave Maria gratia plena Dominus tecum* in the third interval.[5]

---

[1] *Registrum Collegii Mertonensis*, p. 352.   [2] Ibid., p. 485.
[3] William Fitzherbert, Archbishop of York, who died in 1154 and was canonized in 1226.
[4] *Statutes of Cardinal College*, p. 57.
[5] *Statutes of King Henry VIII's College*, pp. 188–9.

The 'bukis for the Quher' of St. Salvator's College at St. Andrew's are listed in an inventory of the late fifteenth or early sixteenth century.[1] They included 'ane gret prykkyt sang buk and tua smallar of prekyt senggyn', and as later additions two sets of part-books described as 'Item off sang bukis with v messis v bukis' and 'Item iiii bukis with iiii messis and antemnis'. At St. Leonard's College it was found impossible to carry out Prior Hepburn's wish that the services should be 'adorned with descant', probably because provision had not been made for a definite choral establishment. The statutes of 1544 ordered High Mass on festivals to be sung in *cantu gregoriano*, Vespers in *cantu gregoriano devote non sincopando nec varia aut impertinentia colloquendo*, while the *Salve* and the commemorations of St. Andrew and St. Leonard in the evening were to be sung by all *alta voce*. Prior John Wynram emphasized this return to a simpler ritual at his visitation in the following year by directing that all members of the college should learn to sing the chant, so that Mass could be sung 'without dissonance', and that difficult Masses should not be attempted.[2] At Aberdeen, on the other hand, Bishop Elphinstone made careful provision for the singing of polyphony at St. Mary's College by requiring that the eight priests who held prebendaries should be skilled in '*cantu gregoriano, rebus factis*[3] *videlicet* prik singin, *figuratione*,[4] faburdon,[5] *cum mensuris et discantu*', or at least in '*cantu gregoriano, rebus factis*, faburdon *et figuratione*'. Every evening at six, between Vespers and supper, all the members of the college were to sing *sollemniter cum organis et cantu*, in the intervals between twelve strokes of the great bell, the three antiphons *Salve regina*, *Angelus ad virginem* and *Sub tuam protectionem*.[6]

[1] Printed in Cant, *College of St. Salvator*, pp. 152–63.

[2] Herkless and Hannay, *The College of St. Leonard's*, pp. 147, 200.

[3] Compare the use of this expression, also as a general term for polyphony, in a document of the Sainte Chapelle, Paris: 'Et cantabitur dictum responsorium [*Gaude Maria*] in pleno [sic] cantu duntaxat sine rebus factis . . . Postea vero in organis cantabitur *Inviolata* cum versiculo et oratione', etc.; printed in Brenet, *Les Musiciens de la Sainte-Chapelle*, p. 43.

[4] Probably ornamentation of plainsong for polyphonic setting in faburden or otherwise. See below, p. 231.

[5] See below, p. 249.

[6] *Fasti Aberdonenses*, p. 60.

Household Chapels

The Old Hall manuscript provided music for the singing of Mass with polyphony in the Royal Household Chapel every day, including ferias. The daily singing of the Lady-Mass may have been added to the duties of the singers after Henry VI reached his majority, contemporary with his founding of Eton and King's, for a payment was made to John Plummer in 1444 for supervising the 'daily Mass of our Lady and divine service in our Chapel of the Household'.[1] The ordinances of Edward IV's chapel point out that 'Oure Lady masse preest and the Gospeller are assigned by the deane, and if the King be present when he redith the Passion on Palme Sonday, it hath ben accustomed the gospeller to be served with a lamprey, and when the chappell synge mattyns overnight, called Blanke Mattyns, or elles solempne dyryges for the Kinge's fader or moder, then is there allowed to them comfettes and wine'.[2] The attendance of the choir at Matins at All Saints and Christmas is confirmed by payments in 1514 to the choristers for singing *Audivi*, and in 1513 to William Cornysh for the singing of *Audivi* on All-Hallows Day and for the singing of *Gloria in excelsis* on the following Christmas Day.[3] In 1474 Edward IV also made ordinances for the household of his four-year-old son, Edward, later the tragic Edward V, in which he ordered that two of the prince's chaplains should 'saye masse and devyne servyce before our sayde sonne' and that 'every day be sayd masse in the hall for the offycers of houshoulde to begin at sixe of the clocke in the morninge and at vii mattins to begin in the chappell, and at nine a masse by note with children'. The 'sonnes of nobles lords and gentlemen being in housholde with our sayde sonne' were to 'arise at a convenyent hower and here theire masse and be vertuously brought uppe and taughte in grammer musicke and other cuninge and exercises of humanitye according to theire byrthes and after their adges'.[4] Henry VII's son Arthur Prince of Wales (1486–1502) also had his own chapel, of which John Nele was dean.[5]

[1] Roper, 'The Chapels Royal', p. 22.
[2] *A Collection of Ordinances*, p. 100.
[3] *Letters and Papers of Henry VIII*, II, ii, pp. 1463–4, 1466.
[4] *A Collection of Ordinances*, p. 29.
[5] In 1496. *Calendar of Patent Rolls 1494–1509*, p. 83.

An exchange of letters between Cardinal Wolsey and Richard Pace, Dean of Henry VIII's chapel, tells of the virtually enforced transfer of a chorister from Wolsey's chapel to the King's. Pace wrote to Wolsey on March 25, 1518:

'My lord, if it were not for the personal love that the King's highness doth bear unto your grace, surely he would have out of your chapel not children only, but also men; for his grace hath plainly shown unto Cornysche that your Grace's Chapel is better than his, and proved the same by this reason that if any manner of new song should be brought into both the said Chapels to be sung *ex improviso* then the said song should be better and more surely handled by your chapel than by his Grace's';

and again on the following day:

'The King has spoken to me again about the child of your Chapel. He is desirous to have it without the procuring of Cornish or other.' Three days later Pace wrote at the King's command to thank Wolsey for the child, and on April 1st to say that 'Cornyshe doth greatly laud and praise the child of your chapel sent hither, not only for his sure and cleanly singing but also for his good and crafty descant and doth in like manner extol Mr. Pygote for the teaching of him'.[1]

The excellence of Henry's chapel was remarked on by Sagudino in a letter to the Signory of Venice giving an account of the reception of the Venetian ambassadors in 1515. On June 6 the King invited the ambassadors and their retinue to Richmond Palace to hear Mass and dine with him: 'so they went to church, and after a grand procession had been made, high mass was sung by the King's choristers, whose voices are more divine than human; *non cantavano ma giubilavano*; and as to the counterbass voices, they probably have not their equal in the world'.[2]

In 1526 Henry ordered that only a part of the Household Chapel should travel with him when he was away from Westminster 'in his castle of Windsor, his Mannors of Bewlye, Richmond and Hampton Court, Greenwich, Eltham or Woodstock . . . at all such tymes . . . the King's noble chappell to be

[1] *Letters and Papers of Henry VIII*, II, ii, pp. 1246, 1249, 1252.
[2] *Calendar of State Papers, Venetian*, ii, p. 247.

kept in the same place, for the administration of divine service, as apperteyneth'. The ordinance continued:

'Nevertheless, forasmuch as it is goodly and honourable that there should be allwayes some divine service in the court, whereby men might be elected unto the devotion, and that it would not only be a great annoyance but also excessive labour, travell, charge and paine to have the King's whole chappell continually attendant upon his person when his Grace keepeth not his hall, and specially in rideing journeys and progresses; it is for the better administration of divine service ordeyned that the master of the children and six men, with some officers of the vestry, shall give their continuall attendance in the King's court, and dayly, in absence of the residue of the chappell, to have a masse of our Lady before noone, and on Sundays and holydayes masse of the day besides our Lady masse and an antheme in the afternoone; for which purpose no great carriage, either of vestments or bookes shall be required: the said persons to have allowance of board wages or bouch of court, with lodge-ing in or neere to the same, and convenient carriage, as in such case hath been accustomed.' [1]

Henry VIII's Book of Payments shows that he paid Fayrfax comparatively large sums for books of polyphonic music in 1516 (thirteen pounds, six shillings and eight pence), 1517 and 1518 (both twenty pounds), and that a priest of London was paid in 1515 for composing 'an anthem of defuse museke' for the King.[2] In 1515 Cornysh received a payment for 'Mr. Gyles who played on the organs in the chapel', and in June of the following year Benet (Benedictus) de Opitiis, 'player at organs', was appointed 'to wait on the King in his chamber'.[3] Payments relating to organs include one of twenty-six pounds, thirteen shillings and fourpence for a new organ at Richmond in 1510, a year's payment in 1514 to William Lewes, organmaker and keeper of the King's instruments, and a payment in 1518 to 'two men of London, for mending the organs at Woodstock, and transporting the organ of Woodstock parish church to the manor of Woodstock, and thence back again to the church'.[4]

---

[1] *A Collection of Ordinances*, p. 160.
[2] *Letters and Papers of Henry VIII*, II, ii, pp. 1469, 1473, 1476.
[3] Ibid., pp. 1467, 1472.   [4] Ibid., pp. 1449, 1478.

The chapel of Cardinal Beaufort is mentioned in the Canterbury Chronicle of John Stone, who records that during the Cardinal's visit to Canterbury in November–December 1438 John Beaufort, Duke of Somerset, the Cardinal's nephew, heard the Lady-Mass *Rorate caeli* sung with polyphony (*cum organo*), in which the Cardinal's chapel took part.[1] About a year before this the Priory of Winchester wrote to Beaufort seeking a place in the chapel of the Cardinal for Robert Bygbroke, a priest who taught the novices singing and played the organ.[2] The chapel of Archbishop Stafford took part in Thomas Goldston's celebration of his first Mass as Prior of Canterbury on Easter Tuesday in 1449, when a Gloria by Gydney was sung (*Et ibidem cantaverunt: Et in terra* Gydney). A John Gydney was one of the two masters of the grammar schools of the city of Canterbury in 1464.[3]

The household chapel choir of Henry Percy, fifth Earl of Northumberland (d. 1527), sang music in five parts, for the gentlemen were divided into tenors, countertenors and basses, and the children into trebles and second trebles in one list, trebles and means in another. The whole choir sang Matins, Mass and Vespers every day, while the Lady-Mass was sung by the master of the children, who was a countertenor, and three other gentlemen, except on Fridays and days on which the Earl was present, when it was sung by the whole choir.[4] On the death of the fifth Earl, Cardinal Wolsey demanded and obtained from his son the books of the Northumberland chapel, which are described in a letter from the sixth Earl to Wolsey's gentleman Thomas Arundel as 'iiii anteffonars, such as I thynk wher nat seen a gret wyll; v grails, an ordeorly, a manual, viii prossessioners, and ffor all the ressidew, they are not worth the sending nor ever was occupied in my lords chapel'.[5] The household of Henry Fitzroy, Duke of Richmond (d. 1536), had four chaplains; the number of singers is not recorded, but the books of his chapel included 'a boke prykked with keryes'

---

[1] *The Chronicle of John Stone*, p. 22.
[2] Register I (1345–1496) in the Cathedral Library, fo. 54.
[3] *The Chronicle of John Stone*, pp. 46, 90.
[4] *Regulations and Establishment of the Household of the Fifth Earl of Northumberland*, pp. 367–76.
[5] Hawkins, *History of Music*, i, pp. 385–6.

and 'a grete Booke of masse, prykked'.[1] An inventory of the books of the Chapel Royal of Scotland in Stirling Castle made in 1505, two years after James IV's new foundation, includes two volumes on parchment with notes '*de ly* faburdone'.[2]

Collegiate Churches

At St. George's, Windsor, payments to one of the clerks for playing the organ at services (*pro divinis in organis exequendis* or *solempnizandis*) are recorded from 1406–7 onwards,[3] and in 1416–17 the chapel bought fifteen sheets of vellum for a book called 'Organboke',[4] which was probably a book of polyphonic choral music. From 1461–3, in 1469, and again for some years after 1477 Thomas Rolfe, a clerk, was paid for playing the organ both *in choro* and *ad missam beate Marie virginis*, and from the time of the refoundation by Edward IV the accounts record new payments to the *informator* and to the choristers for singing the antiphon *Nunc Christe te petimus*, a part of the text of *Sancte Deus, sancte fortis* which was commonly sung as a Jesus-antiphon. A payment to one or more of the clerks for playing the organ appears regularly during this period, and was increased when Richard Woods took over the duties in 1496.[5]

At the visitations of Southwell Minster in 1481, 1484 and 1490 many of the vicars complained about the quarrels in their house and the discord in choir due to Thomas Cartwright's arrogant assumption of superior knowledge of music and his outlandish way of singing faburden. In 1484, for example, Keyll deposed that Cartwright sang faburden in so strange a way that the other singers could not make concord with him, and Rochell reported that while Cartwright sat by the fire in the vicars' hall he upbraided his fellows for their singing, exalting his knowledge above theirs, and his boasts led to brawling

---

[1] *Camden Miscellany*, III, pp. xxiv, 14.

[2] Rogers, *History of the Chapel Royal of Scotland*, p. 78.

[3] Fellowes, *Windsor Organists*, pp. 4–6.

[4] 'Et in xv pellibus de velym emptis in Wyndesore pro uno libro vocato Organboke continento v quaternos quolibet quaterno iii pellium videlicet xii folia vis. iiid.' Bond, *Windsor Inventories*, p. 214.

[5] Treasurer's Rolls.

among the others.[1] It had been observed in 1478 that the singing was unsatisfactory because there were no rulers and no succentor, and at the visitation by Dr. Fitzherbert, the residentiary, in 1503 it was ordered that someone sufficiently skilled should begin the responds, antiphons and other chants, and that the music on feasts of nine lessons, in commemorations and in important octaves should be performed with chant in faburden and with the organ, so that there would be a distinction between services *cum regimine chori* and ferial services.[2] A complaint was made at the visitation in 1508 that Thomas Steill was sometimes unwilling to sing his part in 'pryksonge' at the lectern, and either stood in his stall or sat there reading a book.[3] All this suggests that Southwell was being brought up to date in its musical arrangements, but with some difficulty. In 1519 the deacons and subdeacons were reproved for coming late to Lady-Mass, and George Vincent was reprimanded for being absent from choir very often 'so that the organ was not played at the services, which it was his duty to do'.[4]

There was an organ at Ripon in 1399,[5] and there are records of payments to a vicar for singing Mass in the Lady-chapel and for playing the organ from the mid-fifteenth century onwards.[6] Lawrence Lancaster was paid as organist (*pro lusione super organa*) in 1475–6, and later there was a further payment

[1] 'Dominus Thomas Cartwright cantat faburdon tali extraneo modo quod ceteri chorales nequeunt cum eo concordare'; 'Dominus Thomas sedens prope ignem in domo Vicariorum reprobat consortes suos in cantando et se prae ceteris in scientia cantus commendat, ut ex jactura sua alii ministri excitantur ad rixas'. *Visitations and Memorials of Southwell*, p. 46. Cartwright moved to York and continued his quarrelsome habits there, for in 1499–1500 he and Thomas Becklay, vicars of York, were fined for using 'opprobrious words' to one another. Harrison, *Life in a Medieval College*, p. 73. Cartwright's name is among the vicars of York in 1492 and 1502–3. Bursar's Rolls in the Minster Library.

[2] *Visitations and Memorials of Southwell*, pp. 34, 74.

[3] 'Idem Dominus Thomas non est pronus neque voluntarius interdum ad cantandum le pryksong ad lectrinum sed aliquando stat in stallo aliquando sedet legendo super libros et minime cantat'. Ibid., p. 80.

[4] Ibid., pp. 85, 87.

[5] 'Et in ii corriis equinis emptis pro iiii paribus belows organorum de novo faciendis 2s. 8d.', and other entries. *Memorials of Ripon*, iii, p. 132.

[6] The earliest recorded is in 1447–8: 'Et in solut Thomae Litster capellano pro missa cantanda in capella Beatae Mariae infra ecclesiam Ripon et ad ludendum super organicis per annum, 10s.' Ibid., p. 239.

for 'keeping' the Lady-Mass 'with note and organ' (*cum nota et organis custodienda*).[1] A new statute of 1503 ordered that no vicar or deacon should be admitted unless he could sing plainsong and polyphony (*cantum planum et etiam fractum viz* prykesange), and that the deacons, subdeacons, thuriblers and choristers should attend the schools of grammar and song.[2] At Beverley George Morsell was master of the choristers and 'conduct' of the Lady-Mass and Jesus-Mass in 1531–2.[3]

Polyphonic music was certainly sung at Fotheringhay and Tattersall, for the composer William Typp was precentor at Fotheringhay in 1438, and John Taverner was at Tattersall before going to Cardinal College. Under the revised statutes of 1491 all the vicars of St. Mary Newarke were obliged to sing at Matins and High Mass, and six vicars or more, as the dean should decide, at the daily Lady-Mass in the Lady-chapel, unless it was sung solemnly, probably meaning in polyphony, by the boys and two or three vicars, when the other vicars were excused.[4] The books of St. Mary's collegiate church and almshouse at Ewelme (Oxfordshire), founded in 1437 by William de la Pole, Earl of Suffolk, included a 'large boke of prykked songe, bounden and covered with rede lether'.[5]

In 1517 St. Mary's church in Crail (Fifeshire) was raised into a collegiate church by Sir William Myrton, who provided endowments to maintain a provost, a sacristan, ten prebendaries and four choristers. He also founded a grammar school and a song school, where the scholars were to be taught *discantus* and *precantus*, which probably means singing the solo parts in plainsong. Five years later William Turnour was appointed to the chaplaincy of the Holy Rood in the rood-loft (*in solio*), which carried with it the duty of playing the organ 'according to usage, in the college kirk, in his habit, in the quire, at daily mattins, the Lord's mass [*recte* Lady-Mass ?], *Ave gloriosa*, high mass, and vespers'. The antiphon *Ave gloriosa* was apparently

---

[1] Lancaster was still organist in 1502–3. The names of later organists recorded are John Watson (1511–12), William Swawe (1513–14), Adam Bakhouse (1520–1 and 1525–6) and William Solber (1540–1).

[2] *Memorials of Ripon*, pp. 276, 280.

[3] *Memorials of Beverley*, pp. lxv, civ.

[4] Thompson, *Newarke Hospital and College*, p. 127.

[5] Historical Manuscripts Commission, *Eighth Report*, 1881, p. 629. The statutes of Ewelme are in the *Ninth Report*, 1883–4, pp. 217 sqq.

sung at or before High Mass, and an antiphon was also sung every evening in the aisle of the church, followed by prayers for the soul of the founder.[1]

Secular Cathedrals

A Chapter Act of Lincoln in 1432 refers to four of the vicars as 'singers at the daily mass of St. Mary called *Salve sancta parens*',[2] and an entry of two years later shows that this mass was sung in polyphony.[3] By this time polyphony was also sung at the regular service in choir, since Dean Macworth complained to the Bishop at his visitation in 1437 that some of the canons took the best singers of polyphonic music (*meliores organistas*) with them when they censed the altars in the cathedral, to the detriment of the ritual of the choir (*in divini cultus diminutionem in choro*). Bishop Alnwick ordered the canons to cease this practice and to provide themselves at their own expense with a chaplain or clerk, as laid down in the statutes and customs.[4] When William Horwood was appointed instructor of the choristers in 1477 his duties were defined as teaching them 'playnsong, pryksong, faburdon, diskant and cownter,[5] as well as in playing the organ and especially those whom he shall find apt to learn the clavychordes'.[6] Thomas Ashewell occupied this post in 1508 and William Freeman was appointed to it in 1524, while on March 25 of the same year John Gilbert (instructor, 1518–24) was appointed to play the organ at the Lady-Mass and on Sundays and principal double feasts.[7] In 1535 Robert Dove (Dowffe) was receiving payments for playing the organ at the Lady-Mass and Jesus-Mass, and he was also being paid, with two other vicars, for singing at the Lady-Mass.[8] The posts of instructor and organist were combined in 1539, when James Crawe became master of the choristers and player of the organ (*pulsans organa*) at the Lady-Mass and in the choir

---

[1] *Register of the Collegiate Church of Craill*, pp. 4, 12, 33, 49.
[2] *Lincoln Statutes*, iii, p. 471.
[3] Maddison, *Vicars-choral of Lincoln*, p. 61.
[4] *Lincoln Statutes*, iii, pp. 366, 200.
[5] I.e., improvised descant below the plainsong.
[6] *Lincoln Chapter Acts 1536–47*, p. 31.
[7] Maddison, *Vicars-Choral of Lincoln*, p. 81.
[8] *Lincoln Chapter Acts 1536–47*, pp. 192–5.

on double feasts, feasts of nine lessons and Sundays, and at commemorations of St. Mary and St. Hugh. Crawe or his deputy was to teach the choristers in

'*scientia cantus*, viz. playnsonge, prykyd song, faburdon, diskante and counter and also in playing the organs in the cathedral especially two or three of them whom he or his deputy shall find fit, docile and suitable to be taught to play on the instruments called clavichordes in future provided always that the boys to be taught in this science of organ-playing shall have and find the instruments called clavichordes at their own proper cost and expense'.[1]

Thomas Appleby, who had been appointed choirmaster in 1538, was joint *informator* with 'Master Jaquet' at Magdalen College in 1539,[2] but was reappointed to Lincoln on November 26, 1541.[3]

John Kegewyn's appointment as instructor of the choristers at Salisbury in 1463 carried with it the duty of 'serving the Lady-Mass with organ at the same and other antiphons at all the accustomed times'.[4] Thomas Saintwix or Seintjust (d. 1467), the first recorded Doctor of Music of a university (Cambridge, before 1463),[5] who held many preferments from time to time, was precentor of Salisbury during the last year of his life.[6] A document of 1497 which seems to be the only surviving account roll of the college of vicars of Salisbury during this period shows payments to the organist of the Lady-chapel and to seven vicars for keeping the Lady-Mass.[7] John Wever was instructor of the choristers from *c.* 1509 to 1528,[8] and his successor (1529) was the composer Thomas Knyght, whose duties,

---

[1] *Lincoln Chapter Acts 1536–47*, p. 52.

[2] In 1537: 'Solut Mro Jakett Instructori Choristarum hoc anno L8'; in 1539: 'Solut Mro Jaquet et Mro Applebie Informatoribus Chorustarum L8'. Bloxam, *Register of Magdalen*, ii, pp. 270–1.

[3] *Lincoln Chapter Acts 1536–47*, p. 56.

[4] 'Et quod servabit missam beate marie cum organis ad eamdem et alias antiphonas in omnibus temporibus secundum formam et consuetudinem in ea parte diucius usitatus et observatus'. Salisbury Muniments, Newton Register, p. 57.

[5] Abdy-Williams, *Degree in Music*, p. 153.

[6] Jones, *Fasti Ecclesiae Sarisburiensis*, p. 331.

[7] Salisbury Muniments.   [8] Ibid., Choristers' Accounts.

as prescribed in a deed of 1538, included playing the organ and teaching the choristers 'playnsonge, prycksonge, faburdon or distento'.[1] Knyght was appointed sub-treasurer of the cathedral in 1537, and in 1546 held the prebendary of Ruscombe,[2] continuing his duties as choirmaster, however, at least until 1549.

At Wells annual payments for keeping the organ appear from 1392–3 onwards. Robert Catour, who devised the rules for the choristers afterwards approved by Bishop Bekynton, fulfilled this duty for some fifteen years after 1445, and in 1461–2 he shared the stipend with four other vicars, one of whom was *Ricardus Hugonis*,[3] that is, Richard Hygons, who had been a vicar from 1459.[4] The deed of Hygons's appointment as Master of the Choristers in 1479[5] contains the fullest extant statement of the duties of an *informator* and organist of this period. Hygons was to instruct the choristers in plainsong, mensural music and descant, and to teach playing the organ to those who had the talent. He was to sing at the daily Lady-Mass in the Lady-chapel[6] behind the high altar (which had been completed in 1477), and at the Mary-antiphon before her image at the north side of the choir-door on the accustomed days and times.[7] Immediately after the Mary-antiphon on Sundays he was to direct the choristers in singing the Jesus-antiphon before the great cross in the nave. He was also to be in his place in the second form in choir on the precentor's side, beside the leader of that side (*prope repetitorem*), at High Mass and Vespers on Sundays and festivals, and at Matins when sung in the evening before their proper day. Bishop Bekynton's rules ordered that

---

[1] Robertson, *Sarum Close*, p. 122.

[2] Harward's Memorials, p. 75; Holt Register, p. 17; Choristers' Accounts.

[3] Transcripts by W. E. Daniel of Compotus Rolls, in the Cathedral Muniments.

[4] *Register of Thomas Bekynton*, p. 328: 'Richard Hygons, vicar choral, collated to the sixth chamber on the east side of the Vicars' Close, September 18, 1459'.

[5] Appendix I, p. 425 below.

[6] Ten vicars, chosen by the 'principals', received seven pence a week for singing the service of the Virgin in the Lady Chapel. *Dean Cosyn and Wells Cathedral Miscellanea*, p. 16.

[7] In 1393–4 the choristers were paid twenty shillings for singing the Mary-antiphon in the nave, and in 1417–18 the same for singing the Mary-antiphon 'before the image of the Virgin by the door of the choir'. *Manuscripts of the Dean and Chapter of Wells*, i, pp. 276, 278.

the master was to begin the day's schooling by instructing the choristers in plainsong and polyphony, taking care to give them high or low parts according to the range of their voice.[1]

In 1507 Hygons undertook to pay Richard Bramston, alias Smith, for teaching the choristers, and Bramston was also appointed to 'keep and play the organs' in the choir and Lady-chapel.[2] The act of the Sub-dean and Chapter which ordered John Clausay (Clavelshay) to take over these duties in the following year required him to teach the choristers *ad cantandum et discantandum*.[3] Clausay died soon afterwards, and in 1512 John Gye received a special payment for his diligent instruction of the boys and for his music in the services (*laudibus organicis*).[4] John Gaylard was granted permission to be absent from Matins, except on festivals, for the first quarter of 1514 on condition that he teach the choristers singing,[5] but Bramston apparently retained his office *in absentia* for some time,[6] for in 1531 his leave of absence from the posts of instructor of the choristers and master of the works was confirmed, and on the same day he surrendered both offices for a pension of four pounds, the equivalent of their combined stipends.[7] In 1538 John Smyth was granted a chantry and leave to be absent from Matins, except on festivals, in recognition of his diligence in teaching the choristers and composing music for the services,[8] and was re-

[1] See page 11, n. 3, above.

[2] July 23. Reynolds, *Wells Cathedral*, pp. 223-4.

[3] April 11. Ibid., p. 225. Clausay was already old enough in 1504 to be excused from attendance at Matins on account of his age. Ibid., p. 212.

[4] Gye was afterwards a Canon and Registrar of the Court of the Archdeaconry. *Manuscripts of the Dean and Chapter of Wells*, ii, pp. 231, 245, 259.

[5] Ibid., p. 236.

[6] In 1510, however, complaint was made in the Chapter that Bramston, 'sometime vicar', had come to the cathedral in disguise to steal Farr, one of the best choristers, and it was suggested that a move should be made to obtain the King's protection against 'such unfittyng labours against the Cathedral Church so sett *quasi in culo mundi*'. It was thought that the opportunity should be taken of getting royal permission for the cathedral 'to have any childe in Monasteryes or any other place Withyn the diocese to serve Seynt Andrewe'. Reynolds, *Wells Cathedral*, p. 231.

[7] *Manuscripts of the Dean and Chapter of Wells*, ii, pp. 700-1. He is listed among the vicars in 1542, 1548-9, 1551, and 1553; in 1553-4 Thomas Hooper was executor of his will. Vicars' Minute-Book 1542-93 in the Cathedral Muniments.

[8] 'Nonullos cantus ad divini cultus augmentacionem.'

quired to provide books of polyphonic music (*cantuum crisporum sive diversorum*), commonly called 'square books[1] and pricke song books', for the principal feasts.[2]

By 1507 the vicars of York had to undertake to study polyphonic singing before they were allowed to share in the college revenues; each new vicar was to take an oath that he would learn to sing 'prikson' and faburden if he had a tenor voice, or descant, pricksong and faburden if his voice was not a tenor. There is some evidence that from early in the sixteenth century lay 'singing-men' were employed by the vicars to sing parts in polyphonic music.[3] In 1458 an indulgence of forty days was offered to those attending the Mass and antiphon of the Name of Jesus for the well-being of the King and realm before the crucifix near the south door of the Minster.[4] The payments recorded to the choristers 'for the antiphon' in the vicars' accounts between 1474 and 1519 may have been for the singing of the Jesus-antiphon.[5]

As part of his donations to Chichester Cathedral, Bishop Sherborne provided about 1530 a foundation of four lay-clerks. They were to be singers of polyphonic music, for their voices were to blend well together, and one at least should be a good natural bass, while their combined voices should have a range of fifteen or sixteen notes.[6] The duties of the Sherborne clerks were to sing at High Mass and the Lady-Mass[7] in the Lady-chapel each day, and at Matins on the principal feasts.[8] Sherborne also provided for the singing of an antiphon of St. Katherine by the vicars and choristers on the vigil of her feast

[1] See below, pp. 290–1.
[2] *Manuscripts of the Dean and Chapter of Wells*, ii, p. 248.
[3] Harrison, *Life in a Medieval College*, pp. 63, 238.
[4] *York Fabric Rolls*, p. 240.   [5] See above, p. 84.
[6] 'Statuimus ordinamus et volumus quod sint quatuor clerici laici concinuas voces habentes et musica docti. quorum unus ad minus semper sit basse naturalis et audibilis vocis. aliorum vero trium voces sint suaves et canore. ita quod a commune vocum succentu possint naturaliter et libere ascendere ad quindecim vel sexdecim notas'. Sherborne's Donations, Copy 2 in Chichester, Sussex County Library, fo. 18.
[7] They were required to meet the choristers and their *informator* at Sherborne's tomb daily on their way to the Lady-Mass, and there sing the psalm *De profundis*.
[8] These were Christmas, Epiphany, Easter, Pentecost, Trinity, Dedication of the Church, Translation of St. Richard, and Assumption of the Virgin.

(November 25) at a quarter past seven. In order that the antiphon should be sung with due propriety and devotion, the
informator was to see that each singer was provided with his
part written and noted, and with a candle. At seven the following morning six vicars with the *informator* and the choristers
were to attend a solemn celebration of the Mass of St. Katherine.[1] The *informator* was to have six shillings, in addition to his
special payment for the services, to be spent on refreshments
for the choristers after the Mass, which were to be prepared in
the vestibule or other place nearby, so that the obsequies which
were then being held for the benefactors of St. Katherine's altar
should not be disturbed.[2] A payment to William Samford *pro
antiphona choristarum Nunc Christe*, that is, for the antiphon of
Jesus, besides his stipend, a payment as *informator* and an *ex
gratia* reward, appears in the Chapter Act Book in 1544. In the
same year William Campyon was paid for playing the organ in
choir and in the Lady-chapel.[3]

An inventory of the books of the choir at Exeter which was
made in 1506 shows that Grandisson was still remembered as a
donor, with such later Exeter dignitaries as Bishops Edmund
Stafford and Edmund Lacy and Dean Henry Webber. One of
the polyphonic books, which began with a setting of *Deus
creator*, the Kyrie trope for greater feasts, was used in choir,
and four others, three of which contained music for the Mass,
were kept in the Lady-chapel. The opening words of the other
book in the Lady-chapel, which was donated by Roger Keyes,[4]
are not given in the inventory.[5] The collection of polyphonic
music in the Lady-chapel at St. Paul's in 1445 comprised two
books, one described as *pulcher*, a large roll, seven separate quires,
and a small quire for the organ. Some of these began with a
setting of the Kyrie, the *Deus creator* trope, the Gloria or the

---

[1] 'Ad missam dive Katerine hora septima solenniter decantandam.'

[2] Sherborne's Donations, fo. 15.

[3] Chapter Act Book, C.L.12, fo. 57, in Chichester, Sussex County Library.

[4] Canon of Exeter, 1436; Warden of All Souls, 1442; supervisor of the
building at All Souls and later at Eton; Precentor of Exeter, 1468; d. 1478.

[5] In the choir: 'i magnus Liber Organicus, 2 fo *Deus Creator*'; in the
Lady-chapel: 'i liber Organicus cum armis Rogeri Keys in tercio fo
[blank]; Alius liber Organicus, 2 fo *Domine Fili*; Alius liber Organicus 2 fo
Et in terra'; and 'i liber papiri regalis de prycksong, 2 fo *Et in terra*'. Oliver,
Lives of the Bishops of Exeter, pp. 330 sqq.

Credo, but the identifying cues of three others (*Alma contio, Salus salvandorem* and *Vergente soli*) have no place in the Sarum Lady-Mass, and may have been pieces retained from the earlier *Usus Sancti Pauli*, or *cantica* to be sung at the Lady-Mass instead of the sequence.[1]

Under the statutes (1507) of the Guild of Jesus at St. Paul's, which were drawn up by Dean Colet, the warden and members of the guild undertook to provide payments for the attendance of the minor canons, eight chantry priests, and the six vicars and ten choristers of the cathedral at first Vespers, Matins and Mass on the feast of the Transfiguration (August 6) and the following day, which was the feast of the Name of Jesus, and also at a Requiem Mass on the morning of the next day. All these services were to be sung 'solemnly by note' in the Crypt ('Crowdes') of the cathedral.[2] In addition a cardinal was to sing the Mass of Jesus in the crypt every Friday, and there should be present 'to syng the same by note solempnely Petychanons Vicars vii in numbre and ten Queresters'; 'six of the seid tenne Queresters' were required also to sing 'the service accustomed' at a Requiem Mass which was to be celebrated 'incontinently after the said Masse of Jesu ended'. Under the heading 'For the Salves to be songen daily', the statutes further ordained that 'after Complyn done in the seid Cathedrall Churche, thre Salves shalbe songe solemply daily and yerely in the seid Crowdes in places and dais accustumed, that is to say, before Jesu, oure Ladie, and Seint Sebastian; oon of the Vicaries, Maister of the seid Queresters for the tyme being, to have for his labour yerely xxvis viiid, at iiii termes of the yere by even porcions'.[3]

[1] 'Pulcher liber de organico cantu incipiens *Salus salvandorum*'; 'liber de cantu organico ligatus in tabulis iio fo *Eleyson*'; 'magna pulchra Rotula cum diversis canticis notatis incipiens *Alma concio*'; the seven items each described as 'quaternus de cantu organico' began on the second folio with *Vergente soli, Kirie eleyson* (two), *Et in terra, Deus creator, Patrem omnipotentem,* and one not given; 'minor quaternus pro organis iio fo *Sapientia*'. Simpson, 'Two Inventories of the Cathedral Church of St. Paul', p. 523.

[2] The Chapel of St. Faith in the crypt below the choir was the special chapel of the parishioners. The Jesus-chapel was at the eastern end, and there were also small chapels dedicated to St. John the Baptist, St. Anne, St. Sebastian and St. Radegund. Simpson, *Chapters in the History of Old St. Paul's*, pp. 91–2.

[3] *Charter and Statutes of the Minor Canons of St. Paul's*, pp. 435 sqq. The guild was incorporated by Henry VII; it flourished in the early sixteenth

Two books of polyphonic music appear under the heading *Missalia* in an inventory of the books of the choir of Aberdeen Cathedral in 1436.[1] The singing of an antiphon of the Virgin after the Lady-Mass in Aberdeen was provided for in an agreement of 1537 between Alexander Kyd[2] and William Myrtone, master of the song school. Kyd gave a rental of forty shillings a year

'for the quhilkis the foirsaid sir Wilyame maister of the sang schuyll of the cathedrall kyrk of Abirdene and his successoris God weland sall cause sex bernis of the queir in thair honest surplesis to conveyne at ane alter in the cathedrall kyrk of Auld Aberdene quhilk alter sal be assygyt and schawyne be the said maister Alexander to the said sir Wilyame tyme and plais congruent everilk day bayth feryall and festwall perpetwall tymis to cum. And thair at ye said alter one thair kneys devotlie sall syng *Ave gloriosa* ane anteme[3] of our lade in honour and laud of that glorious lade immediatlie eftir ye lade mess quhene the lade mess sal be sounge, and quhene the lade mess is nocht sounge the feirsaid sex bernis in thair honest habetis at the first bell of the hie mess anent the foirsaid alter sall synge the said anteme *Ave gloriosa* on thair kneis devotlie in plaine singynge one ilk feriall day and in prik singynge one ilk haly day quhene it is abstenit fra laboris.'

If the song school should be closed and the boys away on account of 'universall pest', the money was to go to the vicars, and 'sex of the foirsaid vicaris thair tyme about ilk Saturdaye in prik syngynge sall syng the foirsaid anteme *Ave gloriosa* devotlie

century, its income being £144 6s. 8d. in 1514–15 and £406 0s. 11½d. in 1534–5. Simpson, *Chapters in the History of Old St. Paul's*, p. 93. Henry VIII made regular contributions 'to the proctors of Jhesus yelde in powles'. *Privy Purse Expenses of Henry VIII*, pp. 29, 46, 114, 196.

[1] 'Item duo libri organici primus incipiens in secundo folio *Plasmati humani* et alius liber incipiens in secundo folio *Christeelayson*.' *Registrum Episcopatus Aberdonensis*, ii, p. 136.

[2] Kyd was sub-chanter in 1543 and 1556, and left an endowment for the singing of the Lady-Mass every Wednesday at the altar of St. Michael which he had built. Ibid., pp. 425–5.

[3] In the acceptance of the agreement by the vicars it is called 'hymnus seu prosa'. Ibid., p. 415.

one thair kneis at the foirsaid alter at the first bell of the hie mess'.[1]

The singing of an antiphon in Glasgow Cathedral was provided for in the will (1539) of John Panter, who had been organist and master of the song school there, and who desired that his three-part setting in 'pryckat synging' of [*Ave*] *Gloriosa* should be sung every evening.[2] In 1529 Bishop Gavin Dunbar founded two chaplainries in Elgin Cathedral, the holders of which were to be 'expert in Gregorian chant and reasonably skilled in descant'.[3]

Archbishop Talbot clearly had the establishment of polyphonic singing as one of his objects when he founded the minor canons and choristers of St. Patrick's Cathedral, Dublin. All the minor canons, with the vicars and choristers, were required to be at Matins and the hours services on greater doubles and feasts of nine lessons and at the Commemorations and Masses of the Virgin on doubles and Sundays, and two of them at least on other days. One of them was to sing High Mass each day, unless a 'major' canon were present to do so, and every Friday one of them with the choristers was to sing (*cum nota decantet*) the Mass of the Holy Cross in the rood-loft chapel of the Holy Cross in front of the Crucifix.[4] In 1509 payments were made to John Russell (*dominus*, and therefore probably a minor canon) as *magister choristarum*, to William Herbit as *organista*, to Roger Brown as clerk of the Lady-chapel and for the Mary-antiphon, and to William Growe, a minor canon, *pro scriptura et notatione lirici cantus*. Archbishop Michael Tregury (Archbishop of Dublin, 1449–71) gave an endowment to the vicars in 1472–3 to ensure that 'the Mass of Jesus should be the more honourably performed every Friday in the Cathedral for ever'.[5]

Monasteries

The maintaining of clerks and boys at the cathedral priories and greater monasteries was always connected with the provision of music for votive Masses and antiphons. Three clerks

---

[1] Ibid., pp. 412 sqq.
[2] *Die Musik in Geschichte und Gegenwart*, s.v. 'Glasgow'.
[3] *Registrum Episcopatus Moraviensis*, p. 417.
[4] 'In solio sancte Crucis coram Crucifixo'.
[5] Mason, *History of St. Patrick's*, pp. xxxiii, 90, xxviii–xxx.

were paid for singing in the Lady-chapel at Worcester at various times in 1434–5,[1] but the singing of polyphony there may have been occasional rather than regular during the first half of the fifteenth century, and perhaps until the appointment of John Hampton in 1486. Hampton's duties were to be present in choir on the important Worcester feasts,[2] to take part in processions, to supervise (*observare*) the singing of the daily Lady-Mass, of the Jesus-Mass on Friday, and of the Mary-antiphon *Salve regina* during Lent and the antiphon of the Name of Jesus on Fridays in Lent. He was also to instruct in plainsong and polyphonic music (*in plano cantu et fracto viz* prykd song) the eight choristers who sang the Mary-antiphon daily after Vespers and a Requiem Mass four times a year in the new Lady-chapel built by Bishop Alcock.[3] Hampton's successor, Daniel Boys, who is called 'le Organe pleyr' in the deed of his appointment (1522), had substantially the same duties, but had also to teach the choristers to play the organ. He was to keep the daily Lady-Mass with plainsong, polyphony and the organ (*cum canticis planis fractis et organis*), teach the eight choristers plainsong and polyphonic music, especially that of the Lady-Mass, of the Jesus-Mass, of Vespers and of the usual antiphons, and train any chorister who desired it in descant, both vocal and on the organ,[4] for which the chorister was to pay him twelve pence a quarter.[5]

The accounts of the Master of the Lady-chapel for 1521–2 show payments for two Magnificats, two antiphons, a Mass 'de square note' and a Mass for five voices, and for the writing of a book of polyphonic music.[6] An inventory of the items in the

---

[1] 'In expensis circa Dominum Thomam Whyngle et Dominum Thomam Bryden et Ricardum Synger de Malmesbury cantancium in capelle hoc anno ad diversas vices xxiiiid.' Atkins, *Early Occupants of the Office of Organist of Worcester*, p. 10.

[2] Called 'septem festa', a term borrowed from Evesham, where there were in fact seven such feasts; there were thirteen at Worcester. See *Paléographie musicale*, xii, pp. 48–9, where they are given.

[3] Atkins, op. cit., pp. 12–13.

[4] 'Erudicionem canticorum vocatorum Descant, tam in cantacione quam in ludicione super organum.'

[5] Atkins, op. cit., p. 17.

[6] 'Pro factura duorum *Magnificat* et unius misse de square note et alterius misse de quinque partibus una cum le prickinge ejusdem xiiis. iiiid.; Pro

charge of the Master about a year before the New Foundation of 1541 contains the following:

'a masse boke of [blank] with pryckesong, wheryn is v parts and iiii parts; iiii pryckesong masse bockes of pawper, ii hother bockes [blank] on with antems and salmes[1] yn hym; iiii lyttle pryckesong bocks of masses, v masse bockes of v parts, v bockes with *salve festa dies*, and scrolls belonging to the ii pawper bockes yn them be the v parts of other songs; a [blank] note bocke burdyde; a parchement bocke of salmes burdyde; ii masses of v parts yn parchement skrowlls; a pawper bocke of iiii parts; a pawper bocke with the vitatoris benedict te deum yn pryc-kynge; ther be iii or iiii antems in scrowes'.[2]

The indentures of the appointments to Durham of John Stele (1447), Thomas Foderley (1496), John Tildesley (1502) and Thomas Ashewell (1513) give the duties of the cantor in considerable detail.[3] They are identical in their general provisions, but there are some interesting changes and additions. Stele was to teach 'playnesange, prikenot, faburdon, dischaunte et countre', play the organ and sing the tenor part in the polyphonic music at Mass and Vespers in choir when requested, and attend the daily Lady-Mass in the Gallilee, singing plainsong or polyphony according to the singers present. In the later indentures organ-playing and 'swarenote' were added to the subjects to be taught, and the *Salve regina* in choir was added to the music in which the cantor was to take part. In music sung in choir 'cum priknote, discant, faburdon et organico cantu conjunctim et divisim' he was to sing the tenor or the part best suited to his voice. A new part of the duties was composition, for Foderley and his successors were required to produce every year a new Mass in four or five parts, or an equivalent work, the Prior and precentor approving, 'in honour of God, of the Blessed Virgin Mary, and of St. Cuthbert'. Ashewell did compose a Mass of St. Cuthbert, of which unfortunately only a fragment survives.[4]

The account written *c.* 1593 of the life and ceremonies at

le prykinge unius liber de prikesong ad usum officii hoc anno vis. viiid.; Pro duobus antifonis iiis. iiiid.' Ibid., p. 11.

[1] I.e., probably canticles.

[2] Atkins, op. cit., p. 19.   [3] For references see above, p. 41, n. 5.

[4] British Museum, MS. Add. 30520, fo. 3.

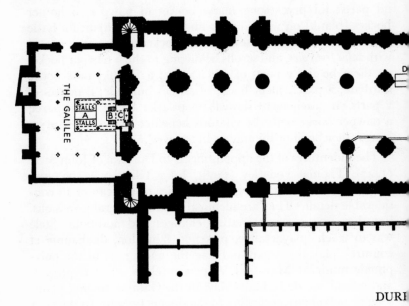

DURH

KEY

A. The Cantarie (Bishop Langley's Chantry-chapel)
B. Bishop Langley's Tomb
C. Altar of Our Lady

D. Loft over with Organ and Desk
E. Jesus Altar
F. Door
G. Rood Doors

Durham before the New Foundation tells of the services which were sung by the cantor and his choir. Every Friday 'after that the evinsong was done in the queir there was an anthem song in the bodye of the church before the foresaid Jesus alter called Jesus anthem . . . by the master of the quiresters and deacons . . ., and when it was done then the quiresters did singe an other anthem by them selves sytting on there kneis all the tyme that ther anthem was in singing before the said Jesus alter'. On the north side of the nave between two pillars there was 'a looft for the master and quiresters to sing Jesus mass every fridaie conteyninge a paire of orgaines to play on, and a fair desk to lie there books on in tyme of dyvin service'. In the 'Cantarie' in the Gallilee

'being all of most excellent blewe marble stood our Lady's alter,

188

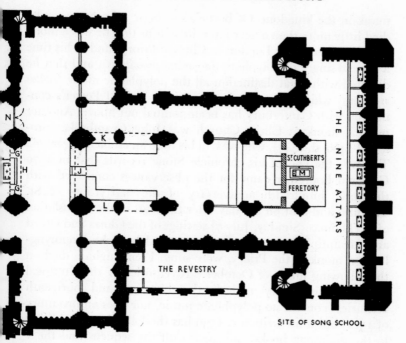

THE NINE ALTARS

ST. CUTHBERT'S

M

FERETORY

THE REVESTRY

SITE OF SONG SCHOOL

CATHEDRAL

KEY

Rood above
Choir Door (Great Organ over)
'The Cryers'
'The White Organs'

M. Shrine
N. 'Trellesdoure' surmounted by iron pikes,
   opened only for processions

a verie sumptuous Monument fynly adorned with curious wainscott woorke . . ., the wainscott being devised and furnished
with most heavenly pictures so lyvely in cullers and gilting as
that they did gretly adorne the said alter when our Lady's mass
was song daily by the master of the song schole [called Mr.
John Brimley, *interlined*], with certain decons and quiristers,
the master playing upon a paire of faire orgaines the tyme of
our Lady's masse'.[1]

In his Chronicle of people and events at Christ Church,
Canterbury, John Stone paid a tribute to the precentor John
Borne (d. 1420), remarking that he was not a singer of poly-
phony (*organista*), but had the most excellent voice of any

[1] *Rites of Durham*, pp. 34, 43.

monk in the kingdom. Of Borne's successor John Stanys, who died little more than a year later, he tells us that he was a monk of Bermondsey near London (a Cluniac Priory) and in his time a superb singer of polyphony (*organista praecipuus*), and that he directed with great distinction all the polyphonic music (*cantus organicus*) which was sung in the Priory. Leonel Power's connection with Canterbury has been pointed out above. Another musical monk at Christ Church was John Crambroke (professed 1406, d. 1447), who was 'in his time an eminent *organista*'. Towards the end of his chronicle Stone records that in 1470 Cardinal Bourchier came for the observances connected with the three hundredth anniversary of the martyrdom of St. Thomas, and that on the day after the feast of the Translation of St. Thomas (Sunday, July 7) settings of the Gloria and Creed and an antiphon *Fragrat virtus* composed by John Frennyngham, a monk of the Priory, were sung. Frennyngham died on the following ninth of October.[1] Inventories of the liturgical books at Canterbury made in the thirteenth and fourteenth centuries[2] contain no polyphonic music, nor does an inventory of 1511, but a list written *c.* 1530 has the following in addition to the plainsong books: 'iiii querys off the sequens and the v boke of v parts with a boke off the base part; the boke of iiii parts with ii queres off the mens and off the basse thereto; iii small querys off thomas maun' [*recte* martyr?]; mr Hawts[3] boke with an old vytatory boke'; and 'the boke that the masse off ii tenors ys In'. Below this list is written: 'In the time of dā John Olph' chawnter and John wood Master off the chyldren in crist's church'.[4]

St. Mary's Chapel in Westminster Abbey had a book of polyphonic music as early as 1415–16,[5] though there is no evidence of stipendiary singers until much later. The duties of Edmund Pynbrygge (1509) and of Thomas Goodman (1510) at Winchester Priory were, besides teaching the boys plainsong and polyphony (*cantus et discantus*), to attend the daily Lady-

[1] *The Chronicle of John Stone*, pp. 11, 12, 188, 112, 114.

[2] In 1294–5, 1321 and 1328.

[3] The composer Sir William Hawte, knight, was connected with Canterbury; see below, p. 415.

[4] Legg and Hope, *Inventories of Christ Church, Canterbury*, p. 164.

[5] 'Solut' fratri Johanni Walden pro novo libro organorum xxs.' Pearce, *Monks of Westminster*, p. 131.

Mass in the Lady-chapel, the Friday Mass of Jesus in the nave, and services in the choir at Vespers on Saturday, at High Mass and Vespers on Sunday, and at first and second Vespers and High Mass on double feasts, singing or playing (*cantando et psallendo vel organisando*) as the precentor should direct. The deed of Matthew Fuller's appointment in 1538 required him to sing and play the organ (*in cantando et organisando*) in choir on double feasts and ferias at High Mass, processions and both Vespers, and at other times at the request of the precentor, as well as at the Lady-Mass and Jesus-Mass.[1] James Renynger's duties at Glastonbury (1534) were to sing and play the organ at the daily Mass, Offices and 'Anteymes' in the Lady-chapel and on festivals in the choir, and to teach six children 'pricke songe and descaunte' and two of them to play the organ, the monastery undertaking to provide 'clavyngcordes'.[2]

The objects of the greater abbeys in supporting singers to perform votive Masses and antiphons in polyphony were to foster the devotion of the people and to add to the renown of their community. Not only would it have been difficult, as Wheathampstead pointed out, to provide enough singers from the community, but also it was questionable whether regulars should be occupied in the study and performance of elaborate music. Cardinal Wolsey put the second of these points very clearly in the statutes for Augustinian canons which he wrote in 1519. Observing that 'plainsong chanted with modest gravity and in a sweet and tranquil style, which draws the souls of listeners to spiritual delight and a longing for the music of heaven, is more to be approved for all ecclesiastics than wanton melodies which please the senses of the listener or elaborate rhythms which excite his admiration for the performers', he strictly forbade the use of polyphony (*cantus fractus vel divisus* pricksong *vulgariter et Anglice dictus*) in choir by the canons or others. Nor were outside singers, whether lay or secular, men or boys, to be allowed in the choir during services. It was permitted, however, that laymen, seculars and boys might sing with polyphony and organ the Lady-Mass and the Mass of the

[1] Winchester Cathedral Library, Enrolment Register 2, fo. 44–44v; Enrolment Register 3, fo. 73.
[2] Deed of appointment (in English) in *The Reliquary*. vi 1892, p. 176.

Name of Jesus, and other such music as it was customary to sing outside the conventual choir in all the monasteries of the kingdom, none of the canons being present except the celebrant. The canons themselves might use a simple setting of the plain-song—and perhaps faburden is meant here—on Sundays and festivals, provided that the integrity of the chant and the clarity of the ritual words were not affected. Wolsey conceded that because of the small number of canons in some Augustinian monasteries an organ could be used in choir, and a layman or secular clerk 'of honest conversation' could be engaged to play it, provided the canons avoided undue familiarity with him.[1]

Polyphony, both vocal and organ, was used at the Augustinian Abbey of St. Mary of the Meadows in Leicester in the late fifteenth century. An inventory of the books in the choir made c. 1493 by Brother W. Charite, the Precentor, includes plainsong books at the high altar and at ten other altars and in the stalls of the Abbot and twenty-two other canons. Under the heading Cantica organica there are a book of polyphony by Brother T. Preston[2] which began with an antiphon, and two books of polyphony by Charite himself, one of which had the words qui caelum et terram at the beginning of the second folio, while the other, which was called by the curious name 'Zon-glouers', began with a Kyrie.[3] The Abbey also possessed two books of organ music which Charite had compiled.[4] There was an establishment of singers at the Augustinian Abbey of the Holy Cross at Waltham in Essex, for a document comprising an inventory of the possessions and a list of wages and gratuities given to lay servants of the monastery at the dissolution shows that there were some twelve singing-men and five choristers,

[1] Wilkins, Concilia, iii, p. 686.

[2] Who may be the composer of the organ music in the British Museum MS. Add. 29996. See below, pp. 192, 217, 364–6, 394–5. In 1543 a Preston was organist and instructor of the choristers at Magdalen and a Preston whose first name is also unrecorded was instructor of the choristers and joint organist with Marbeck at Windsor in 1558–9. Bloxam, Register of Magdalen, ii, p. 190. Fellowes, Windsor Organists, pp. 22–3.

[3] 'Item unus liber de canticis organicis per fr. T. Preston 2° fo quedam antiphona incipiens 2° fo prolem in cruce; Item alius liber de canticis organicis per fr. W. Charite vocat' Zonglouers 2° fo kyrieleyson; Item alius liber de canticis organicis per eundem 2° fo qui celum et terram.' James and Thompson, 'Leicester Abbey Inventories', pp. 46–51.

[4] See below, p. 216.

and that the goods included 'a lytell payre of organes' in the Lady-chapel, and 'a great long payre' and 'a lesser payr' in the choir. Thomas Tallis's name is fourth in a list of seventy laymen, and he signed his name on the last page of a collection of musical treatises which has on one of its pages *Liber sanctae crucis de Waltham*.[1]

The rule of the Brigittine nuns of Syon contained a forthright prohibition of polyphony and of organs in their offices. In the Hours services their singing was to be 'sadde sober and symple withe out brekyng of notes and gay relesynge withe alle mekenes and devocion; but organs schal thei never have none; ther psalmody schal be distyncte and open . . .'[2] Yet the earliest surviving piece of liturgical polyphony for the organ in England[3] is based on the Brigittine version of the offertory *Felix namque*,[4] which differs distinctly from the Sarum version, and may have come from Syon, the only Brigittine house established in England. A possible explanation of this contradictory evidence is that the prohibition did not apply to the brethren who formed part of the community and celebrated Mass.

The survival in Scotland of a choirbook and a set of five part-books shows that the chief polyphonic forms of the early sixteenth century were composed and copied there. The choirbook[5] is a collection of Masses for from three to ten voices, Magnificats and Mary-antiphons for four and five, and a setting of the Jesus-antiphon *O bone Jesu* for the extraordinary number of nineteen. The only composer named is Robert Carver alias Arnat, Canon of Scone,[6] and the manuscript probably belonged to that Augustinian abbey. Carver's compositions include a four-part Mass on *l'Homme armé*, a Mass of St. Michael, *Dum sacrum misterium*, for ten voices dated 1513 (*recte*

---

[1] Fellowes, *English Cathedral Music*, pp. 6–7; *Tudor Church Music*, vi, pp. xii–xiii.

[2] Aungier, *Syon Monastery*, p. 319.

[3] Printed in Dart, 'A New Source of Early English Organ Music', p. 205.

[4] As it appears in Trinity College, Dublin, MS. L.1.13.

[5] Edinburgh, National Library of Scotland, Advocates' Library, MS. 5.1.15.

[6] Robertus Carwor was one of the signers of a deed of lands by the monastery of Scone to John and William Haliburton dated November 4, 1544; *Liber Ecclesie de Scon*, pp. 206–7.

1508 or 1509),[1] a four-part Mass dated 1546 'in his fifty-ninth year', a four-part setting of *Gaude flore virginali*, and the nineteen-part *O bone Jesu*. The compiler drew also on French and English sources, for among the contents are Dufay's *l'Homme armé* Mass, two antiphons by Robert Fayrfax, here anonymous, Magnificats by Nesbett and Walter Lambe and William Cornysh's *Salve regina*, these three also without their composer's names, but identifiable from the Eton choirbook.[2] The part-books are traditionally connected with Dunkeld,[3] and all the music is anonymous, though a blank page at the end of one of the books has the information: 'Robert Doibglas with my hand at the pen William Fischer'. The notation and style of the twenty pieces which form the main contents, and which include fifteen Mary-antiphons, strongly suggest a continental origin. Three identifications support this deduction, for the pieces include Josquin's *Benedicta es*,[4] Jaquet of Mantua's *Ave virgo gloriosa*,[5] and an anonymous setting of *Virgo clemens et benigna*, a complete copy of which is in a Florentine manuscript now in the Biblioteca Vallicelliana in Rome.[6] At the end of the Dunkeld books there are two Masses, both certainly of British origin, the second of which is based on the respond *Jesu Christe fili Dei*.

Cathedrals of the New Foundation

The smaller monasteries were suppressed in 1536, and by 1540 all monasteries and their possessions had been appropriated to the Crown. The nine which were episcopal sees, namely Canterbury, Carlisle, Durham, Ely, Norwich, Rochester, Winchester, Worcester and Christ Church in Dublin, were refounded as secular cathedrals and became known as cathedrals of the New Foundation. Three other monasteries, Chester, Gloucester and Peterborough, became the cathedrals

---

[1] 'In his twenty-second year.'

[2] See the list of contents in *The Eton Choirbook*, i, p. 142.

[3] Edinburgh, University Library, MS. Db.I.7, now bound in one volume, described in a Library catalogue of *c.* 1695 as 'Music of the Church of Dunkeld—5 vols.'

[4] Printed in *Josquin des Prez*, Motets, xi, p. 11.

[5] Printed in *Adriani Willaert Opera Omnia*, iv, p. 117.

[6] See E. Lowinsky, 'A Newly Discovered Sixteenth-Century Motet Manuscript', in *Journal of the American Musicological Society*, iii, 1950, p. 229.

of newly-established sees, and Bath Abbey was secularized, the diocese remaining Bath and Wells. Oxford became a diocese in 1542, and four years later its cathedral was transferred from Oseney, formerly an Augustinian Abbey, to the chapel of Christ Church, which has served from that time both as the cathedral of the diocese and the chapel of the college. Westminster Abbey also became a secular foundation, was joined to the see of London in 1550, and in 1560 became a Royal Peculiar and a collegiate church with a dean and twelve canons. Some monasteries, particularly those in which the parishioners had rights for worship, were continued as parish churches, and at least the parts of their buildings to which those rights applied were preserved.

The musical establishment of cathedrals of the New Foundation consisted of minor canons, lay clerks or vicars, choristers, and a master of the choristers. The number of singers varied according to the resources which the royal warrants put at the disposal of the new dean and chapter. The persons approved by the King in 1541 for the new constitution of Winchester, for example, were a dean and twelve canons, twelve 'Petycanons to synge in the Quere', twelve 'laye men to synge and serve in the Quere daily *Anglice* Vycars', twelve choristers, a master of the choristers (Richard Wynslade or Wynslate), and a gospeller and epistoler.[1] In 1546 the dean and prebends of Christ Church, Oxford, were ordered to provide for eight petty canons, a gospeller and epistoler, eight clerks, a master of the choristers, eight choristers and two sextons.[2] At Worcester from 1544 there were ten minor canons, a master of the choristers (Richard Fyssher), a deacon as gospeller, a sub-deacon as epistoler, eight lay-clerks and ten choristers. At Gloucester the numbers were six minor canons, six lay-clerks, a deacon and sub-deacon, eight choristers and a master.[3]

[1] *Winchester Cathedral Documents, 1541–1547*, p. 54. In Henry VIII's statutes of 1544 the vicars were referred to as 'Laici clerici', and the services were to be 'secundum morem et ritum aliarum ecclesiarum Cathedralium; Ad officio vero noctu decantanda eos obligari nolumus'. Ibid., pp. 130, 138.

[2] An inventory of Christ Church dated May 19, 1545, includes 'a paire of organce, with a torned chane to the same', and an unspecified number of 'prickeson bokes for men and childerne'. Dugdale, *Monasticon*, ii, pp. 166, 173.

[3] Atkins, *Early Occupants of the Office of Organist of Worcester*, p. 20.

The Latin Breviary printed by Edward Whitchurch in 1541 was the first liturgical book of the English Church, but it was still *secundum usum Sarum* and the only change was the exclusion of all references to the Pope and to St. Thomas of Canterbury.[1] The duties of the choir of a cathedral of the New Foundation during the remaining years of the Sarum rite may be gathered from the injunctions of Nicholas Heath, Bishop of Rochester, to his cathedral at his visitation in 1543.[2] 'Imprimis it is or- deyned', they began, 'that all and every the prests clerks and other ministres of the Churche shall endevour theryself as myche as they can to do everything within the Churche wich is appoynted by the ordinall of Sarum to be done.' Then follow injunctions that the master of the choristers should himself 'kepe the orgayns' at Matins, Mass and Vespers on double feasts and on feasts of nine lessons, and should keep the organs himself or by deputy at Commemorations, at which the playing of the organ was to be at the discretion of the chanter; that the 'prests clarks and Choristers with the Master' should sing 'an Anteme in prycksong immediately that Complayn be fully done' on the vigil and the day of principal and double feasts and on every 'holyday' in the year; that on every 'holyday' except principal and greater double feasts, the priests, clerks, master and choristers should sing Lady-Mass 'in pryckesonge with the orgaines', unless High Mass was 'of our Lady', that is, on feasts of the Virgin, when Lady-Mass was to be said; that Prime and the Hours services should be omitted on these holy days, in order that the Lady-Mass should be sung in polyphony; and that on 'woorkedays' the choristers should sing the Lady- Mass in polyphony with the organ.

At Christ Church, Dublin, the canons regular of the monas- tery became the members of the new secular foundation, which included a vicar for each dignitary with the rank of minor canon, four minor vicars, four choristers, and three *clerici chorales*, one of whom acted as master of the boys, organist and

[1] The title was 'Portiforium secundum usum Sarum noviter impressum et plurimis purgatum mendis. In quo nomen Romano pontifici falso adscrip- tum omittitur, una cum aliis que Christianissimo nostri Regis Statuto repugnant.' The shrine of St. Thomas in Canterbury was destroyed and his name ordered to be excised from the liturgy in 1538.

[2] *Use of Sarum*, ii, pp. 234–6.

bedell. The duties of the members and the arrangement of the services, which were modelled on the practice of St. Patrick's, were laid down in a new set of statutes by the King's Commissioners in 1539.[1] When Robert Hayward was appointed as master of the choristers in 1546 he undertook to play the organ and keep the Lady-Mass and antiphon daily and the Jesus-Mass on Friday 'according to the custom of St. Patrick's', to play the organ at Matins on the eight principal feasts and on greater doubles, to procure suitable music at the cathedral's expense, and to teach the choristers pricksong and descant 'to four minims', that is, up to four notes to one upon the plainsong.[2] He was also to teach them to play the Lady-Mass, for which purpose the cathedral provided the necessary instruments.[3]

The Litany in English was issued in 1544,[4] for use instead of the Latin Litanies of Rogation days and times of trouble. In the same year Durham Cathedral bought 'viii ympnall noted ad xviiid.',[5] 'xxiiii latines whereof i dd [dozen] noted with playneson of fyve partes at iiis. the dd',[6] and paid twenty pence 'to the chaunter of Westmynster for pryking the new Latyny in iii, iiii, and v partes in prykeson'.[7]

Parish Churches

There is little evidence that polyphonic music was sung or played in parish churches before the second half of the fifteenth century. From that time larger churches began to provide themselves with the four things necessary for the adornment of their services with polyphony, namely a rood-loft, an organ, additional clerks or 'conducts', and books of pricksong. It had

---

[1] See the extracts printed as Appendix VI, below, p. 437.

[2] 'Quadrupla and Quintupla they denominate after the number of black minims set for a note of the plainsong.' Morley, *Plaine and Easie Introduction*, p. 171.

[3] West, *Cathedral Organists*, p. 28.

[4] Facsimile in Hunt, *Cranmer's First Litany*.

[5] The Sarum *Hymni cum notis* was first printed in 1518, and there were editions in 1524, 1525, 1533, 1541 and 1555.

[6] This entry confirms the existence in 1544 of a printed five-part Litany, otherwise known only from a reference in a copy of Maunsell's *Catalogue of English Books* of 1595. See Fellowes, *English Cathedral Music*, p. 25.

[7] *Durham Account Rolls*, iii, p. 726.

always been essential that the parish priest should have a clerk in minor orders, who was known as the 'parish clerk', to sing or read the epistle at Mass, to alternate (*repetere*) with the priest in singing the psalms at the offices, and to keep the parish school.[1] The additional singers and organ player engaged by a parish church were either clerks in lower orders or laymen,[2] and in either case might be termed 'conducts', since they were stipendiary persons who were not a permanent charge on the parish. In most churches the engagements did not go beyond an arrangement with one or more singers to be present on festivals, usually the Christmas and Easter seasons and the feast of the church's patron saint, and the reward was often refreshment in the ale-house in addition to, or instead of, money. St. Michael's, Cornhill, for example, paid in 1473 'to my Ladye Bokyngham clerkes for their singyng 8d'. At St. Mary-at-Hill, Billingsgate, there were payments in 1484–5 'To singers on St. Barnabas evynyn wyne at Easter and at many other festes of the yer to syngers within the quere vs.'; in 1498–9 to 'Symond Vaireson for helpyng of the quiere all the halydays of Crystmas 3s. 4d.'; in 1502–3 to William Wylde the same sum for a like service at Easter and Whit; in 1534 to 'iii singing men at Easter for helpyng the quyer vs.'; and in 1535 to two singing men for the same at 'ester hollydayes and loo sunday vis.', and to 'vii conducts to sing evensong upon our ladies even xxd.' St. Andrew Hubbard paid in 1496–7 for 'Wyne for singers on the Church holyday 8d.'; in 1528–9 to a 'Conduct on holydays 16d.'; and in 1531–2 'Apone sent Andrewes day to the syngyng men 12d.' The accounts of St. Stephen's, Walbrooke, have entries in 1518 to 'Singers on our Church holyday 20d.', and 'To the syngers on the Invencyon off Synt stevyn 20d.'; in 1526 'To the alehouse over the syngers on Seynt Stephyn Evyn vid.' and 'in Rewarde to the syngers that day 6s. 8d.', and 'Spent on them at the ale house after the last evynsong 7d.' [3]

In 1486 the Dean of the Royal Household Chapel gave per-

[1] Atchley, *The Parish Clerk*, pp. 6–7.

[2] Occasionally a priest, as at St. Mary-at-Hill in 1529–30: 'Brede and Drynk at the hyryng of Sir Symond the Base that cam from Seint Antonys iiiid.' *Medieval Records of a London Church*, p. 349.

[3] Entries from Cox, *Churchwardens' Accounts*, Chapter XV; *Medieval Records of a London Church*. The entries referring to music in the latter are discussed in Baillie, 'A London Church in Early Tudor Times'.

mission for Gilbert Banester and the singers of the chapel to sing at Vespers on Corpus Christi in St. Margaret's, Westminster,[1] and the churchwardens' accounts of St. Margaret's for 1484–6 record that twelve pence halfpenny was spent on 'bread ale and wine on Corpus Christi day for the Singers of the King's Chapel'.[2] At various times between 1510 and 1528 St. Mary-at-Hill rewarded singers from the royal chapel with dinner and sometimes also with drink; this church also borrowed choristers from the church of St. Magnus for St. Barnabas' day in 1478 or 1479, and 'a chyld that songe a trebyll to helpe the quere in crystmas halydayes' in 1493. In 1490 they paid three shillings and four pence, and the 'finding' of their clothes, to two children for their services from Midsummer to Michaelmas.

The Guild of Jesus and the Holy Cross of St. Edmund's church, Salisbury,[3] was responsible for the support of the Jesus-altar there and for the payment of its chaplain and clerk. The earliest surviving account (1476–7) of the stewards of the guild records a payment of twenty-two shillings to some chaplains and clerks for singing the Mass and antiphon of Jesus on Fridays in Lent 'as in former years', and also an amount of eighteen pence to the clerks who sang 'Salve de Jesu' on Fridays in Lent.[4] It appears from the accounts for 1500–1 that these clerks were singers from the cathedral and that the eighteen pence was for the cost of their refreshment, which is referred to as 'drynkynges in Lent after Salve' in 1535–6, when the cost was five shillings and eight pence, and in 1538–9, when it was four shillings. The 'quyrysters' of the cathedral took part in the Salve, and also in the bread and ale, from 1539–40 until the year of the last surviving account of the Guild, which is for 1546–7.[5] The accounts of the churchwardens of St. Edmund's, which are a

[1] Flood, *Early Tudor Composers*, p. 15.

[2] Cox, *Churchwardens' Accounts*, p. 209.

[3] Dedicated to St. Edmund (Rich) of Abingdon, Archbishop of Canterbury 1234–40, formerly Treasurer of Salisbury.

[4] In 1499–1500: 'for bred and ale for preists and Clerkes that syngyth the Salveis every fryday in the lent xxd.' *Churchwardens' Accounts of St. Edmund and St. Thomas Sarum*, pp. 248–9, 252.

[5] Ibid., pp. 271–2. The Churchwardens' Accounts for 1553–4 have: 'paper and yncke to make a Newe Songe for the Salve iid.'; the Salve payments appear in those accounts from 1553 to 1558. Ibid., pp. 100–103.

separate series, mention both organs and a rood-loft in 1443–6,[1] while an inventory of the church's possessions in 1472 contains some fifty service books, including 'i boke for the organes in ii^de fo. *jam tuam*'[2] and a Missal and two 'grayles' (Graduals) for the Lady-Mass.[3] In 1403 the King gave possession of the church of St. Thomas the Martyr in Salisbury to the Dean and Chapter of the Cathedral, and the members of the cathedral body served the church by turn. It may be that the *informator* of the cathedral was afterwards responsible for the music, for Thomas Knyght was paid eight shillings in 1537–8 for his stipend as *organista* of the church.[4]

During the first half of the sixteenth century some parish churches took a further step in the development of their ritual by engaging for longer terms clerks and laymen who presumably sang polyphony on festivals and in votive Masses and antiphons. By 1514–15, for example, the parish clerk at St. Mary-at-Hill had been joined by two conducts, and in 1532–3 three singers served for the full year and two others for more than half of the year and were paid at an annual rate of ten pounds or less. Five years later the accounts list nine singers, of whom Thomas Tallis served for six months and Richard Wynslatt for a quarter; two of the nine served for the full year and others for periods ranging from three weeks to ten months.[5]

Entries referring to books of polyphonic music begin to appear in inventories and accounts of parish churches in the second half of the fifteenth century, for example at St. Margaret's, New Fish Street, London, in 1472[6] and at St. Christopher-le-Stocks, London, in 1488.[7] The 'Bokes of Pricksong'

---

[1] 'Roberto Denby pro factura le Orgelis xis. xd.'; 'i Tinctori pro panno pro le Rode loffte tingendo viiis.' Ibid., p. 358.

[2] *Recte* 'iram tuam'? Cf. *Antiphonale Sarisburiense*, pl. 6.

[3] *Churchwardens' Accounts of St. Edmund and St. Thomas Sarum*, pp. 3–4.

[4] Salisbury Muniments.

[5] This year (1537–8) the church paid 'for xxxvi elles of cloth for vi surplyces for the conductes and iiii for the children at viid. the elle Summa xxis.'

[6] Wordsworth and Littlehales, *Old Service Books*, pl. II (facsimile of an inventory).

[7] 'A Pryk songe boke of paper royall with divers masses therein, begynnyng in the first lyne of the secunde leeffe *Ne filii ūm*', i.e., probably (*Domi*)*ne fili uni*(*genite*) from the Gloria. The church also had 'in the Rode loft a paire of Orgons with the ii peire blewers. The orgons closse, to be shitte with

in an inventory of service-books belonging to St. Laurence, Reading, in 1516 are described as: 'A great boce of vellem bourded for masses of the gifte of Willm Stannford; Another boke bourded of paper with masses & antempins; An old boke bourded with antempins; Anoyther of vellame bordyd with antems & exultavits'.[1] The accounts of St. Mary-at-Hill show that a 'prickid song Booke' was bought in 1483–5; that in 1521–2 John Darlington, a conduct, was paid for a 'pryksonge boke of Kyryes Allelyas and Sequences'; that John Northfolke, also a conduct, supplied 'prykkd song bokes of the which v of them be with Antemys and v with Massis' in 1529–30; and that 'Sir Marke', probably the Marke Fletcher whose name is among the priests in the same account, supplied 'carolles for cristmas' and 'v square bookes' in 1537–8. The inventory of 1553 includes 'x bokes of song to be soung at mas in parchement with v Caroll boks' and 'v littell song bokes in parchement and v song bokes in paist with v song bokes to be sung at mas, in paist'. In 1542 St. Stephen's, Coleman St., London, had 'Item a boke for the organs. . . . Item a boke for Rectores. . . . Item iii hymnalls and olde pricke songe boke'.[2]

The Reformation Inventories of the churches of London show that out of one hundred and nine churches the following nine churches possessed one or more books of polyphonic music: All Hallows the Great, 'v Sawters and xii other pricksong bookes'; Holy Trinity the Less, 'iiii pryke song bokes'; St. Laurence, Pountney, 'iiii bookes for prycksong'; St. Mary-le-Bow, 'iii pricksong bookes'; St. Mary Woolchurch, 'vii small bookes of prycke songe'; St. Michael-le-Quern, 'a pryk songe boke' and also 'a boke of Jhus masse yn parchement'; St. Olave, Hart Street, 'v Salters and iii pryke songe bokes'; St. Peter, West Cheap, 'viii pryksonge bokes'; and St. Peter upon Cornhill, 'iiii synging bokes of Prycksonge'.[3]

close leffes'. Freshfield, 'On the Parish Books of . . . St. Christopher-le Stocks', pp. 118–19.

[1] Kerry, *History of St. Laurence, Reading*, p. 103.

[2] Freshfield, 'Some Remarks upon the Records of St. Stephen, Colman Street', p. 46.

[3] Walters, *London Churches at the Reformation*; for pages see the index under Pricksong.

The Medieval Organ

The study of medieval records has thrown considerable light on the development of the organ as an instrument, on the details of its design and structure, and on the activities of organ builders in the later Middle Ages.[1] On the other hand, comparatively little is known of the function of the organ in the services and its place among the other elements of liturgical ceremonial. The two aspects of the history of the instrument are not unrelated, for the ritual use of the organ was determined not only by its size and resources but also by the particular ritual forms in which it was used. Bound up with both of these sides of its history is the further question of its place in the building, whether in the pulpitum, in a gallery or elsewhere. The position and function of the several organs in a larger church have an obvious relation to the musical needs of the various services sung in the choir itself, in the nave, and in a votive chapel.

To understand the true scale and proportion of the music of the medieval liturgy it is essential to realize that the choir of a large church was an enclosed space designed for the common devotions of the members of its community. It was in effect their private chapel, to which the public were not admitted during the service, and from which, in the case of monastic churches, they were excluded at all times. The western boundary of the choir was a stone choir-screen (*pulpitum*) with a central door (*ostium* or *introitus chori*), built between two of the main columns at either the east or west side of the crossing, or in some cases farther westward in the nave.[2] The choir-screen was under the eastern arch of the crossing in the secular cathedrals, except at Hereford and St. David's, where the choir extended to the first bay of the nave on account of the shortness of the eastern limb of the buildings. There were other exceptions in earlier cathedrals, as in the arrangement at Wells in the twelfth and thirteenth centuries, and that at Old Sarum,[3]

[1] See Hopkins, *The English Medieval Church Organ*; Apel, 'Early History of the Organ'; Sumner, *The Organ*.

[2] The following have been consulted: Bond, *Screens and Galleries*; Hope, 'Quire Screens in English Churches'; Vallance, *English Church Screens* and *Greater English Church Screens*.

[3] The move to New Sarum took place in the time of Richard Poore.

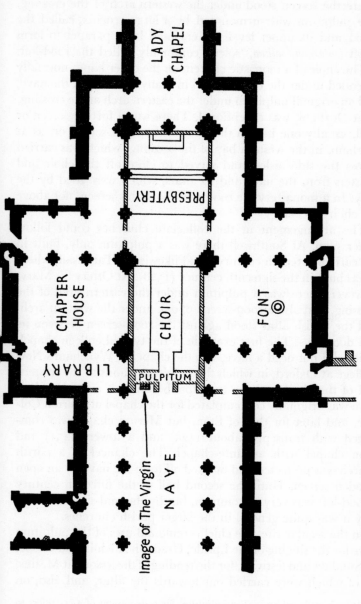

Original arrangement of the choir at Wells. Between 1295 and 1333 the choir was lengthened eastwards, the choir-screen was moved to the east side of the crossing and the present chapter-house was built where the screen stood under the western arch of the crossing. The pulpitum was surmounted by a large crucifix, called the Rood, and its upper level was enclosed by a parapet to form a loft (*solarium, solium*, 'soler') commonly called the rood-loft.

The choir of a monastic church, on the other hand, normally extended under the crossing and in many cases down the nave, and an original pulpitum under the eastern arch of the crossing, as at Durham, was exceptional. There was a further screen or wall, usually one bay to the west of the choir-screen or, as at Durham, in the western bay of the crossing, which was carried across the side aisles, and served to close off the choir and cloisters from the nave and its altars, which were used by the laity. In a monastery the rood was above this screen, not above the choir-screen.

The arrangement in the collegiate churches could follow either plan. At Southwell there was a pulpitum only, built in the early fourteenth century,[1] and likewise at Tattersall, where it was built in the sixteenth century (1528). At Ottery St. Mary, however, there was a pulpitum under the eastern arch of the crossing, and also a rood-screen of oak under the western arch, and the parish altar stood against the rood-screen between its two doorways. The first example of the typical college chapel, which did not need a nave, was the chapel of Wykeham's New College at Oxford, in which the pulpitum stands at the western end of the choir and the transepts become an ante-chapel. A nave was originally contemplated for the chapel of Merton College, and later for that of Eton, but Merton chapel was completed with transepts (about 1425) and a tower (1451) and Eton chapel with an ante-chapel. The chancel of a parish church was protected and marked off from the nave by an open wooden screen. Until the second half of the fifteenth century a rood-loft was very uncommon, but by the mid-sixteenth century it was quite general in the larger parish churches.

In the secular rites the chief ceremonial uses of the pulpitum were for the singing of the Epistle, Gradual, Alleluia and Gospel on Sundays and festivals, for the reading of the lessons at Matins, all of which were carried out towards the altar, and also, on

---

[1] Which replaced an earlier pulpitum, for a document of 1221 refers to clerks reading 'in choro vel in pulpito'; *Visitations and Memorials of Southwell*, p. 208.

occasions, for the ritual which took place before the rood during processions, and which was directed towards the nave. The monastic practice seems to have varied, and though Lanfranc's Constitutions do not mention the pulpitum, the evidence suggests that it was used for reading the lessons at Matins, but not for reading the Epistle and Gospel.[1]

The earliest references to organs in Britain are contained in the writings of Bede (d. 735) and St. Aldhelm (d. 709), in the account by William of Malmesbury, writing c. 1120, of the organs given by St. Dunstan (924–88) to the abbeys of Malmesbury, Abingdon and Glastonbury, and in the description by the monk Wulstan (d. 963) of the enormous organ erected by Bishop Elphege (d. 951) at Winchester, which had four hundred pipes and needed seventy blowers and two players. Among the few records of the existence of organs in the twelfth and thirteenth centuries are a deed of 1172 in which Henry de Blois, Bishop of Winchester, gave the cathedral the revenue of certain churches, among them the 'church of Ellendone for the making of books and the repairing of organs',[2] and a note that Prior Hugh Darlington had *magnum campanile, organa grandiora* made at Durham in 1264.[3] Wulstan wrote of the Winchester organ: 'Like thunder the iron voice batters the ear, so that it may receive no other sound', and other descriptions of the effects of early medieval organs refer to sounds of impressive, and even deafening, volume. Though remarks on the ritual function of the organ in the early Middle Ages are scarce, they give some ground for speculation. According to a summary of the customs of St. Augustine's, Canterbury, which was written in the thirteenth century, the organ was used there on Christmas Day, St. John's day, St. Thomas's day, the Epiphany at High Mass, the feast of St. Adrian (Abbot of Canterbury, d. 710) and its octave, the Purification (if not in Lent) at High Mass, the Annunciation (if in Eastertide), Easter Day, the Translation of St. Augustine at both Vespers and *ad prosam ad evangelium* (that is, in the sequence at Mass),

---

[1] Hope, 'Quire Screens in English Churches', pp. 104–6. Norwich, where the Epistle and Gospel were sung from the pulpitum on feasts, seems to be an exception. *Customary of Norwich*, p. 216.

[2] *Chartulary of Winchester*, p. 2.

[3] *Historiae Dunelmensis Scriptores Tres*, p. 46.

and on the feast of St. Michael in the sequence only.[1] The function of the organ at Vespers is not specified, but its use for the sequence underlines the character of that part of the Mass as an outburst of praise, when not only the voices and the organ but also the bells joined in the festive sound. Another festive use of the organ recorded in monastic annals is with the singing of the Te Deum at times of special rejoicing, as when the Prior of Winchester ordered the community to ring the bells and sing 'a solemn Te Deum to the accompaniment of the organ' for the restoration of Adam of Dalton as Bishop in 1334 after a dispute with the King.[2] The chronicle of St. Alban's, in a description of the reception of an Abbot-elect, tells us that the Te Deum was solemnly begun as he was led into the church and presented to God and St. Alban at the high altar, with all the bells ringing and the shawms ('which we call *burdones*') and the clock sounding.[3] At the reception of Abbot John Moote in 1396 the Te Deum was solemnly sung by the community, 'the organ alternating'.[4]

These few indications seem to point to the use of a comparatively large organ, apparently to alternate with the choir in the performance of sequences, of the Te Deum, and perhaps of hymns, to distinguish occasions of special festivity. Presumably the organist would play the single notes of the plainsong, and if there were two players, as for the organ depicted in the Utrecht Psalter (eighth to ninth centuries)[5] and the Winchester organ, they would perhaps perform the plainsong in parallel fourths or fifths, in the manner of early vocal organum.[6] Such

[1] *Customary of St. Augustine's, Canterbury, and St. Peter's, Westminster*, ii, 293–4, 268. Another reference to the organ reads: 'Quociens organa trahuntur ter in una festivitate, dabit sacrista v. denarios folles trahentibus.' Ibid., p. 259.

[2] *Chartulary of Winchester*, p. 118.

[3] 'Incipiatur solemniter hymnus *Te Deum laudamus* et ducatur modeste et ordinate (assistente Priore ei in uno latere Suppriore in alio cum aliis dignioribus ecclesiae personis propinquius), in ecclesiam et presentatur Deo et Sancto Martyri Albano ad majus altare, pulsato classico sonantibus chalamis (quos "burdones" appellamus) cum horologio.' *Gesta Abbatum*, i, p. 520.

[4] 'Finito vero sermone Hymnus *Te Deum laudamus* per conventum, alternantibus organis, solemniter et devote decantatus fuit.' Ibid., iii, p. 434.

[5] Reproduced in *Die Musik in Geschichte und Gegenwart*, s.v. 'Benediktiner'; Apel, 'Early History of the Organ', opposite p. 209; Sumner, *The Organ*, p. 21.

[6] See Apel, 'Early History of the Organ', pp. 210–13.

an organ would not be on a pulpitum, nor would it be suitable for combining with a group of solo voices.

It is difficult to determine when and where the practice of placing an organ in the pulpitum originated. It is possible that the northern minsters inherited an older tradition, for a pulpitum had been set up at Beverley by Archbishop Ealdred of York between 1060 and 1069,[1] and a York document of 1236 refers to the use of a 'pair of organs' by John the organist.[2] For the secular cathedrals these centuries were a period of building and rebuilding, which in many cases was not completed until the late thirteenth or early fourteenth century. At Exeter, for example, the new choir and presbytery were built between 1270 and 1310, and the existing choir-screen was begun in 1317. In the following year a grant of 1284 by Bishop Quivil to a bell-founder for making the bells and repairing the organ and the clock was confirmed by Royal Patent.[3] From the second half of the fourteenth century onwards the records of secular churches amply demonstrate that the organ used for services in choir was invariably placed in the pulpitum. It seems safe to assume, therefore, that *organa in choro* always means the organ in the pulpitum, and that an organ was never placed on the main level of the choir or presbytery.

In the secular uses bells were rung during the singing of the sequence, but there is no definite indication that the organ was played also. It may not be idle, however, to notice here the striking use of musical imagery in some of the Sarum sequences, in such phrases as *jungat laudibus organi pneuma*; *Syllabatim pneumata perstringendo organica*; *Jungendo verba symphoniae rhythmica, concrepans inclyta harmonia vera caeli lumina*; and *In qua symphonia miscetur et illa quae vere diatessaron prima*. The sequence for the feast of a martyr, *Organicis canamus modulis*, illustrates the ways of God with his saints by a series of musical images. This kind of musical analogy seems to be peculiar to the sequence among forms of liturgical verse, and points to the connection we have suggested between vocal organum and the playing of the organ.

It seems most likely that the motet of the thirteenth and fourteenth centuries was normally performed in the pulpitum

---

[1] Hope, 'Quire Screens in English Churches', p. 51.
[2] Harrison, *Life in a Medieval College*, p. 153.
[3] *Calendar of Patent Rolls, 1317-21*, p. 72.

after the Sanctus and Benedictus, during the canon of the Mass, the neuma in the tenor part being played on an organ. This practice was developed in the secular churches of Paris and northern France and adopted by English secular cathedrals and some of the larger abbeys. The organ in this new era of its liturgical history was a 'positive' organ with one or two rows of pipes, placed in the centre of the pulpitum towards the choir; it was provided with a desk for music, and the singers stood around the player, facing towards the altar. Its main function was to combine with a small group of soloists in the performance of the motet and of the parts of the Mass which the soloists sang in the pulpitum and which were set in polyphony on important festivals.[1]

The evidence for this theory is indirect, for the musical manuscripts give no indication of methods of performance. It may be appropriate to cite here Christopher Wordsworth's description of the pulpitum at Lincoln as he saw it when the organ case was being replaced in 1898. 'The pulpitum', he wrote, referring to the part of it which projects towards the choir,

'is a half octagon capable of holding more than one person if necessary. It is mounted by three broad stone steps, the middle portion of them having been hacked away when an organ was erected in 1826. The pulpitum is of original oak, about the date of the stalls (1380). It has been altered in the present century to support gilded organ pipes. It overhangs the entrance into the choir, and was adapted for singing eastward (*not* towards the nave). Mr. Logsdail assures me, but I was in Lincoln too late to see this, that there were supports for book-desks on the angles above the dean's and the precentor's stalls, as for the Epistle and Gospel. The upper step or platform being wider than the pulpitum would hold several singers if required. There is a still larger stone bench with its back towards the nave where they could sit hidden by the western part of the screen

[1] A significant exception was St. Paul's, where in 1289 Dean William de Montfort forbade the custom, then probably new (the choir-screen was built in the late thirteenth century), of singing polyphony in the pulpitum, and ordered that it should be sung in the presbytery: 'Et quod de cetero in Choro cantent cantus organicos ubi Epistola de more legitur, et non in pulpito, sicut fieri consuevit.' *Charters and Statutes of the Minor Canons of St. Paul's*, p. 104.

till it was time to mount the stone platform in front of them.'[1]

The organ developed rapidly during the fifteenth and early sixteenth centuries, when it was built in a great variety of sizes and brought into use in many more churches. The new organs built on the pulpitum in some of the secular cathedrals were much larger than hitherto, judging by their cost. The chapter of Lincoln resolved in 1442 that their new organ should be the finest obtainable, but only the first payment, of five marks to 'Arnold Organor' de civitate Norwyc', is recorded in the published summary of the acts.[2] A new choir-screen was built at Chichester, probably by Bishop Arundel, and in 1513–14 an organ was installed at a cost of twenty-six pounds, sixteen shillings and eleven pence;[3] a new organ at Lichfield in 1482 cost twenty-six pounds, three shillings and four pence; at Exeter in 1513–14 the cost, including installation, was one hundred and sixty-four pounds, fifteen shillings and sevenpence farthing.[4]

In colleges and collegiate churches the pulpitum, which invariably had an organ, was regarded as essential for carrying out the Sarum rite according to the custom of larger churches. In his final plan for the chapel at Eton Henry VI desired that there should be a space 'be hynde the Provostes stall unto the qwere dore vi fote, for a wey into the Rodelofte for redyng and syngyng and for the Organs and other manere observance there to be had after the Rewles of the Churche of Salesbury'. The pulpitum in King's College chapel, which the founder planned as 'a reredos beryng the Rodeloft departyng the quere and the body of the chirch', was built between 1531 and 1536, and is an early example of Italian Renaissance style in England.[5] According to the contract for the rood-loft at Merton it was 'to be made lyke unto the Rodeloft of Mawdelen College in Oxford', but there were 'to be made in the seide Rodelofft ferre better dorys then ther be in Mawdelyn College aforeseid'.[6]

At Ripon the Lady-chapel organ was in a pulpitum, for the

---

[1] *Ceremonies and Processions of Salisbury*, p. 196.
[2] *Lincoln Statutes*, iii, p. 482.
[3] Sussex County Library, Chapter Act Book C.L.13, fo. 129.
[4] Hope, 'Quire Screens in English Churches', p. 49.
[5] Willis and Clark, *Architectural History of Cambridge*, i, pp. 366, 369, 409.
[6] *Registrum Collegii Mertonensis*, p. 521.

payment to Lawrence Lancaster in 1478–9 is described as *pro missa Beatae Mariae Virginis in capella ecclesiae praedictae vocata* Ladylofte *cum nota et organis custodienda*.[1] Ottery St. Mary had a Lady-chapel at the east end for the daily Lady-Mass required by the statutes, with its own stone pulpitum, which still exists. It is clear from the arrangement of the stairway to this pulpitum that it was not used for reading the Epistle and Gospel, which were read in the presbytery at the Lady-Mass, but solely for musical purposes. In 1545 Ottery St. Mary had 'a paire of organs in the Rodlofte [that is, over the wooden screen at the east end of the nave] praysed at xls.', besides 'a new pair of organs in the quere [that is, on the stone pulpitum] praysed at v lib', and 'a paire of organs in our Lady Chapel praysed at xs.'.[2] An inventory of the Collegiate Church of the Holy Cross, Crediton, made in the same year, has 'A great paire of organes praysed at viili. xiiis. iiiid.' in the choir, and 'a payre of organes praysed at xxs.' in the Lady-chapel.[3]

Durham paid ten shillings for having an organ made in 1377–8, and six shillings and eight pence for the same in 1425–6 and in 1435–6.[4] A list of the amounts spent on building and repairs at Durham between 1416 and 1446 includes an item of twenty-six pounds, thirteen shillings and four pence for making several organs (*factura diversorum organorum*) and one of sixty-nine pounds and four shillings for a new choir-screen (*novum opus vocatum le Rerdoose, ad ostium chori*).[5] An inventory of Meaux Abbey (Cistercian) in 1396 shows that there the larger organ was at the west end of the church (*organa majora in occidentali fine ecclesiae*) and the smaller in the choir (*organa minora in choro*).[6] Westminster Abbey had an organ in the choir in 1422–3, and in 1441–2 a new pair of organs was made for the choir at a cost of six pounds and fourteen shillings.[7] The Islip chapel or

---

[1] *Memorials of Ripon*, iii, p. 260.

[2] Dalton, *Collegiate Church of Ottery St. Mary*, p. 295.

[3] Whitley, 'Inventories of Crediton and Ottery', p. 560.

[4] *Durham Account Rolls*, iii, p. 586.

[5] *Historiae Dunelmensis Scriptores Tres*, p. cclxxiii.

[6] *Chronica Monasterii de Melsa*, iii, p. lxxxii.

[7] In 1422–3: 'In emendacione . . . organorum per fratrem Thomas Gedney xiiis.' Both entries are in the Sacrist's accounts. In 1387–8 there is the entry: 'Et cuidam Nichᵒ ludenti ad organa precepto domini Prioris, xxvis. viiid.' Pearce, *Monks of Westminster*, pp. 133, 135, 99.

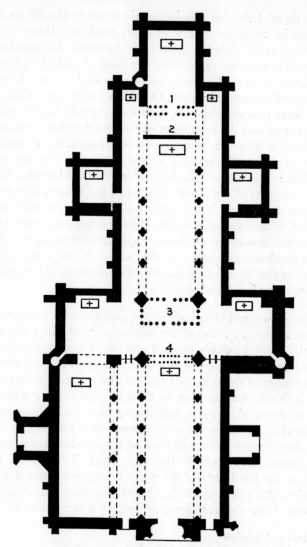

Ottery St. Mary: arrangement of the screens
1. Lady-chapel screen. 2. Reredos of High Altar. 3. Choir-screen. 4. Rood-screen.

chantry, which was built by John Islip (Abbot, 1500–32), consisted of a 'Jhesus Chapell beneath' and a 'Jesus Chapell above',
and the upper chapel, which was a loft with a Jesus-altar of its
own, had 'a payer of Organys with a corten of lynen cloth to

cover them'.[1] At the dissolution there were also 'ii payre of organes in the quyre'.[2] The changes made by Abbot Wheathamstead at St. Alban's apparently included the adoption of the secular manner of reading the Gospel and the provision of a large organ in the choir, for he provided a 'pair of organs' at a cost of seventeen pounds, six shillings and eight pence, and spent forty pounds odd on a 'wooden structure for the placing of the organ and the reading of the lessons'[3] which is elsewhere described as 'a certain new wooden structure at the western end of the choir for the reading of the Gospel'.[4] The organ was installed between 1420, the beginning of Wheathamstead's first abbacy, and 1428, for the chronicler of St. Alban's tells us that 'the new organs made a mighty noise' on the occasion of the visit of Cardinal Beaufort to the Abbey on September 22, 1428.[5]

The fullest account we have of the arrangements in a large monastic church is given by the writer of the reminiscences known as the 'Rites of Durham'. In addition to the organs for the votive masses,[6] Durham had

'3 paire of organs belonginge to the said quire for maintenance of gods service . . . one of the fairest paire of the 3 did stand over the quire dore only opened and playd upon at principall feastes, the pipes beinge all of most fine wood . . . there was but 2 paire more of them in all England of the same makinge, one paire in Yorke and another in Paules . . . also there was a letterne of wood like unto a pulpit standinge and adioyninge to the wood organs over the quire dore, where they had wont to singe the 9 lessons in the old time on principall dayes standinge with theire faces towards the high altar. The second paire stood on the north side of the quire beinge never playd upon but when the 4 doctors of the church was read, viz. Augustine Ambrose Gregorye and Jerome[7] beinge a faire paire of large

[1] *Monks of Westminster*, p. 168.

[2] Hopkins, *The English Medieval Church Organ*, p. 48.

[3] 'In factura unius paris organorum xviili. vis. viiid.'; 'in quadam fabrica lignea pro positione organorum et lectura lectionum praeter pecunias a fratribus datas xliiili. iiis. iiid. obol.' Amundesham, *Chronicle*, ii, p. 259.

[4] Ibid., p. 198.   [5] Ibid., i, p. 28.

[6] See above, pp. 188–9.

[7] I.e., on Sundays and festivals which were not principal feasts. *Rites of Durham*, p. 207.

organs called the cryers. The third paire was dayly used at ordinary service'.[1]

This third pair, according to an addition to the account written in the late seventeenth century, 'were called the White Organs, they were placed on the South side of the Quire towards the Vestry house, and were most, and indeed dayly, used at ordinary service, in the times of Queen Elizabeth and K. James I'. The original account observes that 'the said master [of the choristers] was bownd to plaie on the orgains every principall daie when the mouncks did sing ther high messe and likewise at evinsong, but the mouncks when thei weare at there mattens and service at mydnighte thene one of the said mounckes did plaie on the orgains themeselves and no other', presumably on the 'cryers' or 'white organs' according to the day.[2]

The period when organs were installed in parish churches corresponds exactly to the period of their building of rood-lofts, and there is no doubt that the 'rood-loft solved the problem of accommodating singers of prick-song and organ or other instrumental accompaniment', and that 'this was the primary cause of its introduction and its real duty'.[3] The rood-loft in a parish church was reached by narrow steps opening from the nave; there was no need for access to it from the choir, since it did not fulfil a ceremonial function. The organs at St. Saviour's, Dartmouth, in 1433,[4] at St. Peter Cheap, London, in the same year, at St. Mary's, Sandwich (Kent), in 1444, and at St. Michael's, Cornhill, in 1459 are among the earliest of which there is record.[5] Some idea of relative size may be gathered from the amounts paid for complete instruments, for example in 1455 at St. Margaret, Southwark, six pounds, six shillings and eight pence; in 1517–18 at St. Mary-at-Hill, sixteen pounds, and at St. Andrew, Holborn, for 'little organs', six pounds; in 1519 at All Hallows, Barking-by-the-Tower, fifty pounds, and at St. Petrock, Exeter, ten pounds; in 1520 at All Hallows,

---

[1] Ibid., p. 16.   [2] Ibid., pp. 62–3.

[3] Vallance, *English Church Screens*, p. 68.

[4] Watkin, *Dartmouth*, p. 328. The earliest payments to a player are in 1530 ('to Nicholas the organ player viis.') and 1531 ('to the Organ player for hys beyng here at Crismas iiis. ivd.'). Ibid., p. 312.

[5] Hopkins, *The English Medieval Church Organ*, pp. 35, 52.

Staining, for a pair of new organs and for mending the old, four pounds, six shillings and eight pence; in 1519 at All Saints, Bristol, ten pounds. Some larger churches had both a great and a small organ, as at St. Laurence, Reading, where in 1510 one Berkeleye was paid four pounds 'uppon a bargen of a payre of organnes', in 1512 Richard Turner and John Kent received thirty-two shillings and six pence for an organ, and in 1531 two pence was spent on 'mendyng the stoppes of the grete organs'.[1] Though comparatively few London churches possessed books of polyphonic music at the Reformation, most had one or two organs. In a few cases the inventory notes that one was on the rood-loft, as in St. Mary-le-Bow: 'solde to Thomas Edmondes ii paire of organs and the lofte that the one paire stode on vili. xiiis. viiid.'[2]

The Ritual Use of the Organ

The use of the organ in the liturgy between *c.* 1400 and the Reformation may have retained, at least in part, the earlier 'monastic' tradition of performing plainsong on the organ in single notes. Throughout this period the books 'for the organs' which were listed in inventories were often plainsong service-books, Antiphonal or Gradual, and it seems certain that the use of an organ did not necessarily imply the playing of polyphony, though a well-taught player would probably extemporize on the plainsong as he saw fit and as occasion demanded. It was not, apparently, until *c.* 1475 that it became customary to teach choristers to play keyboard instruments,[3] that is, to apply their knowledge of descant to the keyboard, while the earliest surviving examples of liturgical keyboard music date from *c.* 1520.[4]

The earlier 'secular' tradition of the performance of motets,

---

[1] All these entries except St. Mary-at-Hill and All Hallows, Barking, are from Cox, *Churchwardens' Accounts*, pp. 197 sqq. The contract for the organ at All Hallows still exists; see Hopkins, p. 54.

[2] Walters, *London Churches at the Reformation*, p. 441.

[3] The Durham Account Rolls have an entry in 1416–17: 'Cantori informanti juvenes in organis 2s. 6d.' *Durham Account Rolls*, ii, p. 287.

[4] Apart from the *Felix namque* referred to on p. 193, which may illustrate organ descant of the first half of the fifteenth century.

and of movements of the Ordinary of the Mass composed in motet-fashion, in the pulpitum with the participation of a small organ, came to an end *c.* 1450 with the disappearance of this style of composition. There is no evidence that the great organ took part in the performance of the large polyphonic masses and Magnificats of the period after 1450, nor would it have fulfilled any necessary or useful function by doing so. The extended votive antiphons of the time were sung before an image or crucifix, or in a separate chapel, and the contribution of a small organ to their ensemble would have been pointless. The idea behind the liturgical use of the organ in the later Middle Ages was not that it should act as accompaniment and support to choral music, but that it should be a further adornment of the ritual, sometimes being substituted for and sometimes complementing choral polyphony, or in certain circumstances serving to relieve the singers from the strain of continuous chanting.

The method of substituting the organ for singing in the performance of plainsong may be illustrated in its simplest form by the terms of a will of 1507–8 in which Thomas Miller left a rent of thirteen shillings to St. Olave's, Hart Street, London, with this direction: 'The Clerk of the said church is to have for his labour fourteen pence and so that he can find oon persone to kepe the Quere at same our Lady masse while he plaith at organs or elles that he kepe the quere whiles that same personne pleyes at organs'.[1] In this performance of the music of the Lady-Mass the player of the organ would act as ruler and soloist, the clerk who 'kept the choir' would sing the chorus parts of the plainsong, and they would alternate in certain parts of the Ordinary. Similarly, in the performance in a large church of the music of a votive Mass with a polyphonic choir and the organ, which always took place 'out of choir', the master of the choristers would act as ruler and soloist at the organ, alternating with the choir in the parts of the Ordinary which were not set in vocal polyphony throughout. The value of the organ in easing the work of singers is illustrated by Wolsey's concession to the Austin Canons that their smaller communities might relieve with 'the melody of an organ' the strain of singing several Masses and the canonical hours daily. It was also part of Wolsey's purpose to avoid the danger of lax and inattentive

[1] Provah, *The Annals of St. Olave, Hart Street*, p. 62.

devotion.[1] In the larger monasteries the organ served to adorn the ritual music of festivals, their stipendiary choirs being concerned only with the singing of votive Masses and antiphons out of choir. In the greater secular foundations, on the other hand, choral polyphony was sung in choir on festivals, while the organ supplied polyphonic music on lesser feasts and Sundays, when choral polyphony was not sung.

Unfortunately, only one collection of liturgical organ music has survived in anything like complete form.[2] Its music for the Mass comprises a setting of the Ordinary, partly *alternatim*, and Offertory for Trinity Sunday; an incomplete setting of the soloist's part of the Proper, the Sequence being *alternatim*, for Easter Sunday; and settings of *Felix namque*, the Offertory in the Lady-Mass *Salve sancta parens*, and of Offertories for lesser feasts. For the offices it contains hymns and a Magnificat for Vespers, antiphons for Compline, and hymns and the *Te Deum* for Matins and Lauds. The repertory of organ music at Leicester Abbey is summarized in William Charite's inventory, in which he tells us that he wrote two organ books containing antiphons, hymns, responds, *Te Deum* and several settings of the Magnificat for the offices, and settings of the Kyrie, Sanctus, Agnus Dei, Alleluia and Sequence for the Mass.[3] The tradition of the performance of the Te Deum in a particularly festive manner on occasions of general rejoicing was still maintained, for an account of Richard III's visit to York in 1483 records that the Te Deum was 'begun by the officiating prelate and finished by the choir and the organ'.[4] At the reception of Henry VII in York in 1486 'The

[1] 'Verum quia continuus et immoderatus canendi labor non solum voces psallentium laedit, sed et ipsorum animos ad Deo serviendum inbecilliores efficit, praesertim cum in nonnullis hujus regni cenobiis pauci sint canonici, et nonnunquam tres pluresve missae praeter et ultra horas canonicas sunt cum nota quotidie celebrandae; idcirco nos eorum laboribus in hac parte compatientes, quod in omnibus illorum coenobiis organorum melodia in choris suis, et alibi ad suum relevamen uti . . . non denegamus.' Wilkins, *Concilia*, iii, p. 686.

[2] The early part of British Museum MS. Add. 29996.

[3] 'Item gratis liniavit et notavit omnes antiphonas ymnos responsoria alleluya sequencias *Te deum* certos tonos de *Magnificat kyrieleyson Sanctus* et *Agnus* in duobus libris ordinatis tantum pro organis 2° fo unius *descendit de alterius Noli tardare*.' James and Thompson, 'Leicester Abbey Inventories', p. 57.

[4] Harrison, *Life in a Medieval College*, p. 112.

Archbishop standing in his Trone beganne *Te Deum* etc., which by them of the Quere was right melodiously songen with Organ as accustomed',[1] and at the visit of Cardinal Wolsey to St. Paul's in 1527 'the Lord Cardinall began *Te Deum* the which was solemnlie songen with the King's trumpetts and shalmes as well Inglish men as Venetians'.[2]

A comparison of the surviving repertory of organ settings of hymns[3] with the examples of the same form in vocal polyphony supports the conclusion that one of the chief functions of the organ was to provide polyphony for the offices on less important days, when the polyphonic choir would not be present. There was a relatively small amount of overlap, for of forty-one hymns of which polyphonic settings survive, nineteen exist in organ settings only, sixteen in vocal settings only, and six in both.[4] There are no organ settings of the hymns on the festivals of the Epiphany, Ascension, Whitsunday, Trinity, Corpus Christi, or on any of the feasts of the *Proprium Sanctorum*, while, with the exception of three of those which are common, there are no vocal settings of the hymns which were sung frequently during the periods of the year included in the *Proprium de Tempore*. Similarly, the repertory of polyphonic antiphons for the organ consists of settings of antiphons at Compline,[5] of the canticle-antiphon at Lauds on the vigil of the Ascension,[6] and of that at first Vespers on the feast of St. Laurence.[7] The only one of the

---

[1] Leland, *Collectanea*, iv, p. 191.

[2] Dugdale, *History of St. Paul's*, p. 32.

[3] In British Museum MSS. Add. 29996, 15233 and 30513. The last has been published as *The Mulliner Book*.

[4] These are: *Te lucis ante terminum* (Compline in Advent); *Salvator mundi* (Compline in Lent); *A solis ortus cardine* (Lauds on Christmas Day); *O lux beata Trinitas* (First Vespers on Sunday from Trinity to Advent); *Exsultet caelum laudibus* (Common of Apostles at Lauds); and *Iste confessor* (Common of Confessors at first Vespers).

[5] *Miserere mihi* (psalm antiphon, except during the week after Christmas); *Natus est nobis* (psalm antiphon for that time); *Lucem tuam* (canticle antiphon on doubles from Trinity to Advent and Epiphany to Lent, with some exceptions); and *Glorificamus te* (canticle antiphon on three feasts of the Virgin and at Commemorations except in the Easter season).

[6] *Clarifica me*, of which the only settings are three by Tallis. This antiphon was also sung (without the *Alleluia* which is clearly included in two of the settings) with the *Magnificat* at first Vespers of Palm Sunday.

[7] *Beatus Laurentius*, one setting by Thomas Preston.

six antiphons in this repertory of which vocal settings are known is the Compline antiphon *Miserere mihi*.

Polyphony and Devotion

In this period of a century and a half before the discarding of the medieval rites there was a remarkable growth and flowering of musical culture in all parts of the British Isles. The new foundations gave singers and composers opportunities unknown before, and became the chief centres of the new styles of composition and performance, while the older foundations imposed fresh duties on their singers and appointed teachers to bring them to higher levels of competence and achievement.

In the colleges provision for the chapel establishment and for the adornment of the ritual was a part of the wider purpose of the founders, which was to strengthen the church and the realm by giving free learning to scholars of promise in a context of devotion and regular religious observance. In his *Prefatio* on his foundation of Lincoln College, Bishop Richard Fleming compared the 'dissonant' elements in the church and country (the heresies of the Lollards) to those in the human body;[1] pointing out the danger of their disproportionate growth, he desired that the members of his college should above all seek to exterminate heretical sects. Wykeham in his preamble to the statutes of Winchester, Wayneflete in his *Instrumentum* of the foundation of Magdalen[2] and Elphinstone in his prelude to the statutes of St. Mary's College, Aberdeen,[3] expressed the same purposes, which were to honour God, the Blessed Virgin and the patron saint, to root out error, to nurture the faith and to

[1] 'Ut sicut in microcosmo sunt elementorum spherae harmonicae naturalis quadam dulcedine consonantes, sic humani compago corporis in seipsa elementa continet dissonantium proprietatum, harmonica quadam melodia commixta.' *Statutes of Lincoln College*, p. 7.

[2] 'Ad laudem gloriam et honorem omnipotentis Dei Patris et Filii et Spiritus Sancti ac intemerate beatissime Virginis Marie Matris Christi necnon beate Marie Magdalene Sancti Johannis Baptiste et Apostolorum Petri et Pauli ac aliorum Patronorum Ecclesie Wintoniensis, exterpationemque heresium et errorum, augmentationem Cleri, decoremque sacrosancte Matris Ecclesie cujus ministeria personis sunt idoneis committenda que velut stelle in custodiis suis lumen prebeant et populos illuminent doctrina pariter et exemplo.' Chandler, *Life of Wayneflete*, p. 390.

[3] *Fasti Aberdonenses*, p. 53.

increase devotion. In the secular cathedrals and monasteries, the provision of chapels, altars and musical services outside the choir was a means of fostering the devotion of the laity, especially to the Virgin and to the Name and Passion of Jesus. Abbot Wheathamstead put this purpose clearly when he explained to his community that he wished to institute *organistae* for the singing of the Lady-Mass 'because wherever the Divine Service is more honourably celebrated the glory of the church is increased and the people are aroused to much greater devotion'.[1]

The development of the musical treatment of the Mass, Magnificat, respond, hymn and other ritual forms shows the strongly liturgical side of English polyphony during this period. The votive antiphon, on the other hand, was an extra-liturgical form, detached from the Office though still contained within the framework of a liturgical *memoria*. It was said by individuals and sung in every kind of institution, from the parish guild to the college community. Even more than the strictly liturgical forms of popular devotion, the Lady-Mass and Jesus-Mass, the Mary-antiphon was the universal and characteristic expression of the devotional fervour of the later Middle Ages.

[1] 'Quia ubi Divinum Servitium celebratur honestius ibi vigat decus Ecclesiae, et est populus ad devotionem in multo amplius excitatus.' Amundesham, *Chronicle*, i, p. 106.

V

MASS AND MOTET

The composition of polyphonic music for the Ordinary of the Mass had begun as early as the Winchester Troper. Until the second quarter of the fifteenth century polyphonic settings of the movements of the Ordinary were grouped in the manuscripts according to their words, in the same way as the plainsong chants of the Ordinary were grouped in the Gradual. The Old Hall manuscript, which is a comprehensive collection of settings of the Gloria, Credo, Sanctus and Agnus Dei grouped in this way, has been dated *c.* 1420, mainly because the composer Roy Henry in the manuscript is assumed to be Henry V (reigned 1413–22). It is now generally agreed that Henry VI is out of the question,[1] but the possibility still remains, and has not previously been put forward, that it was under Henry IV (1399–1413) that the greater part of the manuscript was planned and written and that he was the royal composer. An earlier date than 1413–22 is more in keeping with the style of the music in the original layer of the manuscript, for some of the pieces were composed according to the method of English descant current in the fourteenth century, while others show that their composers were in close touch with continental prac-

[1] W. Barclay Squire (in 'Notes on an Undescribed Collection') and the editors of *The Old Hall Manuscript* considered Roy Henry to be Henry VI; see *The Old Hall Manuscript*, iii, pp. x–xiii. Lederer questioned this theory (see p. 221, n. 4, below) and Bukofzer disestablished it; see his *Studies in Medieval Music*, pp. 78–9.

tice of the period surrounding the turn of the century. The earlier date also fits with what we know of the composers who appear in the several stages of the compilation of the manuscript. There is contemporary testimony to Henry IV's talent for music in a chronicle of his reign written by John Strecche, Canon of Kenilworth Priory (Augustinian), who describes him as a brilliant musician.[1] Strecche must be counted a good witness, for both Henry IV and Henry V were often in Kenilworth,[2] and there is earlier evidence of Henry IV's interest in music.[3] While there are many indications of Henry V's encouragement of music and his support of a large musical establishment, there seems to be no contemporary evidence that he had musical ability.[4]

These considerations lead to a dating of the stages in the writing of the Old Hall manuscript which is different from the accepted one. The first layer, which contains pieces in English descant and more elaborate compositions which show decided continental influence, belongs to the reign of Henry IV. The second layer, added by two scribes, contains music by composers who appear in the chapel in the first year of Henry V, and further compositions by two of the first group. This layer may therefore be dated between 1413 and 1432, when there are signs that the chapel assembled by Henry V was being dispersed. The final addition of pieces by Dunstable and Forest may possibly have been made at the time of the chapel's visit to

---

[1] 'In musica micans et mirabilis litteraturis'; British Museum, MS. Add. 35295, fo. 262. The chapter on Henry V in Strecche's *Historia Regum Anglie* is printed by Frank Taylor in *Bulletin of the John Rylands Library*, xvi, 1932, pp. 137 sqq.; the remainder of the chronicle is apparently unpublished.

[2] See Wylie, *England Under Henry IV*, ii, p. 307; iii, p. 318: and Taylor, 'The Chronicle of John Strecche', p. 141. John of Gaunt built the great Hall of his castle at Kenilworth c. 1392.

[3] His father had 'i fistula nomine Ricordo' and his mother sang to the cithara; the Lancastrian household accounts have in 1392–3 a payment of forty shillings to a man presenting a cithara to Henry, and in 1395–6 one of three shillings and four pence to John Davy 'de cam'a dni eunti de Kenill' ad Leycestre pro una cithara dni'. Wylie, op. cit., iii, p. 325; iv, p. 170.

[4] In a rather extravagant treatment of this question V. Lederer (*Über Heimat und Ursprung der mehrstimmigen Tonkunst*, ii, Chaps. III–IV) attributed the manuscript to Henry V's reign, and quoted many literary allusions of the time. None makes the claim that the King was a musician.

France in 1430–1; the next decade was a lean one for the chapel, and the addition is not likely to have been made after Plummer, himself a composer, joined the chapel *c.* 1441.

French and English Style in the Fourteenth and Early Fifteenth Centuries

Contact between English and French households and their chapels may have begun during the papacy of Innocent IV (1352–62) at Avignon. In 1354 the Pope was accepted by both sides as mediator in the war between England and France, and Henry of Grossmont, Duke of Lancaster, led the English plenipotentiaries to Avignon, where for six weeks in 1354–5 he held open house in the style to which Avignon was accustomed.[1] Archbishop Simon Langham, formerly Abbot of Westminster, who took up residence as Cardinal at Avignon in 1368, kept his household and chapel there until his death in 1376, and left legacies to three monks, three priests and a clerk of his chapel.[2] As Henry, Earl of Derby, the future Henry IV went in 1390–3 on expeditions to Prussia and the Holy Land, and his retinue included one or two chaplains and a group of minstrels consisting of trumpeters, pipers and a drummer.[3] Both Henry and his father John of Gaunt were present at the marriage of Richard II to Isabella of France at the Church of St. Nicholas in Calais in 1395, and Henry was again in France from October, 1398, until his return from exile to take the throne in June of the following year. These occasions would have given him an

[1] Mollat, *Les Papes d'Avignon*, p. 356. It was shortly after his return that, on March 4, 1355, he obtained royal letters patent to raise his father's hospital at Leicester into the hospital and college of St. Mary Newarke. Thompson, *Newarke Hospital and College*, p. 27.

[2] 'Item dominis Philippo Johanni et Jacobo monachis capellae meae cuilibet xxx florenos camerae . . . et Johanni de Trisere presbytero . . xl florenos camerae. Item Guisberto de Beert clerico capellae meae . . . xx florenos camerae. Item dominis Philippo et Willelmo presbyteris cuilibet xx florenos c.' Widmore, *History of St. Peter's, Westminster*, p. 184. Among those ordained to the first tonsure by Langham at Canterbury on March 3, 1368, were Johannes Pikard, Jacobus Cook and Johannes Aleyn. *Langham Register*, ii, p. 385. Though the combination of names is striking, it can only be surmise that these may have been three of the composers in the Old Hall book.

[3] *Expeditions to Prussia and the Holy Land made by Henry, Earl of Derby*, p. 132.

opportunity to observe the household chapels of Charles VI, Philip the Bold of Burgundy and John Duke of Berry, with the last of whom Henry was particularly friendly. These chapels were well provided with competent composers and singers, and with organs,[1] while the household accounts of Duke Philip show that Mass was celebrated in his chapel daily and that the organ was customarily played on festivals. In 1397 payments were made for material for the vestments of the Duke's 'prélatz à chanter . . . le divin office aux festes solempnelles en sa chapelle devant lui', and for 'draps d'or sur fonds variés . . . aux messes quotidiennes'. In 1393–4 'maistre Pierre de Pacy, doyen de l'église de Paris, conseiller du roy' obtained for Duke Philip 'unes orgues portatives pour mettre en sa chapelle de son hostel d'Artoiz et les transporter en autres hostels . . . estans audit lieu de Paris et environ pour en jouer devant luy aux festes solempnez ainsi comme il est de coustume'.[2] Twenty-two shillings and six pence were spent in January, 1394, 'pour le apportaige d'unes orgues de l'ostel d'Artoiz à l'église de saint Anthoine pour faire le service devant mon dit seigneur le jour de la feste dudit saint et pour les reporter au dit hostel'.[3] The most costly of such operations was the transporting of an organ from Gand 'destiné au manoir de Conflans' which was brought in 1400 by water to Valenciennes and thence on the backs of 'xii gros varlets' to Paris.[4] On the 'diplomatic' function of Philip's chapel the editor of these accounts remarks: 'Nous ne revenons pas sur la raison très claire de cette dévotion ducale. Ce mode itinérant, qui s'avère de règle à la cour de Bourgogne, s'étend parfois très loin: la musique religieuse est au nombre des moyens de persuasion dont use le diplomate, le politique, en ses tractations délicates.' It seems certain that the development of the music of the Royal Household Chapel under the early Lancastrian kings owed much to the French idea of the manner in which a great Christian ruler should order his daily

[1] See Pirro, *La musique à Paris le règne de Charles VI*; Dannemann, *Die Spätgotische Musiktradition in Frankreich und Burgund*, pp. 1–14. Charles V of France (1364–80) attended Mass 'à chant melodieux et solemnel' in his chapel daily. Marix, *Histoire de la musique de la cour de Bourgogne*, p. 15.

[2] At a cost of sixty pounds. David, *Philippe le Hardi*, p. 112.

[3] Loc. cit.

[4] Each stage took ten days and the cost was some thirty thousand francs. The account has interesting details about the organ. Loc. cit.

and festal observances. The Old Hall manuscript provided polyphonic music for the daily singing of Mass, being in this respect unique, besides motets for festivals and votive antiphons to the Virgin.

The musical evidence that direct contact between English and French composers took place before 1400 consists of a motet by an English composer, named in the text Johannes Alanus, in a notable collection of continental music now in the Musée Condé at Chantilly,[1] and one, or perhaps two, motets by the French composer Mayshuet in the Old Hall manuscript. Alanus has been identified with the canon of Windsor (d. 1373) who bequeathed a book of polyphony to St. George's Chapel; rather improbably with a John Aleyn, piper, who was in the service of Derby during his expedition of 1392[2] and with a Jean Alain who shared with three French minstrels a payment from the Duke of Orleans when the four were in the service of John of Gaunt in 1396;[3] with the Aleyn who contributed a Gloria in descant style to the Old Hall manuscript; and with a John Aleyn who became a minor canon of St. Paul's in 1421 and died in 1437.[4] While his identity is uncertain, there is no doubt about the Englishness of his motet, for the words of the treble part, which begin:

> Sub Arturo plebs vallata
> Plaudat melos, laus ornata
> Psallatur altissimo,
> Anglis conferentur grata
> Eventu piissimo,

go on to praise the skill of a number of English musicians who are listed by name. One of them, Ricardus Blich, may be the Richard Blithe who was a member of the Household Chapel in

---

[1] The piece is also in the Bologna MS. Bibl. G. B. Martini Q15 of *c.* 1430. The Musée Condé manuscript (No. 1047) contains pieces dated 1369 and 1389, and has connections with the courts of Gaston Phébus (1331–91) Count of Foix; John I (1350–95) of Aragon; and Pope Clement VII at Avignon (1378–94). See Reaney, 'The Manuscript Chantilly, Musée Condé 1047'.

[2] *Expeditions to Prussia and the Holy Land made by Henry, Earl of Derby*, p. 269.

[3] Laborde, *Les ducs de Bourgogne*, iii, pp. 123–4.

[4] Bukofzer, *Studies in Medieval Music*, p. 77. There was also a John Aleyne among the King's minstrels in 1421.

1413 and died in 1420.[1] The others are not known from other sources, though 'J. de alto bosco' may be the J. de Bosco who was a singer in the Papal Chapel at Avignon in 1394.[2] The melody of the tenor of Alanus's motet[3] is that of the versicle *In omnem terram exivit sonus eorum*, while the words of the counter-tenor, beginning:

> Fons citharizantium
> Ac organizantium
> Tubal praedicatur
> Musicae primordia
> Scriptis ut historia
> Genesis testatur,

is a roll of great musical theorists from Pythagoras to Franco, to whose successors, in the last verse,

> licet infimus
> Johannes Alanus
> Sese recommendat,
> Quatenus ab invidis
> Ipsum sonis validis
> Laus horum defendat.

The piece has the classical isorhythmic structure, with three statements of the tenor in progressive diminution, but more significant is the fact that it shows a definite tendency towards the sophistication of rhythm which was cultivated in extreme forms by some of the continental composers in the same manuscript:

Ex 22.

---

[1] *Calendar of Patent Rolls, 1416–22*, p. 312.
[2] Haberl, 'Die römische schola cantorum', p. 213, n. 2.
[3] Printed in *Denkmäler der Tonkunst in Österreich*, xl, p. 9.

The Chantilly manuscript has four pieces by Matheus de Sancto Johanne which have French words, and one piece by Mayhuet de Joan with Latin words and a tenor marked *pro papa Clemente*, which must therefore have been composed between 1378 and 1394. At the end of the Old Hall book there are two pieces which clearly form a pair in style and function; the composer of the former of the two, *Arae post libamina—Nunc surgunt in populo*, is given as Mayshuet, and there can be little doubt that this is the same composer. Both are substitutes for the *Deo gratias* at the end of Mass, for the highest part in both pieces begins with a reference to the Mass and ends with the words *Deo gratias*.[1] The tenor of *Arae post libamina—Nunc surgunt* resembles the *clementiam* melody of the Benedicamus, and its texts are sardonic commentaries on the vainglorious and mercenary attitude of singers:

> Cantatores sunt plerique
> Quorum artes sunt iniquae
> Vanam quaerunt gloriam . . .[2]

and:

> Notulas multiplicant et reputant cantatum
> Non amorem Domini puto, sed magnatum.
>
> Vos tales hypocritae numquid aspexistis
> Sanctum Evangelium, in quo perlegistis
> Vere dictum Domini loquentis de istis?
> Amen vobis dicitur mercedem recepistis.

[1] Only two voices, the highest (beginning *Post missarum sollemnia*) and the countertenor, of the second piece have survived. *Arae post libamina* is printed in *The Old Hall Manuscript*, iii, p. 150.

[2] After four six-line verses, the ending has: 'Practicus insignis Gallicus sub Gallicis pennis hunc discantavit cantum; sed post reformavit Latina lingua Anglis saepius fit amoena reddendo Deo gratias.'

Unlike the work of those who 'multiplied small notes', both pieces have a forthright rhythmic and melodic style. In this they are typical neither of the French music of their time nor of the Old Hall music as a whole, which elsewhere gives ample evidence of the melodic elaboration and rhythmic subtlety which were characteristic of French practice in the late four-teenth century.

Motets written as direct substitutes for the *Deo gratias* of Mass are rather uncommon. The best known example is in the *Notre Dame* Mass of Guillaume de Machaut[1] (1300–77), where the tenor, which is isorhythmically disposed, is a slightly varied form of the third *Ite missa est* melody in the Sarum Gradual.[2] The example in the 'Tournai Mass' of before 1350[3] is also based on an isorhythmic treatment of the chant, in this case a slightly varied form of the fourth *Ite missa est* in the Sarum group. Of two further cases in the Ivrea manuscript of the third quarter of the fourteenth century, which has Avignon connec-tions, one has a text (*Post missarum sollemnia*) which is used, with variants, in the latter of the Old Hall pair;[4] the other, which appears to be based on a freely-composed tenor, is also found in the 'Mass of Toulouse', where it is designated *Motetus super Ite missa est*.[5] An English case, the motet *Humanae linguae organis —Supplicum voces percipe—Deo gratias*, is found in a set of frag-ments taken from the fifteenth-century binding of a Fountains Abbey memorandum book for the years 1446–60.[6] The iso-rhythmic tenor is the same melody as that used by Machaut, and both the upper parts end with the word *gratias*. While these pieces are clearly substitute motets for the *Deo gratias*, it is possible that any appropriate motet may have been sung in

[1] Transcription in *Guillaume de Machaut*, iv, p. 20, and *Guglielmi de Mas-caudio Opera*, i, p. 29. There are also modern editions of the Machaut Mass by J. Chailley (Paris, 1948) and A. Machabey (Liège, 1948).

[2] *Graduale Sarisburiense*, pl. 19*; the melody is virtually identical with the seventh Sarum Benedicamus, loc. cit.

[3] Transcription in *Polyphonic Music of the Fourteenth Century*, i, p. 129.

[4] Besseler, 'Studien zur Musik des Mittelalters', I, p. 188.

[5] Transcription in *Polyphonic Music of the Fourteenth Century*, i, p. 138.

[6] British Museum, MS. Add. 40011 B; the contents have been discussed in Bukofzer, *Studies in Medieval Music*, Chap. III. The style of the music in these fragments suggests a date close to 1400, and seven (including one copied twice) of the eighteen surviving pieces are also in the original part of the Old Hall collection.

that place in the ritual. There is no evidence that this continued to be an English practice, but it is interesting to notice that an account of the meeting of Henry VIII and Francis I at the Field of the Cloth of Gold in 1520 tells us that the French 'concluded [Mass] with several motets'.[1]

The First Group of Composers in the Old Hall Manuscript

The first of the four scribes who copied music into the Old Hall manuscript laid out the general scheme of the collection.[2] He gave it the following order: settings of the Gloria; Mary-antiphons; settings of the Credo, Sanctus and Agnus Dei; and five motets, comprising one to St. Thomas of Canterbury, one to the Virgin, one to St. Katherine,[3] and the two *Deo gratias* motets just discussed. Nineteen composers, apart from Mays-huet, appear in the original part of the manuscript, namely, Aleyn, Byttering, R. Chirbury, Cooke, J. Excetre, Fonteyns,[4] Roy Henry, Jervays, Lambe, Leonel (Power), Olyver, Pennard, Pycard, Queldryk, Rowland,[5] Swynford, J. Tyes and W. Typp. Within each group of settings of the Ordinary the scribe arranged the music in two sections, one of which continues the English descant tradition, while the other uses techniques prac-tised by French composers of the time. One of Roy Henry's two

[1] *Letters and Papers of Henry VIII*, III, i, p. 312.

[2] A fourth hand added Dunstable's *Veni Sancte Spiritus*, Forest's *Qualis est dilectus* and part of his *Ascendit Christus* on blank pages between the two groups of Credo settings. For a discussion of the hands, see *The Old Hall Manuscript*, i, pp. ix–xvi.

[3] For which Bukofzer (*Studies in Medieval Music*, p. 71) suggested the occasion of Henry V's marriage to Catherine de Valois on Trinity Sunday in 1420, the tenor of the motet being *Sponsus amat sponsam*, the beginning of the verse of the respond *Virgo flagellatur* at Matins of St. Katherine (November 25). However, the words of the upper parts are a devotion to the saint, and I should place it some years earlier, with the other music in the first hand.

[4] A Michel de Fontaines (d. 1405) was Cantor, i.e., director of the music, and Canon of Sainte Chapelle in Paris; Brenet, *Les musiciens de la Sainte-Chapelle du Palais*, p. 25.

[5] Possibly Philippus Royllart, composer of a motet *Rex Carole—Laetitae pacis* in the Chantilly MS., as Riemann suggested in *Handbuch der Musik-geschichte*, II, i, p. 99. Rex Carolus is Charles V (1364–80). See also Van den Borren, *Le manuscrit de Strasbourg*, p. 55.

pieces stands at the head of the second section of the Gloria settings, and the other at the head of the whole set of Sanctus settings.

The French composers with whose work the 'new' styles in Old Hall may usefully be compared include Nicolas Grenon, who was at the court of Philip the Bold in 1385, in 1403 choirmaster at Laon, in 1408 grammar-master at Cambrai, in 1412 master of the choristers in the chapel of John the Fearless, from 1421 to 1424 choirmaster at Cambrai Cathedral, and from 1425 to 1428 a member of the Papal Chapel in Rome;[1] Billart, who was perhaps the Albertus Billardi who was 'clerc de matines' at Notre Dame, Paris, in 1392;[2] Jo. Asproys or Hasprois, who was at the Papal Chapel in Avignon in 1394;[3] Jean Césaris, who was at Angers Cathedral in 1417;[4] Richard de Loqueville, who was in the service of Duke Robert of Bar in 1410, and choirmaster at Cambrai Cathedral from 1413 to his death in 1418;[5] Jean Tapissier, who was in the service of John the Fearless in 1408;[6] and Johannes Carmen, who was in the chapel of Philip of Burgundy in the last decade of the fourteenth century, the household accounts referring to him as a composer of 'motets et glas',[7] and later at the church of Saint Jacques de la Boucherie in Paris.[8] The fame of three of these composers was celebrated in Le Champion des Dames (c. 1440) by Martin le Franc, who places them in the generation preceding that of Binchois and Dufay:

> Tapissier, Carmen, Césaris
> N'a pas longtemps si bien chanterrent

[1] Dannemann, *Die spätgotische Musiktradition in Frankreich und Burgund*, p. 10. He was apparently still living, and again in Cambrai, in 1449. Reese, *Music in the Renaissance*, p. 13.

[2] Pirro, *La musique à Paris sous le règne de Charles VI*, p. 20.

[3] Dannemann, op. cit., p. 9.

[4] Pirro, op cit., p. 20.

[5] Reese, *Music in the Renaissance*, p. 7; Dannemann, op. cit., p. 10.

[6] Pirro, op. cit., p. 29.

[7] The article 'Carmen' in *Die Musik in Geschichte und Gegenwart* does not refer to Carmen's connection with the Burgundian chapel, which is given in David, *Philippe le Hardi*, p. 113. In 1403 Carmen was paid for copying 'certains himes nouvellement faiz'. *Early Fifteenth Century Music*, p. i.

[8] See Gastoué, *Les primitifs de la musique française*, p. 72. For a discussion of the church music of these composers (except Billart), see Reese, *Music in the Renaissance*, pp. 20–2. Billart's *Salve virgo—Vita via—Salve regina* is printed in *Polyphonia Sacra*, p. 159.

Qu'ilz esbahirent tout Paris
Et tous ceulx qui les frequenterrent.[1]

The continuation of the English descant style in the music of the Old Hall manuscript may be most clearly seen in the settings of the Sanctus and Agnus Dei. Of the first seventeen Sanctus settings only two, Roy Henry's opening piece and one by Chirbury, are not on a plainsong. All are in simple descant style, and their plainsongs provide for every liturgical occasion from greater doubles to ferias. The chant is in the middle part, without ornamentation, in all cases but two; in one of those, a setting by Typp,[2] the chant is used in all three voices, at times a fourth and at times a fifth higher than the original pitch, while in the other, which is by Chirbury, it is set a fifth higher and moved from one part to another without further transposition:[3]

¹ Quoted in Reese, *Music in the Renaissance*, p. 12.
² *The Old Hall Manuscript*, iii, p. 4.
³ Ibid., p. 34, and cf. *Conditor alme*, p. 151 above. A cantus firmus treated in this way is termed 'migrant'. The term is restricted here to cases in which at least a complete phrase or unit of the chant is transferred and in which migration is continuous or habitual. A momentary change in the position of a cantus firmus, which often occurs in these pieces, was merely a crossing of parts, and did not constitute a real change in the method of composition. See Bukofzer, *Studies in Medieval Music*, pp. 47-8, where both kinds of treatment are shown as 'migrant'.

The technical development of this style may be seen in five of the succeeding eight settings of the Sanctus,[1] which are based on plainsongs for feasts and Sundays, and use an ornamented form of the plainsong in the highest voice.[2] This method of ornamentation may appropriately be called *cantus fractus*, for the plainsong is truly 'broken', its notes being separated by others in the manner of variations, or 'divisions' as they were later called. Here the effect of the ornamentation is to achieve a melodic style different from that of the plainsong, and comparison shows that the model for this new style was the secular French chanson:[3]

Ex. 24.

Richard Loqueville

(a) Puis-que — je suis a-mou-reux De vous gra-cieu-se — gen-te —

(b) Plainsong

Ho-san — na in ex-cel - - - sis.

Olyver

Ho - san - - - -

---

[1] *The Old Hall Manuscript*, iii, pp. 58–99. Sturgeon's setting (p. 55) is not in the first hand. The five in question comprise three by Power (pp. 58–75) and two by Olyver (pp. 81–9).

[2] In one of Power's settings (p. 58) the ornamented plainsong is partly in the middle part.

[3] (a) Bodleian Library, MS. Canonici Misc. 213, fo. 93v; (b) *The Old Hall Manuscript*, iii, p. 85.

The method of composition was different from that of simple descant with parts above and below a tenor, since in this style the highest part must be composed first, which was the method of the French chanson. This treatment of plainsong may be regarded as an ancestor of variation technique, and is therefore of great historical interest. It probably arose because the composers wished to make a more festive and 'modern' setting by approximating their descant technique to the style of the chanson while retaining the ritual music as their basis.

Leonel Power's three-part setting in this group[1] is a closer imitation of the French chanson style than Olyver was able to achieve, and is also an early example of another line of development, the writing of two-part sections within a three-part composition.[2] Power set the words *Pleni sunt caeli et terra gloria tua* in the Sanctus and *qui venit in nomine Domini* in the Benedictus for the lesser number of voices, which was to become a standard practice for the next century and a half.[3] The remaining three

[1] *The Old Hall Manuscript*, iii, p. 66. The highest part is an ornamented form of the first Sarum *Sanctus* chant, transposed up a fifth.

[2] For some examples of duets in French compositions, see the Gloria settings with two-part openings by Hugh de Salinis and Loqueville quoted in Dannemann, *Die spätgotische Musiktradition in Frankreich und Burgund*, p. 119. The opening of another Gloria by de Salinis (ibid., p. 120) is in three parts, and the trope, the words of which celebrate the ending of the Schism in 1417, is in two parts. The device of a two-part (or even one-part) opening occurred earlier, in the *introitus* of a few isorhythmic motets by Machaut. See also Bukofzer, *Studies in Medieval Music*, Chapter V.

[3] In this and similar cases the words of the duets were written in red letters instead of black. This probably indicates one singer to a part, corresponding to the indication *unus* in continental manuscripts of the early fifteenth century, and is found later in the Eton manuscript and in the *O quam suavis* Mass.

of the festive settings of the Sanctus comprise one each by Power and Tyes[1] in which the descant method is expanded to four parts, and one by Excetre, apparently on a plainsong, which has not been identified, in the treble.

The settings of the Agnus Dei were set out on an exactly analogous plan, but unfortunately there is a gap in the manuscript and after sixteen settings in simple descant there remain only two complete out of a group of probably eight or nine festive settings. In a setting which is one of the comparatively few four-part pieces in the manuscript[2] Power devised another use of the varied plainsong idea by using an ornamentally expanded version of the chant as the tenor. Olyver's setting,[3] which is in the same style as his two Sanctus settings, is particularly interesting because the plainsong on which it is based is the same melody sung three times, so that the piece is actually three melodic 'variations', one in each of the measures corresponding to our six-eight, three-four and four-four time, on the same chant.

The settings of the Gloria and Credo which were copied by the first writer of the manuscript were also subdivided into a group of descant settings and a group of festive settings, but the systematic use of the plainsongs was not carried out in the Glorias, while in the Creeds it would not have been possible, since the Sarum rite provided only one chant for the Creed. In the only surviving descant setting of the Gloria on a plainsong,[4] and in two settings of the Creed,[5] the plainsong is in the middle part in the normal fashion, while another setting of the Creed uses it in the treble, with occasional notes in the middle voice, without ornamentation.[6] William Typp's descant setting is a compromise between free writing and writing on the plainsong, using notes of the chant intermittently, with transpositions, in all three parts.[7] In many of the descant settings of the Gloria and Creed an effect of overall design is obtained by dividing the piece into three sections in different measures.

[1] *The Old Hall Manuscript*, iii, pp. 76, 94.   [2] Ibid., p. 136.
[3] Ibid., p. 141.   [4] Anonymous. Ibid., iii, p. [8].
[5] Both anonymous. Ibid., ii, pp. 1, 15.   [6] Anonymous. Ibid., p. 8.
[7] Ibid., p. 44. Another setting, which is anonymous (p. 30), seems to use some material from a Credo chant which appears in the modern Roman Ordinary (*Liber Usualis*, p. 71, indicated as of the fifteenth century).

The composers made their most enterprising use of the continental practices of the time in the festive settings of the Gloria and Creed, which can be divided into the three categories of chanson, canon and isorhythm. When they adopted the technique of the chanson they abandoned their traditional descant method, with its three evenly-spaced voices, for the disposition of the parts which had been characteristic of the French secular chanson since Machaut. In structure the chanson consisted of a two-part outline formed by the main melody in the top part (*cantus*) and a slower-moving tenor of rather careful melodic design, supplemented by a countertenor of which the melodic design was of little consequence, since its function was to add a suitable third note to the intervals made by the other two parts and to complement them in rhythm. At the stage in which English composers met this style at the turn of the fourteenth century, the main melody of a chanson could have considerable rhythmic energy, but was not often notable for melodic grace. Its favourite rhythm was triple, corresponding either to our six-eight or three-four, and one of the characteristic rhythmic devices was the use simultaneously or successively of the six-eight and three-four groupings of quavers within a dotted minim, an idiom with which Roy Henry was obviously quite familiar:[1]

Ex.25.

[1] *The Old Hall Manuscript*, i, p. 34. The values referred to are those of the transcription, and are one-quarter of the original. In France, a chanson was normally performed by a combination of voice(s) and various kinds of instruments. In the absence of any evidence for the use of string or

Some English composers became interested in the more complex combinations of rhythms which were a feature of the French secular chanson in the late fourteenth and early fifteenth centuries,[1] and were also used in French sacred music.[2] Power, in particular, wrote one setting each of the Gloria and Credo which are virtually essays, or 'lessons', in mensural proportions:[3]

Ex. 26.

Most pieces in chanson style were divided by changes of measure into several sections; the other means of subdivision, the writing of some sections as duets, occurs in three-part pieces by Excetre,[4] in four-part pieces by Power and Pycard,[5] and in two anonymous four-part Creeds, both of which end with a five-part section.[6] In one of his settings of the Creed[7] Power took direct action, which at first sight is of a rather startling kind, to concentrate the form into two sections followed by an extended Amen by starting the words of the countertenor at *Et in Spiritum Sanctum* and arranging matters so that the cantus

wind instruments in English churches, it must be assumed that parts without words were vocalized or played on the organ.

[1] See *French Secular Music of the Late Fourteenth Century*.

[2] E.g., in Billart's piece referred to in p. 229, n. 6, above.

[3] *The Old Hall Manuscript*, ii, p. 169; the Gloria is in Vol. i, p. 65.

[4] Ibid., i, p. 55; ii, p. 158.   [5] Ibid., i, p. 60; ii, p. 114.

[6] Ibid., ii, pp. 125, 176. The similarity of the former of the anonymous Creeds to Power's four-part Gloria has led to the suggestion that it may also be by Power. Bukofzer, *Studies in Medieval Music*, p. 44.

[7] *The Old Hall Manuscript*, ii, p. 185.

reached that point in the words when the countertenor arrived at the end of the text. This and similar ways of 'telescoping' the text of the Creed were occasionally used in the early fifteenth century, though the later practice of omitting some portions of the text, which was characteristic of English Creeds from c. 1430 to about a century later,[1] was not used in the Old Hall manuscript.

It was only with difficulty that the plainsongs of the Gloria and Credo could be assimilated to the chanson style, for their melodic idioms made them unsuitable for a tenor part, and they could not easily be stylized by ornamentation to make an upper part. In one of the two essays in the solution of this problem Excetre used the latter method to make a three-part setting of the second of the Gloria chants for greater doubles,[2] while in the other the anonymous composer of the second of the four-part Creeds just mentioned used the chant, slightly ornamented, as a second cantus part in the 'full' sections, and more fully ornamented as the upper part of the duets. At least two of the composers, Pycard and Byttering, took up enthusiastically the idea of applying canon, or *fuga* as it was then called, to the setting of the Gloria,[3] though their French contemporaries seem not to have used canon for movements of the Mass,[4] and the only known sacred examples are motets, such as Carmen's *Pontifici decori speculi* in honour of St. Nicholas:[5]

---

[1] See *Missa O Quam Suavis*, pp. xxxiii–xxxvi, and, for a theory as to the possible reasons for the practice, Hannas, 'Concerning Deletions in the Polyphonic Mass Credo'.

[2] *The Old Hall Manuscript*, i, p. 55.

[3] One by Byttering (Vol. i, p. 47) and three by Pycard (ibid., pp. 76, 84, 119). There are two canonic Creeds, both anonymous (Vol. ii, pp. 82, 101), while two other Creeds, by Pycard and Byttering (ibid., pp. 135, 203), are pseudo-canons, and also late examples of hocket technique.

[4] For a reference to two Italian examples, see Strunk, in Bukofzer, *Studies in Medieval Music*, p. 85, n. 57. One of these, with the tenor and countertenor in canon, is transcribed in *Die mittelalterliche Mehrstimmigkeit*, p. 58.

[5] Bodleian Library, MS. Canonici Misc. 213, fo. 26v, transcribed in Stainer, *Dufay and his Contemporaries*, p. 88, and *Early Fifteenth Century Music*, p. 54. The canonic voice is designed in five isorhythmic sections. See also Johannes Ciconia's *O felix templum jubila*, composed in 1400 for the dedication of the new cathedral of Padua, which is written in pseudo-canon; transcription in Van den Borren, *Polyphonia Sacra*, p. 243; discussion in Besseler, *Bourdon und Fauxbourdon*, pp. 78 sqq., and Clercx-Lejeune, 'Johannes Ciconia de Leodio',

Both Pycard and Byttering used this scheme of two canonic parts over two free parts,[1] and by telescoping the text Byttering managed to make his setting one of the shortest of the Glorias in the manuscript:

pp. 120–1. On Ciconia's dates, see Clercx-Lejeune, 'Question de Chronologie', in *Revue Belge de Musicologie*, ix, 1955, p. 47.

[1] *The Old Hall Manuscript*, i, pp. 47, 76. Byttering's canon is not written out in the edition; see Strunk in Bukofzer, *Studies in Medieval Music*, pp. 81–3.

Pycard developed the further possibilities of canonic technique
in a setting with two parts in canon and three free parts:[1]

Ex.29.

and in his technical feat, astonishing for its time, of writing a
five-part setting of the Gloria as a double canon with one free
part.[2] For this piece he provided a part called *solus tenor* to be
sung instead of the canonic tenor and countertenor, so that
the work could be performed by four voices instead of five.[3]
The second of two anonymous settings of the Creed,[4] both of
which are canons for three parts with two free parts, worthily

[1] *The Old Hall Manuscript*, i, p. 119.

[2] Equally remarkable, and probably unique, is Pycard's Sanctus on
fo. 100v, not printed in the edition because thought to be incomplete. It is
actually a canon three-in-one in which the canonic part is a paraphrase of
the plainsong. I have discussed this piece in *New Oxford History of Music*,
iii, Chapter 4.

[3] *Ibid.*, i, p. 84. The upper canon is not in the edition; see Strunk, as
above, pp. 85–6. A *solus tenor* combining countertenor and tenor was used
by Carmen in two four-part motets, reducing them to three parts. One of
these, *Venite adoramus—Salve sancta*, printed in Van den Borren, *Polyphonia
Sacra*, p. 167, dates from *c.* 1409–15. See Besseler, s.v. 'Carmen' in *Die
Musik in Geschichte und Gegenwart*.

[4] *The Old Hall Manuscript*, ii, pp. 82, 101.

represents the culmination of this phase of the cultivation of canon. It is a 'mensuration-canon' in which three parts read from the same music, each interpreting the notation according to a different measure-signature:[1]

Ex. 30.

Pycard's double canon and these anonymous canonic settings of the Credo are quite unparalleled in their technical

[1] Ibid., pp. 110–11. Facsimile in ibid., iii, between pp. xxiv–xxv.

interest outside England at this time, and may represent a
renewal, under continental influence, of the earlier English
interest in rota and rondellus techniques. They belong to the
last phase of a fourteenth-century tradition rather than to the
main movement of style in the early fifteenth century, for
canonic technique played no part in the next stage of the
history of the polyphonic Mass in England.

Isorhythm, on the other hand, kept its interest for composers
until the middle of the fifteenth century, though again its
transference from the motet to the longer movements of the
Mass seems not to have been a general practice in France.[1]
The use of isorhythm in Glorias and Credos in the Old Hall
manuscript is found only in pieces written by the first scribe,[2]
and was an important step towards the emergence some twenty
years later of the idea of setting all the movements of a polyphonic Mass on the same recurring tenor. Among the single
movements in isorhythmic structure in the Old Hall collection,
Typp's Credo on the tenor *Benedicam te Domine* exemplifies a
neatly orthodox design, in which the rhythmic scheme of the
tenor is the same pattern four times:[3]

Ex.31.

Plainsong   Be - ne - di - cam te   Do - mi - ne....

[1] See Harder, 'Die Messe von Toulouse', p. 108, n. 2.

[2] Five settings of the Gloria, by Power (iii, [23]), Pycard (i, 92), Queldryk
(i, 109), Tyes (i, 150), an anonymous (iii, [32]) (the scheme of this is so
similar to that of Power's isorhythmic Credo that it may well be by him),
and another anonymous in which only the Amen is isorhythmic (iii, [27]);
five settings of the Credo, by Pennard (ii, 241; his only piece in the manuscript), Power (ii, 194), Queldryk (ii, 232), Swynford (ii, 213; also his only
piece) and Typp (ii, 224).

[3] Ibid., ii, p. 224. The plainsong (*Antiphonale Sarisburiense*, pl. 107) is the
opening of the third Antiphon at Lauds on the first Sunday after the octave
of the Epiphany.

and the piece is based on three statements of this tenor, laid out in the proportions 12 : 8 : 3, that is, dotted semibreve to semibreve to dotted crotchet in the notation of our example. The successive sections of the upper two parts are also isorhythmically related, for example:

to:

in the first section, and:

to:

in the second section. This isorhythmic treatment of all the parts became the normal practice in the fifteenth-century motet. The melodic style of the piece is clearly related to the chanson, and the text is telescoped. Compared with the established French practice, however, some of the isorhythmic pieces in Old Hall have unorthodox traits,[1] such as the apparently original tenors in pieces by Power, Queldryk and Swynford, a non-repeating tenor in a Credo by Power,[2] and a particularly elaborate scheme in five parts[3] with a pseudo-canon between the two highest by Pycard, as one might expect. Pennard's Credo,[4] which is equally enterprising, involves the rarely-used device of isomelody as well as isorhythm, the second half of the piece being isomelodically related to the first, as may be seen in the Amen, in which the isomelodic variation is carried out in hocket:[5]

Ex. 36.

Treble 1

Et in-car-na-tus est de Spi-ri-tu San-cto

ex ma-ri-a Vir-gi-ne: Et ho-mo fa-ctus est.

Treble 1

a-

Treble 2

a-

Like the large canonic schemes, intellectual adventures of this kind are in the spirit of the previous century, while the later development of the complete Mass on a plainsong tenor stemmed from the more modest three-part settings in which isorhythmic design was combined with the melodic style of the chanson.

[1] See the discussion in Bukofzer, *Studies in Medieval Music*, pp. 56–73.
[2] An anonymous Gloria (Vol. iii, p. [32]) also has a straight-through tenor.
[3] Which can be reduced to four by using the *solus tenor* part.
[4] In four parts, reducible to three.
[5] Vol. ii, pp. 244, 250.

English and French Style from 1413 to c. 1430

Another period of direct contact between English and French musicians began early in the reign of Henry V and ended with the death of John Duke of Bedford at Rouen in 1435. The first occasion was the meeting of all Christendom at the Council of Constance (1414–18). It is recorded that the singers who went with the English bishops to the Council charmed their hearers at Cologne,[1] and that at Constance their music on the feast of St. Thomas of Canterbury made a strong impression. A chronicler of the Council relates that on St. Thomas's Eve in 1416 the English 'ordered four trombonists through the town of Constance at the time of Vespers . . . and sang Vespers in the Cathedral in a laudable manner, with large candles, fine ringing of bells and playing of the organ', or as another version has it 'with sweet angelic singing'.[2] The chapel of Henry V was with him in France from 1417 to 1421,[3] and the composer John Pyamour, who was a clerk in Henry's chapel in 1420, went to France again with Bedford when the Duke returned there after a visit to England in 1427.[4] The most renowned musician in the Duke's service was John Dunstable, composer and astronomer, to whom Abbot Wheathamstead of St. Alban's paid this tribute:

Musicus hic Michalus alter, novus et Ptolomeus,
Junior ac Atlas supportans robore caelos,
Pausat sub cinere; melior vir de muliere
Nunquam natus erat; vitii quia labe carebat,

[1] Pirro, *Histoire de la musique*, p. 57.

[2] 'An sant Thomas aubent . . . sy hiessen ze vesperzit durch die statt Constentz vier prusuner . . . und sungend die vesper zů dem thůmb gar loblich mit grossen brinnenden kertzen, mit schönem gelüt und in den organan' (*another MS* 'und mit engelschem süssem gesang mit den ordnen'). *Ulrichs von Richental Chronik des Constanzes Concils*, p. 97.

[3] See *Calendar of Patent Rolls, 1416–22*, p. 127 (commission to John Colles, clerk of the vestry, and John Water, clerk, to take carriage of the chapel goods to Southampton, December 4, 1417); *Proceedings of the Privy Council*, ii, p. 240 (decision of the Privy Council to the same effect); ibid., p. 236 (provision on February 27, 1422, for payment to the executors of the late Treasurer of the Household, John Rothenhale, for costs incurred in the support and expenses of the Dean and clerks of the King's chapel returning from Rouen to England on January 11–18, 1421).

[4] Bukofzer, *Studies in Medieval Music*, p. 77.

Et virtutis opes possedit unicus omnes.
Cur exoptetur, sic optandoque precetur
Perpetuis annis celebretur fama Johannis
Dunstapil; in pace requiescat et hic sine fine.[1]

The chapel of the royal household went to France for the
visit of Henry VI which began in April, 1430, and ended with
his coronation as King of France in Notre Dame, Paris, by
Cardinal Beaufort on December 16, 1431.[2] Several copies of the
processional antiphon and a copy for the choir of the complete
plainsong for Henry's coronation service,[3] which are preserved
in the French National Archives, show that two significant
changes were made in the traditional plainsong of the English
coronation ritual. The antiphon *Firmetur manus tuas* for the
entrance into the church was replaced by the respond *Ecce
mitto angelum*, no doubt with the visions of Joan of Arc in mind,
and a respond of St. Remigius, patron saint of Rheims, where
Charles VII had been crowned King of France in Joan's
presence on July 17, 1429, was sung as the procession carrying
the holy oil entered from the vestry. The ceremony was carried
out by the English nobles and the two French bishops, Beauvais
and Noyon, who were present; the canons of Notre Dame and
the English clerks took part, and there was an unseemly dispute
between them at the offering of the wine. If Henry VI's chapel
or the Duke of Bedford's sang polyphony during the service, it
is possible that Dunstable's famous motet *Veni sancte Spiritus—
Veni creator Spiritus* and his Credo and Sanctus on *Da gaudiorum
praemia*, which are perhaps the surviving movements of a complete polyphonic Ordinary, were written for the occasion. The
words of the hymn *Veni creator*, which is an essential part of
the Coronation ritual, are sung complete in the countertenor
part of the motet, and its tenor enters with the second line of

[1] Grove, *Dictionary of Music*, 4th ed., ii, p. 112.

[2] *Proceedings of the Privy Council*, iv, p. 39 (April 20, 1430, authorizing
reimbursement of the Cardinal and of the Household Treasurer for their
expenditure on the King's chapel 'ad opem Regis ultra mare'); ibid., p. 30
(warrant for the expenses of Richard Praty and John Carpenter, chaplains
of the King, and John Walden, confessor, who went with him to France).

[3] Headed 'Sequuntur ea que debet chorus ecclesie cantare in conse-
cracione et coronacione regis quando consecratur in ecclesia parisiensi.'
MS. Arch. Nat. L.499, No. 1. See Mahieu, 'Notre-Dame de Paris au
quinzième siècle', pp. 18–19, 21.

the same hymn, leaving out the first three words, which would be sung by the Cardinal. The tenor of the Mass is the melody of the verse of the Trinity respond *Gloria patri genitoque*, which has the appropriate text: *Da gaudiorum praemia, da gratiorum munera, dissolve litis vincula, astringe pacis foedera.*

After its tribute to Tapissier, Carmen and Césaris,[1] Martin le Franc's *Le Champion des Dames* continues:

> Mais oncques jour ne deschanterrent
> en melodie de tel chois
> ce m'ont dit qui les hanterrent
> que G. Du Fay et Binchois.

It is possible that Dufay (d. 1474), who had been a chorister at Cambrai under Loqueville, went to Constance with the chapel of Bishop Pierre d'Ailly of Cambrai, and there found a patron in the elder Carlo Malatesta of Rimini, whose service he had entered by August, 1420.[2] If so, he may have come into contact with English musicians at Constance, though an eminent authority places his first encounter with English music in the years 1426–8, when he was again in Cambrai, and cites the Mass of St. James, in which the term *fauxbourdon* was apparently used for the first time, as the chief evidence of English influence on Dufay's early style.[3] Gilles Binchois (d. 1460), Dufay's most famous contemporary, was with William de la Pole, Earl of Suffolk, in Paris in 1424, went with him to Hainault in the following year, and joined the chapel of Philip the Good of Burgundy in 1430. It is possible that he was in England for a time between these dates.[4]

The Later Composers in the Old Hall Manuscript

The music written into the Old Hall collection by the second and third scribes comprises pieces by Burell, Cooke, Damett, Sturgeon and Leonel Power; music by Cooke and Power had also been in the original layer. The records of the royal household chapel show that John Burell, John Cooke, Thomas

---

[1] See p. 229 above.

[2] An example of Dufay's work in 1421 is the motet *Vasilissa ergo gaude* (*Guglielmi Dufay Opera Omnia*, ii, p. 1), written for the marriage of Cleophe Malatesta and Theodore Paleologus.

[3] Besseler, s.v. 'Dufay', in *Die Musik in Geschichte und Gegenwart*.

[4] Marix, *Histoire de la musique de la cour de Bourgogne*, pp. 176–9.

Damett and Nicholas Sturgeon[1] joined the clerks in 1413, the
first year of Henry V's reign, or perhaps a few years earlier.[2]
The simplest style practised by the composers of this later music
stands on the border between descant style and the style of
the chanson, as may be seen in Burell's Gloria, which combines
the easy flow of the chanson with the spacing of parts characteristic of descant:[3]

Ex. 37.

Treble
Mean

Tenor

Et   in ____ ter - ra ____ pax ho - mi - ni -

bus   bo - nae vo - lun - ta - - - tis.

In their more elaborate settings, such as Sturgeon's Sanctus
with duets,[4] they show themselves quite at ease in the chanson
style, and it is significant that the melodies of the upper parts of
their motets, which are quite orthodox in design, are also in
chanson style. Here the rhythmic energy and variety of design
of the fourteenth-century motet have been abandoned in favour
of a new fluency and grace. The texts of two of the motets refer
to Henry V's campaigns, for Cooke's *Alma proles regia—Christi
miles inclite* on the tenor *Ab inimicis defende nos Christe*[5] invokes
Jesus, the Virgin and St. George for the welfare of the state
and protection against its enemies, while Damett's *Salvatoris*

---

[1] A Nicholas Sturgeon from Devonshire was elected scholar of Winchester
College in 1399, and was then between eight and twelve years old. Kirby,
Winchester Scholars, p. 26.

[2] The Wardrobe Accounts for 1409–12 are missing.

[3] *The Old Hall Manuscript*, i, p. 17. The clefs are C[1] C[3] C[4] (see p. 248, n. 2,
below).

[4] Ibid., iii, p. 55.

[5] From the Litany for Rogation Days in time of war. Bukofzer, *Studies in
Medieval Music*, p. 68.

mater pia—Sancte Georgi on the tenor *Benedictus Mariae filius qui ve*[1] [*sic*] has a prayer for King Henry in both texts, and the text of the *duplum* invokes St. George, *gloriosa spes Anglorum*, to bring victory and peace. This motet and Sturgeon's *Salve mater Domini—Salve templum gratiae* on the tenor *it in nomine Domini*, the texts of which are in praise of the Virgin, form a pair, for Sturgeon's tenor is an exact continuation of Damett's, even to the point of taking up where it left off in the middle of the word *venit*.[2]

The style of this later music shows a movement towards suavity and grace in rhythm and melody and towards care in the treatment of dissonance, which is paralleled by a similar movement in the style of such French composers as Pierre Fontaine, Arnold and Hugh de Lantins, and Gilles Binchois.[3] This common tendency reflects a second stage in the relationship of English to continental music in which the influences were mutual, and in which the effects of English practices on continental writing were at least as strong as those which had earlier worked the other way. It is arguable that this considerable credit on the English side of the account accrued largely from a habit which English composers had of fusing categories and techniques of composition which had normally been distinct in continental practice, such as plainsong with the chanson, isorhythm with the polyphonic Mass, and the chanson with the isorhythmic motet.[4] As in the thirteenth century, England had no art of secular polyphony such as flourished at the continental courts during the fourteenth and fifteenth centuries, and no tradition of the composition of isorhythmic motets for important political or civic occasions, such as were common on the continent. Hence all newly-acquired

---

[1] The Mary-trope of the Benedictus. See above, p. 72.

[2] The letter 'n', as Bukofzer observes, 'got lost in the shuffle'. *Studies in Medieval Music*, pp. 68–70.

[3] For a discussion of the work of these composers, see Reese, *Music in the Renaissance*, pp. 34–42, 86–92.

[4] French composers had earlier adapted the chanson to the Ordinary of the Mass, a style which has been called Ballade-mass. See Dannemann, *Die spätgotische Musiktradition in Frankreich und Burgund*, pp. 79–80. The original corpus of Old Hall shows English composers catching up with this idea, and adopting various methods of reconciling it with their own descant tradition.

techniques and ideas about composition were turned at once to the service of the liturgy, with most fruitful results.

It is remarkable that several sacred compositions by Binchois use ritual forms and plainsong melodies of the Sarum rite,[1] and even more so that his technical methods are closely related to those of the Old Hall composers. Binchois used simple descant on plainsong,[2] the paraphrasing[3] of plainsong in the upper or middle part of simple three-part writing,[4] similar paraphrasing in the tenor part of a piece in chanson style,[5] elaborate ornamentation of a plainsong in the cantus part in a more developed chanson style,[6] and free chanson style with and without duets.[7] It is not possible to suggest a chronology for the church music of Binchois, but such techniques as these are strong evidence of contact, which may well have taken place in the fourteen-twenties, with the music of the English household chapels.

It has often been pointed out that a predilection for parallel thirds and sixths was a characteristic of the English tradition, and there is ample evidence of this in the descants in the Old Hall manuscript. The idea of continuous movement in these intervals seems to have been taken up by French composers and turned into an almost rule-of-thumb method of three-part

---

[1] Reese, *Music in the Renaissance*, p. 90. It may be added that the setting by Binchois of the psalm *In exitu Israel* includes the antiphon *Nos qui vivimus* (*Les musiciens de la cour de Bourgogne*, p. 208), which in the Sarum rite was sung with it at Sunday Vespers throughout the year. *Ordinale Exon*, i, p. 41; music in *Antiphonale Sarisburiense*, pl. 109.

[2] As in the hymn *A solis ortu cardine* (*Les musiciens de la cour de Bourgogne*, p. 188.) The plainsong, without ornamentation, is in the middle part, and the clef arrangement is C³ C⁴ F⁴. English descant was normally written in three different clefs, in accordance with its method of composition; the French chanson was written with the same clef for the tenor and counter-tenor and a higher clef for the cantus.

[3] This term will be used of the writing of a plainsong in a free measured rhythm, without or with only slight ornamentation.

[4] As in the Kyrie *de Angelis* (*Denkmäler der Tonkunst in Österreich*, xxxi, p. 48) and the hymn *Gloria laus* (*Les musiciens de la cour de Bourgogne*, p. 194). In the latter the refrain is set in three parts, the verses in two with the plainsong in the upper part.

[5] As in the Kyrie *Orbis factor* (*absque versibus*) in *Denkmäler der Tonkunst in Österreich*, xxxi, p. 49.

[6] As in the Sanctus. Ibid., p. 53.

[7] As in the Kyrie in *Les musiciens de la cour de Bourgogne*, p. 154, and the Gloria, ibid., p. 163.

writing, under the much-discussed name of *fauxbourdon*.[1] The method is a combination of simple ornamentation of the plainsong in the cantus with parallel movement in thirds and sixths coming to a fifth and octave for the last chord of each phrase, a kind of movement which had been taught and practised in England in the fourteenth century. The middle part in the French form of the method did not need to be written down, since it could be improvised by singing the cantus at the fourth below, though Binchois, for example, wrote out all three parts in some cases, as in his *Magnificat* on the fourth intonation.[2]

In other cases he, or the scribe, indicated *A faulx bourdon*, leaving the middle part to be filled in by the singer.[3] In England, apparently towards the middle of the fifteenth century, 'faburden', which meant singing a part in parallel sixths below the plainsong, with simple ornamentation of its cadences, each phrase beginning and ending with an octave, was added to descant among the elementary methods of part-singing taught to choristers and clerks. Later it was used as a method of improvising on plainsong in choir and in processions, and as a technique of composition ('on the faburden') for organ or choir.[4] By that time the treatment in faburden of the Te Deum, of psalm and canticle intonations, and of well-known hymns must have been familiar to all well-trained singers, and was commonly practised extempore. It should be emphasized that a middle part was not normally implied in English faburden.

[1] See Reese, *Music in the Renaissance*, pp. 64–5, for discussion and references to the literature of the subject.

[2] *Les musiciens de la cour de Bourgogne*, p. 148.

[3] See his *Sancti Dei omnes*. Ibid., p. 218. The comment of the St. Alban's chronicler (see p. 206 above) that shawms were called *burdones* suggests that the term *fauxbourdon* may have been coined to describe a French imitation of the English manner of improvising the instrumental performance of such well-known chants as the *Te Deum*. For a phonological discussion of *fauxbourdon*-faburden, see the articles by H. M. Flasdieck, R. von Ficker and G. Kirchner in *Acta Musicologica*, xxv and xxvi (1953–4), and H. M. Flasdieck, 'Elisab. Faburden-"Fauxbourdon" und NE. Burden-"Refrain" ', in *Anglia*, 74, 1956, which quotes (p. 197) the expression 'te synge a tribull til faburdun' from a letter of as early as *c.* 1427.

[4] The book of the bass part of hymns in Winchester College in 1521 and the book 'voc. le Base' in Magdalen in 1522 may have been faburdens; they are not likely to have been isolated part-books at so early a date.

Dunstable and His Contemporaries

The ripe fruit of this active interchange of ideas and techniques between English and French composers came in the
later music of Power, in the work of John Dunstable, and in
that of a considerable group of composers who were either
Dunstable's contemporaries or immediate followers. Although
this mature style was largely a result of earlier French influence,
it was typically English to continental ears, and Martin le
Franc wrote of its effect on Binchois and Dufay in those terms
in a continuation of the passages from *Le Champion des Dames*
quoted above:

> Car ilz ont nouvelle pratique
> de faire frisque concordance
> en haulte et en basse musique
> en fainte en pause et en muance
> et ont prins de la contenance
> Angloise et ensuy Dunstable
> pour quoy merveilleuse plaisance
> rend leur chant joyeux et notable.

The *contenance Angloise* was well known in many parts of Europe,
for during some forty years after *c.* 1430 music by Dunstable,
John Pyamour, John Benet, John Bedyngham, Forest, John
Plummer, Sandley, Walter Frye and others was copied into
manuscripts in France, Burgundy and northern Italy, sometimes with the casual ascription *Anglicanus* or *de Anglia*. Some
of these composers may have spent their lives abroad, like
Robert Morton, whose extant work consists entirely of French
chansons, and it may always remain uncertain how much of
this great store of expatriate music belongs to the history of
music *in* Britain. On the other hand, had it not survived we
should be left with entirely inadequate notions of the part
which English composers played in one of the key periods of
musical history, for the music of this group shows that they
played an important role in the establishment of one of the
most lasting of all musical forms, the unified polyphonic setting
of the Ordinary of the Mass.[1]

[1] For polyphonic settings of the Ordinary on the continent in the fourteenth century, see Coussemaker, *Messe du XIII* siècle*; Gombosi, 'Machaut's
Messe Notre-Dame'; Harder, 'Die Messe von Toulouse'; Schrade, 'The Mass

From the beginning of the history of the polyphonic Mass in England the Kyrie was left out of the scheme, as in the earlier separate movements in the Old Hall collection, because on festivals it was sung with the particular trope laid down by the Ordinal, which made the Kyrie in some degree a part of the Proper. To make a musical design of the other four movements, their ritual chants were discarded and a plainsong melody appropriate to a certain feast or season was chosen as the tenor, on the analogy of the motet. According to its length, this tenor was used either (1) once in each movement, in the same or (2) in a different rhythm, or (3) more than once in rhythms which were isorhythmically related or (4) not so related but in different measures. Power adopted the first of these plans in his Mass *Alma redemptoris mater*, which appears to be the earliest (*c.* 1430) surviving polyphonic Ordinary on a single tenor, using for his tenor only as much of the melody of the antiphon as he needed, as far as the first syllable of *populo*. He divided the tenor into two sections, one in triple measure and one in duple, and to this bisectional outline he added opening duets in the Credo and Sanctus:[1]

and a duet to begin the third Agnus Dei. He used the two possible groupings in the subdivision of three beats on two levels

of Toulouse'; Chailley, 'La Messe de Besançon'; Schrade, 'A Fourteenth Century Parody Mass'. On the part played by English composers in the early history of the fifteenth-century polyphonic Ordinary, see Bukofzer, *Studies in Medieval Music*, pp. 217–26.

[1] Trent, Castello del Buon Consiglio, MS. 87, fo. 6. The Mass has been edited by Feininger in *Documenta Polyphoniae Liturgicae*, Ser. I, No. 2.

of measure, the dotted minim of the upper parts and the dotted semibreve of the tenor,[1] as in the third and fourth bars of the example. Although the tenor, being the plainsong transposed a fifth down, and the countertenor both have a signature of one flat, the treble has no flat in the signature, a practice for which various explanations have been suggested[2] and which was common in English music until the early sixteenth century.

The Mass *Rex saeculorum* by Dunstable or Power[3] is an example of the second way of disposing a tenor, for the complete melody is used, varied and extended in a different manner, once in each movement. The device of paraphrasing the melody of the tenor before or with its entry, which was merely suggested in Power's *Alma redemptoris* Mass,[4] is also suggested in the Gloria and Sanctus of this Mass, and carried out at length in the opening duet of the Credo:

This idea is another step towards musical unity in the poly-phonic Ordinary, and later became one of the regular ways of

[1] The upper parts are written with the measure signature O, the tenor with ℭ. By a convention which in this period was peculiarly English, after-wards general, the tenor notes must be doubled in length by the singer, the minim (of the original) being read as a semibreve. See Strunk, review of the edition cited, in *Journal of the American Musicological Society*, ii, 1949, p. 109.

[2] See Apel, *Accidenten und Tonalität*; 'The Partial Signatures in the Sources up to 1450'; Lowinsky, 'The Function of Conflicting Signatures'; Hoppin, 'Partial Signatures and Musica Ficta'; Lowinsky, 'Conflicting Views on Conflicting Signatures'.

[3] Printed in *John Dunstable*, pp. 47–57; the differing ascriptions are discussed there, pp. 171–3. The cantus firmus is the antiphon at Terce on the feast of St. Benedict, and is not in the Sarum rite.

[4] See the notes marked with an asterisk in Example 38.

fashioning a common opening for all four movements. The third way of disposing a tenor may be seen in Dunstable's Gloria and Credo on *Jesu Christe fili Dei*,[1] where it is used twice in each movement, the second statement being isorhythmic with the first with the note values halved, as in an isorhythmic motet, so that the two movements are exactly equal in their total length and in the length of their subdivisions.[2] The fourth method was used in an anonymous Mass on *Veterem hominem*,[3] found in a continental manuscript, a passage from which was quoted by Thomas Morley in his 'Plaine and Easie Introduction to Practicall Musicke' (1597)[4] in a context which makes it certain that the composer was English. He disposed the tenor in two statements, not isorhythmically related, one in triple

[1] *John Dunstable*, pp. 35–40. The cantus firmus is the respond at Prime, which had three chants, chosen according to the season and the rank of the day. The chant used for this Mass is that with *Alleluia* which was sung, with a varying verse, from Christmas to the octave of the Epiphany, from Low Sunday to Trinity when the choir was ruled, and on the feasts of Corpus Christi, the Exaltation of the Cross, both feasts of St. Michael, and the Dedication of the Church. *Use of Sarum*, ii, pp. 222, lxxvii.

[2] Of which there are two, one in triple measure and one in duple. The division is made at a point of exact proportion, but does not interrupt the flow of the music. There is a similar change of measure within the isorhythmic period in a Gloria by Tyes in Old Hall (Vol. i, p. 50).

[3] One of a group of antiphons for the octave of the Epiphany which, as Notker relates, were adopted from the Byzantine rite by the order of Charlemagne; see Handschin, 'Sur quelques tropaires grecs traduits en latin'. Music in *Antiphonale Sarisburiense*, pl. 95, and *Die Musik in Geschichte und Gegenwart*, s.v. 'Antiphon'.

[4] Ed. Harman, p. 124. The source of Morley's quotation was discovered by Thurston Dart; see his letter in *Music and Letters*, xxxv, 1954, p. 183.

measure and one in duple, and used both forms once in each movement, e.g.:[1]

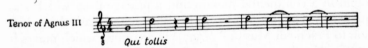

In this Mass the fourth part, which sings only when the tenor does, and therefore only in the four-part sections, is designated *Tenor Bassus*, and the common beginning is clearly realized, all four movements having the same first seven beats in the opening duet.

The movements of a Mass written on a plainsong tenor will sometimes have proportionate lengths, sometimes not. An isorhythmic motet, and therefore also a Mass on a tenor which is disposed isorhythmically, has exactly proportionate lengths by virtue of the repetition of the tenor in the same or proportionately diminished rhythm. Each of Dunstable's two movements on *Jesu Christe fili Dei*, for example, has two main divisions, one with a length equivalent to thirty-four dotted semibreves and thirty-four undotted semibreves, the other to thirty-four dotted minims and thirty-four undotted minims, and the

[1] Trent, Castello del Buon Consiglio, MS. 88, fos. 7v–9. The Mass is printed in *Monumenta Polyphoniae Liturgicae*, Ser. I, Vol. ii, No. 1.

four sections are therefore in the proportions 6 : 4 : 3 : 2. It is interesting to notice that an exactly proportionate division may also occur in movements not based on an isorhythmic tenor, and is found in two of the Masses which have been mentioned. Power divided his *Alma redemptoris* tenor into two continuous sections of fifty-six dotted minims and eighty-four minims, which is the proportion of 1 : 1 in crotchets,[1] and therefore presumably in actual length of performance, while the composer of the *Veterem hominem* Mass designed his tenor in two statements with sixty-two dotted minims in one and ninety-three minims in the other, thus also giving the same number of crotchets in each section. The varied repetitions of the tenor in the *Rex saeculorum* Mass are not related in any exact proportions. Though formal isorhythm went into disuse after *c.* 1450, the use of exact proportions in laying out a tenor remained an optional device in cantus-firmus technique throughout the later Middle Ages.

The first period in the history of the unified Ordinary of the Mass was also the last in that of the medieval motet, and if the motet was normally sung after the Sanctus, as we have assumed, there was an element of cause and effect in the development of one and the disappearance of the other. The movements of the Ordinary were written in exactly or approximately equal lengths, through the use of a recurring tenor, in spite of the great inequality in the lengths of their texts. Whatever may have been the true reason for abbreviating the text of the Creed, that practice contributed to this balance of the movements, as did the lengthening of the settings of the Sanctus and Agnus Dei by means of long passages of music on single syllables, which was a distinct feature of the polyphonic Ordinary. The result was that the time between the Sanctus and the Consecration, which had always been at the disposal of the musicians, was now filled by the singing of the longer polyphonic Sanctus, down to the end of the first Hosanna, and the Benedictus was sung after the Consecration.

The twelve isorhythmic motets of Dunstable[2] were by far the most considerable English contribution to this last period

---

[1] The proportions of these two Masses were pointed out by Strunk in the review cited above, p. 252, n. 1.

[2] Printed in *John Dunstable*, pp. 58–94.

in the history of the form.[1] Unlike those of Dufay, which were roughly contemporary with them, Dunstable's motets give little internal evidence of having been composed for particular occasions or events. They have rather the character of works written for the festivals of saints, and include pieces devoted to St. Alban, St. Germanus,[2] St. Michael, St. John the Baptist, St. Anne, St. Katherine, and the Annunciation and Assumption of the Virgin. His treatment of the design was orthodox, almost invariably having three statements of the tenor in progressive diminution, and the combination of this firmness of structure with his sensitive and imaginative use of the chanson style gives these works a special measure of the beauty of line and radiant serenity which were the distinguishing qualities

[1] There are an isorhythmic motet *Cantemus Domino–Gaudent in caelis* and an isorhythmic drinking song *O Potores exquisiti* in British Museum, MS. Egerton 3307; see Bukofzer, *Studies in Medieval Music*, pp. 145, 175.

[2] The text, as an exception, suggests a particular occasion, which may have been connected with the thousandth anniversary of the death of St. Germanus in 1448, either in Paris or at St. Albans, where St. Germanus was held in special regard.

of the *contenance Angloise*. His *Veni sancte Spiritus et emitte—Veni sancte Spiritus et infunde—Veni creator* on the tenor *Mentes tuorum visita*, the only one of his motets which was copied into a surviving English manuscript,[1] has an additional interest in its unique use of paraphrase, for the treble of the opening duet of each isorhythmic section paraphrases the successive lines of the hymn *Veni creator Spiritus*, from the second and third lines of which he chose his tenor (see Ex. 41).

The Development of the Festal Mass

The establishing of the cantus-firmus method of integrating the movements set the pattern for the composition of the festal Mass for a century to come. English composers held to this basic scheme, taking full advantage of the variety of design possible within it, while their continental contemporaries, particularly Dufay, Obrecht (b. 1452) and Josquin des Prés (d. 1521), explored new possibilities of using given material from both plainchant and secular song. In the dedication of his *Proportionale musices* (*c.* 1476) Johannes Tinctoris of Naples contrasted this conservatism of the English composers with the leading role which Dunstable and his contemporaries had played in European music:

'At this time, consequently', he wrote, referring to the foundation of chapels by Christian princes, 'the possibilities of our music have been so marvellously increased that there appears to be a new art, if I may so call it, whose fount and origin is held to be among the English, of whom Dunstable stood forth as chief. Contemporary with him in France were Dufay and Binchoys, to whom directly succeeded the moderns Ockeghem, Busnoys, Regis and Caron, who are the most excellent of all the composers I have ever heard. Nor can the English, who are popularly said to shout while the French sing, stand comparison with them. For the French contrive music in the newest manner for the new times, while the English continue to use one and the same style of composition, which shows a wretched poverty of invention.'[2]

[1] *The Old Hall Manuscript*, ii, p. 66. It is also in four continental manuscripts; see *John Dunstable*, p. 176.

[2] Translation in Strunk, *Source Readings in Music History*, p. 195, from Coussemaker, *Scriptores*, iv, pp. 153–5.

The saying *Anglici vulgariter jubilare, Gallici vero cantare dicuntur,* which was still current on the continent in the early sixteenth century,[1] is surely intended to point the contrast between the English florid style (*jubilare*) and the more syllabic 'modern' style of the continent, rather than to convey a dislike of the tone-quality of English singers. The style cultivated by the generation after Dunstable involved ever greater refinement and proliferation of detail, and the three Masses of Walter Frye, which were apparently composed on the continent, show some of the directions of this development during the third quarter of the century.[2] In his three-part Mass on *Nobilis et pulchra*[3] Frye decorated and extended the cantus firmus, for which he used the music of both the respond and its verse once in each movement, and also gave the tenor passages of free material in duet with the countertenor. The tenor of his four-part Mass *Flos regalis*[4] is used only as a cantus firmus, with slight elaborations, and the other three parts, the lowest of which is designated *Bassus,* sing in pairs in the duets:[5]

This Mass shows a distinct advance on *Veterem hominem* in the linear interest of the four-part writing and in the artistic use of

[1] Strunk, loc. cit., gives references in 1516 and 1545; see also above, p. 171.

[2] The first initial of the opening piece (Frye's Mass *Summae Trinitatis*) in the manuscript in which they are written (Brussels, Bibliothèque Royale, MS. 5557) bears the arms of Philip the Good (d. 1467) and of Charles the Bold (d. 1477). See Kenney, 'Origins and Chronology of the Brussels Manuscript 5557'.

[3] The first respond at Matins of St. Katherine. This Mass has a Kyrie with the trope *Deus creator.*

[4] The ritual source of the tenor has not been traced.

[5] Brussels, Bibliothèque Royale, MS. 5557, fos. 30v–31.

the melodic idioms of the style. Frye's three-part Mass *Summae Trinitati*[1] is based on a very long respond which is used complete, separated into sections by duets, in the Gloria and Credo, is shortened in the Sanctus and shortened still more in the Agnus Dei. While there is virtually no elaboration of the plainsong, except in an extension towards the final cadence, the tenor was put into rhythm of a kind which makes its movement more like that of the other parts, and their rhythm was correspondingly enlivened:[2]

Ex.43.

Each of Frye's three masses uses a common opening for all the movements.[3]

So great has been the loss of manuscripts of the last quarter of the fifteenth century that practically no material for the history of the festal Mass of that time has survived. We have, for example, no Masses by any of the twenty-five composers in the Eton manuscript except Fayrfax, whose mature music was written in the early sixteenth century, though the King's College inventory shows that Cornysh and Turges also wrote

[1] Ninth respond at Matins on Trinity Sunday; also sung in procession for the reception of a King and Queen, in the Sarum rite. See Wordsworth, *Salisbury Processions*, p. 118.

[2] Brussels, Bibliothèque Royale, MS. 5557, fos. 4v–5.

[3] For the connection of the *Summae Trinitati* Mass with his antiphon *Salve virgo*, see below, p. 305.

Masses, apparently for six voices. From the Magdalen books we have lost two large volumes of Masses in five, six and seven parts, some of which are likely to have been by Davy and his generation.[1] The Eton antiphons give us an idea what their general style would have been, and a fragment of a six-part Mass which has been pieced together from leaves of a late fifteenth-century choirbook, which were afterwards used as covers for a set of part-books written in the late sixteenth century,[2] shows that this style was also used for composing Masses:

Ex. 44.

[1] See below, pp. 431–3 and Index of Musicians, s.v. 'Davy.'
[2] Bodleian Library, MSS. Mus. e. 1–5, written for, and probably by,

John Cuk's Mass *Venit dilectus meus*[1] is a four-part example which, judging by its style, was written in this period. In the Gloria, which exists in part, and in the Agnus Dei, which is complete, the cantus firmus is used rather informally, appearing in the last section in a paraphrased form with a final extension, and in one earlier section of each movement in an abbreviated form. It is not used in all the full sections, as the plainsong usually was in larger forms, and while its rhythmic style is not very different from that of the tenors of Frye's Masses, the elaboration of the melodic lines and the extension of the range of the other parts[2] is considerable, the delight in florid melody and active rhythm and cross-rhythm being particularly noticeable in the solo sections. The cross-rhythm which was a feature of the style of the early fifteenth century was now applied to the further subdivision of the quavers into semiquavers, as in the tenor of the two bars preceding the last part of the Agnus Dei:

Ex.45.

John Sadler. The leaves have been detached and are now catalogued as MS. Mus. e. 21. The clefs of the mean, tenor and second countertenor parts in our reconstruction are deduced from the context; the tenor, which has also lost its clef, makes a poor fit, but the attempt indicates its style. We shall use hereafter the English terms of the period for the various voices, which were bass, tenor, countertenor (in the same range as the tenor, or a third above or below it), mean, treble, quatreble.

[1] In a number of leaves detached from the covers of a volume of Consistory Court Acts in the York Diocesan Registry. See Baillie and Oboussier, 'The York Masses'. The cantus firmus is the sixth antiphon at Matins on the Assumption of the Virgin.

[2] The range of the treble is an eleventh, of the mean a tenth, of the bass an eleventh; the total range is three octaves.

The solo sections used more varied combinations of the parts, and include in this movement duets for treble and bass, treble and tenor, mean and bass, and tenor and bass, and trios for the three lowest parts, the three highest parts, and treble with tenor and bass. There was probably a common opening in all the movements, since the first five notes of the Gloria, which are in duet for tenor and bass, are the same as the first five of the Agnus Dei.

The Festal Mass in the Sixteenth Century

The fundamental principle of late medieval polyphony was differentiation of melody, rhythm and phrasing; this gave an effect of great exuberance and vitality to the full sections, in which the parts surrounded the tenor with patterns of continuously changing melody, of cross-rhythm and of overlapping phrases. The ideas of thematic development, imitation and repetition were minor elements in the making of these patterns, the melodies being formed by a process of continuous renewal and variety. Imitation, when present, was hidden within and incidental to the complex of sound, being concerned with brief and purely decorative figures, and sequence was likewise used only for short and ornamental parts of a phrase. The solo sections were written as passages of vocal chamber music for the more expert singers, in which overt imitation between the parts, which was more frequent in them than in the full choral sections, was used as an additional method of weaving a polyphonic texture. This medieval aesthetic of polyphony, which was bound up with the notion of polyphony as an adornment of the ritual plainsong, persisted in some degree in English choral music until the Reformation, and while it could be modified by the elements of repetition and correspondence in their various forms, the nature of the musical texture was such that it could not be basically changed until the ritual plainsong was abandoned, or used in dismembered units as a source of material for imitative entries. These new elements of repetition and correspondence are increasingly apparent in the festal Masses written between *c.* 1500 and *c.* 1550, and the solution of the technical problems involved is often carried out with great ingenuity and artistry, notably in the work of John Taverner.

Though Taverner composed his festal Masses (*c.* 1520–30) in the most florid style, those of Robert Fayrfax (d. 1521) are in a style which is less florid on the whole than that used by composers who were in mid-career before the turn of the century. Of the five Masses by Fayrfax which have survived complete, *Regali ex progenie,*[1] which was copied into the King's College part-books in 1503–4,[2] and *O quam glorifica,*[3] which was written for proceeding to his degree of Doctor of Music at Cambridge in 1504,[4] are Mary-Masses; the others, *Albanus, O bone Jesu* and *Tecum principium,*[5] are a Mass of St. Alban, a Jesus-Mass and a Mass for Christmas respectively. The only one not based on a cantus firmus is *O bone Jesu,* in which the composer took the opening common to each of its movements from his own Jesus-antiphon *O bone Jesu,* and some of the music of the last section of the Gloria, of the Credo and of the Agnus Dei from the Amen of the same antiphon.[6] Though it is not a

---

[1] Third antiphon at Lauds on the Nativity of the Virgin.

[2] See above, p. 164.

[3] Hymn at first Vespers on the Assumption of the Virgin and through its octave; not in *Antiphonale Sarisburiense.*

[4] In Lambeth Palace Library MS. 1 it is headed: 'Doctor ffeyrfax for his forme in proceadinge to bee Doctor.'

[5] Antiphon at Vespers on Christmas and Epiphany and their octaves.

[6] The identity of all the parts of the common opening with the beginning of the antiphon is assumed from the identity of the mean part, the only part of the antiphon to survive. The connection between the Mass and the antiphon was pointed out in Hughes, 'An Introduction to Fayrfax', p. 99.

'derived' Mass[1] in the full sense, it seems to be the earliest surviving example composed in England of a Mass which has a musical connection with a polyphonic antiphon.

As might be expected, *O quam glorifica* is something of a demonstration of technical skill, in which the treble and tenor were written throughout in duple measure and the other parts in triple measure, so that there is not the usual change from triple to duple measure in the middle of the movements. Each movement was based on one complete statement of the plain-song, which is divided into three sections, the first two corresponding to the first two lines of the hymn. The different measure signatures are merely a matter of notation and do not make cross-rhythms which can be heard as such by the listener. The first full section of the Gloria, for example, in which the tenor was disposed in a succession of dotted crotchets followed by dotted minims, may conveniently be scored with a three-four barring in every part:[2]

Ex.46.

The real essays in proportion in the work, which are quite formal and deliberate in their design, were demonstrated in some of the solo sections, e.g.:[3]

Ex. 47.

[1] See below, pp. 282–3.   [2] Lambeth Palace, MS. 1, fos. 8v–9.
[3] Ibid., fos. 12v–13.

The cantus firmus of the *Regali* Mass was treated in a more orthodox fashion, being set out in two statements, one in triple and one in duple measure, in each movement. The opening of the Benedictus is a fair example of Fayrfax's use of points of imitation, which in this case were made of rather ordinary stuff, in designing a three-part solo section.[1] In *Tecum principium* there are twelve statements of the cantus firmus, all in different rhythmic forms and some with a short final extension, while the basis of the full sections in the *Albanus* Mass, which no doubt arose from Fayrfax's connection with St. Alban's Abbey, is a phrase of nine notes from an antiphon at Matins of St. Alban:[2]

Ex. 48.

The brevity of this theme brings the Mass into a category which may be described as *ostinato*-cantus firmus, on account of the number of repetitions of the theme in the full sections, where it appears forty times. There are thirty statements in the tenor, in direct, inverted and retrograde forms at various pitches,

---

[1] Printed in Walker, *History of Music in England*, p. 37.

[2] A copy with music of this office has not been found, but the theme is identical with the opening of the tenor of Dunstable's St. Alban motet *Albanus roseo rutilat—Quoque ferendus eras—Albanus Domini laudans*, printed in *John Dunstable*, p. 58. See ibid., p. 174, and Hughes, 'An Introduction to Fayrfax', p. 99.

five direct statements at different pitches in each part in turn
at the words *Dona nobis* in the Agnus Dei:[1]

Ex.49.

and finally five direct statements on the last word of the Mass,
pacem, falling by step to the closing cadence.[2]

[1] Lambeth Palace, MS. 1, fos. 23v–24.

[2] See the details of the layout in Hughes, op. cit., pp. 193–4. The music
of the word *pacem* was printed in *Oxford History of Music*, 1st ed., ii,

John Lloyd's Mass *O quam suavis*[1] is a thorough-going example
of what may be called a 'demonstration-Mass' as far as the
writing down of its tenor is concerned, though the listener will
not be conscious of any particular subtleties, but only of writing
of a moderately florid kind, rather in the manner of Fayrfax.
The plainsong melody on which it was based[2] is of such a
length that it is sung twice only, once in the Gloria and Credo
and once in the Sanctus and Agnus. Its rhythm in many of the
full sections is so designed that the actual lengths of the notes
can only be found through the solution and application of a
prescription hidden in a riddle. Some of these 'canons'[3] are *ad
hoc* devices, most are puzzles in numerical order. A fair sample
of the latter type is the final section of the Benedictus, to the
words *in excelsis*, in which the notes of the tenor are written as
breves in the original; the canon is *Hic novenarius per varios
procreatur numeros*, and its meaning is that the notes must actually
have the numbers of semibreves (crotchets in our transcription)
which are indicated in the following quotation:

Ex.50.

Since the singer obviously could not arrive at the right sequence
of the *varii numeri* on the spot, the manner of writing the tenor

pp. 320–1. For the music of the preceding *Qui tollis peccata mundi* see Reese,
Music in the Renaissance, p. 776. It is interesting to compare this treatment
with that of the theme of eight notes in Josquin's Mass *Hercules Dux Ferrariae*
(*Josquin des Prez, Missen*, ii, p. 19) on a *soggetto cavato* (composed before
1499; Reese, *Music in the Renaissance*, p. 236).

[1] The identity of the composer was discovered by R. Thurston Dart.
The Mass is preceded by a puzzle-antiphon (*Ave regina*) with the indication
'Hoc fecit ichannes maris' (sea = flood = Ffloyd or Flud = Lloyd).

[2] The antiphon to the Magnificat at first Vespers on Corpus Christi;
see Collins's introduction to his edition of the Mass, *Missa O Quam Suavis*,
p. xii.

[3] Canon, as defined by Tinctoris, 'est regula voluntatem compositoris
sub obscuritate quadam ostendens'. *Terminorum Musicae Diffinitorium*, ed.
Machabey, p. 9.

is calculated to impress the learned rather than to exercise the wits of the singers, as were the lessons in proportion in the Old Hall manuscript, for example. The manuscript of Lloyd's Mass has all the appearance of a presentation copy of a work designed for the appreciation of the *cognoscenti* as well as for the service of a ritual purpose, and there is nothing to equal its degree of artifice among the surviving English choral music of the period.

The four complete festal Masses by Nicholas Ludford were probably written a few years later than those of Fayrfax, but resemble them closely in style. The Mass of St. Stephen, *Lapidaverunt Stephanum*,[1] and two Mary-Masses, *Benedicta [et venerabilis es]*[2] and *Christi virgo [dilectissima]*,[3] are contained in two of the large choirbooks of the time, both probably written between *c.* 1505 and *c.* 1520, one now owned by Gonville and Caius College, Cambridge,[4] and the other by the Library of Lambeth Palace, while a third Mary-Mass, *Videte miraculum*,[5] is in the Gonville and Caius College book. Ludford's writing is flowing and sonorous, as may be seen from the final section of the *Benedicta* Mass, a mild 'demonstration' of six-eight rhythm in the tenor, which observes closely the number of repeated notes in the original plainsong, against three-four rhythm in the other parts[6] (see Ex. 51).

Though Fayrfax and Ludford composed in a manner which was noticeably more restrained than that of the late fifteenth century, Taverner's writing in the larger forms still retained much of the melodic elaboration and rhythmic interplay of the earlier style, while adding to it new elements of repetition and symmetry in the details of the polyphonic patterns. These elements appeared in his work in two important ways: imitation, or the off-set repetition of a melody in different parts, and sequence, or the successive repetition of a melody in the same

---

[1] First antiphon at Lauds on St. Stephen's Day.

[2] On the verse of the eighth respond (*Beata es*) at Matins on the Assumption.

[3] Ninth respond at Matins on the Annunciation.

[4] MS. 667. At the end is written: 'Ex dono et opere Edwardi Higgons huius ecclesie canonici'. The book was almost certainly written for St. Stephen's, Westminster, where Higgons became a canon in 1518.

[5] Respond at first Vespers on the Purification.

[6] Lambeth Palace, MS. 1, fos. 31v–32.

Ex.51.

part. The technical problem of using imitation in composition on a cantus firmus is that of making the 'point'[1] of imitation fit different parts of the pre-existing melody, and the difficulty of the problem was increased when the composer derived the points from the cantus firmus (thereby furthering the integration of the polyphony) rather than devising points which were independent of the cantus firmus. Both of these methods may be seen in Taverner's Mass *Gloria tibi Trinitas*,[2] where all six parts have a point on *filius patris* which is derived from the cantus firmus, and against the last appearance of this point the

[1] In sixteenth-century terms a 'point' was a figure or theme used in a passage of imitative polyphony, a 'fugue' was the passage as a whole.

[2] The first antiphon at first Vespers of Trinity Sunday, which was also sung as the antiphon to *Quicumque vult* at Prime when the choir was not ruled, except in the octave of Trinity.

second countertenor[1] begins a new and 'independent' point which is imitated by four other parts:[2]

Ex. 52.

In this Mass Taverner departed from the orthodox by putting his cantus firmus in the mean, not in the tenor, and by using it as a basis for solo sections as well as full sections. He used a normal lay-out for the cantus firmus, which is sung three times, in triple time, duple time and in diminution, in each of the first three movements, and twice, in triple time and diminution, in the Agnus Dei, the second section of that movement being free. He used imitation in the solo sections of his larger works rather more than did the composers of the florid style of the late fifteenth century, but less systematically and with freer treatment of the points than did Fayrfax and Ludford. Strict imitation, or 'canon' in the modern sense, which is not found

[1] Or 'sextus', from the fact that it was written in the sixth part-book of a set (Bodleian Library, MSS. Mus. Sch. e. 376–81).
[2] *Tudor Church Music*, i, p. 130.

earlier in solo sections, appears in four passages in the Mass
O Michael.[1]

Repetition in sequence has the effect of giving unity and
symmetry to a melody, as repetition in imitation has to a
passage of polyphony. Taverner frequently varied a sequence,
as he did a point of imitation, by slight changes in the intervals
of the melody, especially when writing against a cantus firmus,
and the opening of the Sanctus of the Mass *Corona spinea* is a
memorable example of this, as well as a sound of truly celestial
quality:[2]

Ex. 53.

He was particularly fond of using a sequence to form an

[1] The cantus firmus is *Archangeli Michaelis interventione*, respond at first Vespers and Matins on the feasts of the Apparition of St. Michael (third respond)
and St. Michael in Monte Tumba (ninth respond). The canons are at the
unison at *Qui tollis* in the Gloria (ibid., p. 199), at the second at *Filium Dei
unigenitum* in the Credo (p. 204), at the unison at the opening of the
Benedictus (p. 216), in each case for two trebles with a free part,
and at the unison for two basses in a four-part section at the opening
of the third Agnus Dei (p. 222). There is a canon at the seventh below
between countertenor and bass, also with a free part, at *in nomine* in the
Benedictus of the Mass 'Small Devotion'.

[2] *Tudor Church Music*, i, p. 175; the cantus firmus had not been identified.

obstinately repeated pattern against a cantus firmus, thus giving
it the more important role of an ostinato, generally in the bass,
as in this passage from the first section of the Agnus Dei of the
Gloria tibi Trinitas Mass:[1]

Ex.54.

where the polyphony is unified by both sequential and imitative use of the points.

Hugh Aston's two surviving Masses, *Te Deum* and *Videte
manus meas*,[2] have something of Taverner's breadth of style and
imaginative use of technique, though they lack his consummate
mastery of line and pattern. The form of the *Te Deum* Mass
comes close to being a set of variations because the composer
formed his cantus firmus almost entirely out of continuous
repetitions of the music of the second phrase (*Te eternum patrem*)
of the Te Deum, which he used nine times in the Gloria, eight
in the Credo, four in the Sanctus and five in the Agnus Dei; it
appears in all the parts except the countertenor. He used the
music of the first phrase of the hymn only to make a common
opening for the Gloria, Credo and Agnus Dei, and the music
of the *Sanctus, Sanctus, Sanctus* (verse 5) of the Te Deum as an

[1] *Tudor Church Music*, i, p. 152.

[2] Antiphon to the Magnificat at Vespers on the Tuesday in Easter Week.
Aston's Masses are printed in *Tudor Church Music*, x.

appropriate basis for the opening of the Sanctus of the Mass, while the rest of the music of the hymn played no part at all in his design. This approach to variations by the repeated use of a liturgical chant may be compared with Taverner's definite adoption of the form of variations on a secular tune in his 'Western Wynde' Mass.[1] Aston's treatment of cantus-firmus technique in his Mass *Videte manus meas* was also unorthodox, since he took advantage of a plainsong theme which has two halves of virtually identical melody to loosen the traditional plan, using only one statement of the cantus firmus in the Credo and one and a half in the Agnus Dei. The work is a fine example of florid linear writing, and of the use of the fast rhythm of triplet quavers to give a cumulative effect to the final sections of the Gloria, Credo and Agnus Dei.

This less formal use of the cantus firmus in a festal Mass may be a symptom of the trend towards free composition in the imitative style. It could not, however, arrive at its final aim within the plan of the festal Mass, for both technical and liturgical reasons, since not only were the structure and style of the festal Mass determined by the fact that it was written on a cantus firmus, but also its liturgical relevance was derived from the particular cantus firmus on which it was based. It was probably due to the strongly liturgical character of English polyphony that the writing of cantus-firmus Masses covered such a wide range of feasts, and survived until the mid-sixteenth century, when this method of composing a Mass had virtually disappeared elsewhere. Some idea of the liturgical range of the festal Masses which have survived in whole or in part may be gathered from the combined contents of two sets of part-books, one a complete set of six[2] containing eighteen Masses, seven of which were copied by William Forrest, petty canon of Christ Church, Oxford, and chaplain to Queen Mary, and the other an incomplete set of four in Peterhouse, Cambridge, containing Masses, Antiphons, Magnificats and a few other ritual forms.[3] Besides the Masses of Fayrfax, Taverner and Aston which have

[1] See below, pp. 283–4.
[2] Bodleian Library, MSS. Mus. Sch. e. 376–81.
[3] Cambridge, Peterhouse MSS. 40, 41, 31, 32, written between *c.* 1540 and 1547 (see below, p. 341, n. 4). See Hughes, *Catalogue of the Musical Manuscripts at Peterhouse*, pp. viii–ix, 2–3.

been mentioned, and Ludford's *Christi virgo* and two incomplete Masses (*Inclina Domine* and *Regnum mundi*), these two collections contain the following: John Norman's *Resurrexit Dominus*; Richard Pygot's *Veni sancte Spiritus*; Robert Jones's *Spes nostra* and Thomas Knyght's *Libera nos*, both for the feast of the Trinity; William Rasor's *Christe Jesu*, perhaps a Mass of St. Thomas of Canterbury; Thomas Ashewell's *Ave Maria*, on an antiphon at Commemorations of the Virgin in Advent; and John Marbeck's *Per arma justitiae*, a Mass for Lent. This last, which has been published,[1] was probably written between *c.* 1535 and 1543, and its design is along traditional lines, except that two of the statements of the cantus firmus are not in the tenor. It is a conservative example of the florid style, with remarkably old-fashioned counterpoint for its time, little imitation in the full sections, and many passages of differentiated polyphony in the solo sections, and shows no great intensity of imagination.

The Shorter Mass

The composition of settings of the Ordinary on a small scale and of separate movements of the Ordinary was practised more or less continuously during this period, though, to judge by the surviving music, only the Kyrie was regularly composed as a separate part of the Ordinary after the early fifteenth century. At that time two movements of the Ordinary might be written to form a pair. There are four such pairs of Gloria-Credo or of Sanctus-Agnus, which are congruent in style and were set down together in a manuscript source in each case, among the works of Dunstable.[2] While the festal Mass derived its liturgical relevance from its choice of cantus firmus, the shorter Masses and Kyries tended to keep a closer relation to the music of the Ordinary by using the plainsongs of the Ordinary as a basis, and thus to maintain the method of the paraphrased and ornamental settings in the Old Hall collection. For example, a ferial Mass of *c.* 1450 for the first three days of Holy Week, in

---

[1] *Tudor Church Music*, x, p. 165. In 1543 Marbeck was accused of holding Calvinist views and writing against the Mass. Ibid., pp. 157–8.

[2] *John Dunstable*, pp. 14–34. For a discussion of earlier paired movements by continental composers see Bukofzer, *Studies in Medieval Music*, pp. 219–22.

three and occasionally four parts, has an ornamentation of the
simple chants in the treble:[1]

Ex. 55.

The problem of the provenance of the manuscript in which
this Mass occurs, the main contents of which are Holy Week
music and carols, has been much discussed.[2] The liturgical
music is based on the Sarum rite, and the presence of carols
suggests that the collection was written for a collegiate church
or household chapel. For liturgical reasons, the theory that it
belonged to the Cistercian Abbey of Meaux seems untenable.
The Cistercian rite was a twice 'reformed' version and con-
flation of those of Metz and Rome, first under the direction of
Stephen Harding and then under that of St. Bernard. The
uniformity of its texts and music was rigorously imposed,[3] and
while some monasteries may have allowed secular rites and
customs in the votive services sung out of choir, it is difficult
to believe that in a Cistercian abbey the ritual of Holy Week
could have been carried out according to a secular Ordinal.[4]

[1] British Museum, MS. Egerton 3307, fos. 17–19. The Kyrie is incomplete
at the beginning; being ferial, the Mass has no Gloria or Credo. It is transcribed in Bukofzer, 'A Newly-discovered Manuscript', pp. 39 sqq., and
discussed in Bukofzer, *Studies in Medieval Music*, Chapter IV, where the
similarity to the style of settings of a Sanctus and Agnus by Binchois on the
same chants is pointed out.

[2] See Schofield, 'A Newly-discovered Manuscript of the English Chapel
Royal, I'; Bukofzer, *Studies in Medieval Music*, Chapter IV; Greene, 'Two
Medieval Musical Manuscripts'.

[3] 'Volumus in nostris de cetero monasteriis tam verbo quam nota ubique
teneri, et mutari omnino in aliquo, auctoritate totius Capituli, ubi ab
universis Abbatibus concorditer susceptum et confirmatum est, prohibe-
mus . . .' Marosszéki, *Les origines du chant Cistercien*, p. 29.

[4] Extracts from a Cistercian Ordinal, including Palm Sunday and Holy
Week, were printed in Rock, *Church of Our Fathers*, i, pp. 413 sqq.

Another method used for shorter Masses was that of setting every second sentence of the text in polyphony for alternation with the original plainsong. This made the ritual chant a part of the performance while giving the composer some freedom of action in the polyphonic sections.[1] There are, for example, a Kyrie by Horwood and two anonymous Gloria-Credo pairs set for *alternatim* singing in a collection of leaves which formed part of a book of Masses of the late fifteenth century.[2] One of the Gloria-Credo pairs has a recurring theme, not used in cantus-firmus fashion, which is a paraphrase of the versicle *Custodi nos*, sung after the hymn at Compline throughout the year (except on double feasts):[3]

Ex. 36.

Cu-sto-di nos Do-mi-ne

The form in which this theme is used in the Mass is written in the manuscript thus:

Ex. 57.

Cu-sto-di nos Do-mi-ne

While this pair was composed in duple measure and is relatively simple in rhythm and texture, with a certain amount of overt imitation, the other Gloria-Credo pair is so florid as to approach at times the style of the festal Masses, e.g.:

Ex 58.

fa - ctum   con-sub-stan - ti-a-lem Pa -

Mean

non fa-ctum Pa-tri: per quem

Tenor
Bass

con-sub-stan-ti-a-lem Pa-tri: per quem

---

[1] In some settings the chant was paraphrased in the polyphonic sections, as in a Gloria by Dufay (Trent MSS. No. 1443; see the index in *Denkmäler der Tonkunst in Österreich*, vii, p. 77).

[2] See p. 261, n. 1, above.

[3] *Ordinale Exon.*, i, pp. 27–8. The chant is taken from the 'Armagh Antiphonal', Dublin, Trinity College, MS. B.1.1, folios not numbered.

Of Horwood's Kyrie, only the treble and tenor, which uses one of the Kyrie chants for Sundays[1] in both paraphrased and ornamental forms, have survived.[2] There is also in this manuscript an anonymous Kyrie written in three parts, below which is a canon explaining that a fourth part is to be deduced by singing one of the other parts in canon six beats behind:

Ex 59.

The troped Kyrie *Deus creator omnium* was also set as a separate item. A collection of polyphonic music of *c.* 1460 in the Pepysian Library at Magdalene College, Cambridge,[3] gives the

---

[1] *Graduale Sarisburiense*, pl. 6*; this chant was also used on the feast of the Conception of the Virgin. Ibid., pl. 8*.

[2] It was for at least three voices, since the treble has rests during the third *Christe.*

[3] MS. 1236; on fos. 10–10v are tables for the date of Easter for the years 1460–1519.

plainsong of the first verse, which also serves for the two following verses, and a two-part setting of the fourth, sixth and eighth
verses, the upper part of which is an elaboration of the plainsong[1] (see Ex. 60).

This may be compared with a three-part setting of about the
same period, also written for alternating plainsong and polyphony, in this case beginning with a polyphonic setting of the
first verse. The fourth verse opens thus:[2]

Ex. 61.

Con - so - la - - tor____

Spi - ri - tus____ sup - pli - ces

The style of the shorter Mass of the late fifteenth and early
sixteenth centuries is exemplified in the Masses *Rex summe* and
Gaudete in Domino by Thomas Packe,[3] both of which include the
Kyrie, in Henry Petyr's 'Playn Song' Mass (not so called in the
manuscript)[4] and in an anonymous Mass on leaves bound up
with manuscript and printed Year Books of Law recently acquired by the Bodleian Library.[5] All four are for three voices.

---

[1] MS. 1236, fos. 33v–34.

[2] On parchment leaves used to cover a copy of the *Valor Ecclesiasticus* of
1534 which was later used by Dugdale; now MS. Archer 2 in the Shake-
speare Birthplace Library, Stratford-on-Avon.

[3] 'Sir' in the manuscript, showing that he was a priest; he is possibly the
same person as Thomas Pyke (Pykke), clerk at Eton 1454–61.

[4] These three are in British Museum, MS. Add. 5665, which also contains carols written before *c.* 1475 (see below, p. 421). The Masses and
other liturgical items appear to have been added about the end of the
century.

[5] The Mass is written on the same paper as the manuscript notes. The
Sanctus is followed by one page of the bass part of a *Stabat Mater*, and the

The Kyrie, Gloria and Credo of the *Rex summe* Mass, which takes its name from one of the plainsong Kyries which were not sung with the words of their trope, were set for *alternatim* singing:[1]

and the material of this and the other two polyphonic sections of the Kyrie recurs throughout the Mass. *Gaudete in Domino* and Petyr's Mass are set for polyphonic singing throughout, with a common opening in each movement. In the Bodleian Mass the Gloria and Credo, which are *alternatim* settings, have a common opening:

Agnus Dei is incomplete. The printed part includes Year Books printed by R. Pynson in 1510 and 1520.

[1] MS. Add. 5665, fo. 73v.

while the Sanctus and Agnus Dei, which are polyphonic throughout, both open with a duet which uses an ornamented form of this beginning. The style of Petyr's Mass is a special case, for he composed the whole of the music with notes of only two lengths, written in a notation adapted from plainsong, in which the symbol ⁑ was to be read as a breve (minim in our transcription) and the symbol ■ as a semibreve (our crotchet), e.g.:[1]

This deliberately 'playn' style was later used by Taverner for his 'Playn Song' Mass (which does not imply a Mass on plain-song themes), and this manner of notation was also used for settings of other ritual forms, notably for the tenor part of responds. The Sanctus and Agnus Dei of each of these Masses were set in a distinctly less simple style than the other move-ments and are about the same length as the Gloria and Credo, in which the words were set almost syllabically.

Taverner's methods of composing a shorter Mass were both varied and enterprising. In two of his five-part Masses, 'Small Devotion' and the 'Meane Mass',[2] he rang the changes on three

[1] MS. Add. 5665, fo. 115v.

[2] Printed in *Tudor Church Music*, i, pp. 70, 50, the latter as *Sine nomine*. The title 'Meane Mass' occurs in one of the Petre part-books (Chelmsford, Essex Record Society O/p Petre MS. 1) and in St. Michael's College, Tenbury, MS. 1464; see *Tudor Church Music Appendix*, pp. 7–8. It is for a mean (compass within the octave upwards from middle C), two counter-tenors, tenor and bass.

ways of treating polyphonic texture: imitation, homorhythm (i.e., 'chordal' style) and antiphony. Antiphony, in polyphony as in plainsong psalmody, means dividing a choir into two groups which sing in alternation.[1] In these Masses a group of voices within the choir occasionally repeats in varied or exact form the music of another group, so that this kind of antiphony is another of the elements of repetition which were introduced into the polyphonic writing of the period. Another technique which involves repetition, that of the rota, had already reappeared in English polyphony about the middle of the fifteenth century,[2] and a passage from the Credo of Taverner's 'Meane Mass' shows antiphony passing into a rota, which is followed by imitation:[3]

[1] On the general history of choral antiphony, see Apel, 'Polychoral Style' in *Harvard Dictionary of Music*.

[2] See below, pp. 302–3.

[3] *Tudor Church Music*, i, p. 58.

The smooth transitions from one to the other tend to hide the differences of technique, but in general rota and imitation may be distinguished from antiphony by an overlap in the music which is repeated, and rota from imitation by repetition of the point at the unison or octave only.

The movements of the 'Meane Mass' were integrated in more than the usual ways, by a recurring ending as well as a common opening, and by a somewhat similar scheme of frequent changes of measure in each movement. In 'Small Devotion', which is both more varied in method and more characteristic in melodic material,[1] the Gloria and Credo use imitative and antiphonal styles, while the melodic lines of the Sanctus and Agnus are so extended that the style approaches that of the large six-part works, with use of sequence, canon and ostinato. For the second half of the *Hosanna* of the Sanctus the composer devised a 'cantus firmus' consisting of seven statements of a rising sequence,[2] and he built the first (*miserere*) *nobis* of the Agnus Dei on an ostinato figure which he used in each of the five parts in succession.[3]

The third of Taverner's five-part Masses[4] was composed by re-working and expanding the music of his own antiphon *Mater Christi sanctissima*.[5] Masses composed by this kind of adaptation of the polyphonic texture of a motet or secular chanson, which

[1] A few passages (beginning and ending of the Gloria; first *miserere nobis* and ending of the Agnus Dei) are derived from his antiphon *Christe Jesu pastor bone*. See below, p. 341.

[2] *Tudor Church Music*, i, p. 89.

[3] The tenor of this Mass is missing, and the editors have supplied a fully appropriate substitute. The recognition of the ostinato character of this passage suggests a small emendation of the tenor at p. 94, bars 11–12, where it certainly had the ostinato figure.

[4] Ibid., p. 99.

[5] See below, pp. 340–1.

was commonly used on the continent during the sixteenth century, have generally been called 'parody' Masses, though recently the rather opprobrious term 'second-hand' Mass and the more appropriate term 'derived' Mass have been applied to them.[1] In this case Taverner made the beginning and the last section of each movement of the Mass correspond to the beginning and end of the antiphon, and did not use the rest of its material in any systematic way, but added a considerable amount of new writing.[2] The four-part Mass 'Western Wynde' is the first surviving English Mass on a secular theme, though such Masses had been common on the continent for nearly a century,[3] and is the earliest of three Masses on this melody, the others being by Tye and Sheppard. It is not a cantus-firmus Mass in the usual sense, but a set of thirty-six variations on the melody, without interludes, carried out in a clearly conceived plan and with constant variety of method and texture. There are nine variations in each movement, disposed in two groups of four with a final variation in triplet quaver rhythm in the Gloria and Credo, and in three groups of three in the Sanctus and Agnus Dei. The melody is ornamented occasionally in the cadence, and is varied only to the extent that in one statement in each movement the third of its phrases, which are in the form A B B', is dropped. In twenty-one variations the theme is in the treble, in ten in the tenor, and in five in the bass,[4] while nineteen variations are full, nine are for three voices, four are partly for three and partly for two voices, and four are for two voices. The positions of the full sections in the Gloria and Credo correspond, being in the first, third, fourth, seventh and ninth variations in both movements; full variations begin the first and end all three divisions of the Sanctus, and come at the end of the first division and in all three variations of the last division of the Agnus. It is clear from these bald

---

[1] K. Jeppesen, review of Reese, *Music in the Renaissance* in *The Musical Quarterly*, xli, 1955, pp. 388–9.

[2] See *Tudor Church Music*, i, pp. lxi–lxii. Again the tenor is missing, but in this case the editors have supplied it only where it could clearly be derived from the antiphon.

[3] The use of secular themes in masses, both as cantus firmus and later by derivation, was common on the continent from Dufay to Palestrina.

[4] Disposed in the four movements thus: treble, 6, 5, 5, 5; tenor, 3, 3, 3, 1; bass, 0, 1, 1, 3.

particulars that the work was conceived and planned as a whole, while its variety of method makes it a notable demonstration of the art of variation by contrapuntal addition. Among the techniques it brings into play are homorhythm, differentiated counterpoint, points of imitation derived from and independent of the theme, counterpoint in sequential ostinato, e.g.:[1]

Ex.66.

and counterpoint in strict ostinato,[2] e.g.:[3]

Ex.67.

In the 'Playn Song' Mass for four men's voices the techniques of imitation, antiphony and homorhythm are used in the Gloria and Credo, while the extension of the melodic lines in the Sanctus and Agnus Dei, with use of sequence, ostinato and imitation, gives those movements an effect which is plain only in the rhythmic sense. Like the Hosanna of the Sanctus in the

[1] *Tudor Church Music*, i, p. 5.
[2] I.e., which is unvaried in pitch and voice.
[3] *Tudor Church Music*, i. p. 16.

PLATE XIII

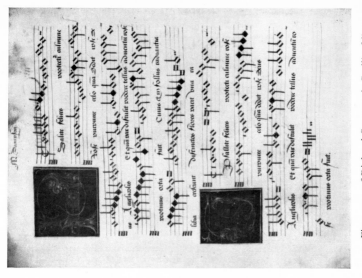

21. First page of Richard Sampson's *Psallite felices*

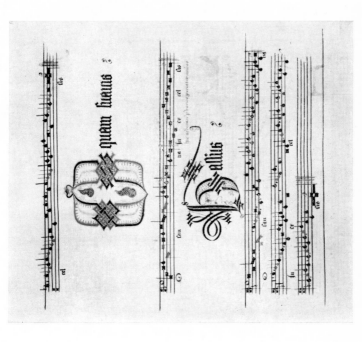

20. Tenor and bass parts of the *Hosanna in excelsis* from the *Benedictus* of John Lloyd's Mass *O quam suavis*

PLATE XIV

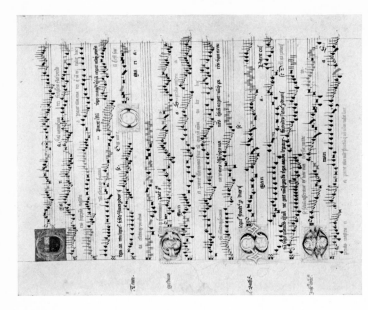

23. First page of John Browne's *O Maria Salvatoris mater*

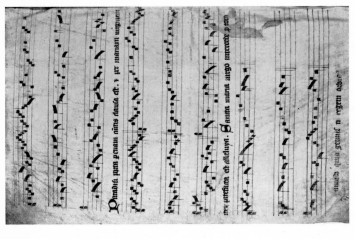

22. Antiphons *Paradisi porta* and *Sancta Maria*

'Small Devotion' Mass, the last section of the 'Playn Song' Mass
is based on an *ad hoc* cantus firmus, a descending scale which is
sung by every part in turn:[1]

Ex.68.

Nicholas Ludford's seven Lady-Masses of *c.* 1520–30,[2] one
for each day of the week, form the only surviving complete
scheme for the daily Lady-Mass throughout the year,[3] including some parts of the Proper as well as the Ordinary, and are
therefore of great interest musically and liturgically. Three of
the part-books have the vocal parts of the polyphony in the
usual way, but the fourth book has, not indeed a fourth part
for the polyphony, but melodies in measured notation and in
the tenor range for the *alternatim* parts of the Kyries, Glorias
and Credos, and the plainsongs of the soloist's part of the Alleluias, of the beginning and odd-numbered verses of the Sequences, and of the whole of the Offertories and Communions.[4]
Only the first words of the texts of these melodies and plainsongs are given, except in the Kyries, and there seems no doubt
that this was the book of the Master of the choir, who would

[1] *Tudor Church Music*, i., p. 49.

[2] The binding of the manuscript in which they were written (British
Museum, MSS. Royal Appendix 45–8) bears the arms of Henry VIII and
Catherine of Aragon.

[3] For some fragmentary survivals, see below, p. 391.

[4] The Offertory *Felix namque* and the Communion *Beata viscera*, sung
daily in the *Salve sancta parens* Mass, are included in the Sunday Mass, the
first of the seven. They are repeated, and those for the other seasons of the
year are given, at the end of the book.

probably use it at the organ. He might play only the single notes of the melodies and plainsongs, but it is rather more likely that he would play extemporaneous descants on them.[1]

All seven settings of the Kyrie were written for *alternatim* performance; the Gloria and Credo of the Wednesday and Friday Masses are in vocal polyphony throughout, the Gloria and Credo of the other Masses being for *alternatim* performance,[2] while all the settings of the Sanctus and Agnus Dei are for voices. The Introit and Gradual of the Lady-Mass changed only with the season, and were normally sung in plainsong,[3] which is not given in these books. The music they contain shows that the performance of the other parts of the Proper and Ordinary was done as follows:

Kyrie	Organ and voices *alternatim*.
Gloria	Voices only on Wednesday and Friday, *alternatim* on other days.
Alleluia	Organ acted as ruler-soloist, voices as chorus.
Sequence	Organ acted as beginner, then *alternatim*.
Credo	Voices only on Wednesday and Friday, *alternatim* on other days.
Offertory	Organ only.
Sanctus and Agnus Dei	Voices only.
Communion	Organ only.

For the most part the style of music is quite florid, as in the opening of the Kyrie of the Sunday Mass:

Ex.69.

---

[1] As has been suggested by Baillie and Oboussier, 'The York Masses', p. 26. The Kyries may have been sung, since the syllables are disposed as for singing.

[2] The Gloria was not sung in Advent and Lent, and the Credo was sung only on the days on which it was sung in the Mass of the day. *Missale Sarum*, col. 766*, and see above, p. 57.

[3] Both the Gradual and its verse were sung by the choir: 'In capella

The tenor parts of the vocal sections in all the Kyries are, as in this example, ornamented forms of the organ melodies with which they alternate, and none have any clear connection with the plainsong Kyries which the Sarum Missal prescribed for the daily Lady-Mass.[1] The same scheme was used in the *alternatim* Glorias and Credos, the tenors of which are, in fact, restatements, varied and unvaried, of the Tenor of the Kyrie of the particular Mass in which they occur. The four vocal movements of the Ordinary of the Wednesday and Friday Masses have a common opening, and the settings of the Sanctus and Agnus Dei in all the Masses are, as usual, in an expansive style which gives them a length commensurate with the Gloria and Credo.[2]

When Tallis derived his five-part Mary-Mass *Salve intemerata*[3] from his Mary-antiphon with that title,[4] he carried out this method of composition in a much more thorough and systematic way than Taverner had done in his 'Small Devotion' and *Mater Christi* Masses. He dismembered the antiphon into sixteen sections, and incorporated all but two of them[5] as complete units into the Mass. This was done in a particularly orderly way, for the sections were incorporated into each movement of the Mass in the same order, with one exception, as they existed in the antiphon, while only the first section of the antiphon appears more than once in the Mass, being sung at the beginning of each movement to make a common opening. The

beatae Virginis per totum annum Gradale cum suo verso cantetur a toto choro'. *Missale Sarum*, col. 762*.

[1] The troped Kyries for lesser doubles, sung *absque versibus*, were distributed among the days of the week; the order is given in *Missale Sarum*, cols. 761*–2*. On the Kyrie melodies in Ludford's Lady-Masses, see below, pp. 290–2.

[2] The settings of the Alleluia and Sequence are discussed below, pp. 376–7, 391–2.

[3] *Tudor Church Music*, vi, p. 3.   [4] See below, p. 335.

[5] The fourth and fifth sections, both in three parts, running from pp. 149–152 of the edition.

Gloria, for example, was composed by putting together seven sections of the antiphon and one new section (in the order 1, 6, new, 9, 10, 12, 11 and 15, where the numbers indicate the order of the sections of the antiphon). The Credo was made of four antiphon sections and two new sections (1, 2, new, 7, new, 14), while the Sanctus and Agnus Dei were each formed of three sections of the antiphon (in the order 1, 3, 8 and 1, 13, 16), with one new section in the last Agnus Dei, ingeniously joined to the last section of the antiphon, so that both works close with the same music.

Apart from the interest of its musical joinery, the *Salve intemerata* Mass is not a work of striking quality, for the best of Tallis is not to be found in his Masses, and the only other surviving example, which has no name, is a rather uncomfortable essay in the Reformation style of 'playn and distincte note, for every sillable one'.[1] Here he alternated imitation and homorhythm in the style of the mid-sixteenth century and made a virtually syllabic setting with careful attention to the rhythm of the words, in the Sanctus and Agnus Dei as well as in the other movements. The treatment of those two movements in particular, with their fairly frequent repetitions of words and sentences, shows how fundamental was the change which was taking place in the ideas of churchmen and composers about the relation of words and music in settings of liturgical forms.

The part-books[2] in which Tallis's *Sine nomine* Mass is preserved contain a considerable amount of music for the Mass, including works by Taverner, Knyght, Appleby, Okeland, Tye, Sheppard, William Whytbrook, who was sub-dean of St. Paul's from 1531 to 1535, and William Mundy, who was a chorister at Westminster Abbey in 1542-3.[3] The books also contain music by Blytheman and Whyte, presumably William Blytheman (d. 1591) and Robert Whyte, who was born about 1535,[4]

---

[1] Cf. Edward VI's Injunction of 1548: '*Item* they shall fromhensforthe synge or say no Anthemes off our lady or other saynts but onely of our lorde And them not in laten but choseyng owte the best and moste soundyng to cristen religion they shall turne the same into Englishe settyng therunto a playn and distincte note, for every sillable one, they shall singe them and none other'. *Lincoln Statutes*, iii, pp. 592-3.

[2] British Museum, MSS. Add. 17802-5.

[3] Pine, 'Westminster Abbey: Some Early Masters of the Choristers', p. 259.

[4] *Tudor Church Music*, v, p. xi.

and can therefore not have been written before the introduction of the English Prayer Book in 1549. The liturgical character of the contents shows clearly that they were written for use with the Sarum rite, and among the compositions by (William ?) Mundy is a setting of *Exurge Christe*, a prayer for the confounding of schismatics and the revival of 'apostolic truth'. The problem of the date of the manuscript is complicated by its including music by Byrd and John Mundy. The former, however, may be Thomas Byrd of the Chapel Royal or the William Byrd who was a chorister at Westminster in 1542–3.[1] Unless it can be shown that the Sarum rite was still in use in some choral foundation in the later sixteenth century, the weight of evidence suggests that the manuscript was compiled for the Marian revival of the old liturgy between 1553 and 1558,[2] though this date would make it necessary to assume that there was an earlier John Mundy than the son of William who died in 1630. The manuscript will be referred to here as the 'Gyffard' part-books, since it appears to have belonged at an early period to a Dr. Philip Gyffard.

Though repetition of words was becoming more common in the music of the Reformation era, as this manuscript shows, it was not always accompanied by as sober a style as is found in Tallis's four-part Mass. Among the settings of the Ordinary is a 'French Mass' by Sheppard,[3] in which he adopts a brisk style, with short points of imitation:

---

[1] Pine, loc. cit.

[2] For Westminster? It contains a votive antiphon of St. Peter (*Et portae inferi*).

[3] Edited by H. B. Collins in Chester's *Latin Church Music of the Polyphonic Schools*, No. 9.

and writes at times in a quick triple rhythm, with even shorter
points:

This work was apparently written on the model of the shorter
Masses of such French composers as Nicolas Gombert (c. 1490–
c. 1560). The same section of the manuscript contains the
'Western Wynde' Masses of Taverner, Tye and Sheppard,
Taverner's 'Playn Song' Mass, Sheppard's Mass 'Be not afraide'
and his 'Playnsong Masse for a Mene', and Appleby's 'Mass for
a Mene'. In a later section there is a group of three Masses,
all bearing the title 'Apon the square', two by William Mundy
and one by Whytbrook. The term 'square' seems to refer to the
melody on which the Kyrie of these Masses is based, for the
melodies which Mundy uses are found in a group of melodies,
set out for the Lady-Mass Kyries of the various days of the
week, written on the fly-leaves of a fifteenth-century Sarum
Gradual.[1] The melodies for Sunday and Thursday in this set
are the same as those used by Ludford in his Sunday and
Thursday Masses, while the Sunday melody is the same as that
of Taverner's Kyrie called *le roy* in the Gyffard part-books,[2]

---

[1] British Museum, MS. Lansdowne 462, fos. 151v–152; see Bukofzer,
Studies in Medieval Music, pp. 191–2. Folio 1v has Sanctus melodies, two of
which are counter parts of Sanctus settings in Old Hall. Ibid., p. 92.

[2] Printed in *Tudor Church Music*, iii, p. 54.

and the melody of the Kyrie of Whytbrook's Mass corresponds to that in Ludford's Mass for Monday. The Kyrie melody of Ludford's Tuesday Mass had earlier been used as the basis of one of the Masses in the York fragments, and the melody of its *Christe* was set in three different ways by Taverner.[1] Another source for three of these melodies is a fifteenth-century manuscript of apparently English origin in the Vatican Library,[2] which has *le roy* and two other melodies which appear in the Sarum Gradual fly-leaves, one of which was used by Mundy in his first Mass:

Ex. 72.
('Square')

Besides the *le roy* title, which may possibly be a reference to the Roy Henry of the Old Hall manuscript, the Vatican manuscript has the name Lambertus,[3] and in the Sarum Gradual the names Lyonel, Dunstaple and Martyn are written beside three of the melodies. While these may be the original composers of the melodies concerned, it is clear from the complex of correspondences which has been outlined that many such melodies became common property and were used as the basis of the Kyrie for the daily Lady-Mass and sometimes also for the

[1] Printed in *Tudor Church Music*, iii, pp. 56–7.
[2] MS. Reg. lat. 1146, fo. 72v–73.   [3] See Bukofzer, op. cit., p. 192.

other movements. The origin of the term 'square', which occurs also in inventories and accounts, is obscure, but it may simply refer to the appearance of the notation in which the melodies were written. The Magdalen accounts for 1532 have a payment to one Bull for 'le prykkyng unam missam et square in scripto gradali' and one to Bull and Norwich for 'prykkyng of squaris in 12 gradalibus in capella'.[1] At Durham the art of descanting on 'squares' was included with faburden and the other techniques of descant among the subjects the cantor was required to teach his singers.[2]

The section of the Gyffard part-books which includes Taverner's Kyrie *le roy* provided a series of separate Kyries and Alleluias for the daily Lady-Mass. Taverner's Kyrie is a good specimen of the relatively florid style of these pieces, other examples of which may be seen in his Alleluias *Salve Virgo* and *Veni electa*,[3] in Tallis's Alleluia *Ora pro nobis*,[4] and in the first section of Okeland's Kyrie:

Ex. 73.

The only example in England of a Mass set in organ polyphony to alternate with plainsong, commonly called an Organ

[1] Macray, *Register of Magdalen*, ii, p. 7.   [2] See above, p. 187.

[3] *Tudor Church Music*, iii, pp. 52–3; the cantus firmus of the former setting resembles both *Salve virgo* and *Virga Jesse floruit virgo* but is not identical with either.

[4] Ibid., vi, p. 88. For a discussion of this set of Alleluias, see below, pp. 377–8.

Mass, is by Philip Ap Rhys of St. Paul's.[1] This is an unpretentious composition, in two and three parts, one of which is always an ornamented form of the plainsong. It comprises the Kyrie *Deus creator omnium*, the other parts of the Ordinary except the Credo, and the Trinity Sunday Offertory *Benedictus sit Deus pater*. In the Kyrie the composer set the odd-numbered verses, leaving the first three words to be sung by the beginner, while in the Gloria the organ begins after the celebrant has sung the opening and the choir *et in terra pax*, and in the Sanctus and Agnus Dei after the beginner has sung the opening. The first Agnus Dei is one of the more interesting sections, and achieves a good effect of rhythmic cumulation:[2]

Ex.74.

[1] In British Museum, MS. Add. 29996; printed in *Altenglische Orgelmusik*, pp. 24–35.   [2] MS. Add. 29996, fo. 34; 'bar-lines' as in the MS.

In the manuscript the Offertory is headed *In die sanctae Trinitatis*. The Sarum Ordinal gives the Kyrie *Conditor* for that day,[1] and the chants on which Ap Rhys based his Sanctus and Agnus Dei are for lesser double feasts according to the Sarum Gradual, though his Gloria is founded on one of the two chants for greater doubles.

[1] *Use of Sarum*, ii, p. 207. Exeter, however, gives *Deus Creator* (*Ordinale Exon*, ii, p. 468). For a discussion of Ap Rhys's Organ Mass, see Stevens, 'A Unique Tudor Organ Mass'.

VI
VOTIVE ANTIPHON AND MAGNIFICAT

Origin and Development of the Votive Antiphon

Fᴿᴏᴍ the beginning of its history the votive antiphon used
ritual texts drawn from the Antiphonal, Processional or
Sequentiary; at a later stage non-ritual words from Books of
Hours and devotional literature were added to its repertory.
The polyphonic votive antiphon probably originated about
the mid-fourteenth century. Thirteenth-century conductus like
Salve mater misericordiae which had a devotional text related to
that of an antiphon may perhaps be regarded as its ancestors,
while a setting of *Mater ora filium*, probably of the early fourteenth century, is an example of the polyphonic treatment of
a text from the Processional which was later used as a votive
antiphon:[1]

Ex. 75.

Ma-ter o - ra— fi - li - um   Ut post hoc ex - si - li - um

[1] In a Sarum Gradual, Bodleian Library, MS. Rawl. liturg. d.3, fo. 71.
It is preceded by poems to the Virgin in sequence form (including *Benedicta
es caelorum regina*) with plainsong, and followed by two other polyphonic
pieces, *Virgo pudicitiae ferens titulum* and *Salve virgo tonantis solium*.

295

A number of devotional pieces to the Virgin with non-ritual texts and music, set out sequence-wise like *Mater ora filium*, have survived.[1] They are probably of the first half of the fourteenth century, and are written in simple descant style.[2] Liturgically, these may still be conductus, or more likely *cantici* to be sung at the Lady-Mass in place of the sequence, rather than votive antiphons in the later sense. It is otherwise with a pair of pieces written in the descant style of the second half of the century, which use both text and plainsong from the ritual. In *Paradisi porta per Evam*[3] the plainsong is in the middle part throughout, transposed up a fifth. This is followed by a setting of *Sancta Maria virgo intercede*[4] which is of particular musical interest as an early example of the treatment of the plainsong by the two lower parts in migrant fashion:[5]

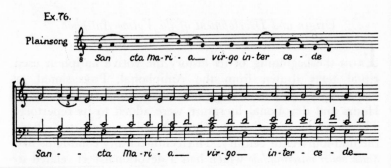

With these two examples we reach the first definite stage in the history of the votive antiphon.

The antiphons which were written by the first scribe of the Old Hall manuscript are in a more developed form of this descant style, like the simplest of the Mass movements in the

---

[1] In leaves in Cambridge, University Library, MS. Ff. 6.16, and Gonville and Caius College, MS. 334/727.

[2] The first pair of verses of *Includimur nube caliginosa* in the Gonville and Caius manuscript is transcribed in Bukofzer, 'The Gymel', p. 82.

[3] The antiphon at the *memoria* of the Virgin on ferias between Low Sunday and Whitsunday. *Ordinale Exon*, i, p. 143; *Antiphonale Sarisburiense*, pl. 252.

[4] One of the antiphons for the *memoria* of the Virgin from the Purification to Ash Wednesday and after Trinity. *Ordinale Exon*, i, pp. 103, 180.

[5] Cambridge, University Library, MS. Kk.1.6, fo. 246v; plainsong in *Antiphonale Sarisburiense*, pl. 493.

manuscript, for the musical development and resources of the antiphon throughout its history were closely related to those of the polyphonic Ordinary. In the simpler descant settings of antiphons a text from a ritual source was set on its own plainsong, which was normally in the middle voice, the only exception being Byttering's *Nesciens Mater,* in which it is shared by all the parts:[1]

Ex.77.

The trend of the descant style towards that of the chanson may be seen in Cooke's *Ave regina caelorum, ave domina,* which combines the idioms of the chanson style with the part-arrangement of descant.[2] Of the three antiphons in a later hand in the Old Hall collection, Cooke's *Stella caeli extirpavit*[3] is a free setting in very simple descant style, Damett's *Salve porta paradisi*[4] is

[1] *The Old Hall Manuscript,* i, p. 157.

[2] Ibid, i, p. 161. The clefs are C[2] C[4] C[5], and there is a change of measure for the middle section.

[3] Ibid., pp. 168-9.

[4] Ibid., pp. 166-7; the text is from the second verse of the sequence *Salve virgo sacra parens.* Bukofzer, *Studies in Medieval Music,* p. 53, n. 21.

intermediate in style, and his *Beata Dei genitrix Maria*[1] takes a step towards a larger form by using duet and full sections in alternation.

The adoption by English composers of the chanson style for the antiphon, as for the Mass, took place when English and French composers were exchanging ideas about style and technique. The antiphon, however, does not seem to have been set in polyphony by continental composers before *c.* 1420. Some of the earliest examples, all in chanson style, are *Ave regina caelorum, mater regis angelorum* by Binchois,[2] *Tota pulchra es* and *O pulcherrima mulierum* by Arnold de Lantins,[3] and *Salve regina* by Hugh de Salinis.[4] The last is remarkable because it is apparently the only setting known by a continental composer to have the trope always included by English composers in settings of this antiphon, treating the trope as solo sections and the exclamations as full sections in the way which was invariable in English settings until the mid-sixteenth century. The pieces by Binchois and de Salinis make some use of their plainsong melody, though neither is completely based on it.

After the Old Hall period English composers sometimes used the plainsong when setting antiphons with ritual texts, employing the same techniques as in single movements of the Mass based on plainsong, but most of the antiphons of the mid-fifteenth century were free compositions. The two antiphons based on plainsong out of fifteen which are contained in a manuscript probably written towards the middle of the century[5] are both examples of the technique of sharing the chant between the parts, e.g.:[6]

Ex. 78.

Plainsong

Spe-ci - o - - sa fa - cta es

[1] *The Old Hall Manuscript*, i, pp. 164–5.

[2] Printed in *Les musiciens de la cour de Bourgogne*, pp. 189–90.

[3] Printed in *Polyphonia Sacra*, pp. 262, 269.

[4] Printed in *Geschichte der Musik in Beispielen*, No. 31.

[5] Bodleian Library, MS. Arch. Selden B.26; the contents of the musical part also include carols, a hymn and secular songs. Facsimiles and transcriptions (save of five of the antiphons) in *Early Bodleian Music*, i and ii.

[6] Selden B.26, fo. 30v. The other antiphon on a plainsong is *Sancta Maria virgo* (fo. 3v), which is also in the Aosta manuscript; see Bukofzer, review of Hughes, *Medieval Polyphony in the Bodleian Library* in *Journal of the American*

Most of these pieces have at least one passage written as a duet
and are divided into two or three sections in different measures.[1]
The rhythmic style of several pieces, including *Speciosa facta es*,
is not far removed from that of the simpler Old Hall antiphons,
though in the free settings the highest part is often quite florid,
and great play is made with the two ways of grouping six
quavers or six semiquavers:[2]

Though none of these antiphons has a composer's name given
here, three, Power's *Ave regina caelorum mater regis angelorum*,
Plummer's *Tota pulchra es* (here incomplete), both in four parts,
and Dunstable's *Beata mater*, have been identified by their
occurrence in continental manuscripts.[3] Plummer's piece, which

Musicological Society, v, 1952, p. 56. In the Oxford manuscript it is followed
by another setting of the same text which is not in Hughes's list of contents.

[1] One, *Funde virgo ter beata*, is in two parts throughout.

[2] Selden B.26, fo. 16v.   [3] See Bukofzer's review mentioned in n. 6, p. 298.

is quite individual in style, is in duple time throughout, and the parts are frequently imitative, unlike the differentiated parts in the normal chanson style. All the antiphons are in praise of the Virgin, with the interesting exception of *Miles Christi gloriose*, which is an antiphon of Thomas of Lancaster, who was executed by Edward II in 1322.[1] Thomas's brother Henry recovered the family titles and estates two years later and in 1330 began the foundation of St. Mary Newarke Hospital and College. He encouraged the popular devotion to the memory of his brother and made efforts to have him canonized as the martyr of Pontefract.[2] The canonization did not take place, but the devotion continued, and this antiphon is part of a rhymed office in honour of 'Saint' Thomas.[3] Newarke College is a likely place for such an antiphon to have been sung in the fifteenth century, and it is conceivable that the manuscript originated there.[4]

The general development of chanson style in England in the first half of the fifteenth century, as in the mature work of Binchois and Dufay, was towards smoothness and grace rather than melodic elaboration. Dunstable maintained this balanced and graceful chanson style when he used plainsong as a basis for an antiphon, as he did in four of the seventeen antiphons which have survived.[5] *Alma redemptoris mater* uses the plainsong at times only,[6] while *Regina caeli* and *Ave regina caelorum, ave domina*[7] have an ornamented form of the plainsong in the treble throughout (see Ex. 80).

Since the effect and intention of ornamenting a plainsong was to transform it into a part with the melodic and rhythmic idioms of the chanson, these three pieces do not differ in style from his freely-composed antiphons, nor from his *Crux fidelis*,[8] an anti-

[1] See Greene, 'Two Medieval Musical Manuscripts', p. 3. The words are: *Miles Christi gloriose/laus spes tutor anglie/fac discordes graciose/reduci concordie/ne sternatur plebs clamose/dire mortis vulnere.*

[2] Thompson, *Newarke Hospital and College*, p. 12.

[3] Printed in *The Political Songs of England*, pp. 268–72.

[4] If so, the first line of the carol 'Alleluia: A newe work is come on hond' (fo. 21v; printed in *Medieval Carols*, No. 30) had an extra appropriateness.

[5] Two of his antiphons are to the Holy Cross, one is to St. Katharine and the others are Mary-antiphons.

[6] *John Dunstable*, p. 106; also printed in Reese, *Music in the Middle Ages*, pp. 418–20, with the notes of the plainsong indicated.

[7] *John Dunstable*, pp. 99, 101.

[8] Ibid., p. 103.

PLATE XV

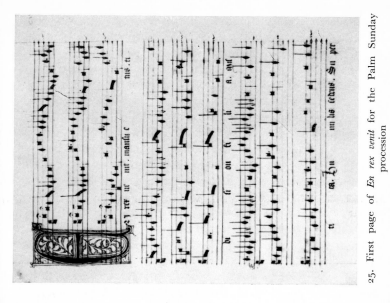

25. First page of *En rex venit* for the Palm Sunday procession

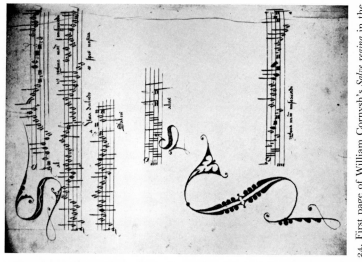

24. First page of William Cornysh's *Salve regina* in the Carver choirbook

PLATE XVI

26. Highest part of John Sheppard's three settings of *In manus tuas*

Ex. 80.

phon of the Holy Cross, which has a paraphrase of its ritual plainsong in the middle part of the full sections and an ornamented form of it in the treble of its duet. The only one of the 'free' antiphons with a distinctly different appearance from its fellows, *Quam pulchra es*,[1] is reminiscent of the earlier descant style in its less graceful melodic lines and its constant use of homorhythm.

Salve regina[2] is the most extended of Dunstable's antiphons, and its length is largely due to the addition to the normal text of the trope of three four-lined rhyming verses beginning *Virgo mater ecclesiae*, which was adopted for the votive use of this antiphon in England and is almost invariably found with it in Processionals and Books of Hours.[3] Its effect is to extend the text which follows the word *ostende* to a length equalling that up to *ostende*, and to give this second portion the form of alternating verses and exclamations. The singing of the verses by soloists in the plainsong performance of this antiphon was a

---

[1] *John Dunstable*, p. 112.   [2] Ibid., p. 115.

[3] The hymn from which the trope was derived contains six verses, as printed in *Analecta Hymnica*, xxiii, p. 57. For the usual Sarum plainsong version with five verses, see *Eton Choirbook*, i, p. 141. Polyphonic settings seldom have more than three verses. See also Harrison, 'An English Caput', pp. 204–6.

monastic, if not also a secular custom,[1] and it was natural to write them as solo sections in polyphonic settings.[2] Dunstable made no use of the plainsong in his setting, while Power used it only in the exclamations:[3]

Power's *Mater ora filium* shows him writing in chanson style with the same assurance as he did in his *Alma redemptoris* Mass:[4]

and Plummer's antiphon to the mother of the Virgin, *Anna mater matris Christi*, like his *Tota pulchra es*, has passages which suggest either a revival of the rondellus technique or an adap-

---

[1] E.g., *Ordinale of St. Mary's, York*, i, p. 27; Aungier, *History of Syon Monastery*, p. 333: 'all schalle knele excepte . . . the sustres that be tabled or assygned by the chauntres to synge the verses of *Salve Regina* or *Regina celi* which schal be songen standynge at the deske'.

[2] The invariable use of the trope in English settings makes it likely that the anonymous settings in the Trent manuscripts published in *Denkmäler der Tonkunst in Österreich*, xxvii, pp. 60, 74, and also the settings of three verses of the trope (all based on its plainsong) in Trent MS. 90, fos. 350–2, are by English composers.

[3] *John Dunstable*, p. 152. It is ascribed to Dunstable in Trent MSS. 90 and 92; see ibid., pp. 192–3. The mode is the same as the plainsong, and the opening phrases resemble it in their general outline.

[4] *Denkmäler der Tonkunst in Österreich*, xl, p. 212, revised slightly from the manuscript (Trent MS. 92, fo. 181v).

tation of the technique of canon and pseudo-canon found in
some of the Old Hall music:[1]

Ex.83.

At its best the English polyphonic antiphon of this period
combined the sensitive melodic lines of the chanson style with
elements of the English descant tradition, with very expressive
results in some cases, as in the remarkable ending of Forest's
Tota pulchra es:[2]

Ex.84

[1] In leaves bound in at the end of an English treatise on the Mass of the
second half of the fifteenth century (Bodleian Library, MS. Add. C.87). The
composer's name is spelt Plomer here, Polmier and Polumier in continental
manuscripts. The first eight lines of this antiphon are taken from the eighth
and sixth responds in the rhymed office of St. Anne; see *Breviarium Sarum*,
iii, pp. 551, 549.

[2] *Denkmäler der Tonkunst in Österreich*, xl, p. 80.

The use of a plainsong cantus firmus for the setting of an antiphon along the same lines as those employed for single movements of the Mass also began in this period. It does not seem that this was done with the idea of relating a text of general use to a particular festival, as with the Mass. Forest's *Ascendit Christus*,[1] for example, has a tenor which is a paraphrased form of *Alma redemptoris*, but the text of the antiphon itself, which in its ritual position is the canticle antiphon at first Vespers of the Assumption, had a more definite festival context than the tenor. The idea may simply have been to lend

[1] Printed from the Modena manuscript, where it is ascribed to Dunstable, in *John Dunstable*, p. 148. The last scribe of the Old Hall manuscript copied Forest's *Qualis est dilectus tuus* (printed in *The Old Hall Manuscript*, ii, p. 77) after Dunstable's *Veni Sancte Spiritus*; he next began to copy *Ascendit Christus*, but left off, putting Forest's name in the margin, before he had finished the treble part. Bukofzer (*Die Musik in Geschichte und Gegenwart*, s.v. 'Forest') identified the composer, whose first name is not recorded, with John Forest, Dean of Wells and a benefactor of Lincoln College. There is no definite evidence that they were the same person.

the antiphon more dignity and scope by applying to it the technical method of the cantus-firmus Mass, and in this respect Forest's piece may be regarded as a pioneer work in the history of the large antiphon. Its tenor moves rather faster in relation to the other parts than was usual in the later antiphon, when the other parts had developed a more florid style, but it thereby achieves the structural use of a plainsong melody without sacrificing the equanimity and balance characteristic of the chanson style:[1]

Ex.85.

Walter Frye's *Salve virgo mater pia*, a somewhat later piece, has a similar treatment of a plainsong. This work is a particularly striking example of the relation in design between antiphon and Mass, for the tenor of the Gloria and Credo of Frye's own Mass *Summae Trinitati* is identical in all the details of its melody and rhythm with the tenor of this antiphon, and the common opening of the movements of the Mass was taken from the opening of the antiphon. This makes the Mass a very early example of the derived Mass.[2]

[1] The piece ends before the complete melody of *Alma redemptoris* has been sung; on this point and its connection with a Credo by 'Anglicanus', see Bukofzer, *Studies in Medieval Music*, p. 41.

[2] The antiphon is anonymous in Trent MS. 88, fos. 7ov-71; the recognition of the identity of the tenors and the corollary that Frye was the composer of the antiphon are due to Bukofzer. See his article 'Frye' in *Die*

There is at least one example of the isorhythmic method of disposing the plainsong tenor of an antiphon, John Benet's *Gaude pia Magdalena*,[1] which is based on the tenor *O certe precipuus*, the respond at first Vespers on the feast of St. Mary Magdalene, using only the music of those three words. The tenor is stated three times in progressive diminution in the same scheme of proportions as that of Dunstable's *Veni sancte Spiritus*, and, as there, the upper parts over each of the isorhythmic halves of the tenor are also isorhythmically related. The quotation shows the beginning of the section composed on the third statement of the tenor:

Ex. 86.

This piece combined the features of the antiphon and the isorhythmic motet at a time when the former was waxing and the latter had almost waned.

During the second half of the fifteenth century the large-scale antiphon was established as a work similar in style and comparable in size and design to a single movement of a festal

Musik in Geschichte und Gegenwart, where the opening of the antiphon is quoted alongside the beginnings of the Gloria and Credo of the Mass.

[1] In the same set of leaves as Plummer's *Anna mater matris Christi*. The poem is in a Book of Hours and Psalter, MS. 20 in the John Rylands Library, Manchester, with others on the same model, including antiphons to St. John Baptist, St. Katharine, St. Nicholas, St. Thomas of Canterbury, and one to St. George beginning *Georgi martir inclite/te decet laus et gloria*.

setting of the Ordinary. The tenor, whether it was a measured form of a plainsong or an original melody, was the basis of the full sections, as may be seen in an anonymous *Gaude flore virginali* which is an early example (*c.* 1450–60) of a four-part antiphon of large design based on an original tenor. Though written in a continental manuscript, it is probably by an English composer, because of its style and because its text has the variations which are peculiar to it in English Books of Hours and polyphonic settings:[1]

Ex.87.

The Eton Antiphons

Our knowledge of the style of the large antiphon in England in the late fifteenth century is due entirely to the preservation of the Eton choirbook.[2] Although a *Gaude flore virginali* by Dunstable, his only recorded five-part work, which is listed in the index, has unfortunately been lost, the surviving contents of the manuscript provide some material for the history of the form between the Dunstable period and *c.* 1485–1500, when the greater part of the music was composed. Two of the forty antiphons which are complete[3] are by William Horwood (d. 1484), and one is by Gilbert Banester (d. 1487). These three, and also Horwood's *Gaude virgo mater Christi*, the last page of which is missing, were written on original tenors, and are probably the

---

[1] Trent MS. 89, fo. 170v. The work is given as two pieces (Tr. 617, 618) in the catalogue in *Denkmäler der Tonkunst in Österreich*, vii, p. 51.

[2] Complete edition in *The Eton Choirbook* (in course of publication).

[3] Thirty-nine complete in the manuscript, and one, Walter Lambe's *O Maria plena gratia*, in a complete copy, anonymous, in the Lambeth Palace Library, MS. 1. Fourteen others survive in various states of incompleteness; for details, see Harrison, 'The Eton Choirbook', pp. 168–75.

earliest antiphons in the collection. Horwood's *Salve regina* has a
tenor and countertenor (called *Bassus* in the manuscript) in the
same clef, and above them a countertenor, mean and treble;
this is the same disposition of the parts as in our last example,
with a treble added. It is the only piece in the manuscript in
which the two lowest parts have this tenor-countertenor relationship, and on this ground as well as on grounds of style it is
possibly the oldest of Horwood's pieces here. Imitation is virtually absent, even in the solo sections, e.g.:

where the tenor is clearly the basic part, the others being added
with contrasting line and rhythm. There are occasional points
of imitation, freely treated, in Horwood's other antiphons, in

Banester's, and also in Hugo Kellyk's seven-part *Gaude flore virginali*, which, to judge by its style, is also one of the earlier pieces in the manuscript. The clearest case of imitation in Horwood's writing is this passage from his *Gaude flore virginali*: where he uses points which became common coin in the next century.

The words of the latter part of Banester's *O Maria et Elizabeth* are a prayer for the king and for peace and loyalty in the church and state.[1] This is the only allusion of its kind in the manuscript, and the earlier part of the text, which is a poem on the Visitation of the Virgin (July 2), may possibly imply a reference to the pregnancy of Elizabeth of York with the boy who was born on September 19, 1486, and became Arthur, Prince of Wales:[2]

Ex. 90.

---

[1] 'Protege quesumus athletam regem nostram N', etc.

[2] Flood (*Early Tudor Composers*, p. 15) suggests that this piece was written for the marriage of Henry and Elizabeth.

Like Banester's music, Kellyk's is old-fashioned in its idioms, but he works the material into a texture of seven melodious parts in a remarkably competent way:

Ex. 91.

Horwood's *Gaude virgo mater Christi* is the most mature in style of the works in this group; the melodies of the parts in the solo sections are well balanced, and there is a fine ability to combine sonority and line in such a full section as this:

Ex. 92.

The Eton music shows the extension in the range of pitch in choral music which came with writing for five and more parts, with the highest parts for boy trebles and the lowest parts in the modern bass range. The written pitch of the Old Hall music and of that of Dunstable's time had tenor C as the lowest normal note, the B flat a tone below being rarely written. Though the actual pitch was partly a matter of convenience, it is clear that the range of polyphony until the second half of the fifteenth century corresponded to that of the tenor and countertenor voices of today. The normal compass of four-part polyphony in the mid-fifteenth century may be seen in the anonymous *Gaude flore virginali* quoted above,[1] which extends two octaves and a third, or seventeen notes, upwards from tenor C; the regular compass of pieces in five or more parts in the Eton manuscript is twenty-two or twenty-three notes. The compass of each piece is given in these terms in the manuscript, together with the number of voices, both in the index and at the head of the piece, probably to show which works needed trebles and which could be sung by men only or, with transposition, by boys only. A few five- and six-part antiphons keep within the range of fourteen or fifteen notes, but none of the four-part antiphons exceeds fifteen notes. Of the ten four-part Magnificats, only one of which remains complete, six had a range of twenty-one or twenty-two notes, one of seventeen, and three of

[1] Ex. 87, p. 307.

fourteen. The sonority obtained from the wider range in the full sections and the greater possibilities of textural contrast in the solo sections were among the major 'discoveries' of the later medieval composers, whose liking for the sound of rich and full chords is also evident in the common practice of dividing one or more parts at important cadences.

All the music in the manuscript, with the exception of Wylkynson's nine-part *Salve regina*, was composed before 1502, the year of the death of Provost Henry Bost, whose arms are in the initial of the mean part of Davy's *O Domine caeli terraeque*.[1] Wylkynson's nine-part *Salve regina*, which is signed with his name and is probably in his hand, is in 'white' notation, and has picture initials pasted on which are not the work of the illuminator(s) of the rest of the manuscript. It is a later addition, datable between 1502 and 1515.[2] The antiphons which show the maturity of the florid style include thirty-six complete pieces by fourteen composers, namely, in the order of the extent of their contribution to the manuscript: John Browne, Walter Lambe, Richard Davy, Robert Wylkynson, William Cornysh, Robert Fayrfax, Edmund Turges, Fawkyner, Nicholas Huchyn, Robert Hacomplaynt, John Hampton, Richard Hygons, Edmund Sturton and John Sutton. Exactly half of these thirty-six antiphons were written on a cantus firmus taken from plainsong,[3] while three others, all by Lambe, used the plainsong of their particular texts with a technique compounded of paraphrase, ornamentation and migration. The standard method of disposing the tenor in two statements in different measures was used in more than half of the eighteen cantus-firmus pieces, the slight variants which were introduced being the addition of an extra phrase from (or partial statement of) the tenor in five

---

[1] See Squire, 'On an Early Sixteenth Century Manuscript', p. 89.

[2] For a discussion of evidence which suggests that there were two stages in the compilation of the book, see Harrison, 'The Eton Choirbook', pp. 163–4.

[3] While a cantus-firmus Mass bears the name of its plainsong as the title, which is usually given in the manuscripts, the identity of the cantus firmus of an antiphon is virtually never given there. The only exception in Eton is Lambe's fragmentary *O regina caelestis gloriae*, where the simultaneous cantus firmi are both marked. So far, it has been possible to identify all but four of the eighteen tenors concerned, as well as two used in incomplete pieces. For details, see *The Eton Choirbook*, iii, Editorial Commentary.

cases and a return to perfect time for the final section of the piece in three. Both of these variants were used by Lambe in his *O Maria plena gratia*, where the final section in triple measure is based on a partial restatement of the cantus firmus.

The way in which a plainsong melody was divided up and disposed as the cantus firmus of an antiphon was related to the length and sequence of thought of its text, and while a number of conventions had been established for the treatment of the Ordinary of the Mass and were regularly observed, the troped part of the *Salve regina* was the only case of such a convention being established for the antiphon. The first step would presumably be to decide what parts of the text would be set as full sections, and to dispose the tenor accordingly. In his first *Salve regina*, for example, which is one of the most clearly-balanced settings of that text, Browne disposed the antiphon *Maria ergo unxit* as his cantus firmus in this fashion:

Ex. 93.

313

Here the framework of the composition was made in two sections of equal time-value,[1] assuming that the final notes with pauses are to be regarded as *extra tempus*. The disposition of the parts in the solo sections would be planned so as to give them an appropriate variety of texture, and written with such lengths as to make the piece a balanced whole. Browne made the change from triple to duple measure at the end of the first verse of the trope, though it was most often made at the beginning of this verse, and designed the whole piece so that not only the two statements of the cantus firmus but also the two main sections are virtually of equal length. In his other setting of *Salve regina*, on the antiphon *Venit dilectus meus*, Browne made the change of measure after the first exclamation, *O clemens*, which he based on the first five notes of the plainsong as an extra insertion between its two statements. His layout of this cantus firmus is not symmetrical, but the two sections of the piece are again almost exactly the same length.

A carefully calculated disposition of the cantus firmus was also used by Wylkynson in his *Salve regina* for nine voices and by Sutton in his setting for seven voices, both based on three statements of their plainsong. Wylkynson equalized the lengths

[1] Equal, that is, if we assume that the dotted minim of perfect measure was the equivalent of the semibreve of imperfect measure. Similarly symmetrical arrangements to that in Ex. 93 result from this assumption in a few other cases, and an approximately equal length for the two main sections of the piece results in virtually all cases. There seem to be good empirical grounds for the conclusion that the effect of the stroke of diminution in the measure signatures was to indicate the relation $\lozenge\cdot$ in $\Phi = \circ$ in $\mathbb{C}$, as compared with the earlier relation $\circ\cdot$ in O $= \circ\cdot$ in C. See also above, pp. 254-5.

of the division of the cantus firmus (*Assumpta est Maria*) under each measure signature, thus:

Statement I, 51 bars		Statement II, 27 bars[1]	Statement III
3/4 39 bars		4/4 39 bars	3/4 16 bars

Sutton, on the other hand, made the first two statements of his plainsong (*Libera nos*) equal in length and the sections of different measure into which they were divided unequal, thus:

Statement I, 32 bars	Statement II, 32 bars		Statement III
3/4 43 bars	4/4 bars	3/4 11 bars	3/4 · 16 bars[2]

The composers of the other twenty-five texts, apart from the *Salve regina*,[3] in the manuscript (only two, *Gaude flore virginali* and *Stabat mater dolorosa*, were set more than once) disposed the full and solo sections so as to agree with the form and content of the words. In the case of a metrical text the verse or group of verses was a regulating factor, and the relation between the text and the lay-out of the cantus firmus, as well as the varied treatment of the solo sections, may best be seen in a reduction of these elements to a diagrammatic form such as is reproduced on the following page. Browne's *O Maria salvatoris mater*, on an unidentified cantus firmus, has six verses in each of the two main sections, and the diagram also shows the cumulative addition of the parts in the first two verses from the fourteenth bar onwards, the broken texture of the fourth and fifth verses, in which the lines of the poem were grouped by the sense (or a possible interpretation of it) and not by the verse, and the remarkable exclamatory full section in the course of the ninth verse. In Davy's *Salve Jesu mater vera* on an invented tenor, which has a plainer overall plan than Browne's *O Maria*, the full section in the third verse is built up gradually, that in verse eleven is reserved so as to give special emphasis to the last

---

[1] In the treble part in a solo section.   [2] Under a sign of double diminution.

[3] For the lay-out of the other three settings of *Salve regina* based on a plainsong, by Hacomplaynt, Huchyn and Hygons, see Harrison, 'An English "Caput" ', pp. 209–14.

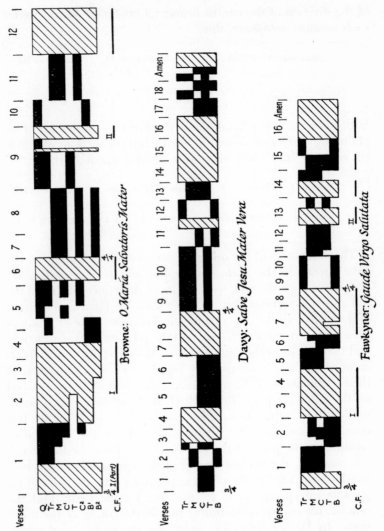

Diagrams, drawn to scale, of antiphons in the Eton Choirbook. The letters at the left indicate the voices. Full sections are shown by diagonal lines; solo sections are in black. The horizontal lines represent the lay-out of the cantus firmus.

line *Quid Maria patitur*, and the concluding full section is also unusually short. Fawkyner's *Gaude virgo salutata* on the antiphon *Martinus Abrahae sinu* has a well-balanced scheme, and its judicious choice of parts for the solo sections contributes greatly to the lightness and clarity of its general effect. The third of the four sections into which the second statement of the cantus firmus was divided is exceptional in being the basis of a solo section rather than of a full section.

Among the pieces which use a scheme other than the standard double *cursus* in laying out a plainsong as the tenor are Sturton's *Gaude virgo mater Christi*, on one statement of *Alma redemptoris mater*; Davy's *In honore summae matris* on *Justi in perpetuum vivent*, a lengthy respond which has one complete statement, with a partial restatement in triplet quavers for the Amen; and Davy's *Virgo templum Trinitatis* on three statements of the St. Martin antiphon *O virum ineffabilem*, disposed in such a way that the ends of the statements do not coincide with the ends of the sections of the piece, a rather exceptional treatment.

The three pieces by Lambe which use ornamentation and sharing of the plainsong proper to the words are interesting examples of the continued practice of these characteristically English techniques in the late fifteenth century. In *Nesciens mater* he used the plainsong as the cantus firmus of the full sections, but otherwise the piece is a free composition, apart from momentary paraphrase at the opening and momentary ornamentation in the mean part in one other passage.[1] In *Ascendit Christus* he used the chant in both solo and full sections, in the former as material for ornamentation, and in the latter in ornamented forms and also as momentary cantus firmus in the countertenor, tenor and bass parts:

Ex. 94.

[1] At 'sola virgo', bars 63–5.

Lambe's *Salve regina* is a more extended essay in this mixture of free composition and writing on a plainsong, in which the chant is used as a cantus firmus for some of the full sections, as in *O pia;* as a shared and partly ornamented cantus firmus for other full sections, for example in *Vita dulcedo et spes nostra salve;* and as melodic material for some of the solo sections, as in the setting of the lines *Virgo clemens, virgo pia, Virgo dulcis, O Maria.* Other examples of Lambe's technical skill are his combination of two plainsongs to make a double cantus firmus in his six-part setting of *O regina caelestis gloriae,*[1] of which unfortunately only one page has survived, and his demonstration of rhythmic proportions in some passages of his four-part setting of *Gaude flore virginali,* where he continued the tradition of the essay in proportions practised by Power and other Old Hall composers, which was still taught in the age of Thomas Morley and John Farmer.[2] In the course of two of these passages, one a few bars after the other, Lambe presented the singers with examples of the proportion 3 : 2 in terms of the quaver, crotchet and minim, having written the tenor of the full sections throughout the piece in duple proportion to the other parts (see Ex. 95).

The rhythmic elements in the florid style reached the highest point of their development in the music of the Eton collection. They were the result of a continuous process of elaboration of the style of Dunstable and the later Old Hall composers, which had combined the practice of composition around a plainsong

---

[1] Johannes Regis (*c.* 1430–85), master of the choristers at the Church of Our Lady in Antwerp from 1463 and afterwards secretary to Dufay and canon of Soignies, composed a Mass with *Ecce ancilla Domini* and *Ne timeas Maria* as a double cantus firmus and other antiphons in pairs in the same way. The work is printed in *Johannis Regis Opera Omnia*, i, p. 25.

[2] In his *Divers and Sundry waies of two parts in one*, London, 1591.

tenor characteristic of fourteenth-century descant with the melodic idioms and disposition of voices characteristic of the continental chanson. The rhythmic values used for paraphrasing a plainsong in the tenor remained virtually constant during the fifteenth century, with the minim as the unit of movement. By the end of the century, however, the rhythmic values of the other parts had evolved from the idioms of the chanson into a great variety of groupings of the smaller note-values, as in Browne's *O regina mundi clara* (see Ex. 96), which exemplifies the complexity and vigour of the rhythmic counterpoint in a full section in the florid style. In many of the solo sections the composers used a still more extensive vocabulary of ornamental melodic idioms, and achieved an effect of delicate vocal chamber music in a truly 'coloratura' style, as in Fawkyner's *Gaude rosa sine spina* (see Ex. 97), where the treatment of the bracketed figure is reminiscent of the rondellus technique of the thirteenth century.[1] Interchange and imitation of a

[1] Compare Plummer's use of this device in his *Anna mater matris Christi*, p. 303 above.

characteristic melodic idiom were practised in solo sections as well as in full sections like that quoted above from Browne's *O regina mundi clara*, as in this passage from the same piece:

Ex.98.

in which the point is a peculiarly English cadential ornament of the fifteenth century.[1]

As a rule the solo sections were made of free material not connected with the cantus firmus, but in some cases the composer adapted the idea of the recurring opening of the movements of a Mass by deriving the main voice or voices of an opening solo section from the beginning of the cantus firmus, as Browne did in his *Stabat Mater*:

Ex 99.

In some instances material for solo sections other than the opening one were derived from the cantus firmus in the same way as in Wylkynson's nine-part *Salve regina*:[2]

Ex.100.

[1] See also Lambe's *Salve regina*, bars 96–7; Cornysh's *Salve regina*, bars 98–100.

[2] See also bars 112–16 of the same piece, and Hacomplaynt's *Salve regina*, bars 14–16, Mean.

and in settings of *Salve regina* the familiar plainsong of the antiphon occasionally had an effect on the melodic material of the polyphony, as in Hacomplaynt's setting:

Although the depiction of words by melody had no greater place in medieval polyphony than it had in plainsong, Fawkyner's little figure for the serpent in his *Gaude rosa sine spina* is a clear case of musical illustration:

and makes one inclined to believe that the last syllable of the word *pereamus* in his *Gaude virgo salutata* was not dropped merely by chance:

The relation of the rhythm of the words to musical rhythm varies between the extremes of syllabic setting and extended vocalization. The general principle was to set the beginning of a sentence syllabically in an appropriate rhythm, and to extend the rest of the musical sentence by vocalizing, rather in the manner of a 'modernized' neuma, and almost always on the penultimate syllable.[1] Repetition of words was quite exceptional. The singing of a syllable on the first of a group of quick notes rather than after the last (as in modern practice), e.g.:

Ex.104.

Pa - rit il - la___

was a common idiom, later used in the setting of English words until well on in the seventeenth century.

The other technical features of the polyphony of the later Middle Ages were bound up with the theory and practice of the modes of plainsong, with the modifications in modal practice which resulted from the introduction of accidentals within the modes, and with the new problems in the treatment of intervals and chords which arose with the increase in the number of parts. In the Eton antiphons the third and fourth modes, which had E as their final, were not used, and the composer of the only piece which was based on a plainsong in the third mode (in the transposed position ending on A), Browne's *O regina mundi clara*, avoided that mode by writing the piece in the first mode, with the final D.[2] The modes with a major third above the final (modes five to eight on the finals F and G) occur about three times as often as the first and second modes, which had a minor third, and the last chord of all main sections of a piece, almost without exception, had a major third, changed by an accidental if necessary, whatever was the mode of the

---

[1] Hence the aptness of the Italian visitor's description of English singing: 'non cantavano ma giubilavano'. See p. 171 above, and compare the use of *jubilare*, p. 258 above.

[2] Lambe wrote a third mode cadence, with G sharp, in his *Salve regina* (bar 55) and in his *Stella caeli* (bar 90); these are the only occurrences of G sharp in the manuscript. *Stella caeli* is in an almost 'pure' fifth mode without B flat.

piece. While it would be misleading to suggest that there was any regular connection between the composer's choice of mode and the subject of his text, it may be noted that all the settings of *Stabat mater* were written in the second mode transposed down a fifth, and that Davy wrote all his pieces except his *Stabat mater* in the seventh or eighth mode.

The factors involved in the use of accidentals were a complex of the practice of plainsong, of the necessities and developing idioms of polyphony, and to a limited extent of the impulse to use them to express the thought of the words. In a piece in the fifth or sixth mode, for example, B flat was normally written throughout, as sometimes in plainsong. On the other hand, the transposition of the second mode down a fifth to G, which did not occur in plainsong and required the use of B flat,[1] arose in polyphony from the need to accommodate the range of the mode to the range of the tenor voice.[2] The reverse of this method of adjusting mode to range was also used, by keeping the normal pitch of the mode in the writing of the music, thus setting the voices at a pitch which required downward transposition in performance.[3] This practice of writing in the 'high

[1] A few second mode chants were transposed *up* a fifth ('in acutas et superacutas aliquando transmutatur, et tunc facit finem in alamire per b quadratam'. *Use of Sarum*, ii, pp. xii, xvi) to avoid the low B flat, which was not written in plainsong.

[2] The range of the second mode, according to the Sarum Tonale (*Use of Sarum*, ii, p. xi), was from the fifth below the final to the sixth above (G to B) in antiphons, and to the seventh above (rarely) in responds. The tenors in the transposed second mode in Eton (it is not used in the untransposed position) range from C to F (in the three *Stabat mater* settings, Hacomplaynt's *Salve regina* and Hampton's *Salve regina*), from C to D (in Cornysh's *Gaude virgo*), and from C to G (in Fayrfax's *Salve regina*). Other transpositions in Eton are of the fifth, sixth and seventh modes to C. The transposition in Browne's second *Salve regina* arises from the plainsong, which is itself in the sixth mode transposed up a fifth, being one of the 'variationes in acutas constitutas' (see *Use of Sarum*, ii, pp. xl–xli). The examples of 'mixed' modes, in addition to Browne's *O regina mundi clara*, are Wylkynson's nine-part *Salve regina* (tenor in seventh mode on F; piece in fifth mode) and Browne's six-part *Stabat virgo* (tenor in fifth mode; the piece appears to be in seventh mode on C).

[3] Presumably a third or a fourth, as convenient. In a valuable series of four articles on 'Pitch in the 16th and Early 17th Centuries', considered mainly in relation to the pitch of the organ, Arthur Mendel rejects the theory of transposition by a third. In purely vocal performance, however,

clefs' was most often adopted when the tenor was in the seventh mode,[1] and in such cases the written pitch of the treble part took it up to the high B or C, making transposition in performance unavoidable.

The composers of the Eton music followed a long-established practice when they set the lowest part of a piece with a constant B flat and one or more of the upper parts with a more or less constant B natural.[2] This flattening of the B below C on the second space in the bass clef with almost complete consistency, whatever the mode,[3] gave rise to the idiom of 'false relation'. The setting of a bass part under a tenor singing F, for example, called for B flat as one of the possible notes, and if the upper parts were in a mode which normally used B natural, a situation arose in which false relation could become an established idiom, as in this passage:

Ex. 105.

there seems no reason why any convenient pitch, perhaps given by the organ, should not have been used.

[1] Eton Nos. 27, 31, 37. The other cases of high clefs are in Mode VIII (No. 17, highest note B flat); Mode V (No. 3; highest note A); Mode I (No. 21; highest note A); and Mode I on G (No. 19; highest note B flat). In two pieces with normal clefs (Nos. 2, 31) the treble goes to A; otherwise the limit is F or G. The numbers refer to the catalogue of the manuscript in *Annales Musicologiques*, i, pp. 169 sqq.

[2] And correspondingly with two flats in the bass and one above when the mode was transposed a fifth down.

[3] The only antiphon in which the B natural at this pitch is 'normal' is Kellyk's *Gaude flore virginali*, which is in the fifth mode on C.

from Davy's *Virgo templum Trinitatis*, which is in the eighth mode. This effect was obviously enjoyed for its own sake, and became accepted in other contexts. It was used, for example, to give cumulative tension to the final full section of a piece, and in this case was sometimes pressed to the most extreme form in which technical deftness could bring it off, as in the Amen of Davy's *Stabat mater*:

Here, and in similar instances in pieces in the second mode on G, the false relation resulted from the writing of B natural in the upper parts instead of the B flat proper to this transposition of the mode.

This technique of introducing into a mode the idioms of another mode was used by Browne in several passages in which he 'imported' the flat seventh degree, which was idiomatic in the seventh mode, into cadences in the fifth or sixth mode. The most remarkable of these instances is the close of his *Stabat juxta Christi crucem*, where he created a situation of extreme tension by writing the normal and the flattened forms of the seventh degree simultaneously:

Sturton's writing of D flat in his *Gaude virgo mater Christi*, the most extreme accidental in the manuscript and its only occurrence, may have been suggested to him by the rare use of just such an importation in the chant which he used as his cantus firmus. The usual way of writing the Sarum form of *Alma redemptoris mater* was in the transposed position of the fifth mode up a fifth on C, in the G clef.[1] In the version of the chant which Sturton used, B flat as a flattened seventh not proper to the mode occurs at the word *genitorem*.[2] Presumably the plainsong was transposed in the service books in order to introduce the flattened seventh at this point, for if it were written in the normal position the note would be E flat, which was not admitted in plainsong notation. Sturton wrote the antiphon as his cantus firmus at the normal pitch of the fifth mode, which is that of the tenor voice, and the E flat in question comes shortly after he had written E flat as bass to B flat in the tenor, so that his D flat appears in a context which may be summarized thus:

Ex.108.

The expression of words by 'foreign' notes is no less rare in the music of this time than their depiction by melodic lines. At times accidentals of this kind were used where the words

[1] See *Use of Sarum*, ii, p. xxxv (beginning of this antiphon) and p. xxxii: 'Huius (toni) eciam cantus frequenter in acutas et in superacutas transmutatur, et tunc facit finem in cesolfaut causa toni et semitoni'.

[2] As in *Antiphonale Sarisburiense*, pl. 529.

would not seem to suggest them,[1] while at others it is difficult for us not to feel that their effect is particularly appropriate to the words, as in Sturton's treatment of *mortem pati*,[2] or in such a passage as this from Browne's first *Salve regina*:

Ex.109

The Eton music, like the chapel for which it was created, is a monument to the art and craftsmanship of many minds united in the object of carrying out the founder's vision of perpetual devotion. From its study and performance there emerge some distinct impressions of the musical personalities among the composers who contributed most significantly to the expression of that devotion. Browne's technical command, the deeply penetrating quality of his imagination, and his capacity for strikingly dramatic expression place him among the greatest composers of his age, while Lambe's wise and experienced mastery is capable of reaching heights both of emotion and technique. Davy excels in sure and rapid craftsmanship and in the joyful exuberance of its use, and Cornysh in the versatility of a talent which, though not remarkable for depth or consistency, ranges from the sensuous warmth of the *Salve regina* to the flamboyance of the *Stabat mater* and the simplicity of the *Ave Maria mater Dei*. Wylkynson can be admired for his more than respectable competence as a well-schooled *informator*-composer, and his high level of ability is shared by most of those whose attainments can be judged only from one or two examples of their work.

Among the memorable passages in the music of the more distinguished of the Eton composers are the first section and the magnificent Amen of Browne's *Stabat mater*, a work of inexhaustible interest; the opening of his first setting of *Salve regina*, where 'the music unfolds like a flower responding to the

---

[1] As, for example, in the curious passage on *ecclesia* in Browne's second *Salve regina*, bars 84–6. [2] Bars 74–6 in his *Gaude virgo mater Christi*.

sun';[1] the closing cadence of Lambe's *Salve regina*; and the astonishing effect of the momentary vision of a new tonal panorama which Davy created in two passages of his *In honore summae matris*, the former of which may be quoted:

Ex.110.

The Votive Antiphon in the Sixteenth Century

Three five-part antiphons by Fayrfax, in addition to his *Salve regina* in the Eton book, remain complete: *Aeternae laudis lilium*, *Ave Dei patris filia*, and *Maria plena virtute*.[2] All three have free tenors, and like his Masses are noticeably less florid than the Eton antiphons. The first is on the Visitation, and is thought to be the 'Anthem of oure Lady and St. Elizabeth' for which Fayrfax was paid twenty shillings at St. Albans in 1502 from the privy purse of Queen Elizabeth.[3] It was written, without

[1] Walker, *History of Music in England*, p. 33, where the passage is quoted.

[2] See Hughes, 'An Introduction to Fayrfax', p. 95, with the following emendations: the *Stabat mater* in Harley 1709 is by Davy; Fayrfax's *Salve regina* has survived only in Eton; *Ave cujus conceptio* in Harley 1709 is anonymous; *Ave lumen gratiae* is incomplete in Eton; the anonymous *Ave Dei patris filia* in Lambeth MS. 1 is not the same work as that attributed elsewhere to Fayrfax.

[3] On March 28; *Privy Purse Expenses of Elizabeth of York*, p. 2. One of Fayrfax's incomplete antiphons, *Lauda vivi alpha et O filia supernissima*, ends

the composer's name, into the large choirbook of *c.* 1510 which is now in the library of Lambeth Palace, and which contains six other large antiphons: Lambe's six-part *O Maria plena gratia* (here anonymous and in Eton with the composer's name but incomplete), Sturton's six-part *Ave Maria ancilla Trinitatis,* and four anonymous five-part pieces. Sturton's antiphon, which is based on *Gloria tibi Trinitas,* opens with anticipations in three of the parts of the beginning of the cantus firmus, which later became well known as that of the instrumental *In nomine.*[1] The piece is in the first mode, without flat as signature in any of the parts save for one line in the treble, and has many instances of false relation:

Ex. 111.

Taverner's *Ave Dei patris filia,*[2] his only surviving large antiphon on a cantus firmus, was based on the chant of the Te Deum, and it is interesting to compare his treatment with Aston's in his *Te Deum* Mass. While Aston based twenty-six sections of his Mass on the second phrase of the Te Deum chant, Taverner used each of its five different phrases once only, in their due order, so that there is no element of recurrence in his cantus firmus, and he based the Amen of the antiphon on

with a prayer for Henry VIII. Sad to say, all of the five antiphons known to be by Ludford lack one or more voices.

[1] See Reese, *Music in the Renaissance,* p. 779.

[2] *Tudor Church Music,* iii, p. 61.

the last verse of the Te Deum, *In te Domine speravi*,[1] including the neuma of the fourth mode.[2] Although the style of the full sections is basically non-imitative, there are two clear instances of the anticipation of the cantus firmus by other parts,[3] and a few of mutual imitation around the cantus firmus, one involving the perpetration of a musical pun on the words *ut sol*, which are set to their appropriate notes in the hexachords on G and C:[4]

Ex.112

Imitative treatment of the solo sections is no more frequent, on the whole, than it was in the Eton music, but here the solo sections are somewhat less elaborate in style. The setting of the penultimate syllable of *preconizatur*, which comes immediately before our last quotation, is characteristic of Taverner in its effective use of sequence and its close pursuit of three points, the last of which is a typical 'ending-point' in his vocabulary. His setting of the Amen is a good example of the cumulative effect of repetition, in this case a double ostinato in the treble

---

[1] The lay-out, both of the cantus firmus and of the complete piece, seems to be an example of calculated proportions. The cantus firmus is disposed thus: $(60 \times \text{♩.}) + (30 \times \text{o}) + (48 \times \text{♩.})$; the complete piece has $(113 \times \text{♩.}) + (113 \times \text{o}) + (48 \times \text{♩.})$.

[2] In the *Liber Usualis* the Te Deum is indicated as third mode (p. 1834); in the Sarum Tonale it was in Mode IV. *Use of Sarum*, ii, p. xxii.

[3] By the treble at the opening, and by the bass (and treble in diminution) before the first entry of the cantus firmus.

[4] Josquin des Prés did this on G–D at the words *electa ut sol* in his *Virgo prudentissima*; the passage is in *Josquin des Prez, Motetten*, p. 135. See Reese, *Music in the Renaissance*, p. 255.

and bass against the cantus firmus of the tenor (the mean and countertenor are omitted):

Ex. 113.

Taverner's *Gaude plurimum*[1] shows some further development of imitative technique and some use of antiphony,[2] while the division of the music into successive points of imitation, which are rather freely treated, is clearly perceptible in the full sections of his *O splendor gloriae*,[3] an antiphon of the Trinity.[4] Although this is virtually in the imitative style, the parts do not yet repeat words or phrases,[5] except in a passage written as a free rota, in which the voices imitate each other in irregular order at the octave or unison[6] (see Ex. 114).

Hugh Aston's *Gaude virgo mater Christi*,[7] which has a non-

---

[1] *Tudor Church Music*, iii, p. 78.

[2] At *sempiterni patris* the bass repeats the previous countertenor phrase, and the mean repeats the bass's *benignus hominem edidisti* (ibid., p. 79). The treatment of *Gaudemus itaque* (p. 85) is antiphony with overlap, and in the final full section (pp. 90–1) the tenor repeats the treble's phrase on *eandem tecum caelestem gloriam.* [3] Ibid., p. 99.

[4] Compare the requirements of Wolsey's statutes for Cardinal College, p. 168 above.

[5] There are some exceptions, but it should be noted that all three manuscripts on which the edition is based are dated after 1580.

[6] *Tudor Church Music*, iii, pp. 108–9.

[7] Ibid., x, p. 85. His three incomplete antiphons (*Ave Maria ancilla Trinitatis*, *Ave Maria divae matris Annae filia*, and *O Baptista vates Christi*) are printed in the same volume, pp. 114–51. A treble part with the words *Ave domina sancta Maria* has not been printed; see Hughes-Hughes, *Catalogue of Musical Manuscripts in the British Museum*, i, p. 463.

Ex.114.

metrical prayer at the end of the usual metrical text, also exists as an antiphon of St. Anne with an alternative text beginning *Gaude mater matris Christi*.[1] He set it in florid style, with considerable use of imitation, up to the end of the poem, but much of his setting of the prayer is in antiphonal style, and the general impression is of a certain inconsistency of method. However, there are some interesting points, such as his use of rests to clarify imitations in the full sections and the surprising survival of a fifteenth-century cadence idiom in which one of the parts leaps an octave:[2]

Ex.115.

(no-) -   -   *bis*

[1] In Bodleian Library, MSS. Mus. e. 1–5.
[2] *Tudor Church Music*, x, p. 95.

The long and well-made Amen is based on an ostinato shared by four parts and consisting of a short figure which is melodically expanded:

Ex.116.

is then used in diminution, and is finally treated as a point worked out in an extended stretto. Aston used the same idea of an expanding ostinato in the bass of the Amen of his *Ave Maria divae matris Annae filia*, which begins thus:[1]

Ex.117.

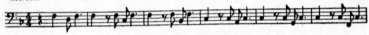

and is then developed into a more continuous part based on this figure.

Aston's *Te Deum laudamus* was originally a setting of the Marian text which imitated the Te Deum and began *Te matrem Dei laudamus.*[2] It appears with those words in the earlier manuscripts, and the later substitution of the Te Deum text, which differs considerably from that of the hymn, turned it into an antiphon of the Trinity.[3] Aston gave his setting the style and design of a large antiphon, basing all save one of the full sec-

---

[1] *Tudor Church Music*, x, p. 136.

[2] For references to this and other imitations of the Te Deum, see *Muchelney Memoranda*, p. 7, n. 2, and Corbin, *Essai sur la musique religieuse portugaise*, p. 352, n. 1. *Te matrem Dei* was the first piece in a book of Antiphons in Magdalen; see the inventory below, p. 431.

[3] See *Tudor Church Music*, x, p. xviii. The mean part-book British Museum, MS. Harley 1709, gives Asshwell as the composer. About 1600 John Baldwin copied two three-part sections of this work, with the Marian text, into his manuscript collection, now in the Royal Music Library in the British Museum. He gave Taverner as the composer, and the two items were published, as *Tu ad liberandum* and *Tu angelorum domina*, among Taverner's works in *Tudor Church Music*, Vol. iii. The former is Aston's music (ibid., x, pp. 107–8) transposed down a fourth, and the latter is the following section (ibid., pp. 108–9). There are two other misattributions to Taverner in the same volume; *Rex amabilis*, again from Baldwin, is actually a section of Fayrfax's *Maria plena virtute*, and *Esto nobis* (from British Museum, R.C.M. MS. 2035) is a section of Tallis's *Ave Dei patris filia* printed in ibid., vi, p. 166.

tions on one or two statements of the plainsong of the second verse of the Te Deum, a fourth higher than the original pitch and somewhat ornamented. At the word *Sanctus* he used the corresponding phrase of the Te Deum as the cantus firmus, and in the last section put the plainsong of *In te Domine* in the bass, bringing the piece to an end in the seventh mode. The first few notes of the opening duet of the antiphon are the same as those of the opening of his *Te Deum* Mass, but the material and the design differ thereafter and the Mass is not 'derived' from the antiphon. Nevertheless, the connection is enough to suggest that the original title of the Mass may also have been *Te matrem Dei laudamus,* and that the two works form a pair such as Aston was required to submit as his Oxford Bachelor of Music exercise in 1510.[1]

Tallis's antiphon *Salve intemerata,* the source of his derived Mass with the same title, was written on an original tenor. It is not a successful work, for the style of the polyphony falls awkwardly between differentiation and integration, lacking the linear and rhythmic vitality of the earlier style and the logic and coherence of the later, while the rhythm sags at intermediate cadences through lack of overlapping phrases, and the themes are uneven in interest. His only other surviving complete antiphon,[2] the six-part *Gaude gloriosa Dei mater,*[3] is, on the other hand, one of his finest pieces, and a crowning work in the history of the votive antiphon. All its themes have character, and some move with a rare exuberance which springs from his daring treatment of rising intervals; the flow of the rhythm is always maintained, and the form, which is on a very large scale, is handled with great skill. The maturing of his style is shown in such points as the gradual addition of the voices from the duet which begins at *Gaude virgo Maria* to the apt entry of the first full section on the word *omnia,* in the varied texture of the solo sections and the long sweeping lines of the full sections, in his use of cumulative sequence:

[1] See the transcript of the entry recording his supplication, ibid., x, p. xiv.

[2] *Ave Dei patris filia* (ibid., vi, 162) and *Ave rosa sine spinis* (ibid., p. 169) are still incomplete. For parts of these which have been found since the edition was printed, see *Tudor Church Music Appendix,* pp. 43–9.

[3] *Tudor Church Music,* vi, p. 123.

Ex. 118.

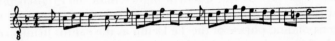

and, in the Amen, of extended ostinato. Although there is no cantus firmus, and the tenor is integrated into a texture which uses both imitation and differentiation with great resource, the work is definitely in the florid style, owing a lot to Taverner but thoroughly characteristic of the mature Tallis in its combination of strength and expressiveness.

A number of large antiphons composed between the early years of the century and *c.* 1545 were copied into the Peterhouse part-books, from which the tenor book has unfortunately been lost. Besides antiphons by Fayrfax, Ludford, Taverner, Aston and Tallis, this collection includes Mary-antiphons by Richard Bramston (*Mariae virginis fecunda viscera*), Arthur Chamberlayne (*Ave gratia plena Maria*), R. Hunt (*Stabat mater*), Edward Martyn (*Totius mundi domina*), John Marbeck (*Ave Dei patris filia*), John Mason[1] (*Ave Maria ave fuit prima salus* and *Quales sumus O miseri properantes*), John Norman (*Euge dicta sanctis oraculis*), William Pasche (*Sancta Maria mater Dei*), and Richard Pygot (*Salve regina*);[2] Jesus-antiphons by Walter Erley or Erell (*Ave vulnus lateris*) and John Mason (*Vae nobis miseris*); and an antiphon of St. Augustine (*Exsultet in hac die fidelium ecclesia*) by Hugh Sturmys. The four parts of Marbeck's *Ave Dei patris filia* which survive in the Peterhouse books and his complete Jesus-antiphon *Domine Jesu Christe* have been printed,[3] and show him using more 'modern' techniques, such as imitation and contrapuntal homophony, than he did in his Mass *Per arma justitiae*. The Mary-antiphon, which may well be the earlier, is the more successful work. In *Domine Jesu Christe* he often seems to miss the main point of imitative technique, the overlap of the entries, and tends to fall back on a cliché in his closes, except in that of the first main section, which uses effectively a short ostinato figure in the tenor and bass.

---

[1] 'Cicerstensis', i.e., of Chichester, in the Index of the manuscript.

[2] Pygot's *Gaude pastore*, the bass part of which survives in British Museum, MS. Add. 34191, is an antiphon of St. Thomas of Canterbury.

[3] *Tudor Church Music*, x, pp. 200, 215.

The Shorter Votive Antiphon

Throughout this period more modest settings of votive antiphons were composed, presumably for smaller choirs and for less important occasions. Walter Frye's *Ave regina caelorum mater regis*,[1] for example, was one of the most widely known examples of the mature chanson-antiphon; it was copied into thirteen continental manuscripts and made into three arrangements for organ. Obrecht used its tenor as the basis of his antiphon and Mass of the same name, and it was depicted in a Flemish painting of *c*. 1450.[2] In England descant technique, with the plainsong as the middle part of three, was still used for the setting of short antiphons in the late fifteenth century, as may be seen in Richard Mower's *Regina caeli*:[3]

Ex.119.

In this form of descant technique the tenor was the exact plainsong, and was written in the note-symbols of plainsong, a method which was commonly used until the Reformation for such ritual items as responds, but seldom for votive antiphons. Some of the free antiphons in the same collection as Mower's piece are much plainer in style than his, while others use a limited range of melodic idioms in an expressive way, as in this passage from an anonymous three-part setting of *Gaude virgo mater Christi*:[4]

[1] Transcription in Reese, *Music in the Renaissance*, pp. 94–5.
[2] See ibid., pp. 94, n. 307, 191, 200.
[3] British Museum, MS. Add. 5665, fo. 56v.   [4] Ibid., fo. 104v.

Ex.120.

Besides a few Mary-antiphons, this manuscript contains a setting of *Gaude sancta Magdalena* by Thomas Packe and an anonymous setting of the short Jesus-antiphon *Nunc Christe te petimus*.[1]

In February, 1516, Benedictus de Opitiis left his post of organist at the church of Our Lady (later the Cathedral) in Antwerp, where he had been in February, 1514, if not earlier, and from March 1 he was established as court organist to Henry VIII. Five years previously Richard Sampson had been in Antwerp on a diplomatic mission, and after a period in the service of Wolsey (1513–16) and another as proctor of Tournai (from 1517), he became Dean of St. Stephen's, Westminster, in 1520 and Dean of the Chapel Royal in 1523, going on to hold other deaneries and eventually the bishopric of Chichester. Compositions by these two men were written into a relatively small but finely executed manuscript which bears the date 1516,[2] and which begins with a setting of a poem in honour of Henry VIII (*Salve radix varios producens germine ramos*) in the form of a canon four-in-two set down in two circles with a rose within each. This is followed by a lengthy four-part piece by Sampson, also

---

[1] This text was the third of three verses sung with the respond *Libera me domine* at Matins of the Dead. It was set as an antiphon both with and without the words *Sancte Deus*, etc. See, for example, Taverner's *Sancte Deus*, in *Tudor Church Music*, iii, pp. 139–40.

[2] British Museum, MS. Royal 11 E. xi.

to words in praise of the King (*Psallite felices*), of which this passage is a fair sample:

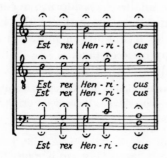

It seems very likely that these two composers met in Antwerp, and that Sampson's 'praise-motet' was modelled on the work of Benedictus, who in the year before he left Antwerp contributed two pieces to a publication by Jan de Geet of Antwerp entitled *Lofzangen ter ere van Keizer Maximiliaan en zijn kleinzoon Karel den*

Vijfden.[1] Not only the style of the music but also the notation of the manuscript are very similar to those in the Antwerp publication. Sampson's motet is followed by three Mary-anti-phons—Benedictus's four-part *Sub tuum praesidium*,[2] Sampson's five-part *Quam pulchra es*,[3] and an anonymous four-part setting of *Haec est praeclarum vas*—while the rest of the contents of the manuscript are two settings of texts from the psalms, which do not fit into any particular place in English liturgical practice. They are, in fact, motets in the sense of that word which was normal on the continent but was not used in England until the late sixteenth century, although works of their type began to be written about the time of the Reformation.

It was in the smaller musical forms, both sacred and secular, that the Renaissance style of imitative polyphony in duple measure was first practised in England, and the interest of the early Tudor kings in foreign arts was one of the means by which it became known. A collection of secular chansons by Nether-lands composers had been made for Prince Arthur (1486–1502),[4] and, as was the convention in such *chansonniers* on the continent, several Mary-antiphons were included. Some years after the Sampson-Benedictus manuscript was written, an anthology of motets by continental composers, including two secular pieces, was made and splendidly illuminated in the Flemish style for Henry VIII.[5] The effects of such importations on English music are more apparent in the smaller sacred forms, in carols, and in the secular court music than in works in the large florid style, which absorbed the techniques of imitation and antiphony without suffering any basic change.

Taverner's short antiphon *Mater Christi sanctissima*,[6] for ex-

[1] Published in facsimile, with an introduction by W. Nijhoff, Gravenhage, 1925. See also the facsimiles in Hans Albrecht, s.v. 'Benedictus de Opitiis', in *Die Musik in Geschichte und Gegenwart*.

[2] This piece is also in the Antwerp print.

[3] Also composed in the Netherlands style, as Wooldridge pointed out in *Oxford History of Music*, first edition, ii, p. 322; the first part is printed there, pp. 323–4.

[4] Now Cambridge, Magdalene College, Pepys MS. 1760.

[5] British Museum, MS. Royal 8 G. vii. The pomegranate, badge of Catherine of Aragon, appears in the decoration, and one of the pieces contains a prayer for the Emperor Charles, elected in 1519; hence the book may be dated between 1519 and *c.* 1528.

[6] *Tudor Church Music*, iii, p. 92.

ample, which was the source of his derived Mass, is clearly distinguished from his large antiphons by its use of homophony, antiphony and short points of imitation, and his *Christe Jesu pastor bone*[1] by being set in almost 'playn song' fashion in antiphonal style with free imitation in the last section. At first sight this piece seems to be a Jesus-antiphon with a second section in the form of a prayer for Henry VIII, which begins *Fundatorem specialem serva regem nunc Henricum*, but its original words were almost certainly those of the antiphon of St. William of York[2] which began *O Wilhelme pastor bone* and continued with virtually the same words as Taverner's work,[3] while the prayer may originally have been a prayer for Wolsey as founder of Cardinal College.[4] Two of the other four short antiphons by Taverner, which lack their treble and tenor parts, are settings of texts prescribed in both the original and revised statutes of the College; he set the *Ave Maria*[5] with the pauses required for the ringing of the bell, and the text of his *Sancte Deus* agrees with the form given in Wolsey's statutes.[6]

Sancte Deus was also composed by Tallis, in an expressive setting for four voices with two trebles,[7] and by Philip van Wilder, a Netherlands musician who lived in London from 1525 onwards and appears in the court accounts of Henry VIII as a lutenist from 1529 onwards. At the end of the Gyffard part-books there is a group of short antiphons comprising seven Mary-antiphons, two Jesus-antiphons and an antiphon of St. Peter. The title and the opening notes of Tye's *Sub tuam protectionem* would lead one to expect that it was a setting of the

---

[1] *Tudor Church Music*, iii, p. 73.

[2] See discussion of the statutes of Cardinal College, above, p. 168.

[3] The text is in *York Processional*, p. 196, as the antiphon *in exitu chori* on the feast of St. William. It is also in a Sarum Book of Hours, Manchester, Rylands Library, MS. Lat. 127. These agree in reading *pater, mundum*, and *gaudia* for the *fautor, semper*, and *gloriam* respectively of Taverner's setting.

[4] The prayer for Henry is in the Peterhouse part-books, one of two sources of the work; these books must therefore have been written between *c.* 1540 and 1547. The other source is the later part-books, Oxford, Christ Church MSS. 979–83, which read 'et Elizabetham nostram Angliae reginam serva' for the sentence *Fundatorem*, etc.

[5] *Tudor Church Music*, ii, p. 134.

[6] Ibid., p. 139. Taverner's other two short antiphons are *Sub tuum praesidium* (ibid., p. 144) and *Fac nobis secundum hoc nomen suave* (ibid., p. 135), an antiphon of the Name of Jesus. [7] *Tudor Church Music*, vi, p. 98.

(1) Dotted minim in M.S.

Mary-antiphon which began with those words, but the text is adapted as a Jesus-antiphon, and the music continues as a free setting, with a flexible use of imitation:

Ex. 122.

Robert Carver's nineteen-part *O bone Jesu* is a remarkable example of sonorous and resourceful part-writing which, while not free of technical errors, is not nearly so faulty as his modern editor[1] would have us believe. We may be sure that his choir revelled in its sound[2] (see Ex. 123).

The setting of *Gaude Maria* by Robert Johnson,[3] a Scottish priest who was banished to England, apparently for heresy, before the Reformation, shows in its 'pairing' of parts and systematic imitation that he had moved closer to the Franco-Netherlandish style than had Carver and most of his English contemporaries (see Ex. 124).

This and other pieces by Johnson and his Scottish contemporaries show that musical style in Scotland during the first half of the sixteenth century was affected by French music of the time. There were cultural ties with the French court, and the copying of French music into Scottish manuscripts has already been noticed.[4]

The Magnificat

The large number of pieces of sacred polyphony of this period which are not comprised under the headings of Mass, motet or

[1] J. A. Fuller-Maitland (Year Book Press, London, 1926); now superseded by the edition in *Music of Scotland 1500–1700* (*Musica Britannica*, XV), ed. K. Elliott, 1957.

[2] Edinburgh, National Library of Scotland, MS. Adv. 5.1.15.

[3] In the Gyffard part-books.

[4] See above, p. 194.

344

votive antiphon have, with few exceptions, the common feature that they are settings of a part, and not of the whole, of the ritual text with which they are concerned. The decision as to which part of the text was set in polyphony and which left in plainsong depended on the ritual form of the particular item, and since in such cases plainsong and polyphony were integral parts of the same piece, the polyphony was most often written on the plainsong it replaced, in either a plain or ornamented form. For convenience, the various categories of ritual polyphony will be discussed in the order in which they were arranged in our second chapter.

Complete psalms were not set in polyphony for use in their normal liturgical position in the Offices, but only where they formed part of a procession or other special ceremony. The composition of music to words selected from the psalms, which was not uncommon on the continent after *c.* 1450, was not practised in England until immediately before the Reformation, and it may be that such 'psalm-motets' as Tye's *Miserere mei Deus* and *Omnes gentes plaudite*, which were both biblical and didactic, were beginning at that time to replace the votive antiphon in some churches. The plan of some of these pieces, such as Robert Johnson's *Domine in virtute tua* and Sheppard's *Beati omnes*, corresponds to that of an antiphon with psalm *Ipsum*.[1] Johnson's work is a setting of the first eight verses of the twentieth psalm in which the words and music of the first verse are repeated at the end.

A Magnificat of the second half of the fourteenth century which may be the earliest surviving polyphonic treatment lacks the first verse but, as far as it survives, sets all the succeeding verses. It is in simple descant style, and has the first intonation of the canticle in the middle voice. Apart from repeated notes to accommodate the varying number of syllables, the music is the same for each verse:[2]

Ex. 125.

Plainsong

Et ex - sul-ta-vit spi - ri-tus me - us: in De - o sa-lu-ta-ri me-o.

[1] See above, p. 59. *Domine in virtute* was the ninth antiphon, with psalm *Ipsum*, at Matins on the first Sunday after the octave of the Epiphany.

[2] Cambridge, University Library, MS. Kk.1.6, fo. 247.

Et ex - sul - ta - vit___ spi - ri - tus me - us___

in De - o sa - lu - ta - ri me - o.___

Another setting, which exists only in fragments, shows that a more elaborate style of free composition was also used in this period:[1]

Ex. 126.

a - ni - - - ma___

__ me - - - a___ Do - (minum)

The style of the Magnificat in the first half of the fifteenth century may be judged from the setting in the second mode by Dunstable, the only one of that period known to be by an English composer, in which he set the odd-numbered verses in three parts, leaving the first word to be sung by the beginner:[2]

Ex. 127.

(Beginner)   (Choir)

Plainsong

Ma - gni - fi - cat a - ni - ma me - a Do - mi - num.

ma - gni - fi - cat   a - ni - ma___ me - a   Do - - - mi - num.

a - - ni - ma___ me - a   Do - mi - num.

[1] On a fly-leaf of the Bodleian Library MS. Lat. Th. e. 30.
[2] *John Dunstable*, p. 95.

and used virtually the same music for the other odd-numbered verses, varying the rhythm by writing the fifth and seventh verses in duple measure. He adopted the same scheme for the even-numbered verses, which he set as duets, the sixth and eighth verses being in duple measure. Hence the last verse, which was the second half of the *Gloria patri*, was a duet, which in performance would be followed by the antiphon in the second mode. The highest part of the polyphony throughout, both in trios and duets, is an elaboration of the Magnificat intonation of that mode.[1]

A canticle intonation could be turned into a treble part in polyphony by even simpler and more functional methods, as in this verse from Christopher Anthony's Magnificat *primi toni* of *c.* 1450:[2]

Ex. 128.

and also in less simple ways, as in this passage from the same piece:

Ex. 129.

Anthony may have been English, but in any case his setting illustrates, as does the next example by an anonymous composer from the same continental manuscript, the common lines

---

[1] Dunstable's setting may be compared with four by Binchois (*Les musiciens de la cour de Bourgogne*, pp. 131–53) and two by Dufay (*Denkmäler der Tonkunst in Österreich*, vii, pp. 169–78), which also treat all the verses.

[2] Trent MS. 90, fos. 375v–376.

of development in England and on the continent of the composition of the Magnificat, of which specimens in English manuscripts of this period are lacking. Anthony's piece followed the practice of setting only the even-numbered verses, which was almost invariable after the mid-fifteenth century,[1] and about the same time composers began to set the canticle in four parts, with the elaborated intonation in the tenor, as in:[2]

Ex. 130.

This technique of setting the Magnificat was the equivalent of that used in the festal Mass and large antiphon, and opened the way for its development into a larger form written in the florid style. In the full sections of such settings the composer elaborated the intonation into a tenor of a length appropriate to the dimensions of his setting and made the solo sections

---

[1] Consequently the Magnificat was listed and referred to as *Et exsultavit*, as in the index of the Eton choirbook. The only English Magnificat in which the odd verses are set (beginning *anima mea*) is a fragmentary one in Bodleian Library, MS. Lat. liturg. a. 6.

[2] Trent MS 91, fos. 58v–59. Verses four and ten have the same music (in duple measure for three voices), as also have verses six and twelve (in triple measure for four voices); verses two and eight are single.

of free material. The tenor of every full section of a Magnificat in the eighth mode, for example, was in effect a variation on the intonation of that mode:

Ex.131.

and by the time of this setting by Horwood, which is one of the sadly few left of the original twenty-four in the Eton manuscript,[1] the writing of the fourth, eighth and first half of the last verse as solo sections, and the use of duple measure for the fourth and sixth verses, were established conventions.

A four-part Magnificat of this period has been preserved in a volume of Proceedings of the Mayor's Court of Dartmouth (Devonshire).[2] It is in the fifth mode on F, though its tenor, which is clearly the basis of the composition, does not seem to be closely related to the Magnificat intonation of that mode:

Ex.132.

The music is contemporary with the Court records, for it ends on the sixth folio, on the verso of which the records of the Court

[1] Four, by Horwood, Kellyk, Lambe, and William Monk of Stratford, are complete; two, by Fayrfax (marked 'Regale' in the index) and Nesbett (complete, without the composer's name, in the Carver choirbook), can be supplied from other sources.

[2] MS. 1981 of the Town of Dartmouth, now in the City Library, Exeter.

begin with a judgement of October 4, 1484. It may be that it was customary in some places to open a series of court sittings with a service, for in the first year of Edward VI Christ Church Cathedral, Dublin, was granted funds to increase the choir by six priests and two choristers, in return for which the choir sang in the Law Courts on the first day of every term.[1]

The treatment of the Magnificat at the height of the florid style may be seen in a setting by Cornysh in the eighth mode on C, and in one by Turges in the sixth mode, both in the Caius College manuscript. Cornysh used the extraordinarily wide range of three octaves and a fifth, writing C below the bass clef for the second basses in two places and a treble part which goes up to G. His piece is not consistently florid in the solo sections, but breaks out here and there into purple patches such as:[2]

The following passage from Turges's Magnificat, which is perhaps the most florid work of this period in any form, shows the

[1] Lewis-Crosby, *Annals of Christ Church*, p. 44.
[2] Cambridge, Gonville and Caius College, MS. 667, p. 116.

unusual rhythmic situation of a series of triplet quavers beginning at a half-beat in the basic crotchet measure:[1]

The two settings by Fayrfax[2] and one by Ludford are in a less
florid style than this, but the three by Taverner, in the first
mode for six voices, in the second mode for five voices, and in
the sixth mode for four men's voices, are among his most
elaborate and inspired works.[3] The six-part setting is particularly extended, e.g.:

[1] Cambridge, Gonville and Caius College, MS. 667, pp. 126–7.
[2] The 'Regale' Magnificat has been edited by Dom Anselm Hughes
(London, 1949).
[3] *Tudor Church Music*, iii, pp. 3–25. The tenor of the five-part setting and
most of the highest part of the six-part setting have been supplied by the
editors.

The same style of expansive ornamentation pervades the only surviving organ setting of the Magnificat,[1] which, unlike the vocal settings, begins after the beginner has sung the first word, and supplies the odd-numbered verses thereafter. This anonymous piece is a formidable and extended setting designed in pairs of verses which have the same kind of musical treatment. Thus the first, a half-verse corresponding to *anima mea Dominum*, and the third are set as contrapuntal duets, the fifth, which begins:

Ex. 136.

and the seventh are essays in proportion, while the ninth and eleventh are in imitative style.

Tallis's four-part setting,[2] while it is by no means a large work and makes frequent use of imitative texture, has the extended melodic lines and the spontaneous motives of the differentiated style. His five-part setting,[3] on the other hand, has the syllabic treatment and clear working out of carefully chosen points which are characteristic of the Renaissance style. It is paired by a common opening with a Nunc dimittis in the same style, which begins like the Magnificats with the second verse and continues with the even verses, and which is one of the few remaining settings of the Latin text of this canticle. Tallis's two settings of the Magnificat bring out strongly the contrast between the old style and the new as they existed side by side during the last decade or so of our period.

[1] British Museum MS. Add. 29996, fo. 25v, under the title 'The viii tune in C faut'.

[2] *Tudor Church Music*, vi, p. 64.   [3] Ibid., p. 73; the tenor is supplied.

VII
OTHER RITUAL FORMS;
THE CAROL

Ritual Antiphon

O<small>N</small> some occasions of special ceremonial importance an antiphon and the psalm-verses which were sung with it were both set in polyphony. One of the earliest examples is a setting in the Pepys manuscript of the Nunc dimittis with the antiphon *Lumen ad revelationem* for the ceremony of the distribution of candles on the feast of the Purification.[1] In the antiphon the middle part is based on the plainsong, while in the canticle, in which only the second half of each verse is set, it is the upper part which carries the intonation. Since this was one of the few cases in which the antiphon was sung complete before the psalm and also after each verse, the music would be performed in this way:

Ex. 137.

Plainsong

Lu-men ad re-ve-la-ti-o-nem gen-ti-um....

Lu-men ad re-ve-la-ti-o-nem
Lu-men ad re-ve-la-ti-o-nem gen-ti-um

Lu-men ad re-ve-la-ti-o-nem gen-ti-um

[1] Cambridge, Magdalene College, Pepys MS. 1236, fos. 55v–56.

The Gyffard part-books contain a group of four anonymous settings of the antiphon *Asperges me* and two verses and the *Gloria patri* of the psalm *Miserere mei Deus*, sung at the aspersion before Mass on Sundays except from Easter to Trinity.[1] In two of these the first half of each verse was left in plainsong, as in the Nunc dimittis just quoted, while in the others the whole text was set in polyphony, as may be seen in two passages from the third setting, in which the first half of the first psalm-verse was set in a remarkably florid style for so late a date:[2]

Ex. 138.

[1] The antiphon was sung complete after each of the two verses, but after

A setting of *Vidi aquam egredientem*, which was sung with one verse and the *Gloria patri* of the psalm *Confitemini Domino*[3] at the aspersion between Easter and Trinity, in the same manuscript,[4] uses the monorhythmic form of the plainsong as its basis, and the anonymous composer seems to have taken special delight in false relations:

Ex. 139

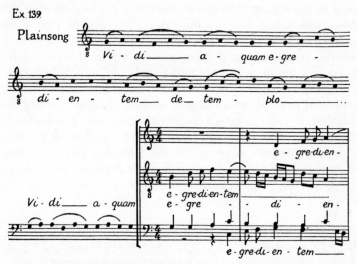

the *Gloria patri* only its second half, from *Lavabo me*, was repeated. *Missale Sarum*, col. 32**.

[2] Plainsong from the Sarum Gradual of 1527; the beginner's *Asperges me* as in Add. 17802-5.

[3] The last return in this case was from the words *Et omnes ad quos pervenit. Missale Sarum*, col. 33**.

[4] There is an earlier setting, which also begins at the third word, in the choirbook in Lambeth Palace, MS. 1.

Another case of polyphonic treatment of both antiphon and psalm is that of the psalms *Laudate pueri* and *In exitu Israel* with the *Alleluia* antiphons which were sung with them during the procession to the font at Eastertide. A setting of the former in the Pepys manuscript, which is liturgically the most varied and interesting collection of the fifteenth century, has the antiphon *Alleluia Alleluia Alleluia*, the psalm and the *Gloria patri* composed in three parts throughout, omitting the beginning of the psalm, which was sung by the rulers. The middle part is an ornamented form of the plainsong, and the single *Alleluia* which ends the verses is treated differently each time it recurs. John Sheppard's setting in the Gyffard part-books, which deals only with the even-numbered verses and the single *Alleluia* which was joined to each, is an example of the technique of using the faburden of a plainsong intonation as the bass of a polyphonic composition. This technique may be illustrated from the first verse of Sheppard's piece, where the faburden and the chant, which is not, of course, sung with the polyphony but only in alternation with it, are related in this way:

Ex. 140.

356

The bass of each verse is virtually the same thing, while the other parts vary, so that the method of composition is essentially the writing of contrapuntal variations on a ground. The setting in the same collection of *In exitu Israel*, with the single *Alleluia* to end each verse, which was made jointly by Sheppard, Byrd[1] and William Mundy, was also written for *alternatim* singing and was similarly based on the faburden of the intonation, so that in this case three composers wrote variations on the same ground. Sheppard composed seven verses, Byrd three and Mundy four, including the first verse of the *Gloria patri*.[2]

At least one setting of each of the antiphons with verses, *Media vita* and *O rex gloriose*, which were sung with the Nunc dimittis during the last four weeks in Lent, has survived, though both are incomplete.[3] Sheppard composed the full sections of his six-part *Media vita*,[4] which comprise the words of the antiphon itself, on the monorhythmic form of the plainsong, and the missing tenor part can be supplied without difficulty. He wrote one of the verses, however, without using the chant, and the other two with a free use of its motives. This fine work is written in an appropriately severe style, though not without the energy and linear interest characteristic of all this composer's writing for the Sarum ritual, as the passage on the next page shows.

Sheppard composed two seven-part settings of the antiphon *Libera nos salva nos*,[5] which was sung, with the psalm *Magnus Dominus* (Ps. 47), as the sixth antiphon at Matins on Trinity Sunday. While it is possible that these were intended as votive antiphons, the fact that in both cases he left the first two words to be sung in plainsong and used the chant as a basis makes it more likely that they were sung in the ritual position, when the antiphon was performed complete after the psalm. In one of the settings the lowest part is the plainsong in monorhythm, and in the other it is the faburden of the plainsong.

[1] See above, p. 289.

[2] The Byrd contribution to this symposium is printed in *Tudor Church Music*, ix, p. 298, and in *William Byrd*, viii, p. 42. See also Stevens, 'Processional Psalms in Faburden'.

[3] John Mason's setting of *O rex gloriose* is in the Peterhouse part-books.

[4] In Oxford, Christ Church, MSS. 979–83.

[5] Both in Oxford, Christ Church, MSS. 979–83, and therefore lacking one part.

Ex. 141.

Another ritual antiphon which was set in vocal polyphony was *Miserere mihi Domine*, the psalm-antiphon at Compline throughout the year, though it is likely that polyphonic settings were used only during Lent, when the choir attended Compline. One of the settings in the Pepys manuscript has a long and well-controlled treble which was evolved from the chant:[1]

Ex.142.

while John Norman's setting shows the method of writing in a very florid style of abstract decoration around the plainsong:[2]

Ex.143.

[1] Cambridge, Magdalene College, MS. Pepys 1236, fos. 91v–92.
[2] British Museum, MS. Add. 5665, fo. 145.

359

This method is closely related to one of the ways of setting a plainsong for the organ, that of writing a rapid and purely decorative part against the melody played in monorhythm, as in one of John Redford's settings:[1]

Ex.144.

However, a more usual way of treating a plainsong for the keyboard was to put it in the middle or lowest of three parts in either a monorhythmic or decorated form, and write counterpoints on one or more points upon it. If only one point were used the effect was that of an ostinato, as in this pleasant *Miserere* by Redford:[2]

Ex.145.

[1] British Museum, MS. Add. 29996, one of a series of fourteen *Miserere* settings; the composers named are Kyrton, Redford, E. Strowger (whose setting is a canon two in one on the plainsong), and Philip Ap Rhys (as 'P.R.'). Two of the Redford settings are also in *The Mulliner Book*, as No. 7 (with a rapid part below the plainsong) and No. 53 (with two points over an ornamented form of the plainsong). The latter is there entitled '*Miserere* with a meane'; in the keyboard context mean signifies a middle part, which may or may not be the plainsong, shared by the two hands.

[2] British Museum, MS. Add. 29996, fo. 8; 'bar-lines' as in the manuscript.

It will be noticed that here the composer used ornamentation of the plainsong to produce movement where it was needed as well as deftly to work in his point. In his setting of the longer melody of *Glorificamus*,[1] which was the canticle antiphon at Compline at Commemorations of the Virgin (except in Eastertide) and on three of her feasts, Redford used one point, which involved a suspension, for half of the piece. He did not maintain this ostinato treatment throughout, and thereafter his counterpoint is more loosely made, and lacks consistency. Tallis, on the other hand, used the ostinato method with complete success in his three settings of *Clarifica me pater*,[2] the canticle antiphon at Lauds on the vigil of the Ascension, in all of which the plainsong, somewhat decorated, is the tenor of four parts, and a single point is maintained against it throughout.

For settings in a style which was more idiomatic to the keyboard the composers combined and contrasted these and other methods. Richard Wynslate's *Lucem tuam*, for example, begins quietly with a point over the plainsong:[3]

Ex. 146.

[*Lu - cem tu - am, Domine*]

Soon he pursues a short motif:

Ex. 147.

[*(conce)-de, ut de - sti-(tutis)*]

[1] *The Mulliner Book*, No. 54.
[2] Ibid., Nos. 99, 101, 104.
[3] British Museum, MS. Add. 29996, fo. 19v; for plainsong, see above, p. 102.

and later brings a shift of rhythmic grouping:

ending with a return to the idea of the repeated motif:

Vocal polyphony was seldom used for the antiphonal chants of the Mass, though the Pepys manuscript provides exceptions in the form of two settings of the Communion *Beata viscera* for the Assumption of the Virgin[1] and one setting of *Vera fides geniti*, the Communion on the Nativity of the Virgin,[2] all anonymous. *Vera fides* is based on an ornamented form of the plainsong sung as the middle part of three, while one of the settings of *Beata viscera* is free after the first few notes and the other has three parts over the plainsong sung in monorhythm[3] (see Ex. 150).

The only surviving vocal setting of an Introit in this period is one of an anonymous and unique set of pieces for the Proper of the Mass of the Name of Jesus in the Gyffard part-books,

[1] Also sung in the Mass *Salve sancta parens*.
[2] Also sung in the Mass *Salve sancta parens* at Eastertide.
[3] Cambridge, Magdalene College, Pepys MS. 1236, fos. 86v–87.

Ex.150.

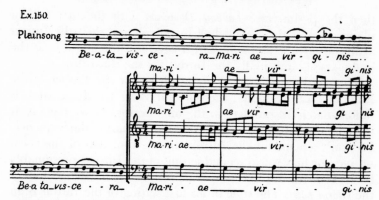

which also includes the Gradual, Alleluia and Sequence.[1] All the settings are based on their plainsongs, which were put in the tenor part in plainsong notation, to be interpreted monorhythmically, and the composer set the parts of the ritual sung by the choir, not the parts of the soloists. He laid out the Introit *In nomine Jesu* on the full plan of its double repetition, with first the beginning by the ruler and continuation by the choir:

Ex.151.

[1] In Hughes-Hughes, *Catalogue of Manuscript Music in the British Museum,*

then the psalm-verse *Laudate Dominum* with the first half in plainsong and the second half in polyphony, then the Introit again (*ut supra*), the *Gloria patri* treated in the same way as the psalm-verse, and finally the Introit for the third time.

Thomas Preston's set of organ pieces for the Proper of the Mass of Easter Sunday, the only surviving set of the kind, is unfortunately incomplete in the manuscript. As we have it, it includes the Introit, Gradual, Alleluia and part of the Sequence. Preston's scheme for the Introit differs from that of the vocal setting, for he wrote a second setting of the Introit, presumably for its returns, but not a separate setting of the second half of the *Gloria patri*. The style of his first setting of the Introit is an interesting form of the idea of an essay in rhythm and figuration upon the plainsong, in which the chant is decorated and put into a series of free and flexible rhythms, while the other part deals with a succession of changing rhythmic and melodic ideas,[1]

Ex. 152.

Plainsong

Re-sur - re-xi _____ et_ad-huc te-cum sum, ____ Al - le - lu - ya,...

(Beginner)

Re-sur - re-xi _____

ii, p. 272, the group is listed under the title of the Introit *In nomine Jesu,* and the other pieces are not listed separately. They are discussed below, pp. 378, 393.

[1] British Museum, MS. Add. 29996, fo. 62v; the Gradual, Alleluia and Sequence, which is incomplete, are discussed below.

appearing at the beginning, and later

Ex. 153.

and

Ex. 154.

His setting of *Tu cognovisti*, which is the second half of the psalm-verse *Domine probasti me*, and his second setting of the Introit are in the more usual imitative style with the decorated plain-song in the tenor, the former being carried through on one point, the latter on a series of some nine points. In contrast to the complete absence of vocal treatments, more organ settings of Offertories have survived than of any other ritual form but the hymn, and it is not surprising to find that the Offertory *Felix namque* for the Mass *Salve sancta parens*, which was cele-brated with music more often than any other Mass, was the most often set. Preston's series of eight settings form an im-pressive contribution to these essays in the keyboard treatment of a long plainsong melody. Four of the eight are treatments of the monorhythmic plainsong in each of four parts in turn:[1]

Ex. 155.

Plainsong
Beginner   (Choir)

Fe - - lix nam - - que es sa-cra _____ ..

_____
[1] British Museum, MS. Add. 29996, fo. 53v.

and there is a second setting on the chant in the bass, in triple measure.[1]

Respond

Settings of the responsorial chants of the Mass and Office had the most ancient and continuous tradition in the history of medieval polyphony in Britain, for examples are found in every century from the two-part organa of the Winchester Troper to the Office responds of Tallis and Sheppard. It was natural that during the period of the growth of secular choirs in the later Middle Ages polyphony should be applied to those responds of the secular Office which had special ceremonial treatment, such as the Christmas respond *Hodie nobis caelorum rex* and the All Saints respond *Audivi vocem*. As in earlier centuries, only the solo parts were set, the rest being sung by the choir in plainsong, and in most fifteenth-century examples the polyphony elaborated, or at least made occasional reference to, the plainsong which it replaced:

1 Printed in *Altenglische Orgelmusik*, p. 6.

me - di - a - no - - cte cla - - -

After verse, respond is repeated from *Oleum*

These passages are from one of the three settings by John Tuder in the Pepys manuscript,[1] which also contains no fewer than five anonymous settings of *Gloria in excelsis*, the verse of *Hodie nobis*. In this respond the opening was not normally set, for a reason which will be apparent if the method of its ceremonial performance be recalled, and even when the music was on the whole only distantly related to the chant the plainsong melody always made itself felt at the words *et in terra pax*:[2]

Ex. 157.

The only other responds of the Office in the Pepys collection, *In pace in idipsum* with the *Gloria patri*, and *In manus tuas*,[3] which

[1] Fos. 100–100v. For a discussion of two settings of *Audivi* in the earlier MS. Egerton 3307, one of which is not based on the plainsong, see Bukofzer, *Studies in Medieval Music*, pp. 125, 135, 139–40. In the setting of this respond a break was regularly made before the words *Ecce sponsus*, where the singers turned from the altar to the choir. See above, p. 107.

[2] Pepys MS. 1236, fos. 11v–12.

[3] There are two settings of each; both the settings of *In manus tuas* are by William Corbronde, while the *In pace* settings are anonymous. Only one part is extant of each of two further anonymous settings of *In pace*.

were sung at Compline in Lent, were treated on the same lines. We meet three of these texts again in the work of Taverner, where the plainsong is sung virtually without ornament and surrounded with florid counterpoint. It is not hard to imagine how enchanting was the effect of his *Audivi* and *Gloria in excelsis*, both for four high voices, when sung with their appointed ceremonial:[1]

Ex. 158.

Tallis used a different technique in setting these three responds, and the comparison is instructive, for Taverner surrounded the chant with contrasting lines, while Tallis adapted it to the purposes of imitative polyphony, making a point out of each phrase of the plainsong melody:[2]

Ex. 159.

[1] *Tudor Church Music*, iii, p. 47.
[2] Ibid., vi, p. 90.

In the work of Taverner we meet the earliest examples of a method of setting Office responds which seems, at first sight, to be liturgically improper because it appears to reverse the roles of soloists and chorus, but which is actually analogous to the way in which Ludford set the Alleluia in his Lady-Masses for choir and organ. In *Dum transisset sabbatum*, the third (and last) respond at Easter Matins, Taverner set the respond in polyphony and left the soloists' beginning and verse to be sung in plainsong.[1] This can be explained as a recognition of the accomplished fact that the choir of a secular foundation such as Cardinal College was now a polyphonic choir, and therefore ritual polyphony, which had been for centuries the preserve of soloists, was now given to the choir, and replaced its plainsong as it had previously replaced the plainsong of the soloists. The effect was to restore the kind of contrast between choir and soloists which was originally contemplated by the liturgy. In making a choral setting of a respond the composer had to provide for a break in the flow of the polyphony at the point where the respond was taken up after the verse, which was at the words *ut venientes* in *Dum transisset*, as may be seen in Robert Barber's setting of that text:[2]

Ex.160.

This method, with the monorhythmic disposition of the plainsong which invariably went with it, was used in the increasing number of responds of the Office which were set in polyphony during the last decades of the Sarum rite. Tallis wrote settings in this style of *Dum transisset*, of *Loquebantur variis linguis* for first Vespers of Whitsunday, of *Videte miraculum* for first Vespers and Matins of the Purification, of *Homo quidam*

[1] *Tudor Church Music*, iii, pp. 37, 43. In the former the opening is not given, though the words are written; the correct treatment may be seen in the alternative version for four parts, ibid., p. 40.

[2] British Museum, MSS. Add. 17802-5.

fecit coenam for first Vespers of Corpus Christi, of *Candidi facti sunt* for first Vespers of feasts of Apostles, and of *Honor virtus et potestas* for Matins of Trinity Sunday.[1] This impulse towards the further adornment of the ritual of the Offices is most marked in the work of Sheppard, for responds form a very considerable proportion of his music to Latin words.[2] Most of those which survive were written in a set of part-books from which the tenor book has disappeared,[3] but thanks to the monorhythmic method of writing the plainsong this is not as serious a loss as it might have been, and it is possible to reconstruct with certainty those responds in which the cantus firmus was in the tenor.[4] The simplicity of this operation and the vigour of Sheppard's style are both illustrated in the opening of his setting of *Reges Tharsis*, sung as the respond at first Vespers and as the third respond at Matins of the Epiphany:

Ex. 161.

[1] All are printed in *Tudor Church Music*, vii. The title of the last is given as *Virtus honor* and the first word of *Homo quidam* has not been supplied. The last two responds mentioned were printed in the Byrd-Tallis *Cantiones Sacrae* of 1575, though it seems unlikely that they were composed after the accession of Elizabeth I.

[2] The beginnings are not normally given in the manuscripts, and must be supplied to show the proper title in each case. In the list of Sheppard's works in Grove, *Dictionary of Music*, s.v. 'John Shepherd', the additions shown in brackets should be made to the following titles: (*Non conturbetur*) *cor vestrum*; (*Laudem dicite*) *Deo nostro*; (*Christi virgo*) *dilectissima*; (*Reges Tharsis*) *et insulae*; (*Impetum*) *fecerunt unanimes*; (*Filiae*) *Hierusalem* (*venite*) (*Justi*) *in perpetuum*; (*Spiritus Sanctus*) *procedens a throno*; (*Gaude Gaude Gaude Maria*) *virgo cunctas* (*haereses*). The verse *Gloria in excelsis* should not be listed under Masses.

[3] Oxford, Christ Church, MSS. 979–83.

[4] The following have been completed in this way: *Non conturbetur* II, *Dum*

As a rule, settings of those responds which had a longer tradition of polyphony, such as *Gloria in excelsis, Audivi, In pace* and *In manus tuas*, were still done in the older way of solo polyphony and choral plainsong. Sheppard's three settings of *In manus tuas* in the Gyffard part-books show the old and new methods side by side. In the first he set the soloist's part, which consisted of the words *In manus tuas; Redemisti me, Domine Deus veritatis*:

Ex. 162.

while in the other two he set the part of the choir, consisting of the words *Domine commendo spiritum meum*, which in both cases

transisset I, *Reges Tharsis, Impetum fecerunt, Spiritus Sanctus procedens* I and II, *Verbum caro* and *Gaude Gaude Gaude Maria* (with prose *Inviolata*).

are marked in the manuscript '*In manus* Corus M[r] Sheparde':

Ex. 163.

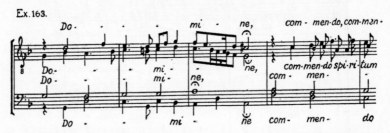

In the later Middle Ages settings of the responds of the Mass were still confined almost entirely to the Alleluia, but again the Pepys manuscript provides an exception, an anonymous setting of the Gradual *Benedicta et venerabilis* for the Vigil of the Assumption.[1] Two points about this piece, which deals only with the soloist's beginning and the verse *Virgo Dei genitrix*, may be noted: the use of unison at *genitrix* and at *in tua se clauset* later in the verse, which is rare in ritual polyphony, though less so in carols and secular polyphony; and the deliberate form of cadence at *factus*, an idiom which is also found in the Alleluias in this manuscript, where it has a function which does not seem to apply here:[2]

Ex. 164.

[1] Also sung in the Mass *Salve sancta parens*; however, since the Gradual of the Lady-Mass was sung throughout by the choir (see above, p. 286, n. 3) this setting must be for the feast.

[2] Cambridge, Magdalene College, Pepys MS. 1236, fos. 75v–76. The Sarum Customary does not expressly say that the last word and neuma of

The settings by Sheppard and John Ensdale of the Easter
Gradual *Haec dies* (the latter is in the Gyffard collection) may
be assumed to have been sung at Vespers rather than at Mass.
Ensdale's piece is marked *in die pasche* and follows in the manuscript John Mundy's setting of the *Kyrie*, also marked *in die
pasche*, with which Vespers began during Easter week. Both
Sheppard's and Ensdale's settings treat only the words of the
Gradual, omitting the plainsong beginning, and not those of
the verse, and both are based on the plainsong, which does not
include the neuma on the last syllable of the ending *laetemur in
ea* in either setting.[1] Ensdale put the plainsong in the bass,
Sheppard in the tenor, and while Ensdale wrote elaborate runs
on the word *exsultemus*:

the verse of the Gradual were sung by the choir, in the same way as those
of the verse of the Alleluia; see *Use of Sarum*, i, p. 70, and cf. *Missale Sarum*,
col. 8. This setting is evidence that they were, as are also the settings of this
Gradual and of the Gradual *Propter veritatem* in the St. Andrew's manuscript.

  [1] Cf. above, p. 63.

Sheppard's setting (in six parts) is more integrated in style.[1]

All but a few of the settings of the Alleluia which survive were composed for the Lady-Mass, and one of the earliest examples in our period is a two-part setting, made in the first half of the fifteenth century, of the Alleluia *Salve virgo* for the weekly Lady-Mass from the Purification to Septuagesima and Trinity to Advent.[2] Only the beginning and the words of the verse up to *caelorum* were set, leaving the complete Alleluia and the last two words *et domina* of the verse, with the neuma, to be sung in plainsong by the choir. The upper part is based throughout on the plainsong, the beginning:[3]

Ex. 166.

and the second half of the verse being set in triple measure and the first half of the verse in duple measure. The Pepys manuscript contains a complete set of Alleluias for the daily Lady-Mass,[4] as well as settings of the Alleluia *Surgens Jesu* for the

[1] It has been published by Chester, edited by H. B. Collins.

[2] For the weekly Lady-Mass 'quacunque feria contigerit'; if it were celebrated daily, this Alleluia was sung on Friday. *Missale Sarum*, cols. 780*–781*.

[3] British Museum, MS. Egerton 3307, fo. 46.

[4] In the following order: *Post partum, Virtutes caeli, Ora pro nobis, Salve virgo, Virga Jesse, Veni electa, Ave Maria* (these on fos. 31v–33v) and *Per te Dei genitrix* (fo. 43). See the order in *Missale Sarum*, col. 781*.

Mass of the Name of Jesus and of the Alleluia for certain feasts, including *Dulce lignum* for the Finding of the Holy Cross, *Ascendens Christus* for the Ascension, *Paraclitus Spiritus* for the Monday in Whitsun week, and *Dies sanctificatus* for the Transfiguration.[1] In these settings, all anonymous, the Alleluia and the ending of the verse, which had the same plainsong neuma, were set to the same music. In some pieces the whole of the Alleluia melody was used, in others only its opening, as far as the jubilus, as may be seen in these two settings of the Alleluia *Post partum*, which also show the different methods of performance that seem to be implied:[2]

[1] The manuscripts normally give the closing words of the verse, since they were sung in polyphony. In the Pepys manuscript these closing words are the only clue to the identity of the verses, except in the cases of *Dulce lignum* (title given at the end), *Ascendens Christus* ('De Ascensione' at the end) and *Paraclitus Spiritus* ('Spiritus Paraclitus' at the end). This manuscript also contains settings of the Alleluias *Laudate pueri* and *Confitemini* for Eastertide, which are discussed below, pp. 378–9, 409.

[2] Cambridge, Magdalene College, Pepys MS. 1236, fos. 52v, 32.

Choir: polyphony, 'pro nobis'; then soloists' beginning
(polyphony), followed by Sequence.

The order of the Alleluias in Ludford's cycle of daily Lady-Masses[1] corresponds to that prescribed in the Sarum Missal, and the method of performance is quite clear, observing the division between solo (here organ) and chorus (here vocal polyphony) laid down in the Missal. The polyphonic sections were based on their plainsongs, used in ornamental forms in the tenor, and since a sequence was always sung the repeat of the Alleluia in each case ended at the first note of the neuma, as in the Alleluia *Post partum* for the Monday Mass:

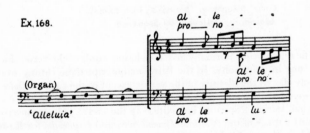

Ex. 168.

¹ In British Museum, MSS. Royal Appendix 45–8.

376

The latest in date of these Alleluias for the Lady-Mass are four pieces by Sheppard, two each by Taverner and William Mundy, and one each by Knyght, Tallis and Tye.[1] Again, some settings deal with the whole of the Alleluia melody, others with its beginning only, as may be seen by comparing Sheppard's setting of the Alleluia *Veni electa*:

Ex. 169.

with Taverner's.[2] Knyght's Alleluia *Obtine sacris*, which is one of the most attractive of the set in its freshness and spontaneity,

[1] In British Museum, MSS. Add. 17802–5. This manuscript gives no indication of the words of the verses, neither of their openings nor endings; they must be identified by comparison with the plainsong melodies.

[2] Printed in *Tudor Church Music*, iii, p. 53.

illustrates the mid-sixteenth-century manner of ornamenting a plainsong in the tenor and the freely imitative style of the parts which were set around it:

The choral sections of the Gradual *Constituit Deus pater* and the Alleluia *Dulce nomen* of the Proper of the Jesus-Mass in the same manuscript were set in polyphony, as were those of its Introit. Hence the Gradual[1] was sung with alternating plainsong and polyphony in the following way: the beginning of the Gradual in plainsong;[2] the complete Gradual in polyphony; the verse *Adiuva nos* in plainsong[3] up to the last word *tuum*; the neuma on that word in polyphony. The Alleluia was treated in the same fashion, but the neuma of the last word *sibilum* of the verse was given a different setting, as in the Gradual, although its melody is the same, after the first few notes, as that of the Alleluia. There was no repeat of the Alleluia, since the sequence *Dulcis Jesus Nazarenus* followed.

Between the Epistle and Gospel at the Mass of Easter Eve and the Mass of the eve of Whitsunday the Ordinal prescribed both the Alleluia *Confitemini Domino* and the Tract *Laudate Dominum*.[4] The upper part of the setting of this Alleluia in the

---

[1] Called 'grale' in the manuscript.

[2] Not given in the manuscript.

[3] Indicated in the manuscript by the first two words, without music.

[4] *Use of Sarum*, ii, p. 167; *Ordinale Exon*, i, p. 323 ('Epistola *Si consurrexistis*, et legatur in pulpito. Qua lecta, duo clerici de superiore gradu in capis sericis ibidem dicant *Alleluya*. Chorus idem repetat. ℣. *Confitemini domino*. Sequatur Tractus *Laudate dominum*.') and p. 330 ('Ep. *Factum est cum Apollo*. *Alleluya*. ℣. *Confitemini domino*, sicut in vigilia Pasche').

Egerton manuscript, which is for two voices, appears to be based on the whole melody of the Alleluia, and is followed by a setting of the verse up to the last word *ejus*, which was evidently to be sung by the choir in plainsong. The actual method of performing this Alleluia, however, is made clear by the setting in the Pepys manuscript, for it was a special case in which the Alleluia was sung in full by two soloists and repeated in full by the choir before the soloists sang the verse. The Pepys setting is for two voices, and is followed by another setting for three voices which is marked *chorus*, and then by the verse, set for two voices up to *misericordia*, leaving out the last word. The setting by Sheppard in the Gyffard part-books, where it is marked *vigilia pasche*, seems to be the only other surviving treatment of this text. Sheppard composed the Alleluia in imitative style on a point derived from the plainsong:

Ex.171.

and the verse on free points, with a florid passage on the word *saeculum*:

Ex.172.

The only settings of responsorial chants for the organ are the Gradual and Alleluia which form part of Preston's Proper for the Mass of Easter Sunday. The organ takes the role of the soloists, having the first two words of the Gradual and the verse without the last word:[1]

---

[1] British Museum, MS. Add. 29996, fo. 64v.

in sae -   *cu·lum -*]

and likewise supplying the opening of the Alleluia and the two
verses *Pascha nostrum* and *Epulemur*, without the final neuma in
each case. In the Gradual, Preston carried the keyboard treatment of the plainsong to a stage beyond that of the rhythm-
cum-figuration style he used in the Introit, making it an essay
in proportions which requires complete rhythmic independence
in the player's two hands. He set both of the Alleluia verses in
imitative style in three parts.

Tract

Although the Tract was not normally a subject for polyphonic setting, there is a single example, a three-part piece
bearing the title *Tam peccatum*,[1] which John Baldwin copied
into his anthology now in the Royal Music collection in the
British Museum, and which he attributed to Taverner. These
words are the beginning of the fourth verse of the tract *Dulce
nomen Jesu Christi* for the Jesus-Mass from Septuagesima to
Easter, which is unusual among tracts in having a non-biblical
text. Though the attribution must be somewhat suspect on account of Balwin's errors in similar cases, the music is interesting
as an ostinato using a simple figure treated in quasi-isorhythmic
fashion.

Hymn

When the chanson style and technique were applied to the
English descant method of setting a hymn, the effect was analogous to the ornamented treble style of the Mass and antiphon,
as may be seen in the only surviving setting of a hymn by
Dunstable:[2]

[1] Printed in *Tudor Church Music*, iii, p. 126.
[2] *John Dunstable*, p. 95; original notation and transcription in Wolf,
Handbuch der Notationskunde, i, pp. 382–3.

This also shows the practice, henceforth almost invariable, of writing down the setting or settings for the even-numbered verses, leaving the others to be sung in plainsong. Most fifteenth-century settings used this method of the decorated treble, often very elaborate, as in this anonymous setting of the hymn at first Vespers of the Ascension in the Selden manuscript:[1]

If the composer wrote different music for two or three verses, the technique became that of contrapuntal variations on a theme, as with Gilbert Banester's settings of the three even-numbered verses of *Exsultet caelum laudibus*, the hymn at Lauds for Common of Apostles:[2]

[1] Bodleian Library, MS. Arch. Selden B. 26, fo. 30.
[2] Cambridge, Magdalene College, Pepys MS. 1236, fos. 15v–17v.

Two other ways which were less usual in the fifteenth century were that of *fauxbourdon*,[1] consisting of a part written in sixths and octaves below the tune with a third part moving in fourths below it, as in an anonymous setting in the Pepys collection of the second verse of *O lux beata Trinitas*:[2]

and that of the monorhythmic cantus firmus, as in this treatment of the tune of *Salvator mundi Domine* by an anonymous composer, also in the Pepys manuscript:[3]

---

[1] In the continental sense, distinct from the English faburden.
[2] Pepys MS. 1236, fo. 11.
[3] Ibid., fos. 64v–65. A transcription of three parts, omitting the part next below the treble, was printed in *Hymns Ancient and Modern*, Historical Edition, p. xxxvi.

Ex. 178.

As a rule, the vocal polyphonic hymns of the sixteenth century, which are almost all by Tallis or Sheppard, used the plainsong in the treble in a monorhythmic or slightly ornamented form, or disposed in a more or less persistent rhythmic pattern, as in Tallis's setting of the same hymn:[1]

Ex. 179.

[1] Printed in *Tudor Church Music*, vii, pp. 242–5.

Here the tune is more ornamented than usual, and the same is true of Tallis's *Jam Christus astra ascenderat*[1] for first Vespers of Whitsunday, in which he disposed the melody in the second and fourth verses, which have identical music, in such a way as to make a strict canon between the treble and countertenor:

Ex. 180.

Some fifteen hymns by Sheppard, for five to eight voices, have survived, but all save two lack their tenor part. Because the regular method of setting was to put the tune in the treble (there are single instances in Sheppard of the tune in the mean and in the bass) we are in a much less fortunate position with Sheppard's hymns than we were with his responds, for only one of his hymns had a monorhythmic plainsong in the tenor,[2] and can therefore be restored with certainty. One of the two which remain complete is a fine setting of *Aeterne rex altissime*, with a monorhythmic cantus firmus in the treble, which begins:[3]

[1] Printed in *Tudor Church Music*, vii, p. 285. The titles of the Tallis hymns given in the edition are those of the second verse of the hymn, except in the case of *O nata lux*; the actual titles of the others must be discovered before the plainsong and full text can be supplied. The following are the titles of the Tallis hymns: *Illae dum pergunt* is *Sermone blando angelus*; *Procul recedant somnia* is *Te lucis ante terminum*; *Adesto nunc* is *Salvator mundi*; *Solemnis urgebat* is *Jam Christus astra ascenderat*; *Haec Deum caeli* is *Quod chorus vatum*; *Hic nempi mundi* is *Deus tuorum militum*; *Tu fabricator omnium* is *Jesu salvator saeculi*. The first three were printed in the *Cantiones Sacrae* of 1575, where Tallis included a setting of each of the two tunes of *Procul recedant* (see *Hymns Ancient and Modern*, Nos. 163, 34), which are, of course, two different pieces.

[2] One of his two settings of *Deus tuorum militum*.

[3] Oxford, Christ Church, MSS. 979–83 (attributed to Tallis in St.

Ex.181.

The titles of organ settings of hymns were always indicated
by the opening words of the first verse, which shows that the
first and remaining odd-numbered verses were supplied on the
organ, and not, as with vocal polyphony, the even-numbered
verses. This is confirmed by the fact that the only collection of
organ music which is liturgically ordered[1] provides three verses
for *Salvator mundi*, a hymn with five verses, two for *Te lucis ante
terminum*, which has three, and four for *Christe qui lux es*, which
has seven.[2] Since the Customary directed that the singing of a
hymn should continue from the point where the beginner left
off, the organ must have been regarded in this case as both
ruler and continuer. Redford's setting of *Te lucis ante terminum*
in the Mulliner book, which begins with the second line of the

Michael's College, Tenbury, MS. 344); the other is the second of his settings of *Deus tuorum militum*, in the same manuscript.

[1] British Museum, MS. Add. 29996 as far as fo. 67v.

[2] There are three other examples of the kind, *Conditor alme siderum*,
Verbum supernum and *Iste confessor*. There are also settings which give only
one verse and others which have fewer than the number of odd-numbered
verses.

tune,[1] seems to be the only case which provides for a vocal beginning and an organ continuation.

These sets of verses called for variety of technique in the successive treatments of the same tune. For example, Redford's three verses for *Verbum supernum prodiens a patre*, the hymn at Matins during Advent, are a duet based on the decorated plainsong for the first verse, a more florid duet on the decorated faburden of the plainsong for the second verse:[2]

Ex.182.

and an imitative treatment, with three points on the plainsong as a 'meane', for the third verse. This last verse was copied into the Mulliner book,[3] but not the first two. Thomas Mulliner was not concerned with the needs of the Latin ritual, and his choice of a single verse from a set in this and in two other cases[4] shows the direction of the changing musical taste of his time. In all three instances he chose a verse in three parts in imitative style, which is the most frequent style of the hymns in his collection. Other methods found there include ostinato, the essay in proportions, and abstract figuration of a *moto perpetuo* kind. While Redford's ostinato figures generally have an instrumental sound and are usually pursued in one part,[5] Tallis's are vocal in sound and are shared between the parts, as in his settings of other ritual forms. The style of unfolding motives

---

[1] Stevens, *The Mulliner Book*, p. 46.

[2] British Museum, MS. Add. 29996, fo. 13v, there anonymous; see Grove, *Dictionary of Music*, s.v. 'John Redford'.

[3] *The Mulliner Book*, No. 66.

[4] The fourth verse of *Christe qui lux* in Add. 29996 is *The Mulliner Book*, No. 31, and the third verse of *Veni redemptor* is *The Mulliner Book*, No. 47.

[5] E.g. *Aeterne rerum*, *Jam lucis* and *Aeterne rex altissime*; *The Mulliner Book*, Nos. 74, 75, 69. The last is printed in Walker, *History of Music in England*, p. 69.

which is seen in the first two verses of Redford's *Verbum supernum* is seldom to be found in Mulliner's collection, though there is a clear case in the first of William Blytheman's four verses for *Aeterne rerum conditor*, the hymn of nine verses at Lauds on Sundays from Epiphany to Lent, which is the only group of hymn-verses in the Mulliner book which has the appearance of a set.[1]

Two choral settings of the Te Deum have survived, both arranged for *alternatim* singing, the polyphony beginning with the second verse. Taverner's five-part setting lacks the tenor, but its restoration has been possible since the tenor had the plainsong in every verse but one.[2] The melody of verses eleven to twenty was changed by the addition of the note a tone higher than the cadence note of the plainsong, evidently to make a more manageable cadence in the polyphonic setting. Hence these verses have a cadence F D E instead of F D, the setting being based on the chant transposed down a tone:

Ex 183.

---

[1] *The Mulliner Book*, Nos. 49–52.
[2] *Tudor Church Music*, iii, p. 26.

At the 'antiphon' *Aeterna fac* the melody is put in the bass at a fourth lower than the expected pitch, which gives it a cadence on A, and the final 'antiphon' *In te Domine speravi*, with the neuma, is also at this pitch, this time in the tenor range, so that the music from *Tu patris* to the end is kept in the fourth mode with the final A. It is interesting to compare Taverner's Te Deum with the anonymous four-part setting which is the first piece in the Gyffard part-books. This work was written on the faburden of the plainsong, a method equivalent to that of the psalm *In exitu* in the same manuscript; it is not at all behind Taverner's setting either in the flexible use of imitation or in the melodic interest of the points:

Ex.184.

The cadences are treated in the same fashion as in Taverner's setting, the faburden of *Tu patris sempiternus*,[1] for example, showing that the cadence with the additional note is assumed:

Ex.185.

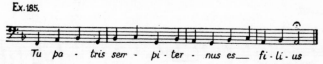

Again, the same transposition is made at *Aeterna fac* as in Taverner's setting, though in this section and in *In te Domine*

---

[1] It will have been noticed that each phrase of a faburden always ends with a cadence falling one step, whatever may be the cadence in the plainsong. Every cadence in the plainsong which did not rise one step was ornamented in performance so that it did.

the bass is the actual plainsong and not its faburden. Some bars of the final section illustrate the linear and rhythmic vigour of the counterpoint:

Organ settings of the *Te Deum* were regularly written on the faburden of the chant, but the faburden could be put in any part of the texture, and the variety of treatment was naturally greater than in the vocal settings. The range of style may be judged from three consecutive verses of Avery Burton's setting, based on the faburden of the plainsong transposed down a second, in which it will be seen that the cadences in the part of the chant which begins at *Tu rex gloriae* are treated in the same way as in the vocal settings:[1]

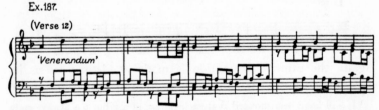

[1] British Museum, MS. Add. 29996, fo. 23v. The first verse in the example is followed by a verse (also *Venerandum*) in the manuscript, which is marked 'A verse more then nedythe'.

Organ settings also had regularly a transposition of the chant at *Salvum fac* which was equivalent to that in the vocal settings at *Aeterna fac*. They began with the half-verse following the beginner's singing of the first three words of the hymn, and hence did not treat the same succession of verses as did vocal settings. It was in keeping with the instructions of the Customary that in no case did the organ act as beginner of the Te Deum.

Sequence and Prose

While the sequence at the votive Masses of Jesus and of the Virgin seems commonly to have been sung in polyphony, it was quite unusual to sing a polyphonic sequence on a festival, if we may judge from the rarity of surviving examples.[1] The remains of a set of Lady-Mass sequences of the second half of the fifteenth century,[2] unfortunately in a very fragmentary state, show that they were set for *alternatim* performance and in a moderately florid style. The sequences in Ludford's set of daily Lady-Masses[3] appear in the following order: *Ave praeclara, Post partum, Ave Maria, Laetabundus, Hac clara die, Ave virgo singularis* [*sic*] and *Hodierne lux diei*. Here *Ave virgo singularis* is apparently a slip for *Ave mundi spes Maria*, of which it is the second verse, the verses which follow it in the ruler's book being the remaining

[1] There are fragmentary remains of a setting of the sequence for Ascension Day in Bodleian Library, MS. Eng. misc. 291. The setting begins at *Nam quadraginta*; for the text of this sequence, see *Missale Sarum*, col. 413. For the sequence-hymn *Alma chorus*, see below, p. 393.

[2] Also in MS. Eng. misc. 291.

[3] In British Museum, MSS. Royal Appendix 45–8.

odd-numbered verses of that sequence. With this emendation the order corresponds to that of the Sarum Missal with the omission of the sequence *Salve sancta parens*, which the Missal gives after *Laetabundus*. In Ludford's settings the sequence is begun in the normal manner, the organ acting as beginner, and thereafter supplying the odd-numbered verses:

Since the verses of a sequence go in pairs to the same music, the tenor of each vocal verse is an ornamented form, in this case a fifth lower, of the plainsong which was played immediately before on the organ.

Thanks to John Baldwin's bent for copying examples of three-part polyphony we have two single sequence verses by Taverner, one entitled *Jesu spes poenitentibus*, from a sequence *Dulcis Jesu memoria* for the Mass of the Name of Jesus, the other beginning *Traditur militibus*, from *Coenam cum discipulis*, the sequence for the Mass of the Five Wounds of Jesus.[1] These were very probably copied from complete *alternatim* settings for four voices, composed on a plan similar to that of the settings in Ludford's Lady-Mass cycle, as doubtless were also Tye's three-part *Tellus flumina* and four-part *Unde nostris eya*,[2] both verses from the

---

[1] *Tudor Church Music*, iii, pp. 123, 132; for the texts of these sequences, see *Missale Sarum*, cols. 850, 752*.

[2] In Oxford, Christ Church, MS. 45.

sequence *Post partum* of the Mass *Vultum tuum.* The Gyffard part-books contain an anonymous setting of *Alma chorus Domini,* the sequence for the Thursday after Whitsunday,[1] and a setting of *Dulcis Jesus Nazarenus* is included in the Proper of the Mass of the Name of Jesus. In the former the monorhythmic form of the plainsong was used in the bass, and in the latter in the tenor, as in the other pieces of the set. The final lines of *Alma chorus* may be quoted to show the strong style of the piece and its remarkable Amen, where the bass, which is the faburden of the plainsong, is written in normal mensural notation, not as elsewhere in plainsong symbols, and forces the rhythm into a triple grouping without a change of measure-signature:

Ex. 189.

[1] *Alma chorus* was also sung as the hymn at Compline on Whitsunday and the three days following, and as the hymn at Compline on the feast of the Name of Jesus. The polyphonic setting is discussed in this section, in agreement with its musical form, though since it has an Amen it was certainly written for use as a hymn, probably for the Whitsuntide use since it

The only surviving organ setting of a sequence is, like *Dulcis Jesus Nazarenus*, one of a group of pieces for the Proper of a Mass, Preston's set for the Easter Sunday Mass, and is unfortunately incomplete. Preston took advantage of the alternating verses of the lengthy Easter sequence *Fulgens praeclara* to write a series of essays in figuration and proportion.[1] Though shorter than his first setting of the Introit *Resurrexi* in the same set, the opening section of the sequence is similar to it in style,[2] while other verses use various kinds of persistent figuration, as in the second verse, which are sometimes worked out in some form of 3 : 2 proportion, as in the verse *Dic impie Zabule*, on the same melody as the following verse *Igneis nexus loris*:

Ex. 190.

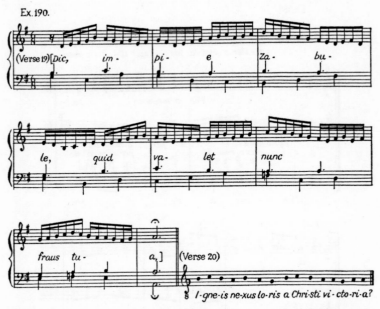

follows in the manuscript a setting of the Whitsun respond *Spiritus sanctus procedens*. Amen was never sung after a sequence; see *Missale Sarum*, col. 11.

[1] Facsimiles and discussion in Stevens, 'Further Light on *Fulgens Praeclara*', where the writer suggests the printed Sarum Gradual of 1532 as the earliest source of the plainsong used by Preston. However, it occurs in virtually the same form in earlier sources, e.g. in Manchester, John Rylands Library, MS. Lat. 24 (text in *The Sarum Missal*, p. 467), in the fifteenth-century York Gradual Bodleian MS. Lat. liturg. b. 5, and in the printed Sarum Gradual of 1527.

[2] The setting leaves the first word to be sung by the beginner in plain-

Although the setting has lost some verses at the end, it is of great interest as a compendium of the contrapuntal devices of the period.

There are five settings in the Pepys manuscript and one setting by Taverner of the prose at Matins of St. Nicholas, *Sospitati dedit aegros*, which is the only prose of which more than one setting remains in our period. All six treat not merely the alternate verses but the whole text of the prose,[1] and also the words *sospes regreditur*, the closing words of the respond *Ex ejus tumba* in which the prose was inserted, which in the ritual performance followed the prose and completed the sense of its last verse. The verse *Catervatim ruunt populi* of this respond was an exception to the general rule in that it was sung by the whole choir, and the prose *Sospitati* was also performed in a different way from other proses, being sung by the whole choir *alternatim*.[2] Hence the complete polyphonic setting of the prose and the ending of the respond was preceded and followed by choral plainsong:

Ex.191.

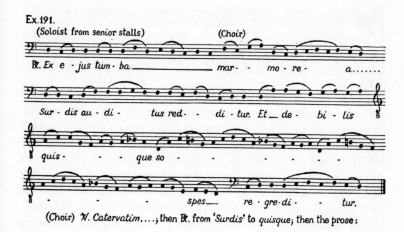

(Choir) ℣. *Catervatim....*; then ℞. from '*Surdis*' to *quisque*; then the prose:

song, and takes up the music at *praeclara*. It is based on the plainsong a fourth lower than the original, and the alternating verses must have been sung at that pitch. For the full text see *Missale Sarum*, cols. 360–1.

[1] The first setting in the Pepys manuscript (fos. 19v–20) seems to be an incomplete setting rather than an exception to the rule. The manuscript has only the first three of the eight verses (fo. 19v) and the concluding words *Sospes regreditur* (fo. 20).

[2] See above, p. 69.

This shows the first verse, with the plainsong which preceded it, of the most elaborate of the settings in the Pepys manuscript,[1] in which the anonymous composer set the second and fifth verses for two voices, and changed to triple measure for the seventh and eighth verses. The end of the eighth verse was followed by the setting of the last two words of the respond:

Ex.192.

the neuma which the prose replaced being omitted, and the first verse of the *Gloria patri* and the last return to the respond at *et debilis* were then sung in plainsong. Walter Frye's *Sospitati*, which is one of the five in this manuscript and the only work known to be his which has survived complete in his native country,[2] is a simpler setting, and probably earlier than the one just quoted. He wrote only two settings for the first four verses, and one of these 'double-duty' verses has the plainsong ornamented in the tenor, a rather unusual treatment in this manuscript:[3]

[1] Cambridge, Magdalene College, MS. Pepys 1236, fo. 82v.

[2] The first few notes of his English chanson 'So ys emprinted', which survives in various forms in continental manuscripts, are in Bodleian Library, MS. Ashmole 191, fo. 196v. See Bukofzer, *Studies in Medieval Music*, p. 94, and his article 'Walter Frye' in *Die Musik in Geschichte und Gegenwart*.

[3] Cambridge, Magdalene College, MS. Pepys 1236, fos. 84v–85.

Ex.193.

Taverner composed a different setting for each verse of his five-part *Sospitati*,[1] writing three of the verses in three parts, and the piece is a fine example of resourceful craftsmanship. He used the plainsong in the sixth verse and in *sospes regreditur* as a cantus firmus, in the first, third and fifth verses as the basis for extended melodic lines, in the second verse as material for imitative points, and in the fourth verse as a free canon:

Ex.194.

the seventh and eighth verses being set in free florid counter-point.

Sheppard's six-part *Gaude, gaude, gaude Maria* with the prose *Inviolata*[2] for second Vespers on the feast of the Purification is the sole surviving example of a polyphonic setting of both

---

[1] *Tudor Church Music*, iii, p. 110; to be revised by ibid., *Appendix*, p. 35.
[2] In Oxford, Christ Church, MSS. 979-83.

respond and prose, only the verse *Gabrielem archangelum scimus* and the *Gloria patri* being sung in plainsong. This is perhaps his finest work, and must be accounted one of the masterpieces of the last years of the Sarum rite. It is based throughout on the plainsong transposed down a fifth as a monorhythmic cantus firmus, and the treatment is an interesting demonstration of the manner of joining the beginning and end of a prose, without breaks, to the words and music of a respond. The respond, which begins thus:[1]

Ex. 195.

[1] The Sarum Breviary gives the three *Gaudes* when the respond was sung at Vespers with the prose, one *Gaude* when it was sung at Matins. *Breviarium Sarum*, iii, cols, 145, 143. The music for the Vespers form is not given in *Antiphonale Sarisburiense*, and is supplied here from the Sarum Processional, British Museum, MS. Harley 2911, fo. 71v.

is first set complete, and would be followed by the singing of the verse in plainsong. The polyphonic setting, which as usual does not show the verse, then gives the return to the respond at *Dum virgo* with the same music as before, which this time runs straight through into the prose where it is inserted after *Et post partum virgo*, thus:

Ex. 196.

The second verse of the prose, *Quae es effecta*, is also set for the full chorus, while the third verse has a beautifully tender setting for four high voices, disposed as two gymels[1] of trebles and means, with bass:

[1] The term used in English late medieval manuscripts for a duet of two soloists from the same section of the choir. See above, p. 154.

Ex. 197.

The fourth verse has the same music as the third, the gymels exchanging parts, and the next four verses are set in pairs in the same fashion, the fifth and sixth for the same voices as the third and fourth, and the seventh and eighth for five voices, two gymels and the countertenor. The last verse of the prose, *O benigna quae sola*, is set for the full choir, and goes without a break into the last words of the respond, *inviolata permansisti*, set to the same music as before.

Lesson

The Pepys collection contains three settings of the troped lesson *Laudes Deo* which was sung in the pulpitum at the Midnight Mass of Christmas. In each case the words which were sung before and after the lesson and one or more parts of the trope which was inserted into it are set for two voices,[1] although the Missal provided that the opening and closing words were to be sung by two singers together and the words of the lesson and the trope *alternatim*. In the first of these settings the chant of the words which precede the lesson is used in an ornamented form in the upper part:

[1] The first setting (fos. 3v–5v) treats *Fulserunt* only; the second (fos. 76–7) *Fulserunt* and *Messias*; the third (by Garnesey, fos. 78v–80) *Fulserunt, Ab arce, Messias, Qui creavit, In Hierusalem* and *Judex cum venerit*. In each case this is in addition to the opening (*Laudes Deo*) and closing (*Ab ortu solis*) texts of the trope; for the complete text see *Missale Sarum*, cols. 50–1.

Ex. 198.

but in the section of the trope beginning *Fulserunt et immania*, the music and words of which were drawn from the sequence for the same Mass, the plainsong is put in the lower part:

Ex. 199.

A unison beginning is used in each of the other two settings, one of which is by Garnesey:

Ex. 200.

Sheppard and Robert Johnson still observed the convention of two-part setting for this trope, and their settings[1] are interesting as examples of fairly extended two-part writing in the mid-sixteenth century. Sheppard worked on the basis of free imitation on points derived from the plainsong:

[1] In Oxford, Christ Church, MSS. 45 and 982 respectively.

Ex.201.

John Tuder's setting of the Lamentations in the Pepys manuscript,[1] in which only one voice is given, provided for the complete set of three lessons, each ending with *Jerusalem, Jerusalem
convertere ad Dominum Deum tuum,* for each of the three days on
which the Lamentations were sung at *Tenebrae.* He did not set
the announcement (*Incipit Lamentatio,* etc., or *De Lamentatio,* etc.)
which was part of the plainsong and was always included in
later settings, but he set the Hebrew letters in phrases of some
length. This latter convention was firmly established by the
time of the great settings of Tallis and Robert Whyte, which are
among the most impressive and moving works in the larger
style of the mid-sixteenth century. Tallis's music,[2] a fine example of the effective use of both antiphony and extended
imitation, comprises the first two lessons of the *Tenebrae* of
Maundy Thursday with their announcements, apparently from
two different sets, since they are in different modes.

The two anonymous Passions according to St. Matthew and
St. Luke in the Egerton manuscript are the earliest polyphonic
settings of the Passion known in any country.[3] In these, as in
later English settings, the composer set only those parts of the
Gospel which were marked *a(lta)* in the service-books, and
hence his text comprised the words of the Jews and the disciples, and of all individuals except Christ and the Chronista or
narrator. The Egerton settings were written in a simple and
solemn descant style, without any use of the plainsong and
without any of the melodic idioms of the chanson style:[4]

[1] Cambridge, Magdalene College, Pepys MS. 1236, fos. 36–42.

[2] *Tudor Church Music,* vi, pp. 102, 110.

[3] Unfortunately only the early choruses (as far as *Ave Rabbi*) of the St.
Matthew setting have survived; the St. Luke is complete, and is transcribed
in Bukofzer, 'A Newly Discovered 15th-Century Manuscript', pp. 39 sqq.

[4] British Museum, MS. Egerton 3307, fo. 16.

Ex. 202.

Num-quid e - go sum,—— Do - mi - - - ne?

Although Richard Davy's setting of the St. Matthew Passion
in the Eton choirbook[1] is in four parts and the style is less
simple, this tradition of appropriate restraint and sobriety is still
apparent, quiet strength and clear annunciation taking the
place of the floridity and jubilation of his antiphons:

Ex. 203.

Between Davy's work and the anonymous St. Matthew Passion
in the Gyffard part-books there is no noticeable change of
style; the later setting has the same directness of treatment and
control of the quicker rhythms, and the impression of restraint
is strengthened by the old-fashioned style of the counterpoint:

Ex. 204.

Processional Music

The parts of the ritual of processions which were set in polyphony during our period comprise the hymn or prose *Salve festa*

[1] It is incomplete at the beginning; two voices begin at *Hic dixit, possum
destruere templum* and all four at *Non licet mittere eos.*

dies for various festivals, and a number of items which were proper to the time between Palm Sunday and Whitsunday. The chant of *Salve festa dies* was always the same though the words for the various feasts differed, and the earliest polyphonic setting, which is in the Egerton manuscript, gives under one composition the words for Easter, Ascension, Whitsunday, Corpus Christi and St. George's day. The music comprises a three-part setting of the refrain, settings in three parts of the first and third verses and in two parts of the second and fourth, ending with a new three-part setting of the refrain, and has an ornamented form of the plainsong in the treble throughout.[1] Thus the opening and closing refrains and the verses were sung in polyphony, and the intermediate refrains probably in choral plainsong. On the other hand, all but two of the six settings of *Salve festa dies* in the Pepys manuscript, and all the surviving settings of later date, are concerned only with the refrain. The two which treat a verse or verses as well as the refrain are both settings of the *Salve* for the feast of the Dedication of a Church, one having three verses which relate to the feast of Corpus Christi,[2] and the other the usual first verse of the *Salve* for the Dedication festival, *Hic est aula Dei*. Two of the other settings in the Pepys collection are among the rare examples of four-part writing in that manuscript. Both are quite independent of the plainsong melody, and the opening of one, which is also for

[1] See Bukofzer, *Studies in Medieval Music*, pp. 123–4; the beginnings of the two settings of the refrain are quoted there, p. 142.

[2] This shows that the manuscript was written for a place dedicated to Corpus Christi, and therefore almost certainly for Corpus Christi College, Cambridge. There do not seem to have been any churches dedicated to Corpus Christi, the colleges at Cambridge and Oxford (founded 1516) being the only cases. The setting is found on fos. 23v–27, in the following order:

> Te merito criste iubilans laudat chorus iste
> cui vitam caro dat tua sancta caro. ('verte')
>
> Salve festa dies toto venerabilis evo
> qua sponso sponsa iungitur ecclesia.
>
> Rex sedet in sena turba cunctis duodena
> se tenet in manibus se cibat ille cibus. ('verte')
>
> Fit caro de pane vinum cruor hec duo plane
> cristus discipulis dat memoranda suis.

Corpus Christi, shows that its style has similarities to that of Horwood's pieces in the Eton choirbook:[1]

Ex. 205.

An anonymous setting of *c.* 1500 of the *Salve* for the Dedication festival shows a very simple way of making a three-part piece on the plainsong:[2]

Ex. 206.

while Sheppard's characteristically vigorous setting of the Easter *Salve* for four male voices has no melodic connection with the chant:[3]

---

[1] Cambridge, Magdalene College, Pepys MS. 1236, fos 57v–58. Horwood's *Salve regina* has the same disposition of clefs as this piece, with a 'countertenor' in C³ added. Our example may also be compared with the four-part verse from *O redemptor* in the Egerton manuscript quoted and discussed in Bukofzer, *Studies in Medieval Music*, pp. 136–7.

[2] British Museum, MS. Add. 5665, fo. 120, in 'plainsong' notation (see above, p. 280). There is also a three-part setting, in normal notation, in this manuscript (fos. 106v–107).

[3] In the Gyffard part-books.

Ex.207.

It is written in the transposed form of the mode of the chant, and its ending shows that it requires the plainsong to be sung a fourth higher than the written pitch.

In the only surviving setting of *En rex venit*,[1] sung at the first station of the Palm Sunday procession, which is in the Egerton manuscript, polyphony is applied to the parts of the ritual which were sung by the three clerks, that is, the opening sentences, which begin thus:[2]

Ex.208.

[1] Apart from a single part in Shrewsbury School, MS. Mus. iii. 42, which, like the liturgical part of the Egerton manuscript, is concerned chiefly with music for Holy Week. Some of the music is plainsong, some measured, and the manuscript is remarkable in being a part-book, one of a set of three, of a date (possibly 1430–60) much earlier than part-books came into general use. This form may have been adopted on account of the plays (see p. 99, n. 1, above), each player's part being in one book. The contents are listed in K. Young, *The Drama of the Medieval Church*, ii, pp. 520–1.   [2] British Museum, MS. Egerton 3307, fo. 8.

and the verses *Hic est qui de Edom* and *Hic est ille*, the second of which has an effective use of emphasis by pauses:[1]

Ex.209.

In the two settings of *Gloria laus et honor* for three voices which are in the Egerton collection,[2] the opening refrain, and probably also the final one, and all the verses, were sung in polyphony, and the other refrains in plainsong by the choir, as the Ordinal directs.[3] Both compositions are free in part, and in part based on the ornamented plainsong, while the setting in the Pepys collection, by Tuder, uses the chant in an enterprising way:[4]

Ex.210.

---

[1] British Museum, MS. Egerton 3307, fos. 9v–10.

[2] The former of the two is incomplete; for a restoration of its beginning and a description of both settings, see Bukofzer, *Studies in Medieval Music*, pp. 120–2.

[3] 'Hiis finitis assunt pueri in eminenciori loco canentes *Gloria laus*. Chorus idem repetat post unumquemque versum. Pueri ℣. *Israel es tu*', etc. *Use of Sarum*, ii, p. 161.

[4] Cambridge, Magdalene College, MS. Pepys 1236, fos. 96v–96bis.

and becomes quite florid at times. The verses of this piece appear to use the chant in an ornamented form at the fourth above the normal pitch:

Ex 211.

The method of imitative writing on a monorhythmic cantus firmus may be seen in settings of *Gloria laus* by Tye and Blytheman for two trebles, mean and tenor, where the plainsong is in the mean, and in another setting by Blytheman,[1] where it is used in each of the four parts in turn:

Ex. 212.

The verse *Unus autem* of the antiphon *Collegerunt*, which was sung at the next station of the Palm Sunday procession at the north-west door, has three surviving settings, all of the fifteenth century,[2] and all using the method of ornamenting the plainsong, generally, but not entirely, in the highest of the three parts.[3] The antiphon *Ave rex noster* for the fourth station of this procession, at the rood, was a choir chant, and was apparently not set in polyphony.

The hymn with refrain for the procession with the chrism

---

[1] All three are in the Gyffard part-books.

[2] One is in the Egerton manuscript and two are in Pepys.

[3] In the second and longer of the settings in the Pepys manuscript (fos. 68v–70) the ornamented plainsong is a fourth higher than the original pitch.

on Maundy Thursday, *O redemptor sume carmen*, has a polyphonic setting in the Egerton manuscript, in which the refrain is based on the plainsong while the verses are freely composed.[1] The settings in the same collection of two processional pieces for Holy Saturday, *Inventor rutili* and *Rex sanctorum*, both of which are in the form of refrain and verses, are based throughout on the chant with a different setting for each verse, and thus take the form of melodic variations on the plainsong.[2] One of the two settings of *Inventor rutili* in the Pepys manuscript is a varied form of the Egerton setting, and this seems to be the only musical connection between the two manuscripts, though they have much in common liturgically. While this setting gives the refrain only, the other setting in Pepys is of the complete text, for one voice, and is also in the form of variations on the chant. The verse *Crucifixum in carne* of the antiphon *Sedit angelus*, which was sung at the rood on Easter Sunday morning by three from the senior stalls (turning towards the people),[3] and the verse *Laudate pueri* of the Alleluia which was sung at the font in the procession of Eastertide Vespers by three boys (turning to the east), both have polyphonic treatments in the Egerton manuscript.[4] The setting of *Laudate pueri* ends before the last word *domini*, and appears not to be based on the chant which it replaces. The psalms *Laudate pueri* and *In exitu Israel*, both with an *Alleluia* antiphon, which were sung while going to and returning from the font in this procession, also had polyphonic settings, which have been discussed earlier.

As we have seen, a twelfth-century setting of *Dicant nunc Judei*, the verse of the antiphon *Christus resurgens* for the procession on Easter Sunday morning with the cross which has been taken from the *sepulchrum*, is one of the oldest surviving pieces of polyphony in medieval Britain.[5] The fifteenth-century settings, one in the Egerton manuscript for three voices[6] and one in Pepys for two,[7] are closely related to the plainsong, while the only identified composition by John Cornysh treats

---

[1] Bukofzer, *Studies in Medieval Music*, p. 123; part of the verse *Stans ad aram* is transcribed there, p. 136.

[2] Ibid., p. 123.   [3] *Use of Sarum*, ii, p. 168.

[4] The former is discussed in Bukofzer, *Studies in Medieval Music*, p. 124.

[5] See above, p. 117.

[6] Bukofzer, *Studies in Medieval Music*, p. 125.   [7] At fos. 54–5.

an ornamental form of the chant in the manner of a duet in the florid style:[1]

Ex. 213.

The long history of this Easter processional antiphon comes to a fitting close with superb settings of the complete antiphon and verse by Thomas Knyght and John Redford in the Gyffard part-books. Both surround the monorhythmic plainsong with vigorous counterpoint, which in Redford's setting tends to the pursuit of short ostinato points, suggesting the influence of the keyboard style on which his fame chiefly rests:

Ex. 214.

The chants of the various forms of *Kyrie eleison* used in processions on Rogation days and on St. Mark's day were sometimes sung in an appropriately simple counterpoint or in faburden. The style of the counterpoint may be judged from the beginning of one of the settings in the Pepys manuscript, which has a three-part setting of each of the three usual litanies:[2]

[1] British Museum, MS. Add. 5665, fos. 120v–121; there is another two-part setting in this manuscript at fos. 142v–143.

[2] At fo. 55; the plainsong is taken from the Processional referred to in the next footnote.

410

Ex.215.

That this method of writing is closely related to faburden becomes clear if the tenor of this example be compared with actual faburdens of this chant which happen to have been written down, though it seems certain that they would normally have been improvised. In one case the faburdens of the Rogation Kyries were noted in the lower margins of the pages containing their plainsongs in a Sarum Processional of the late fifteenth century, now in the Bodleian Library,[1] while another form of the faburden of this chant was written at the end of a fifteenth-century Sarum Processional now in the Library of Lambeth Palace, with faburdens of two other Rogation Kyries, the three being headed 'Faburdon'.[2] Example 216 shows the plainsong, ornamented at the cadences as it would have been in faburden singing, together with the faburden from the Bodleian Processional, the faburden from the Lambeth Palace Processional transposed up a fifth, and the tenor of the Pepys setting, also transposed up a fifth for more convenient comparison:

[1] MS. Rawl. liturg. e. 45, fos. 57v–61v.

[2] Lambeth Palace Library, MS. 438, fo. 180v. They have been discussed by Bukofzer in *Geschichte des englischen Diskants*, pp. 123–4, and 'Fauxbourdon Revisited', p. 31. In his article Bukofzer deduced 'a treble that may possibly be the melody' of the first of the faburdens in Lambeth; his deduction came close to the original, which in the form added in the late fifteenth century to a manuscript Sarum Ordinal of the end of the fourteenth century (Salisbury Cathedral Library, MS. 175, fo. 214v; Frere did not include these melodies in *Use of Sarum*) reads thus:

Ex.215 a.

Ex. 216.

This juxtaposition shows that there was room for slight differences in the making of a faburden, and that the composer of the Pepys setting used the faburden as his tenor, as did Banester in his *Exsultet caelum* (Ex. 176 above). These are remarkably early instances of English faburden technique.

The Pepys manuscript contains a setting of *Ab inimicis nostris defende nos Christe*, an optional part of the Litany for Rogation Days in time of war, the first part of which had been used by Cooke as the tenor of his isorhythmic motet *Alma proles regia—Christi miles inclite* in the Old Hall manuscript. This setting is divided in four sections in conformity with the text, and is another example of the unusual method of ornamented plainsong in the tenor part:[1]

Ex. 217.

[1] Fos. 46v–47; plainsong from Bodleian Library, MS. Rawl. liturg. d. 3, fo. 14.

Apostles' Creed and Lord's Prayer

Two unique polyphonic settings of ritual items which may be added here are an Apostles' Creed by Robert Wylkynson, written, probably in his own hand, on the last page of the Eton choirbook, and a Lord's Prayer by Philip van Wilder in the Gyffard part-books. The latter was printed in Tylman Susato's fourth book of *Ecclesiasticae Cantiones quatuor vocum*, published in Antwerp in 1554. It is a pleasant setting in imitative style for three trebles and a tenor, which does not use the chant of the *Pater noster*:

Wylkynson's piece is a real curiosity. The Apostles' Creed was said at Compline daily, and this setting may have been written for Compline in Lent, when the choir attended, for it is based on a cantus firmus consisting of the first phrase of *Jesus autem*

Ex 219.

(End)

'ut supra'

transiens, the antiphon to the Magnificat on Monday in the first week in Lent. To this phrase of chant are added twelve parts entering in succession in the manner of a rota with the text *Credo in Deum*, each section of which is marked in the

414

manuscript with the name of the Apostle who was traditionally
said to have supplied it. The effect when sung is that the phrase
Jesus autem transiens has truly passed 'through the midst' and
remains at the end (see Ex. 219).

Benedicamus

Polyphonic settings of the Benedicamus were uncommon in
the later Middle Ages. All but one of the examples which exist
are in the Pepys manuscript, which contains eighteen settings
for two and three voices, anonymous save two by 'W. Haute
Knyght' and one by J. Nesbet. In some the upper part is an
elaboration of one of the Benedicamus chants, while others are
free compositions, and include several effective essays in the
use of characteristic motives. Though canon was a rare technique in this period, one of the settings is a canon two in one
over a tenor written in the idiom of the continental 'trompette'
parts, followed by a canon over a pedal:[1]

Ex. 220.

(1) ACB in MS.

One of Hawte's settings is in the form of a pseudo-canon three
in one[2] (see Ex. 221) while Nesbet's is a treatment of the
in perenni melody of the Benedicamus with the Easter Alleluia,
beginning in cantus-firmus style and ending with a passage of
free ornamentation[3] (see Ex. 222):

[1] Cambridge, Magdalene College, Pepys MS. 1236, fos. 124v–125.
[2] Ibid., fo. 127.   [3] Ibid., fo. 126v.

Ex. 221.

Ex. 222.

Carol

We have no direct information about the use of Benedicamus substitutes after the period of the thirteenth- and fourteenth-century ordinals. The disappearance of the conductus in the second half of the fourteenth century and the appearance of the votive antiphon at the same time might suggest that the antiphon replaced the conductus as a festal substitute for the Benedicamus, but the practice of institutions and the character of the texts of the antiphons make it clear that this could not have been the main function of the votive antiphon. On the other hand, the words of some polyphonic carols, a genre which appeared about the time the conductus was going out of use, make it likely that the sacred carol of the fifteenth century took over from the conductus the role of Benedicamus substitute on

certain festivals. The carol has been defined as 'a song on any
subject, composed of uniform stanzas and provided with a
burden', which was sung at the beginning and after each verse.
In some cases the verses end with a recurring line, called
refrain as distinct from the self-contained burden.

Historians of the carol as a form of poetry have agreed in
ascribing the initial impulse in the cultivation of the sacred
carol to the activity of the Franciscans.[1] The appearance of the
earliest pieces of devotional polyphony to English words was
contemporaneous with the first period of their preaching in
England, and it has been suggested that the Latin poems in the
'Red Book of Ossory', which Bishop Richard de Ladrede of
Kilkenny, a Franciscan, wrote between 1317 and 1360 for the
minor clergy of his cathedral to replace the improper secular
pieces they had been singing, were intended especially for the
three days after Christmas, the Circumcision and Epiphany.[2]
As we have seen, these had been days of special licence, which
was restricted by the statutes of Bishop Odo de Sully of Paris
and by the ordinals of the English secular cathedrals to a relatively free choice of music as a substitute for the second Benedicamus at the Offices.[3] The great majority of the polyphonic
carols of the fifteenth century are for this festal season from
Christmas to the Epiphany, and include, besides carols for those
two feasts, carols of St. Stephen, St. John, the Holy Innocents,
St. Thomas of Canterbury and the Circumcision. There are a
few carols of the Blessed Virgin, one or two of which seem
particularly appropriate to the Annunciation, though they
would all have also been relevant to Christmas. Carols sung in
choir during this period would almost certainly have been substitutes for the Benedicamus, and the texts of some polyphonic
carols strongly suggest that this was their function. The famous
'Agincourt' carol *Deo gratias Anglia*[4] has the refrain-line *Deo
gratias*. The Latin carol *Deo gratias persolvamus* in the Selden
manuscript[5] ends with the lines *Benedicamus Domino, Deo gratias,*

---

[1] Greene, *Early English Carols*, pp. cxxi sqq.; Chambers, *English Literature
at the Close of the Middle Ages*, pp. 81–2.

[2] Chambers, loc. cit.   [3] See above, pp. 108–9, 121.

[4] *Medieval Carols*, No. 8. The theory of the editor (p. xiv) that carols
were sung in ritual processions is untenable, since the ordinals laid down
the chants to be sung for processions throughout the year.

[5] Ibid., No. 22.

the last two words being the refrain. In the Egerton manuscript both the burden and the last verse of *Novo profusi gaudio*,[1] which has Latin, French and English words, end with *Benedicamus Domino*; the penultimate line of *Parit virgo filium*[2] and the first line of the last verse of *Exsultavit cor*, which refers to the prowess in battle of Henry V,[3] are *Benedicamus Domino*; the last line of *David ex progenie*[4] is *Benedicat Domino*; and the burden of *Verbum patris*[5] is the first two lines of the established Benedicamus trope of the Christmas season, *Verbum patris hodie Processit ex virgine*. Thus the movement begun by the friars was taken up in other communities, and provided Benedicamus substitutes acceptable to church authorities for use in the Christmas season and on occasions of national prayer or thanksgiving.

There is also a considerable number of 'moral' and convivial carols which could not have been introduced into a service, and were probably sung at banquets in royal and aristocratic households and at evenings of recreation in colleges and collegiate churches. In earlier times carols are mentioned as songs which could be danced to at court entertainments, as in 'Sir Gawayne and the Green Knight',[6] written probably in the last quarter of the fourteenth century:

> Justed ful jolilé thise gentyle knightes
> Sythen kayred to the court caroles to make,[7]

and

> Daunsed ful drezly wyth dere carolez.[8]

In the same poem conductus and carols are mentioned together:

> Much glam and gle glent up therinne
> About the fyre upon flet, and on fele wyse
> At the soper and after, mony athel songez
> As condutes of Krystmasse and carolez newe
> With al the manerly merthe that mon may of telle.[9]

---

[1] *Medieval Carols*, No. 47. [2] Ibid., No. 73.
[3] Ibid., No. 61; the second verse begins 'Henrico Quinto prelio', but the rest of the verse was not written in.
[4] Ibid., No. 46. [5] Ibid., No. 67.
[6] Ed. J. R. R. Tolkien and E. V. Gordon, 1925.
[7] Lines 42–3. [8] Line 1026. [9] Lines 1062–6.

One of Wykeham's statutes for Winchester College, which was copied or adapted by many of the new foundations of the fifteenth century, including All Souls, St. John's (Cambridge), Eton and Magdalen, allowed the fellows and scholars to have a fire in hall on greater feasts and important college occasions, and to remain after supper singing songs and entertaining one another with 'poems, chronicles of kings, the wonders of the world and other recreations suitable to the clerical state'.[1] An account of a royal banquet on Twelfth Night in 1487 tells us that 'At the Table in the Medell of the Hall sat the Deane and those of the Kings Chapell, which incontynently after the Kings first course sange a Carall'.[2] It was for use at such times that convivial and didactic carols, and those which while festal were not in the full sense devotional, were written in the same collections as those which were substitutes for the Benedicamus during the Christmas season.

The polyphonic carols of the late fifteenth and early sixteenth centuries are markedly different in style and subject from the earlier carols, for their favourite theme was the Passion of Our Lord and they were personal in expression and pietistic in tone. There is nothing to suggest that these 'Carols of the Passion' were sung in the ritual; their place is with the household music of the court, and they were a part of the late medieval devotion to Jesus which had its liturgical expression in the Jesus-Mass and antiphon. Their chief source is the manuscript called the 'Fayrfax book',[3] which has carols by Browne (probably John, but possibly William, who was a gentleman of the Household Chapel between 1503 and 1511),[4] Davy, Cornysh, Banester and Sheryngham, and courtly and convivial pieces by Browne, Davy, Fayrfax, Turges, Tuder ('Tutor'), Hampshire, Newark and Thomas Phelypps. Similarly the 'XX songes ix of iiii

---

[1] 'In festis principalibus . . . liceat gracia recreationis in cantilenis, et aliis solaciis honestis moram facere condecentem, et poemata, regnorum cronicas, et mundi huius mirabilia, ac cetera que statum clericalem condecorant seriosius pertractare.' Kirby, *Annals of Winchester College*, p. 489.

[2] Leland, *Collectanea*, iv, p. 237.

[3] British Museum, MS. Add. 5465; the texts are published in B. Fehr, 'Die Lieder des Fairfax MS.', in *Archiv füir das Studium der neueren Sprachen*, cvi, 1901, pp. 48 sqq. For printed transcriptions of the music, see Reese, *Music in the Renaissance*, p. 768, n. 25.

[4] Lafontaine, *The King's Musick*, pp. 2–5.

partes and xi of thre partes' of 1530, the only polyphonic music printed in England before the Reformation,[1] contained sacred and secular songs, devotional carols and instrumental pieces by Fayrfax, Cornysh, Ashewell, Pygot, Taverner, Jones, Robert Cowper and John Gwynneth. The publishing of this collection shows that a musical repertory of the kind sung in the early Tudor court had by that time a fairly wide use in the more affluent and musically cultured households of the realm.

The musical development of the polyphonic carol went along the same lines as that of the short antiphon and the processional music, though at a rather slower pace. Most of the carols, all anonymous, in the two collections of the first half of the fifteenth century, a roll at Trinity College, Cambridge,[2] and the Selden manuscript in the Bodleian Library,[3] are written for two voices in the simple descant style which was established by the end of the fourteenth century. When a third part was added, usually in a refrain, it was a middle part in the descant fashion, though the composers adopted from the beginning the rhythmic and melodic idioms of the chanson:[4]

Ex. 223.

The carols in the Egerton manuscript,[5] which are also anonymous, generally have the longer and more graceful melodies

---

[1] The bass book and the first page of the treble are in the British Museum, the first and last pages of the mean in Westminster Abbey Library. There are some facsimiles in E. B. Reed, *Christmas Carols Printed in the 16th Century*, 1932, pp. 4 sqq. The texts are printed in *Anglia*, xii, pp. 589 sqq.

[2] Cambridge, Trinity College, MS. O.3.58.

[3] All are printed in *Medieval Carols*. The name Childe, perhaps the composer, is written above 'Y-blessed be that Lord' in the Selden manuscript.

[4] *Medieval Carols*, No. 41.

[5] They are discussed in Bukofzer, *Studies in Medieval Music*, pp. 148–69.

and the interweaving tenor and countertenor parts, written in the same clef,[1] of the mature chanson style:[2]

Ex.224.

Ver-bum Pa- tris___ ho - - - di - e___

Some of the carols in the collection called the 'Ritson' manuscript after Joseph Ritson, who owned it in the eighteenth century, bear the name of Richard Smert and others appear to be the joint work of Smert and John Trouluffe. Smert was a vicar-choral of Exeter from 1428 to 1465 or later,[3] and rector of the parish church of Plymtree near Exeter from 1435 to 1477, when he resigned. A John Treloff was one of the five canons of the prebendal church of St. Probus, which was attached to Exeter Cathedral, during the episcopate of John Bothe, Bishop of Exeter from 1465 to 1478.[4] The Ritson carols are similar to the more mature examples in the Egerton collection, being in chanson style and in triple measure, with the exception of the second refrain of *Ave decus saeculi*,[5] which is in duple measure. The only instance of four-part writing is the second refrain of 'O blessed Lord full of pity', where the countertenor has almost the function of a bass, being in a lower clef than the tenor and taking the lowest notes at the cadences:[6]

Ex.225.

O bles-sed Lord, full of___ pi - - ty

---

[1] With three exceptions: *Qui natus est* (*Medieval Carols*, No. 51) has a middle part of the descant type, while *Omnis caterva* (No. 70) and *Comedentes convenite* (No. 71) have three different clefs with a middle part of the chanson countertenor type.   [2] Ibid., No. 67.

[3] Calendar of Documents of the College of Vicars Choral, in the Cathedral Library.   [4] *Monasticon Diocesis Exoniensis*, p. 63.

[5] *Medieval Carols*, No. 86.   [6] Ibid., No. 116.

The carols in the Fayrfax book show a decided change in musical style. They are regularly in duple measure and sometimes treat the refrain in a shortened or varied form, as in 'Woefully array'd' by William Cornyshe,[1] a setting of words 'rather doubtfully ascribed to John Skelton',[2] to which the composer's warm and intimate style was well suited. In the first two lines of the third verse he used a homorhythmic treatment with striking effect:[3]

Ex. 226.

while for the end of the last verse and the shortened final refrain he used a familiar point, and closed on a form of the suspended cadence which he wrote at the end of the first section of his *Salve regina* in the Eton choirbook:[4]

---

[1] 'William Cornysshe Junior' in the manuscript, which suggests that it was written before the death of William senior in 1502; it also contains a carol by Edmund Turges in praise of Prince Arthur (d. 1502).

[2] Chambers, *English Literature at the Close of the Middle Ages*, p. 107; see also Brown, *Religious Lyrics of the Fifteenth Century*, p. 326.

[3] British Museum, MS. Add. 5465, fo. 65v.   [4] Ibid., fo. 66v.

Ex. 227.

The Break with Medieval Tradition

The change from the Latin to the English liturgy brought to a close the varied repertory of ritual music associated with plainsong. Though the Anglican 'Service' incorporated in its Communion service something of the musical tradition of the shorter Mass, little musical continuity with the style of the festal Mass was possible once the extreme reforms of Edward VI's reign (1547–53) had come into effect. The Marian revival was shortlived and by the fifteen-sixties the new Morning, Communion and Evening services had opened a new chapter in the history of English church music. The Anglican anthem and Magnificat inherited in some degree the liturgical tradition of the Latin votive antiphon and Magnificat, but again there was virtually no continuity of style with the larger votive antiphon and Magnificat of earlier Tudor times. The style inherited by the English anthem was that of the earlier psalm-motet, shorter antiphon and carol. The social function of the carol passed to the polyphonic songs of the Elizabethan age, and its characteristic mixture of sacred and secular is still found in Thomas Whythorne's 'Songes of three, fower, and five voyces' of 1571, which includes 'moral' songs and metrical psalms, and in Byrd's 'Psalmes, Sonets, & songs of sadnes and pietie, made into Musicke of five parts' of 1588, which stand between the medieval carol and the madrigal, the household music of a later age.

APPENDIX I

Deed of Appointment of Richard Hygons as Master of the Choristers at Wells (1479)[1]

Omnibus Christi fidelibus presens scriptum indentatum visuris seu audituris Johannes Gunthorp Decanus Ecclesie Cathedralis Wellensis capitulumque eiusdem Salutem in Domino sempiternam ac eidem Scripto fidem credulam adhibere Noveritis Nos de confratris nostri Magistri Thome Overay dicte Ecclesie precentoris assensu et consensu expressis dedisse et concessisse hocquoque presente scripto nostro confirmasse Ricardo Hugons Civitatis Wellensis in Comitatu Somersetensi civi et inhabitatori viro in cantu scientifico Annuum redditum sive annuam pensionem iiii librarum xiiis iiii denariorum legalis monete Anglie Ad terminum vite sue sub modis formis condicionibus et provisionibus subscriptis eidem annuatim per manus communarii dicti Ecclesie Cathedralis pro tempore existentis Ad quatuor terminos usuales scilicet Natalis Domini Pasche Sanctorum Johannis Baptiste et Michaelis Archangeli equalibus porcionibus fideliter persovendam prima solutione huius incipiente in festo Natalis domini proxime futuro Viz lxvis viiid de pensionibus redditibus et proventibus decano et capitulo prefate Ecclesie Cathedralis in et ad Usum supportacionem et sustentacionem choristarum et tabulariorum illius Ecclesie Cathedralis pro tempore existencium domusque eorundem necnon aliorum operum in ea parte incumbenciam legitimam datis concessis et appropriatis Ac xxvi solidos viii denarios de terris pratis domibus redditibus et proventibus nostris apud Estwalles Wellie olim Orum ys lyvelode nominatis exeuntibus et proventuris Unum quoque quindecim edificiorum seu messuagiorum decenter et honorifice prope cemeterium Ecclesie Cathedralis antedicte sumptibus et expensis bone memorie domini Thome de Bekyngtona quondam Bathonensis et Wellensis Episcopi edificatorum quod ipse Ricardus modo occupat et inhabitat situm et situatum inter edificia sive messuagia adnunc per Johannem Howse ex parte orientali et

[1] Wells Museum, MS. 22, now in the Cathedral Library. The text printed here is from the MS. 'Transcript of Documents in the Museum', Vol. i, pp. 77–80.

Johannem Seward ex parte occidentali eciam ocupata et inhabitata
in et ad Valorem Summe xxvis viii denariorum Pro huius valoris
redditu sive pensione supradictus Ricardus Hugons hec onera
subibit. Primo instruet et informabit diligenter et studiose iuxta
vires dictos Choristas et tabularios omnes et singulos pro tempore
existentes in bonis et virtuosis moribus in cantu plano fracto et
discantu lusu quoque organorum iuxta eorum disposicionem et
capacitatem. Secundo. dietim presens erit in superpellicio suo honesto et condecenti in missa beate marie virginis in Capella eiusdem
sita et situata ex parte orientali summi altaris prefate Ecclesie
Cathedralis ac prope et retro ipsum ibidem cantando et psallendo.
Ac eciam in Antiphona eiusdem beate marie virginis ante imaginem
suam prope hostium chori dicte Ecclesie Cathedralis ex parte
boreali eiusdem positam et situatam certis diebus et temporibus
antiquitus decantari solita quando et quotiens huiusmodi Antiphona ibidem decantatur—causa legitimi impedimenti cessante in
hac parte—iudicio precentoris illius Ecclesie Cathedralis pro tempore existentis approbanda Postquam quidem Antiphonam sit
decantatam statim et immediate idem Ricardus Hugons quolibet
die dominico in quo seu in crastino die tunc sequente festum duplex
non continget Aut in quo die dominico Exequie mortuorum
solemnes in prefata Ecclesia Cathedrali non celebrabuntur faciet
Antiphonam de Jesu ante crucem maiorem in navi eiusdem Ecclesie
Cathedralis existentem per dictos choristas et tabularios more
hactenus in ea parte consueto et solito decantari. Tertio. presens
erit in Choro antedicto in superpellicio honesto et condecenti locum
servans et tenens in gradu inferiori ex parte Cantoris superscripti
prope repetitorem eiusdem Chori singulis diebus dominicis et
festivis in missis altis et utrisque vesperis—primis et secundis Ac
in matutinis in festis Sancte Trinitatis Corporis Christi Nativitatis
Sancti Johannis Baptiste Apostolorum Petri et Pauli et Translationis
Sancti Thome Martyris ibidem psallendo et cantando ad honorem
dei et Chori eiusdem cessante causa legitimi impedimenti exponenda
et declaranda decano si presens fuerit Ac in ipsius Absentia Sub-
decano et in Utriusque eorum absentia presidenti Capituli pro
tempore existenti. In casu et eventu quibus huiusmodi missis vesperis et matutinis seu eorum alicui in festis principalibus et maioribus
duplicibus commode interesse non possit abesseque velit et desideret
petita desuper licencia et obtenta ab eo cui causam suam huiusmodi
habet exponere et declarare Si vero in festis minoribus duplicibus
festivis seu aliquibus diebus festivis et dominicis causa impedimenti
legitimi subsistat quod in prefatis missis vesperis et matutinis seu
eorum aliqua presens esse non valeat causam ipsam Precentori
supermemorato seu eius deputato exponat licenciamque in ea parte

ab eo postulet et obtineat. Quarto. quod quando et quotiens prefatus Ricardus Hugons velit devillare licentiam petet et obtinebit a Cantore dicte Ecclesie pro tempore existente seu eius deputato ac in sua huiusmodi absencia semper ordinabit et providebit de honesto scienti et docto viro in ipsius loco ad informandum et docendum et instruendum Choristas et Tabularios supermemoratos diligenter utiliter et attente suis sumptibus et expensis. Quinto. quod quando et quotiens continget dictum Ricardum Hugons infirmitatem corporis pati seu incidere temporalem quominus durante ipsa infirmitate valeat personaliter instruccioni et informacioni predictorum Choristarum et Tabulariorum debite intendere ut tenetur pro toto et omni tempore huiusmodi infirmitatis doctum honestum et scientem virum inveniet et in loco illius subrogabit ad suplendum debitum suum in informacione et instruccione eorundem suis eciam sumptibus et expensis. Sed si quod absit continget ipsum Ricardum Hugons perpetuam infirmitatem pati seu adversa corporis valitudine continua et incurabili laborare sic quod non poterit debitum officii sui huiusmodi facere et exequi ut premittitur tunc percipiet dumtaxat annuatim per manus communarii prenominati Ad quatuor Anni terminos superscriptos equalibus porcionibus xxvi solidos viii denarios de pensionibus redditibus et proventibus Decano et Capitulo ipsius Ecclesie ad Usum supportacionem et sustentacionem permissis datis concessis et appropriatis habebitque edificium seu messuagium super plene descriptum et nunc per eundem Ricardum Hugons occupatum et inhabitatum durante vita sua Proviso semper quod si dictus Ricardus Hugons fuerit negligens et remissus in informando docendo et instruendo prefatos Choristas et Tabularios licebit Precentori Ecclesie antedicte pro tempore existenti eum alloqui et admonere ad sui emendacionem et reformacionem in ea parte Cui precentori idem Ricardus Hugons in hiis que concernunt debitum officii sui huius humiliter obediet et parebit Proviso eciam quod si idem Ricardus Hugons animo pertinaci antedicta onera seu eorum aliquod neglexerit aut recusaverit perimplere et observare Ac de et super hoc legitime coram Decano et Capitulo prefate Ecclesie Cathedralis pro tempore existente convictus fuerit extunc presens nostra concessio pro nulla habeatur viribusque careat et vigore. Et si contingat predictum redditum seu pensionem quatuor librarum xiii solidarum quatuor denariorum a retro fore in parte vel in toto per quindecim dies post aliquem terminum terminorum supra scriptorum extunc bene licebit prefato Ricardo Hugons in quatuordecim aliis edificiis sive messuagis supermemoratis et eorum quolibet distringere et districciones sic captas abducere asportare et penes se retinere quousque de huius modi redditu seu pensione sic a retro existente sibi plenarie fuerit satisfactum et persolutum In cuius rei testimonium Uni parti huius scripti indentati penes ipsum Ricardum Hugons remanenti Nos prefati Decanus et Capitulum Sigillum nostrum commune apponi fecimus. Alteri uni parti eiusdem Scripti penes Decanum et Capitulum et Successores nostros remanenti idem Ricardus Hugons sigillum suum apposuit. Hiis testibus Magistro Johanni Middilton Officiali Archdiaconi Wellensis ac dominis Ricardo Huchyns Johanne Comb et Johanne Towker Capellanis Vicariis choralibus Ecclesie Cathedralis supermemorate Datum quo ad Sigilli mei Ricardi Hugons antedicti appositionem Wellie septimo die mensis Decembris Anno domini millesimo Quadringentesimo Septuagesimo nono.

APPENDIX II

Deed of Appointment of Thomas Ashewell as Cantor at Durham (1513)[1]

Haec indentura facta inter Thomam, permissione Divina Priorem ecclesiae cathedralis Dunelmensis, ex una parte, et Thomam Hashewell cantorem, ex parte altera, testatur, quod idem Thomas est retentus et firmiter juratus ad serviendum dicto Priori et successoribus suis, bene et fideliter usque ad terminum vitae suae, sub forma infrascripta; videlicet quod idem Thomas Hashewell illos monachos Dunelmenses et octo pueros seculares, quos Prior Dunelmensis, vel ejus deputatus, assignaverit sibi ad discendum, assidue et diligenter et meliori modo, quo sciverit, tam ad modulandum super organa, quam ad planum cantum et organicum, decantando scilicet planesong, priknott, faburdon, dischant, swarenote, et countre, quantum in ipso est gratis laborabit et informabit. Ac prefatos monachos et octo pueros, ut premittitur, quater omni die feriato, videlicet bis ante meridiem et bis post meridiem, diligenter et sufficienter docebit eorumque lecciones [ut praefertur, audiet], nichil ab eis de dictis scienciis suis occultando. Tenebitur itaque idem Thomas Hashewell omnibus et singulis missis, vesperis, et *Salve regina*, in choro ecclesiae cathedralis Dunelmensis predictae, cum priknote, dischaunte, faburdon, et organico cantu conjunctim et divisim celebrandis, a principio praedictorum cantuum usque ad finem illorum, nisi ipsum aliqua legitima causa impediat, personaliter interesse, modulando ibidem super organa, si necesse fuerit [sive admonitus seu assignatus fuerit], tenoremque ad cantus supradictos canendo, aut aliam partem voci suae magis congruentem, a precentore seu ejus locum gerente assignatam. Et tenebitur cotidie personaliter interesse missae beatae Mariae Virginis [a principio usque ad finem] cum nota in Galilea Dunelmensi celebrandae, canendo ad eandem missam planum cantum sive organicum, meliori modo quo sciverit et poterit, sicut contigerit alios ibidem cantare pro tempore, nisi legitima et magna causa ipsum impediat. Et si talis causa emerserit, quod ibidem alternis vicibus interesse non poterit, alium peritum

---

[1] Reprinted from *Historiae Dunelmensis Scriptores Tres*, p. ccccxiii; words in brackets from John Tildesley's indenture, ibid., p. cccxcviii.

habilem et ydoneum ejus loco [et officio] subrogabit. Tenebitur eciam ad vocacionem praecentoris praefatae ecclesiae cathedralis Dunelmensis seu ejus locum tenentis pro cantibus previdendis [tociens quociens ad hac praemunitus fuerit]. Insuper idem Thomas, quolibet anno, durante termino supradicto, quamdiu bene et comode laborare poterit, unam novam missam quatuor vel quinque parcium, vel aliquid ei equivalens, sicut praefatis Priori et precentori pro tempore existentibus visum fuerit, in honorem Dei, beatae Mariae Virginis, et sancti Cuthberti facere tenebitur. Pro quibus omnibus et singulis serviciis bene et fideliter impendendis et sustinendis, dictus Prior pro se et successoribus suis concessit dicto Thomae Hashewell decem libras monetae Angliae ad quatuor anni terminos, scilicet ad festum annunciacionis beatae Mariae Virginis, sancti Johannis Baptistae, sancti Michaelis Archangeli, et nativitatis Domini, per equales porciones, una cum tribus ulnis de secta generosorum clericorum quolibet anno ad nativitatem Dom in recipiendis; habendum et tenendum supradictas decem libras et trei ulnas panni praefato Thomae a dicto Priore et successoribus suis apud monasterium Dunelmense ad terminos supradictos solvendass quamdiu omnia et singula premissa modo et forma praenotatis et, bene perimpleverit. Si vero contingat dictum Thomam in tantam debilitatem morbo incidere, vel infirmitate, quod praemissa facere seu perimplere nequeat, extunc idem Thomas erit contentus percipere annuatim de praefato Priore et successoribus suis pro tempore incumbenciae suae quinque marcas usualis monetae Angliae. In cujus rei testimonium sigillum commune capituli nostri praesentibus est appensum. Data Dunelmi, in domo nostra capitulari, vicesimo iiiito die mensis Decembris, anno Domini millesimo quingentesimo terciodecimo.

APPENDIX III

Extract from a Magdalen College Inventory (1522)[1]

Duo libri missarum pro hominibus et pueris in papiro, 2º fo. primi *tis gracias*,[2] 2º fo. secundi *Eleyson*. Unus liber pro hominibus tantum vel pueris tantum in papiro, 2º fo. *Kyrie*. Unus liber non ligatus, 2º fo. *magnam gloriam*.[3] Item unum librum unius partis tantum voc. le Base, 2º fo. *Kyrie*.[4] Item 8 quaterni de sancto Swythuno,[5] 14 de nomine Jhū, 5 de visitacione beate Marie.

Item sunt novem libri pulcherrimi cantuum fractorum, quorum duo sunt majores, in quibus sunt misse septem parcium sex parcium et quinque parcium, 2º fo. primi. *Et in terra*,[6] 2ᵈᵒ fo. secundi, *bone voluntatis*;[6] duo libri minores missarum cum sequenciis Alleluya et Kyryeleson quatuor parcium, pro missis beate Marie, 2ᵈᵒ fo. primi, *Euge*,[6] 2ᵈᵒ fo. secundi, *Euge*. Item duo magni libri, Psalmorum[7] Magnificat et Nunc Dimittis ac Antiphanarum septem parcium sex parcium et quinque parcium, secundo fo. primi *Et exultavit*, secundo fo. secundi *Et exultavit*. Item duo libri Antiphanarum quinque parcium et quatuor parcium, secundo fo. primi *Te matrem Dei*, secundo fo. secundi, *Sancta*. Item magnus liber Missarum Antiphanarum et Psalmi Magnificat cum sequenciis et aliis pro missis beate Marie, pro viris tantum vel pueris tantum, secundo fo. *Kyryeleson*. Isti libri fuerunt empti infra annum Domini millesimum quingentesimum decimum octavum et annum Domini millesimum quingentesimum vicesimum quartum.

[1] Reprinted from Macray, *Magdalen Register*, ii, p. 209. The second paragraph is an addition, probably of 1524.

[2] Probably for *te gracias*, with which the first full section of a Gloria often began.

[3] From the Gloria.

[4] Squares or faburdens?

[5] Bishop and Confessor, d. 863; patron saint of Wayneflete's Cathedral of Winchester.

[6] The second verse of *Ave praeclara*, the Sequence of the Sunday Lady-Mass, begins *Euge caeli porta*.

[7] I.e. canticles.

APPENDIX IV

Extract from a King's College Inventory (1529)[1]

An inventarye of the pryke songys longynge to the Kyngys College in Cambryge

5 greate bokys coverde wyth rede lether conteynynge the most solemne antems off v partes.

iiij smallar bokys coverd wyth lether havynge Cornys and Copers massys.

iij bokys of parchmente conteynynge *Salve festa dies En rex venit Rex sanctorum. Crucifixum.*[2]

iiij bokys of papyr havynge Sequenses and Taverners Kyries.

vi bokys off parchemente conteynynge Turges massys and antems *Pontificem.*[3] *O per omnia.*[4] *Summe dei.*[5] *Cristi virgo. Alma redemptoris. Cristi virgo. Quia devotis.*[6] *Qui tres pueros.*[7] Water Lambes *Exultavit.*[8] *Nunc dimittis* off the same. *Exultavit. Alma redemptoris. O cristi pietas.*[9] a masse *Recordare.*[10] Horwood's *Gaude.*[11]

---

[1] Reprinted from *The Ecclesiologist*, xxiv, 1863, p. 100, with slight emendations from the original.

[2] Holy Week music in three-part settings; compare the collections in Egerton 3307 and the Shrewsbury part-book.

[3] *Pontifices almi* is the seventh antiphon at Matins of St. Nicholas.

[4] Fifth antiphon at Lauds of St. Nicholas.

[5] Seventh respond at Matins of St. Nicholas.

[6] Fifth antiphon at Lauds of St. Katherine.

[7] Verse of the respond *Summe Dei confessor Nichole*.

[8] There is a five-part Magnificat by Lambe in the Eton choirbook.

[9] Antiphon to the Magnificat at second Vespers of St. Nicholas. The melody is the same as that of *O quam suavis*; see *Missa O Quam suavis*, p. xi.

[10] *Recordare Domine testamenti* (which was set by Richard Bramston in Add. 17802–5) is the eighth respond at Matins on the first Sunday after Trinity; *Recordare mei Domine et erue me* is the seventh antiphon at Matins on Passion Sunday. There are also Offertories *Recordare mei Domine omnipotentatui* on the twenty-second Sunday after Trinity and *Recordare quod steterim* on the Saturday before Palm Sunday.

[11] The Eton choirbook contains Horwood's *Gaude flore virginali* and his *Gaude virgo mater Christi* (incomplete); both are for five voices.

Haycomplaynes *Gaude*.[1] *Congaudentes*.[2] *O gloriosa*.[3] Dunstabylls *Exultavit*.[4] *Summe dei. Exultavit* Morgan. *Quia viderunt. Ascendit cristus. O pastor*.[5] *Tibi laudes*.[6] *Exultavit*. Also *Quia viderunt. Exultavit* ffarfax. *Quia viderunt* off the same. *Cristi virgo*. Wylkynsons *Salve decus*.[7] The Masse *Regale*. The masse *Lux eterna*.[8] *Ne derelinquas*.[9] *Summe Dei*.

vj bokys of squaris off ye wych ij be papyr ye reste parchmente. A boke wyth a blake coverynge in parchment havynge *Dicant nunc. Laudate pueri. In pace. In manus. Verbum patris refulgens*[10] and a masse off Taverners for chyldren.

iiij bokys in papyr off carrolls. Nowell.

vj bokys conteynynge a masse of Pygottys a nother off Cornyshys and an anteme off Davys.

ij Bokys havynge a masse Regale, a nother A dew mes a mowrs,[11] and Taverners Kyries with the Sequensis.

A boke conteynynge thes songys folloynge. *Laudes deo*.[12] The prose for Christmas day *Verbum patris*.

[1] The only surviving composition by Hacomplayne (Hacomblene, Hacomplaynt) is his *Salve regina* in Eton.

[2] *Congaudentes exsultemus* is the sequence on the feast of St. Nicholas.

[3] *O gloriosa domina* is the hymn at Lauds on feasts of the Virgin and at Commemorations of the Virgin except at Christmastide; *O gloriosa genitrix* is the antiphon to the Benedictus at Lauds for Commemorations of the Virgin from the Purification to Advent.

[4] Certainly a lost composition, not the three-part work in *John Dunstable*, p. 95.

[5] The antiphon to the Magnificat at first Vespers of St. Nicholas.

[6] *Tibi laus* is the seventh respond at Matins on Trinity Sunday.

[7] Wylkynson's five-part *Salve decus castitatis* (now fragmentary) is in the Eton choirbook.   [8] See above, p. 164.

[9] *Ne derelinquas me Domine pater* is a respond at ferial Matins in August; *Ne derelinquas me Domine Deus* is the Introit for Wednesday after the second Sunday in Lent.

[10] Apparently for boys, and perhaps a variant on the Benedicamus substitute *Verbum patris* for Holy Innocents.

[11] There is a four-part song 'Adew mes amours' by Cornysh in British Museum, MS. Add. 31922.

[12] Probably the troped lesson at Midnight Mass; *Laudes Deo devotas* is the sequence for Friday after Whitsunday.

APPENDIX V

Extracts from a Winchester College Inventory (1531)[1]

LIBRI COLLEGII BEATE MARIE PROPE WINTONIAM PRO CAPELLA

Antiphonaria ex parte domini Custodis

Item i magnum antiphonarium iacens coram domino custode, 2do folio *Spiritui*

Item aliud antiphonarium iacens coram magistro schole et sociis senioribus, 2do fo. *incipient*

Item aliud antiphonarium iacens coram 30 socio, 2do fo. *debeamus*

Item aliud antiphonarium iacens coram sociis junioribus, 2do fo. *venit*

Item aliud antiphonarium iacens coram conducto, 2do fo. *seculorum*

Item aliud antiphonarium iacens coram hostiario et clerico, in iibus voluminibus, 2do fo. prime partis *hoc modo*, 2do fo. secunde partis *per singulos*

Item aliud antiphonarium iacens coram scholaribus, 2do fo. *donec*

Antiphonaria ex parte Vicecustodis

Item i antiphonarium iacens coram vicecustode, 2do fo. *portarum*

Item aliud antiphonarium iacens coram sociis senioribus, 2do fo. *vis et reg*

Item aliud antiphonarium iacens coram sociis junioribus, 2do fo. *tencia*

Item aliud antiphonarium iacens coram conducto, 2do fo. *tegente*

Item aliud antiphonarium iacens coram clericis, 2do fo. *quam ad*

Item aliud antiphonarium iacens coram scholaribus, 2do fo. *tato*

Item aliud antiphonarium pro rectore chori, 2do fo. *tunc*

Item aliud antiphonarium pro organista, 2do fo. *Domine* (struck out)

Item aliud antiphonarium novum ordinatum pro chorustis, 2do fo. *facite*

Item aliud antiquum antiphonarium pro chorustis, 2do fo. *ati* (struck out)

. . . .

---

[1] In the College Muniments.

434

Gradalia ex parte domini Custodis

Item i gradale iacens coram domino custode, 2do fo. *temporibus*
Item aliud gradale iacens coram sociis senioribus, 2do fo. *dicatur*
Item aliud gradale iacens coram sociis junioribus, 2do fo. *temptantis*
Item aliud gradale iacens coram conducto, 2do fo. *omnibus*
Item (blank)

Gradalia ex parte Vicecustodis

Item i gradale iacens coram vicecustode, 2do fo. *temporibus*
Item aliud gradale iacens coram sociis senioribus, 2do fo. *orationes*
Item aliud gradale iacens coram sociis junioribus, 2do fo. *quatuor*
Item aliud gradale iacens coram conducto, 2do fo. *supradicto modo*
Item aliud gradale iacens coram clericis, 2do fo. *In hoc ha*

Gradalia pro chorustis

Item i gradale, 2do fo. *Deus*
Item aliud gradale, 2do fo. *vestigia*
Item aliud gradale, 2do fo. *in ira mea* (struck out)

Processionalia

Item i processionale 2do fo. *ex te sanctum*
(seventeen others, of which three are struck out)
v non reperimus precedentis inventarii
Item ix processionalia impressa similia, 2do fo. *bus vel in locis*
Item aliud impressum, 30 fo. *Deus invicte*
Item iii libri himnorum impressi similes, 30 fo. *exiens*
Item 2º psalteria scripta, unum 2do fo. *cum exarserit*
Item aliud, 2do fo. *et nunc reges*
Aliud, 2do fo. *me fac*

Manualia et Pontificalia

. . . .

Collectaria

. . . . . .

Libri Evangeliorum et epistolarum

. . . .

Ordinalia

. . . . . .

Item 2° libri notati, unus missarum, alius antiphonarum, ex dono
   magistri Pers[1] quondam socii collegii
Item iiii libri notati responsoriorum consimilis quantitatis
Item alius liber imnarum partis basse, cum multitudine bossorum
   in lateribus, ex dono magistri Barnake[2]

Legende

. . . . . .

Missalia

. . . . . .

[After sections headed Jocalia et vasa argentea, Cruces de argento
   cum baculis, Calices, Cruces de Cupro, Candelabra de
   Laten:]

Organa

Item i par organorum in parte boreali chori ex dono domini
   Johannis Webbe[3]
Item aliud par organorum in pulpito
Item i par organorum in capella Fromond

. . . . . .

---

[1] John Pers of Taunton; Scholar, 1480; Scholar of New College, B.C.L.;
Fellow of New College, 1487–93; Fellow of Winchester, 1505.

[2] Ralph Barnake, Scholar of Winchester, 1495; Scholar of New College;
Fellow of Winchester, 1500–17; Warden, 1520–6.

[3] Fellow, admitted 1494.

APPENDIX VI

Extracts from the Statutes of the New Foundation of
Christ Church Cathedral, Dublin (1539)[1]

Regulae et constitutiones pro melius ordinanda Ecclesia Sancte
Trinitatis et pro mutando priorem et conventum in Decanum et
Capitulum sicut proposita sunt a Regis Henrici octavi Commis-
sionariis. [Robert Payneswick, Prior, became Dean; Richard Bale,
Sub-prior, Precentor; Walter Whyte, Seneschal and Precentor,
Chancellor; and John Mosse, Sub-precentor and Sacrist, Treasurer.]

. . . .

Likewise that the other regular canons being in number eight, and
four chorister boys, shall be called by the name of Vicars Choral,
who shall be present at the divine offices there by day and night,
and shall *collegialiter* exercise hospitality within the precincts of the
said College, in like manner as the Vicars Choral of the Church of
St. Patrick's; assigning to the said eight for the same and their
cloathing 53l. 13s. 4d. and for the sustentation of the four boys
6l. 13s. 4d. per annum. . . .

The said eight Vicars Choral shall be in the ministry and shall
perform similar duties as in the Church of St. Patrick. The first
shall be styled Sub-dean and Dean's Vicar, to which office we
appoint John Curragh *presbyter*, which John shall be president of
the said vicars choral . . . he shall also be a secular canon of the
said Church, shall have a Stall in the Choir, a place and voice in
the Chapter *secundum stalli sui gradum* in the Election of the Archbishop and Dean and all other capitular acts. . . .

Likewise we ordain that one of the Vicars Choral shall be precentor's vicar, called succentor, whose office shall be to instruct the
boys of the choir in singing; he shall have the second place after the
Dean's Vicar in Choir, Chapter and at table, shall order the table of
weekly services, and such other matters as are arranged by the
Succentor in St. Patrick's Cathedral, to which office we appoint
Dominus John Kerdyff. . . .

[The Chancellor shall have a Vicar Choral, who shall have the

[1] From an eighteenth-century translation in the National Library of
Ireland, MS. 98, fos. 44–50.

third place in rank, and shall] emend and correct *libros chori falso latino et incongruo corruptos* . . . to which office we appoint Christopher Bathe, whom we make hereby a minor canon, commonly called a petit Canon. . . .

[Dominus Oliver Grant is appointed Treasurer's Vicar Choral and a minor canon, with fourth place in Choir, Chapter and at Table.]

Likewise we ordain that the other regular canons, in number four shall be personally present at divine offices, especially *quando Missae cum cantu celebrantur*, each of whom shall receive yearly 46s. 8d. from the funds above named, and shall have their daily refections at the tables of the vicars. . . .

We will that the four above mentioned Choristers shall attend diligently to the offices enjoined by the Precentor or master of the boys, to whom they shall shew due reverence. Likewise we will that they be present in the Daily Mass of the Blessed Virgin Mary and in all other masses *cum fractum habeant cantum*, likewise in Vespers *pro cantandis responsoriis* and *in Missis gradalibus*. . . .

We appoint that one of the Dignitaries shall celebrate every *sexta feria* a Mass *De nomine Jesu* in the *summo mane* in lieu of the first Mass, before the Image of the Crucifix in the accustomed place, and this solemnly *cum solemni cantu*.

We appoint likewise that the four principal vicars in their turns *per omnes hebdomadas* shall serve and celebrate Mass at the principal altar daily, and shall celebrate a mass *cum cantu plano* for the State of the King at the said altar three times per week; likewise that the other four minor vicars in their turns per week shall officiate daily at the Mass of the Blessed Virgin Mary except on the great and principal feasts in which we wish one of the Dignitaries to celebrate if conveniently they can; if not we leave it to the disposition of the Dean and Precentor.

Likewise the said Vicars minor shall one of them daily except Friday celebrate or cause to be celebrated in said church *submissa voce* one other mass, called the Mass of the Holy Cross, vulgarly stiled 'The Roode Mass', at the accustomed time and place. Likewise the said Vicars minor every Thursday (*Die Jovis*) shall celebrate a Mass *cum cantu et Choristis et aliis ministris prout decet et consuetum est*. Likewise said vicars with two of the principal Vicars who shall be free that week from the service of the High Mass shall celebrate on Mondays, Wednesdays and Saturdays at the altar of the Holy Ghost one mass for the soul of Walter Kelly formerly Mayor of Dublin, for the soul of Alison Ward *cum ab hac luce migraverit*, and all other benefactors of said church.

Likewise that three *clerici chorales habeantur* in said cathedral, of whom the first shall be learned in the musical art *tam ad pulsatione Organorum quam in cantu plano et fracto, pariter et in sufficienti discantu pro instructione puerorum*, who shall be master of the Boys under the praecentor and shall minister in the daily mass of the Blessed Virgin Mary and in the high Mass, and as often as any Mass *cum cantu fracto* shall be celebrated; he shall have the office of Bedell in the said Cathedral carrying *Virgam* before the Dean when he shall come to celebrate the divine offices, and also before the other dignitaries when they shall perform the divine offices in the Choir, and shall have for his pay yearly 6l. 13s. 4d.

Likewise a second *Clericus* who shall be called Sacrist, whose office it shall be to strike the bells at the proper hours; he shall be present day and night, at the Mass of the Blessed Virgin Mary every day for assisting the singers there, in like manner at the High Mass.

Also a third Clerk, whose office to strike the bell *campanum Mariae* at the first Mass, and assist the prebendary celebrating the same, and to administer to him the wine water and bread; he shall do the same at the Mass of the Blessed Virgin Mary and the second Mass.

. . . .

12 December 31 of the King
John Allen Canc. R
Georgius Dublin
Willimus Brabazon

BIBLIOGRAPHY

ADLER, G.: *Handbuch der Musikgeschichte*, 2 vols., 1930.

Altenglische Orgelmusik, ed. D. Stevens, 1953.

AMUNDESHAM, J.: *Chronicle*, ed. H. T. Riley, Rolls Series, 1870.

Analecta Hymnica Medii Aevi, ed. G. M. Dreves, C. Blume and H. Bannister, 55 vols., 1886–1922.

The Ancient Laws of the Fifteenth Century for King's College, Cambridge, and Eton College, ed. J. Heywood and T. Wright, 1850.

ANGLÈS, H.: 'Latin Chant before St. Gregory', in *New Oxford History of Music*, ii, 1954.

Antiphonale Sarisburiense, ed. W. H. Frere, 1901–26.

APEL, W.: *Accidentien und Tonalität in den Musikdenkmälern des 15. und 16. Jahrhunderts*, 1937.

—— 'Early History of the Organ'. *Speculum*, xxiii, 1948.

—— 'From St. Martial to Notre Dame'. *Journal of the American Musicological Society*, ii, 1949.

—— *Harvard Dictionary of Music*, 1944 (London, 1951).

—— *The Notation of Polyphonic Music, 900–1600*, 4th ed., 1949.

—— 'The Partial Signatures in the Sources up to 1450'. *Acta Musicologica*, x–xi, 1938–9.

ATCHLEY, C.: *The Parish Clerk, and his Right to Read the Liturgical Epistle*, 1924.

ATKINS, I.: *The Early Occupants of the Office of Organist and Master of the Choristers of the Cathedral Church of Worcester*, 1918.

AUNGIER, G. J.: *The History and Antiquities of Syon Monastery*, 1840.

BAILLIE, H.: 'A London Church in Early Tudor Times'. *Music and Letters*, xxxvi, 1955.

—— and OBOUSSIER, P.: 'The York Masses'. *Music and Letters*, xxxv, 1954.

BATIFFOL, P.: *History of The Roman Breviary*, trans. A. M. Y. Baylay, 1912.

BESSELER, H.: *Bourdon und Fauxbourdon*, 1950.

—— *Die Musik des Mittelalters und der Renaissance* (*Handbuch der Musikwissenschaft*, ed. E. Bücken), 1931–4.

—— 'Studien zur Musik des Mittelalters'. *Archiv für Musikwissenschaft*, vii and viii, 1925, 1926.

BISHOP, E.: 'Holy Week Rites of Sarum, Hereford and Rouen Compared', in *Liturgica Historica*, 1918.

—— 'On the Origin of the Prymer', in *Liturgica Historica*, 1918.

BLOXAM, J. R.: *A Register of the President, Fellows, Demies, Instructors in Grammar and Music, Chaplains, Clerks and Choristers and other Members of Saint Mary Magdalene College in the University of Oxford*, ii, 1857.

BOND, F.: *Screens and Galleries in English Churches*, 1908.

BONNIWELL, W. R.: *A History of the Dominican Liturgy*, 1944.

BOYS, W.: *Collections for an History of Sandwich*, 1792.

BRENET, M.: *Les Musiciens de la Sainte-Chapelle du Palais*, 1910.

Breviarium ad Usum Sarum, ed. F. Proctor and C. Wordsworth, 3 vols., 1879–86.

BRODRICK, G. C.: *Memorials of Merton College*, 1885.

BROWN, C.: *Religious Lyrics of the Fifteenth Century*, 1938.

BUKOFZER, M. F.: 'Fauxbourdon Revisited'. *The Musical Quarterly*, xxxviii, 1952.

—— 'The First Motet with English Words'. *Music and Letters*, xvii, 1936.

—— *Geschichte des englischen Diskants und des Fauxbourdons nach den theoretischen Quellen*, 1936.

—— 'The Gymel, the Earliest Form of English Polyphony'. *Music and Letters*, xvi, 1935.

—— 'Interrelations between Conductus and Clausula'. *Annales Musicologiques*, i, 1953.

—— 'A Newly Discovered Fifteenth-Century Manuscript of the English Chapel Royal—Part II'. *The Musical Quarterly*, xxxiii, 1947.

—— *Studies in Medieval and Renaissance Music*, 1950.

—— ' "Sumer is icumen in": a Revision'. *University of California Publications in Music*, ii, 2, 1944.

Calendar of Entries in the Papal Registers relating to Great Britain and Ireland: Petitions, i, 1896; *Letters*, vi, 1904; *Letters*, viii, 1909.

Calendar of the Manuscripts of the Dean and Chapter of Wells, ed. W. H. B. Bird and W. P. Baildon, 2 vols., 1907, 1914.

Calendars of the Patent Rolls preserved in the Public Record Office. The volumes are shown by the years covered.

Calendar of State Papers and MSS. relating to English Affairs existing in the Archives and Collections of Venice, ii, ed. R. Brown, 1867.

Camden Miscellany III, Camden Society, 1855.

CANT, R. G.: *The College of St. Salvator*, 1950.

Catalogue of Muniments of the Lichfield Vicars, ed. J. C. Cox, in *Collections for a History of Staffordshire*, William Salt Society, 1886.

Cent Motets du XIIIe siècle, ed. P. Aubry, 3 vols., 1908.
Ceremonies and Processions of the Cathedral Church of Salisbury, ed. C. Wordsworth, 1901.
CHAILLEY, J.: 'La messe de Besançon et un compositeur inconnu du XIVe siècle: Jean Lambelet'. *Annales Musicologiques*, ii, 1954.
CHAMBERS, E. K.: *English Literature at the Close of the Middle Ages*, 1947.
—— *The Mediaeval Stage*, 2 vols., 1903.
CHANDLER, R.: *The Life of William Wayneflete*, 1811.
The Charter and Statutes of the College of Minor Canons in St. Paul's Cathedral, London, ed. W. S. Simpson, 1871.
Chartulary of Winchester Cathedral, ed. A. W. Goodman, 1927.
Chronica Monasterii de Melsa, ed. E. A. Bond, 3 vols., 1866.
The Chronicle of John Stone, Monk of Christ Church 1415–1471, ed. W. G. Searle, 1902.
Churchwardens' Accounts of S. Edmund and S. Thomas, Sarum, ed. H. J. F. Swayne, 1896.
CLARK, J. M.: *The Abbey of St. Gall*, 1926.
Clement Maydestone's Directorium Sacerdotum, ed. W. Cooke and C. Wordsworth, 2 vols., Henry Bradshaw Society, 1901–2.
CLERX-LEJEUNE, S.: 'Johannes Ciconia de Leodio', in *Report of the Fifth Congress of the International Society for Musical Research, Utrecht, 1952*, 1953.
El Còdex musical de Las Huelgas, ed. H. Anglès, 3 vols., 1931.
A Collection of Ordinances and Regulations for the Government of the Royal Household, made in divers Reigns from King Edward III to King William and Mary, 1790.
A Collection of all the Wills . . . of the Kings and Queens of England, ed. J. Nichols, 1780.
COOK, G. H.: *Mediaeval Chantries and Chantry Chapels*, 1947.
CORBIN, S.: *Essai sur la musique religieuse portugaise au moyen age*, 1952.
COUSSEMAKER, C. E. H. DE: *Scriptorum de Musica medii aevi nova series*, 4 vols., 1864–76; facsimile edition, 1931.
—— *Messe du XIIIe siècle*, 1861.
COX, J. C.: *Churchwardens' Accounts from the Fourteenth Century to the Close of the Seventeenth Century*, 1913.
The Customary of the Benedictine Monasteries of St. Augustine, Canterbury, and St. Peter, Westminster, ed. E. M. Thompson, 2 vols., Henry Bradshaw Society, 1902–4.
The Customary of the Cathedral Priory Church of Norwich, ed. J. B. L. Tolhurst, Henry Bradshaw Society, 1948.
Customs of Augustinian Canons, ed. J. W. Clark, 1897.

DALTON, J. N.: *The Collegiate Church of Ottery St. Mary, being the Ordinances and Statutes, 1338–9*, 1917.

DANNEMANN, E.: *Die spätgotische Musiktradition in Frankreich und Burgund vor dem Auftreten Dufays*, 1936.

DART, R. T.: 'A New Source of Early English Organ Music'. *Music and Letters*, xxxv, 1954.

DAVID, H.: *Philippe le Hardi*, 1947.

Dean Cosyn and Wells Cathedral Miscellanea, ed. Dom A. Watkin, Somerset Record Society, 1941.

Denkmäler der Tonkunst in Österreich, vii, ed. G. Adler and O. Koller, 1900.

—— xxvii, part 1, ed. R. von Ficker and A. Orel, 1920.

—— xxxi, xl, ed. R. von Ficker, 1924, 1933.

DITTMER, L. A.: 'An English Discantuum Volumen'. *Musica Disciplina*, viii, 1954.

Documenta Polyphoniae Liturgicae Sanctae Ecclesiae Romanae, Ser. I, No. 2, ed. L. Feininger, 1947.

DOWDEN, J.: *The Medieval Church in Scotland*, 1910.

Dufay and his Contemporaries, ed. J. F. R. and C. Stainer, 1898.

DUGDALE, W.: *History of St. Paul's*, with additions by H. Fells, 1818.

DUNCAN, L. L.: 'The Will of Cardinal Bourgchier, Archbishop of Canterbury, 1486'. *Archaeologia Cantiana*, xxiv, 1900.

—— and HUSSEY, A.: *Testamenta Cantiana*, 1906–7.

John Dunstable, Complete Works, ed. M. F. Bukofzer (*Musica Britannica*, viii), 1953.

Durham Account Rolls, ed. J. T. Fowler, 3 vols., Surtees Society, 1898.

Early Bodleian Music, ed. J., J. F. R. and C. Stainer and E. Nicholson, 3 vols., 1901.

Early Cambridge University and College Statutes, ed. J. Heywood, 1855.

Early English Harmony, ed. H. E. Wooldridge, 1897.

Early Fifteenth-Century Music, ed. G. Reaney, 1956.

The Early Statutes of the Cathedral Church of the Holy Trinity, Chichester, ed. M. E. C. Walcott, 1877.

Educational Charters and Documents, 598–1909, ed. A. F. Leach, 1911.

EDWARDS, K.: *The English Secular Cathedrals in the Middle Ages*, 1949.

The Eton Choirbook, ed. F. Ll. Harrison (*Musica Britannica*, x–xii), 1956–8.

Expeditions to Prussia and the Holy Land made by Henry Earl of Derby, ed. L. T. Smith, Camden Society, 1894.

FARMER, J.: *Divers and Sundry waies of two parts in one, to the number of fortie, uppon one playn Song*, 1591.

Fasti Aberdonenses: Selections from the Records of the University and King's College of Aberdeen, 1494–1854, 1854.

FELLOWES, E. H.: *English Cathedral Music from Edward VI to Edward VII*, 1941.

—— *Organists and Masters of the Choristers of St. George's Chapel in Windsor Castle*, 1939.

—— *The Vicars and Minor Canons of His Majesty's Free Chapel of St. George in Windsor Castle*, 1945.

FLOOD, W. H. G.: *Early Tudor Composers*, 1925.

French Secular Music of the Late Fourteenth Century, ed. W. Apel, 1950.

FRERE, W. H.: 'The Connexion between English and Norman Rites'. *Journal of Theological Studies*, iv, 1903; reprinted in *Walter Howard Frere, A Collection of his Papers on Liturgical and Historical Subjects*, 1940.

—— 'The Newly-found York Gradual'. *Journal of Theological Studies*, ii, 1901; reprinted as above.

—— 'York Service Books'. *York Minster Historical Tracts*, xix, 1927; reprinted as above.

FRESHFIELD, E.: 'Some Remarks upon the Book of Records and History of the Parish of St. Stephen, Coleman Street'. *Archaeologia*, l, 1887.

GASTOUÉE, A.: *Les primitifs de la musique française*, 1922.

Geschichte der Musik in Beispielen, ed. A. Schering, 1931.

Gesta Abbatum Monasterii S. Albani, ed. H. T. Riley, 3 vols., Rolls Series, 1867-9.

GIBSON, S.: *Statuta Antiqua Universitatis Oxoniensis*, 1931.

GOMBOSI, O.: 'Machaut's Messe Notre-Dame'. *Musical Quarterly*, xxxvi, 1950.

Graduale Sarisburiense, ed. W. H. Frere, 1894.

The Great Register of Lichfield Cathedral, ed. H. E. Savage, William Salt Society, 1926.

GREENE, R. L.: *The Early English Carol*, 1935.

—— 'Two Medieval Musical Manuscripts: Egerton 3307 and some University of Chicago Fragments'. *Journal of the American Musicological Society*, vii, 1954.

GRÖNINGER, E.: *Repertoire-Untersuchungen zum mehrstimmigen Notre Dame-Conductus*, 1939.

GROVE, G.: *Dictionary of Music and Musicians*, 5th edition, ed. E. Blom, 9 vols., 1954.

HABERL, F. X.: 'Die römische "schola cantorum" und die päpstlichen Kapellsänger bis zur Mitte des 16. Jahrhunderts'. *Vierteljahrsschrift für Musikwissenschaft*, iii, 1887. Also in *Bausteine zur Musikgeschichte*, iii, 1888.

HANDSCHIN, J.: 'Die mittelalterlichen Aufführungen in Zürich, Bern und Basel'. *Zeitschrift für Musikwissenschaft*, x, 1927.
—— 'Sur quelques tropaires grecs traduits en latin'. *Annales Musicologiques*, ii, 1954.
—— 'The Summer Canon and its Background'. *Musica Disciplina*, iii, 1949.
—— 'Trope, Sequence and Conductus', in *New Oxford History of Music*, ii, 1954.
—— 'The Two Winchester Tropers'. *Journal of Theological Studies*, xxxvii, 1936.
—— 'Zur Geschichte der Lehre von Organum'. *Zeitschrift für Musikwissenschaft*, viii, 1925–6.
—— 'Zur Geschichte von Notre Dame'. *Acta Musicologica*, iv, 1932.
—— 'Zur Leonin-Perotin Frage'. *Zeitschrift für Musikwissenschaft*, xiv, 1931–2.
HANNAS, R.: 'Concerning Deletions in the Polyphonic Mass Credo'. *Journal of the American Musicological Society*, v, 1952.
HARDER, H.: 'Die Messe von Toulouse'. *Musica Disciplina*, vii, 1953.
HARRISON, F.: *Life in a Medieval College*, 1952.
HARRISON, F. LL. : 'An English "Caput"'. *Music and Letters*, xxxiii, 1952.
—— 'The Eton Choirbook'. *Annales Musicologiques*, i, 1953.
HARVEY, J.: *Gothic England*, 1947.
—— *The Plantagenets*, 1948.
HAWKINS, J.: *General History of the Science and Practice of Music*, 5 vols., 1776.
The Hereford Breviary, ed. W. H. Frere and L. E. G. Browne, 3 vols., Henry Bradshaw Society, 1903–13.
HERKLESS, J., and HANNAY, R. K.: *The College of St. Leonard*, 1905.
Historia et Cartularium Monasterii Sancti Petri Gloucestriae, ed. W. H. Hart, 3 vols., 1863–7.
Historiae Dunelmensis Scriptores Tres, ed. J. Raine, Surtees Society, 1839.
Historical Anthology of Music, i, ed. A. T. Davison and W. Apel, 1949.
Historical Manuscripts Commission, Eighth Report, 1881; *Ninth Report*, 1883–4.
HOPE, W. ST. J.: 'Quire Screens in English Churches'. *Archaeologia*, lxviii, 1917.
HOPKINS, E. H.: *The English Medieval Church Organ*, 1888.
HOPPIN, R. H.: 'Partial Signatures and Musica Ficta in Some Early 15th-Century Sources'. *Journal of the American Musicological Society*, vi, 1953.
HUGHES, DOM A.: *Catalogue of Musical Manuscripts at Peterhouse, Cambridge*, 1953.

HUGHES, DOM A.: 'An Introduction to Fayrfax'. *Musica Disciplina*, vi, 1952.

—— *Medieval Polyphony in the Bodleian Library*, 1951.

HUGHES-HUGHES, A.: *Catalogue of Manuscript Music in the British Museum*, 3 vols., 1906–9.

HUNT, J. E.: *Cranmer's First Litany, 1544, and Merbecke's Book of Common Prayer Noted, 1550*, 1939.

Hymns Ancient and Modern, Historical Edition, ed. W. H. Frere, 1909.

JAMES, M. R.: 'Chapel Inventories'. *Etoniana*, xxv–xxxiii, 1920–3.

—— 'Organs and Organists in the College Accounts'. *Etoniana*, xxiv, 1919.

—— and THOMPSON, A. H.: 'Catalogue of the Library of Leicester Abbey'. *Transactions of the Leicester Archaeological Society*, xxi, 1940–1.

John of Gaunt's Register, 1372–1376, ed. S. Armitage-Smith, 2 vols., Camden Society, 1911.

John of Gaunt's Register, 1379–1383, ed. E. C. Lodge and R. Somerville, 2 vols., Camden Society, 1937.

JONES, W. B., and FREEMAN, E. A.: *History and Antiquities of St. David's*, 1856.

Josquin des Prez, Werken van, ed. A. Smijers, 1935–   .

JULIAN, J.: *A Dictionary of Hymnology*, 1915.

JUNGMANN, J.-A.: *Missarum Sollemnia*, 3 vols., 1951–4.

KANTOROWICZ, E. H.: *Laudes Regiae*, 1947.

KENNEY, S. W.: 'Origins and Chronology of the Brussels Manuscript 5557 in the Bibliothèque royale de Belgique'. *Revue Belge de Musicologie*, vi, 1952.

KERRY, C.: *A History of the Church of St. Lawrence, Reading*, 1883.

KIRBY, T. F.: *Annals of Winchester College*, 1892.

—— *Winchester Scholars*, 1888.

KNOWLES, DOM D.: *The Religious Orders in England*, 2 vols., 1950, 1955.

LABORDE, L.: *Les ducs de Bourgogne*, 3 vols., 1852.

LAFONTAINE, H. C. DE: *The King's Musick*, 1909.

LEDERER, V.: *Über Heimat und Ursprung der mehrstimmigen Tonkunst*, 1906.

LEGG, J. W., and HOPE, W. ST. J.: *Inventories of Christ Church, Canterbury*, 1902.

LELAND, J.: *De rebus Britannicis Collectanea*, ed. T. Hearne, 6 vols., 1774.

Letters and Papers, Foreign and Domestic, of Henry VIII, i–iv, vii, 1864–1920.

LEVY, K. J.: 'New Material on the Early Motet in England'. *Journal of the American Musicological Society*, iv, 1951.

LEWIS-CROSBY, E. H.: *The Cathedral of the Holy Trinity commonly called Christ Church, Dublin*, n.d. [*c.* 1950].

Liber Ecclesie de Scon, Bannatyne Club, 1843.

Liber Protocollorum M. Cuthberti Simonis . . . A.D. 1499–1513, also Rental Book of the Diocese of Glasgow A.D. 1509–1570, ed. J. Bain and C. Rogers, 2 vols., Grampian Club, 1877.

Liber Sancti Jacobi: Codex Calixtinus, ed. Dom G. Prado and W. M. Whitehill, 1944.

Liber Usualis, ed. Benedictines of Solesmes, 1950.

Lincoln Cathedral Statutes, ed. H. Bradshaw and C. Wordsworth, 3 vols., 1892–7.

Lincoln Chapter Acts 1536–47, ed. R. E. G. Cole, Lincoln Record Society, 1917.

LOWINSKY, E.: 'Conflicting Views on Conflicting Signatures'. *Journal of the American Musicological Society*, vii, 1954.

—— 'The Function of Conflicting Signatures in Early Polyphonic Music'. *The Musical Quarterly*, xxxi, 1945.

—— 'A Newly Discovered Sixteenth-Century Motet Manuscript at the Biblioteca Vallicelliana in Rome'. *Journal of the American Musicological Society*, iii, 1950.

LUDWIG, F.: *Repertorium Organorum Recentioris et Motetorum Vetustissimi Stili*, i, 1910.

—— 'Über die Entstehung und die erste Entwicklung der lateinischen und französischen Motette in musikalischer Beziehung'. *Sammelbände der internationalen Musikgesellschaft*, vii, 1905–6.

LYTE, H. C. M.: *A History of Eton College*, 4th ed., 1911.

Guillaume de Machaut, Musikalische Werke, ed. F. Ludwig and H. Besseler, 4 vols., 1926–54.

MACRAY, W. D.: *A Register of the Members of St. Mary Magdalen College, Oxford*, New Series, ii, 1897.

MADDISON, A. R.: *A Short Account of the Vicars-choral, poor-clerks, organists and choristers of Lincoln Cathedral from the 12th century to the Accession of Edward VI*, 1878.

MAHIEU, B.: 'Notre-Dame de Paris au XVᵉ siècle'. *Les Chroniques de Notre-Dame*, ix, 1947.

MARIX, J.: *Histoire de la musique et des musiciens de la cour de Bourgogne sous le règne de Philippe le Bon*, 1939.

MAROSSZEKI, S. R.: *Les origines du chant cistercien* (*Analecta Sacri Ordinis Cisterciensis*, viii), 1952.

Guglielmi de Mascaudio Opera, i, ed. G. de Van, 1949.

MASON, W. M.: *The History and Antiquities of the Collegiate and Cathedral Church of St. Patrick near Dublin*, 1820.

Medieval Carols, ed. J. Stevens (*Musica Britannica*, iv), 1952.

The Medieval Records of a London City Church, ed. H. Littlehales, Early English Text Society, 1904–5.

Memorials of Beverley Minster: The Chapter Act Book of the Collegiate Church of St. John of Beverley, 1286–1347, ed. A. F. Leach, 2 vols., Surtees Society, 1898, 1903.

Memorials of Henry V, King of England, ed. C. A. Cole, Rolls Series, 1858.

Memorials and Chapter Acts of the Collegiate Church of SS. Peter and Wilfrid, Ripon, ed. J. T. Fowler, 5 vols., Surtees Society, 1875–1908.

MENDEL, A.: 'Pitch in the 16th and Early 17th Centuries'. *The Musical Quarterly*, xxiv, 1948.

MILMAN, H. H.: *Annals of St. Paul's Cathedral*, 1869.

Missa O Quam Suavis, ed. H. B. Collins, 1927.

Missale ad usum Ecclesiae Herfordensis, ed. W. G. Henderson, 1874.

Missale ad Usum Insignis et Praeclarae Ecclesiae Sarum, ed. F. H. Dickinson, 1861–83.

Die mittelalterliche Mehrstimmigkeit, ed. H. Husmann (*Das Musikwerk*, ed. K. G. Fellerer), n.d. [1955].

MOLLAT, G.: *Les Papes d'Avignon*, 1924.

The Monastic Breviary of Hyde Abbey, ed. J. B. L. Tolhurst, 6 vols., Henry Bradshaw Society, 1930–42.

Monasticon Anglicanum, ed. W. Dugdale; new edition, ed. J. Caley, H. Ellis and B. Bandinel, 6 vols. in 8, 1817–30.

Monasticon Diocesis Exoniensis, ed. G. Oliver, 1846.

Monumenta Monodica Medii Aevi, i, ed. B. Stäblein, 1956.

Monumenta Polyphoniae Liturgicae Sanctae Ecclesiae Romanae, Series II, No. 1, ed. L. Feininger, 1951.

MOORMAN, J. R. H.: *Church Life in England in the Thirteenth Century*, 1946.

MORLEY, T.: *A Plaine and Easie Introduction to Practicall Musicke*, ed. R. A. Harman, 1952.

MOSER, H. J.: *Musiklexikon*, 2 vols., 1955.

Muchelney Memoranda, ed. B. Schofield, Somerset Record Society, 1927.

The Mulliner Book, ed. D. Stevens (*Musica Britannica*, i), 1951.

Les musiciens de la cour de Bourgogne au XVᵉ siècle, ed. J. Marix, 1937.

Die Musik in Geschichte und Gegenwart, ed. F. Blume, 1949– .

The Old Hall Manuscript, ed. A. Ramsbotham, H. B. Collins and Dom A. Hughes, 3 vols., 1933–8.

An Old St. Andrew's Music Book, ed. J. H. Baxter, 1931.

OLIVER, G.: *Lives of the Bishops of Exeter and a History of the Cathedral*, 1861.

OLLARD, S. L.: *Fasti Wyndesorienses; the Deans and Canons of Windsor*, 1950.

Ordinale Exon, ed. J. N. Dalton, 4 vols., Henry Bradshaw Society, 1909–40.

The Ordinale of St. Mary's Abbey, York, ed. L. McLachlan and J. B. L. Tolhurst, 3 vols., Henry Bradshaw Society, 1936–51.

The Ordinale of the Nuns of Barking, ed. J. B. L. Tolhurst, 2 vols., Henry Bradshaw Society, 1927–8.

Paléographie musicale, ed. Benedictines of Solesmes, 1889– .

PALMER, T. F.: *Collectanea I*, Somerset Record Society, 1924.

PANTIN, W. A.: *Chapters of English Black Monks*, 3 vols., Camden Society, 1931–7.

PEARCE, E. H.: *The Monks of Westminster*, 1916.

Piae Cantiones, ed. G. R. Woodward, 1910.

PINE, E.: *The Westminster Abbey Singers*, 1953.

—— 'Westminster Abbey: Some Early Masters of the Choristers'. *The Musical Times*, xciv, 1953.

PIRRO, A.: *Histoire de la musique de la fin du XIVe siècle à la fin du XVIe*, 1940.

—— *La musique à Paris sous le règne de Charles VI*, 1930.

The Political Songs of England, ed. T. Wright, Camden Society, 1839.

Polyphonia Sacra, ed. C. Van den Borren, 1932.

Polyphonic Music of the Fourteenth Century, i, ed. L. Schrade, 1956.

Polyphonies du XIIIe siècle, ed. Y. Rokseth, 4 vols., 1935–9.

Privy Purse Expenses of Elizabeth of York; Wardrobe Accounts of Edward the Fourth, ed. N. H. Nicolas, 1830.

The Privy Purse Expenses of Henry VIII, ed. N. H. Nicolas, 1827.

PROVAH, A.: *The Annals of the Parishes of St. Olave Hart Street and Allhallows Staining*, 1894.

RABY, F. J.: *A History of Christian-Latin Poetry from the Beginnings to the Close of the Middle Ages*, 1953.

RAYNAUD, G.: *Recueil de motets français des XIIe et XIIIe siècles*, 2 vols., 1881–3.

REANEY, G.: 'The Manuscript Chantilly, Musée Condé 1047'. *Musica Disciplina*, viii, 1954.

REESE, G.: *Music in the Middle Ages*, 1940.

—— *Music in the Renaissance*, 1954.

Johannis Regis Opera Omnia, ed. C. Lindenburg, 2 vols., 1956.

Register of Thomas Bekynton, 1443–1465, ed. H. C. M. Lyte and M. C. B. Dawes, 2 vols., Somerset Record Society, 1934–5.

Register of the Collegiate Church of Crail, ed. C. Rogers, Grampian Club, 1877.

Register of Simon Langham, Archbishop of Canterbury, 1366–88, Canterbury and York Society, 1952.

Registrum Annalium Collegii Mertonensis 1483–1521, ed. H. E. Salter, 1923.

Registrum Episcopatus Aberdonensis, 2 vols., 1845.

Registrum Episcopatus Glasguensis, ed. C. Innes, 1843.

Registrum Episcopatus Moraviensis, 1837.

Registrum Statutorum et Consuetudinum Ecclesiae Cathedralis Sancti Pauli Londiniensis, ed. W. S. Simpson, 1873.

The Regulations and Establishment of the Household of Henry Algernon Percy, the Fifth Earl of Northumberland, ed. T. Percy, 1770.

Rentale Dunkeldense, ed. R. K. Hannay, 1915.

REYNOLDS, H. E.: *Wells Cathedral*, 1880.

Rites of Durham, ed. J. T. Fowler, Surtees Society, 1903.

ROBERTSON, D. H.: *Sarum Close*, 1938.

ROCK, D.: *The Church of Our Fathers*, ed. G. W. Hart and W. H Frere, 4 vols., 1903–4.

ROGERS, C.: *History of the Chapel Royal of Scotland*, 1882.

ROPER, E. S.: 'The Chapels Royal and their Music'. *Proceedings of the Musical Association*, liv, 1927.

The Sarum Missal, ed. J. Wickham Legg, 1916.

SCHMIDT, H.: 'Zur Melodiebildung Leonins und Perotins'. *Zeitschrift für Musikwissenschaft*, xiv, 1931.

SCHOFIELD, B.: 'A Newly Discovered Fifteenth-Century Manuscript of the English Chapel Royal—Part I'. *The Musical Quarterly*, xxxii, 1946.

—— 'The Provenance and Date of "Sumer is icumen in".' *Music Review*, ix, 1948.

SCHRADE, L.: 'A Fourteenth Century Parody Mass'. *Acta Musicologica*, xxvii, 1955.

—— 'The Mass of Toulouse'. *Revue Belge de Musicologie*, viii, 1954.

—— 'Political Compositions in French Music of the 12th and 13th Centuries'. *Annales Musicologiques*, i, 1953.

SIMPSON, W. S.: *Chapters in the History of Old St. Paul's*, 1881.

—— 'Two Inventories of the Cathedral Church of St. Paul, London'. *Archaeologia*, l, 1887.

SMITS VAN WAESBERGHE, J.: *Gregorian Chant*, n.d. [1949].

SMOLDON, W. L.: 'Liturgical Drama', in *New Oxford History of Music*, ii, 1954.

'Some Early Scottish Composers'. *The Musical Antiquary*, ii, 1910.

SQUIRE, W. B.: 'Notes on an Undescribed Collection of English 15th-Century Music'. *Sammelbände der internationalen Musikgesellschaft*, ii, 1901.

—— 'On an Early Sixteenth Century Manuscript of English Music in the Library of Eton College'. *Archaeologia*, lvi, part i, 1898.

Statuta et Consuetudines Ecclesiae Cathedralis Beatae Mariae Virginis Sarisberiensis, ed. C. Wordsworth and D. Macleane, 1915.

Statuta et Consuetudines Ecclesiae Cathedralis Sarisberiensis, ed. E. A. Dayman and W. H. R. Jones, 1883.

Statutes and Constitutions of the Cathedral Church of Chichester, ed. F. G. Bennett, R. H. Codrington and C. Deedes, 1904.

Statutes of the Colleges of Oxford, printed by desire of H.M. Commissioners for inquiring into the State of the University of Oxford, 1853.

STEVENS, D.: 'Further Light on *Fulgens Praeclara*'. *Journal of the American Musicological Society*, ix, 1956.

—— *The Mulliner Book, A Commentary*, 1952.

—— 'Processional Psalms in Faburden'. *Musica Disciplina*, ix, 1955.

—— 'A Recently Discovered English Source of the 14th Century'. *The Musical Quarterly*, xli, 1955.

—— 'A Unique Tudor Organ Mass'. *Musica Disciplina*, vi, 1952.

STOKES, G. T.: *Ireland and the Anglo-Norman Church*, 1889.

STRUNK, O.: *Source Readings in Music History*, 1950.

SUMNER, W. L.: *The Organ*, 1952.

TAYLOR, F.: 'The Chronicle of John Strecche for the Reign of Henry V (1414-23)'. *Bulletin of the John Rylands Library*, xvi, 1932.

THOMPSON, A. H.: *Newarke Hospital and College*, 1936.

—— 'The Statutes of Fotheringhay College'. *The Archaeological Journal*, lxxv, 1918.

TINCTORIS, J.: *Terminorum musicae diffinitorium*, ed. A. Machabey, 1951.

Tudor Church Music, ed. P. C. Buck, E. H. Fellowes, A. Ramsbotham, R. R. Terry and S. T. Warner, 10 vols., 1923-9; *Appendix with Supplementary Notes*, ed. E. H. Fellowes, 1948.

Ulrichs von Richental Chronik des Constanzes Concils, 1414 bis 1418, ed. M. R. Buck, 1882.

Use of Sarum, ed. W. H. Frere, 2 vols., 1898, 1901.

VALLANCE, A.: *English Church Screens*, 1936.

—— *Greater English Church Screens*, 1947.

Valor Ecclesiasticus tempore Henrici VIII auctoritate regia institutus, 6 vols., 1810-34.

VAN DEN BORREN, C.: *Le Manuscrit musical M.222 C.22 de la Bibliothèque de Strasbourg*, 1924.

VAN DIJK, S. J. P.: *Latin Liturgical Manuscripts and Printed Books; Guide to an Exhibition held during 1952*, Bodleian Library, Oxford, 1952.

—— 'Saint Bernard and the *Instituta Patrum* of Saint Gall'. *Musica Disciplina*, iv, 1950.

Visitations in the Diocese of Lincoln, ed. A. H. Thompson, 3 vols., Lincoln Record Society, 1940–7.

Visitations and Memorials of Southwell Minster, ed. A. F. Leach, Camden Society, 1891.

WAGNER, P.: *Die Gesänge der Jakobusliturgie zu Santiago de Compostela*, 1931.

—— *Introduction to the Gregorian Melodies*, i, trans. A. Orme and E. G. P. Wyatt, 1901.

WAITE, W. G.: *The Rhythm of Twelfth-Century Polyphony*, 1954.

WALKER, E.: *A History of Music in England*, ed. J. A. Westrup, 1952.

WALTERS, H. B.: *London Churches at the Reformation*, 1939.

WATKIN, H. R.: *Dartmouth*, i (*Parochial Histories of Devonshire*, v), Devonshire Association for the Advancement of Science, Literature and Art, 1935.

WELLESZ, E.: *Eastern Elements in Western Chant*, 1947.

WEST, J. E.: *Cathedral Organists*, 1921.

WHITLEY, H. M.: 'Inventories of the Collegiate Churches of the Holy Cross, Crediton, and Our Blessed Lady of Ottery'. *Reports and Transactions of the Devonshire Association*, xxxiv, 1902.

WIDMORE, R.: *History of the Church of St. Peter, Westminster*, 1751.

WILKINS, D.: *Concilia Magnae Britanniae*, 4 vols., 1737.

Adriani Willaert Opera Omnia, iv, ed. H. Zenck, 1952.

WILLIAMS, C. F. A.: *Degrees in Music*, 1893.

WILLIS, R., and CLARK, J. W.: *The Architectural History of the University of Cambridge*, 3 vols., 1886.

Winchester Cathedral Documents, 1541–1547, ed. G. W. Kitchin and F. T. Madge, 1889.

The Winchester Troper, ed. W. H. Frere, Henry Bradshaw Society, 1894.

WOLF, J.: *Handbuch der Notationskunde*, 2 vols., 1913, 1919.

WOOLDRIDGE, H. E.: *The Polyphonic Period*, i and ii (*Oxford History of Music*, i and ii, 1st ed.), 1901, 1905.

Worcester Antiphonary, ed. A. Mocquereau (*Paléographie Musicale*, xii), 1922–5.

The Worcester Fragments, ed. L. A. Dittmer, 1957.

Worcester Mediaeval Harmony, ed. Dom A. Hughes, 1928.

WORDSWORTH, C.: 'Lincoln Inventories'. *Archaeologia*, liii, 1892.
—— and LITTLEHALES, H.: *The Old Service-Books of the English Church*, 1904.
WYLIE, J. H.: *History of England under Henry IV*, 4 vols., 1884–98.

YARDLEY, E.: *Minevia Sacra*, ed. F. Green, 1927.
York Fabric Rolls, ed. J. Raine, Surtees Society, 1859.
The York Missal, ed. W. G. Henderson, 2 vols., Surtees Society, 1874.
The York Processional, ed. W. G. Henderson, Surtees Society, 1875.

REGISTER AND INDEX OF MUSICIANS

In addition to British musicians mentioned in the text, this list includes composers (in capitals), holders of university degrees in music, masters, informators and organists. If no office is shown, that of clerk is to be understood. An asterisk indicates that there is an entry in Grove's *Dictionary*. As a rule, information given there is not repeated here. Names of Chapel Royal musicians are from lists kindly supplied by Mr. John Harvey and Dr. A. R. Myers, the printed Calendars of Patent Rolls and Close Rolls, the *Letters and Papers of Henry VIII*, and Lafontaine. References to Leach are to his *English Schools at the Reformation* (London, 1896); those to Sterry are to his *Eton College Register, 1441–1698* (Eton, 1943). Names of graduates in music are from Williams; other references will be found in the Bibliography. In other cases the information is from unpublished archives. The year in medieval accounts was normally counted from Michaelmas to Michaelmas, divided—at Christmas or January 1, Easter or March 25, and June 24—into four terms. Where dates enclose three or more years it is not to be assumed that the records are complete for the whole period.

*Cotell (Cutell), Richard, 12, 113, 149–50, 152

St. Paul's, minor canon 1394–5, cardinal, 1395

Couch, Robert

New Coll, inf 1535 (*Valor Eccl.*)

*COWPER, ROBERT, 35, 140

King's, 1492–6 (as Cooper, Coopar); the will of a R.C. was proved in 1541 (*Test. Cant.*)

Crambroke, John, 190

Canterbury, monk 1406–d. 47

*Crane, William

Crawe (Crowe), James, 177–8

Lincoln, inf 1539 (Maddison)

CUK, John (*see also* Cooke), 261–2 (Ex. 45)

A John Cooke was *succentor vicariorum* at York 1452–5 (Harrison)

DAGGERE, WILLIAM

His song 'Downbery down' is in Brit. Mus. Add. 31922

DAMETT, THOMAS, 20, 22, 87, 245–7, 297–8

Chapel Royal, 1413–31; Windsor, Canon 1431– d. 37 (Ollard)

DARK, JOHN

His Magnificat is in Cambridge, Peterhouse part-books

Darke

New Coll, inf 1484–5

Darlington, John, 201

St. Mary-at-Hill, London, 1521–2; Eton, inf 1522–3, clerk 1544–50 (Dec)

Davy, John

Lincoln, org 1489, inf 1490 (Jan 14) (Maddison)

*DAVY (DAVYS), RICHARD, 36, 162, 164, 260, 312, 315–17, 324–6 (Exs. 105–6), 328–9 (Ex. 110), 403 (Ex. 203), 419

Magdalen, inf and org 1491–2; in 1495–6 Magdalen paid for binding a 'liber de canticis et missis et antiphonis domini Ric. Davy'; Exeter, VC 1497–1500

Dawke, John

B.Mus. Oxford 1511

Derby, Robert, 161

Winchester Cath, clerk (and org?) 1444

Ditty, Walter

Eton, 1530 (June)–40, inf 1530 (Sept)–40

Dore, William, 161

Winchester Coll, org 1542

Dove (Dowffe), Robert, 177

Lincoln, VC 1520–d. *c.* 1537, inf 1528, org 1535 (Maddison)

DRAKE, RALPH, 43

Muchelney, master *c.* 1500; one voice-part of his 'Frere Gastkyn' is in Brit. Mus. Royal App. 58 (early 16th cent, after 1504)

Draper, John

Supplicated B.Mus. Oxford 1516–17

*DUNSTABLE, JOHN, 25, 147, 155, 221, 228, 243–4, 250, 252–8 (Exs. 39, 41), 265, 274, 291, 299–302 (Ex. 80), 306–7, 311, 318, 346–7 (Ex. 127)

Ede, Richard

Canon regular, supplicated B.Mus. Oxford 1506–7

Edmund, 32

Winchester Coll, inf 1396–7

Edmunds, William, 21

Windsor, installed 1478 (Apr 19), inf 1479–80; Eton, 1484; Chapel Royal, 1490

EDWARDS

His respond *Terrenum sitiens* is in Cambridge, Peterhouse part-books

Elwell, John

Eton, inf 1457–61

*ENSDALE (ENSDALL), JOHN, 373–4 (Ex. 165)

ERLEY (ERELL), WALTER, 336

EXCETRE, JOHN, 22, 228, 233, 235–6

Chapel Royal, 1374–96

Exce(s)tre, William, 21, 25

John of Gaunt's Chapel, 1383; Chapel Royal, 1392–1402

Farford, Thomas

Lincoln, chor 1448, VC 1455–d. 71, sometime inf (Maddison)

*FARMER, JOHN, 318

*FARTHYNG (FARDYNG), THOMAS, 24–5, 35, 163

King's, chor 1477–83, clerk 1493–9; Chapel Royal, 1511–20

FAWKYNER, 312, 316, 319–20 (Ex. 97), 322 (Exs. 102–3)

*FAYRFAX, ROBERT, 24, 42, 164, 172,194,259,263–8 (Exs. 46–9),270, 273,312,324,334,336,351,419–20

Firtun, John
St. Stephen's, Westminster, and Chapel of the Duke of Norfolk; Mus.B. Cambridge 1516

FLUYD, see LLOYD

Foderley, Thomas, 41, 187
Durham, master 1496–1502

FONTEYNS, 228

FOREST, 221, 228, 250, 303–5 (Exs. 84–5)

Forest, William
Winchester Coll, 1464–9 (as John in 1465, 1468)

Foukys, W., 10
Lincoln, inf 1431

Fowler, John
Exeter, VC 1432–3; Chapel Royal, 1433–4

FOWLER, JOHN, 24
Chapel Royal, 1451–67; presumably the composer in the Pepys MS.

Fowler, John
Chapel Royal, 1499 (gospeller), 1504, 1518 (late gospeller)

Foxe, Robert
Westminster, master from 1542–3 (Pine)

Francis, John, 158
New Coll, inf 1427–9, 1436–43

Freeman, William, 177
Lincoln, chor 1485, poor clerk 1495, inf 1524 (Maddison)

FREN(N)YNGHAM, JOHN, 43, 190
Canterbury, master (?) 1455–d. 70; no compositions survive

*FRYE, WALTER, 250, 258–9 (Exs. 42–3), 337, 396–7 (Ex. 193)

Fryvyll, Humphrey
King's, 1495–9; Mus.B. Cambridge 1495–6, Mus.D. 1505

Fuller, Matthew, 44, 191
Winchester Cath, master 1538, VC until 1558 (Chapter Act Book)

Fyssher, Richard, 195
Worcester, master 1543–9 (Atkins)

Games
Magdalen, inf 1547–51

GARNESEY, 401 (Ex. 200)

Gaylard, John, 180
Wells, inf 1514 (Jan–Mar)

GEDNEY, see GYDNEY

Genyngs, George
Eton, 1526 (June)–7 (June), inf 1526 (Sept)–7 (June); King's, 1528–34 (as Genyns)

Gilbert, John, 177
Lincoln, inf 1518, org 1524 (Maddison); B.Mus. Oxford 1510–11

Gilbert, Richard
Wimborne Minster, org 1495 (Cox)

Godwin, Robert, 32
Winchester Coll, Fellow 1541–50, inf 1542

Goodman, Thomas, 44, 190
B.Mus. Oxford 1505; Winchester Cath, master 1511, VC 1541–56 (Chapter Act Book)

Goole, see Coole

Grenacres (Grenakers), John
Magdalen, inf 1535

Green (Grene), Richard, 41
Worcester, org 1468–84 (Atkins)

Grene, William
King's, 1492–8; Westminster, master c. 1532–c. 43 (Pine)

Growe, William, 185
St. Patrick's, Dublin, minor canon 1509

Gustinian, 160
New Coll, org 1542–3

*GWYNNETH, JOHN, 420

GYDNEY, JOHN(?), 173
No compositions survive

Gye, John, 180
Wells, inf 1512

Gyles, John, 172
Chapel Royal, 1511, org 1515

HACOMBLENE
(HACOMPLAYNT), ROBERT, 36, 312, 315, 321–2 (Ex. 101), 324, Ill. 5
b. St. Andrew's, London; Eton, scholar 1469 (aged 13)–72; King's, scholar 1472, B.A. 1475–6, M.A. 1480, B.D. 1490, D.D. 1507, Fellow 1475–93, Provost 1509–d. 28 (Sept 8) (Sterry)

the Prentes composer of a Magnificat in Cambridge, Caius College MS. 667

Prentys, Richard, 22
Chapel Royal, 1393, Dean 1402–8

Preston, 192
Magdalen, inf 1543

*PRESTON, THOMAS, 192, 217, 364–6 (Exs. 152–5), 394–5 (Ex. 190)
In the Inventory of Leicester Abbey c. 1493

PROWETH, STEPHEN
Two voice-parts of his antiphons *O bone Jesu* and *Plaude potentissime* are in Cambridge, Univ. Lib. MS. Dd. xiii. 27 and St. John's Coll MS. 234

Prynne, Nicholas
Wells, VC 1547–55, org 1547–8

*PYAMOUR, JOHN, 22, 243, 250
Chapel Royal, 1420–1; Chapel of Duke of Bedford, 1427; d. before July 4, 1431

PYCARD, 228, 235–40 (Ex. 29), 240, 242

*PYGOT(T), RICHARD, 24, 26, 171, 274, 336, 420

Pynbrygge, Edmund, 44, 190
Winchester Cath, master 1510–11

Pypis
Mus.B. Cambridge 1497

QUELDRYK, 228, 240, 242

*RASOR (RASAR, RASER), WILLIAM, 35, 274
King's chor 1493–6, clerk 1509–15

Raynold, Walter
New Coll, inf 1423–4 (3 terms)

*REDFORD, JOHN, 13, 360–1 (Exs. 144–5), 386–8 (Ex. 182), 410 (Ex. 124)

Renynger, James, 44, 191
Eton, 1528–9 (2 terms): Glastonbury, master 1534; a James Runyger was master and org at St. Dunstan-in-the-East, London, 1547–8 (Leach)

Retford, John, 10
Lincoln, inf 1429, 1434

Richmunde, William
Queen's, Oxford, org 1518

Robert, John
New Coll, inf 1423 (2 terms)–5

Robynson, John
Fotheringhay, org 1546 (J. C. Cox in *Arch. Jour.*, lxi, 1904, p. 273)

Rochell, Robert, 174
Southwell, VC 1484–1503

Roke, Adam
Eton, 1448–61, 1468–9; Windsor, 1461–3, inf 1462 (June)–3, resigned 1476 (Nov 18)

Rolfe, Thomas, 174
Windsor, c. 1460–9 (resigned July 31), 1476 (re-admitted Apr 1)–84, inf 1461–2 (June), org 1461–9, 1477–84

Roper, George, 165
Magdalen, 1519–24

Rowland, Robert
Eton, 1526 (June)–7, inf 1526 (June–Sept), 1527 (June–Sept)

ROWLARD, 228

Russell, John, 185
St. Patrick's, Dublin, master 1509

RYSBY, HENRY, 35
Eton, 1506–8; presumably the composer of 'Whoso that wyll hymselff applye' in Brit. Mus. Add. 31922

Saintwix (Seintjust), Thomas, 178
Mus.D. Cambridge 1463; Salisbury, Precentor 1466, d. 1467

Salesbury, 25
Archbishop of Canterbury's Chapel, 1396

Samford, William, 11, 182
Chichester, inf 1544

*SAMPSON, RICHARD, 24, 338–40 (Ex. 121), Ill. 21

SANDLEY (STANDLEY), 250
His *Missa ad fugam* and *Quae es ista* are printed in *Documenta Polyphoniae Liturgicae*

Savage, John
King's, conduct and inf 1472–4

Saxy, Robert
Eton, inf 1452–3, Succentor 1457–61

Scherar, William, 15
Dunkeld, VC early 16th cent

Scherman, Thomas
Supplicated B.Mus. Oxford 1508–9

Schete, John
New Coll, inf 1394–5

Sharpe, Richard
Eton, 1512–15; King's, 1517–24 (as

William or John), 1524–9; a R. S. was org Coll Church of the Trinity, Stratford-on-Avon, 1545–8 (Leach)

*SHEPPARD (SHEPHERD), JOHN, 36, 165–6, 283, 288–90 (Exs. 70–1), 345, 356–7 (Ex. 140), 366, 370–2 (Exs. 161–3), 373–4, 377 (Ex. 169), 379–80 (Exs. 171–2), 384–6 (Ex. 181), 397–400 (Exs. 195–7), 401–2 (Ex. 201), 405–6 (Ex. 207), Ill. 26
Not a Fellow of Magdalen 1549–51

*SHERYNGHAM, 419

*SMERT, RICHARD, 421
Exeter, VC 1428–c. 65

Smith, John
Eton, 1523 (Jan)–5, inf 1523 (Sept)–5

Smyth, John, 180
Wells, VC 1534–44, org 1534–5, inf 1538

Smythe, Richard
Montgomery, org 1547–8 (Leach)

Solber, William, 176
Ripon, org 1540–1

SOULEBY (SULBY), HENRY
Eton, 1444–5; Chapel Royal, 1446–51; perhaps the composer Soursby (also Sorbi) in the Trent and Aosta MSS.

Stanys, John, 190
Canterbury, Precentor d. 1421 (Dec 19)

Steill, Thomas, 175
Southwell, VC 1508–23

Stele, John, 41, 187
Durham, master 1447

Stephen
Magdalen org 1529

Stevenson, John, 15
Dunkeld, Canon early 16th cent

Stonyng, Michael
Ottery St. Mary, secondary 1545 (Dalton)

*STONYNG, OLIVER, 35
Eton, Fellow 1530–47, Precentor 1533–5; formerly of Magdalen; presumably the composer Stonings (Stenings)

STRATFORD, WILLIAM, Monk of Stratford (see also Parker), 349

STROWGER, E., 360

*STURGEON, NICHOLAS, 20, 22, 231, 245–7
Elected scholar of Winchester Coll 1399, aged 8–12 (Kirby)

STURMYS, HUGH, 336

*STURTON, EDMUND, 312, 327–8 (Ex. 108), 330 (Ex. 111)

Summer
Eton, inf 1521 (3 terms)

SUTTON, JOHN, 35, 312, 314–15
Magdalen, M.A., Fellow 1476; Eton, Fellow 1477–c. 79; a Sutton was Mus.B. Cambridge 1489 (Grace Book Δ)

Swawe, William, 176
Ripon, org 1513–14

SWYNFORD, 228, 240, 242

SYGAR, JOHN, 35, 164
King's, conduct 1499–1501 and 1508–15; presumably the composer of a Magnificat, now fragmentary, in the Eton Choirbook

Sylvester, John
B.Mus. Oxford 1521–2; Westminster Abbey, master 1522

Synet, Thomas
New Coll, inf 1434–5

Synger, Richard, of Malmesbury, 186
Worcester 1434–5

*TALLIS, THOMAS, 24, 44, 193, 200, 217, 287–8, 292, 334–6 (Ex. 118), 361, 366, 368 (Ex. 159), 369–70, 377, 384 (Ex. 179), 402

*TAVERNER, JOHN, 27, 30, 37, 176, 263, 268–73 (Exs. 52–4), 280–5 (Exs. 65–8), 287–8, 290–2, 330–3 (Exs. 112–14), 334, 336, 340–1, 351 (Ex. 135), 368–9 (Ex. 158), 377, 381, 388–9 (Ex. 183), 392, 395, 397 (Ex. 194), 420

Tattersall, 1525

Taylor, Thomas
Supplicated B.Mus. Oxford 1531

Thatcher (Catherow), John, 11
Salisbury, inf 1462

Thetford, John of, 10
Lincoln, inf 1395

Thomas, John
Magdalen, inf and org 1498–1500

Tildesley, John, 41, 187
Durham, master 1502

TROULUFFE, JOHN, 421
St. Probus, Exeter, Canon c. 1465–c. 78

Tucke, John, 44, 158
New Coll, Fellow 1500–7, B.A.;

INDEX OF TITLES

GENERAL INDEX

479

Talbot, Archbishop Richard, 17, 185, Ill. 3
talea, 148
taperer, *ceroferarius*, 14, 94
Tapissier, Jean, 229, 245
Tattershall, Collegiate Church, 27, 176, 204
Temporale, 5, 53–4, 100, 114
Tenebrae, 70, 402
Tewkesbury, Abbey, 38
third form, *tertia forma*, also called first form, *prima forma*, 12, 51, 89
Thorne, Nicholas, 79
thurifer, *thuribularius*, 9, 12, 14, 17–18, 94, 176
Thurlby, 160
Tinctoris, Johannes, 257
Tonale, 18, 59, 100–3, 324, 331
tonus, see mode
Tournai, 338
Tract, 54, 57, 63–4, 79, 106, 116, 378, 381
trahere (organa), 112, 206
'trebill', 115, 199, 249
Tregury, Archbishop Michael, 185
Trèves, 120
triplex, triplum, 113–14, 121, 126, 136
Trisere, Johannes de, 222
trombone, 243
Troper, *Troparium*, 100, 115, 133
trumpet, 217
Trumpington, William de, 78
truncatio, 149
Tuam, Cathedral, 16
Tunsted, Simon, 115
Turner, Richard, 214
Turstin, 46

Utrecht Psalter, 206

valectus, 41; see also *clericus valetus*
Valenciennes, 223
variation, 231, 233, 272–3, 283–4, 357
variation, *variatio* (of mode), 101–2, 105
Vaughan, Bishop Edward, 16
Venice, 171
Venitarium, see Invitatory
versiculus, 56, 162, 169
vicarius, 5
Villiers, George, 29
virilis vox, 18
Visitation to the sepulchre, 98, 117, 134

Volpiano, William of, 46
vox puerilis, 14

Walden, John (chaplain), 244
—— (monk), 190
Walter, 161
Waltham, Bishop John, 84
Waltham Holy Cross, Abbey, 38, 44, 192–3
Ware, Richard de, 113
Water, John, 243
Waverley, Abbey, 38
Wayneflete, Bishop William, 33, 161, 218
Webber, Henry, 182
Wells, Cathedral, 3, 6–11, 33, 51, 76, 179–81, 202–3, Ill. 2
Westminster, Abbey, 38, 43, 78, 82, 113, 190, 195, 197, 210–12, 222, 288–9
——, Chapel of St. Stephen, 19, 28, 198, 201, 268, 338
——, Palace, 19, 171
——, St. Margaret, 199
Wheathamstead, John, 42, 191, 212, 219, 243
Whitby, Abbey, 38
Whitchurch, Edward, 196
White Canons, *see* Premonstratensian Order
White, Sir Thomas, 86
Whithorn, Cathedral, 14
Whyngle, Thomas, 186
Whyte, 167
William of Malmesbury, 205
William of Volpiano, 46
Wilmer, 29
Winchcombe, Abbey, 135
Winchester, Cathedral, 2–3, 43–4, 133, 161, 173, 190–1, 194–5, 205–6
——, College, 31–4, 103, 159–61, 218, 246, 249, 419
——, Collegiate Church of St. Elizabeth, 77
Winchester, David, 44
Winchester Troper, 115–16, 120, 129
Windsor, Castle, 171
——, Chapel of St. George, 19–21, 28, 34–5, 50, 112, 163, 174, 192, 224
Wodeford, John, 21
Wolf, Johannes, 42
Wolsey, Cardinal Thomas, 14, 26–7, 36–7, 168, 171, 173, 191–2, 215, 217, 332, 338, 341